In Odd We Trust

CREATED BY

DEAN KOONTZ

WRITTEN BY **QUEENIE CHAN** AND **DEAN KOONTZ**

ILLUSTRATIONS BY **QUEENIE CHAN**

DEL REY

BALLANTINE BOOKS

NEW YORK

A Del Rey Trade Paperback Original

Text copyright © 2008 by Dean Koontz
Illustrations copyright © 2008 by Queenie Chan

Published in the United States by Del Rey Books, an imprint of The Random House Publishing Group, a division of Random House, Inc., New York.

DEL REY is a registered trademark and the Del Rey colophon is a trademark of Random House, Inc.

ISBN 978-0-345-49966-0

Cover Design by David Stevenson

Also by Dean Koontz

Odd Hours • The Darkest Evening of the Year • The Good Guy • Brother Odd • The Husband • Forever Odd • Velocity • Life Expectancy • The Taking • Odd Thomas • The Face • By the Light of the Moon • One Door Away From Heaven • From the Corner of His Eye • False Memory • Seize the Night • Fear Nothing • Mr. Murder • Dragon Tears • Hideaway • Cold Fire • The Bad Place • Midnight • Lightning • Watchers • Strangers • Twilight Eyes • Darkfall • Phantoms • Whispers • The Mask • The Vision • The Face of Fear • Night Chills • Shattered • The Voice of the Night • The Servants of Twilight • The House of Thunder • The Key to Midnight • The Eyes of Darkness • Shadowfires • Winter Moon • The Door to December • Dark Rivers of the Heart • Icebound • Strange Highways • Intensity • Sole Survivor • Ticktock • The Funhouse • Demon Seed

DEAN KOONTZ'S FRANKENSTEIN
Book One: Prodigal Son • *with Kevin J. Anderson*
Book Two: City of Night • *with Ed Gorman*

Also by Queenie Chan

The Dreaming, volumes 1–3

CONTENTS

In Odd We Trust

Chapter 1

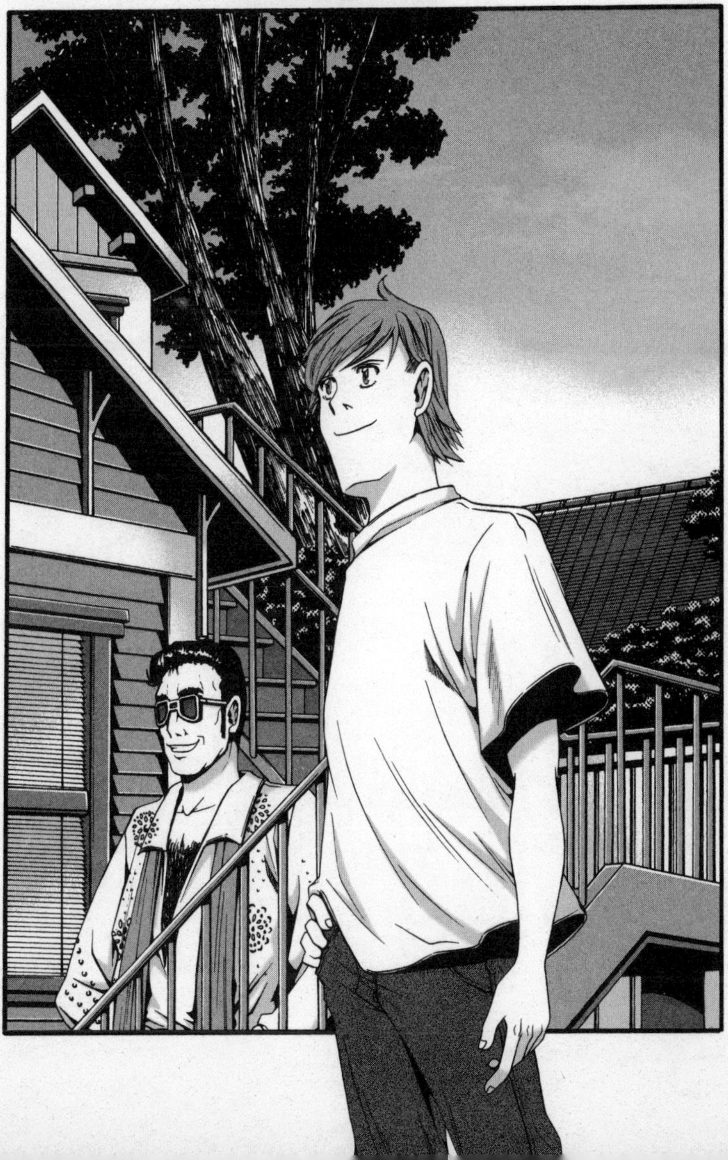

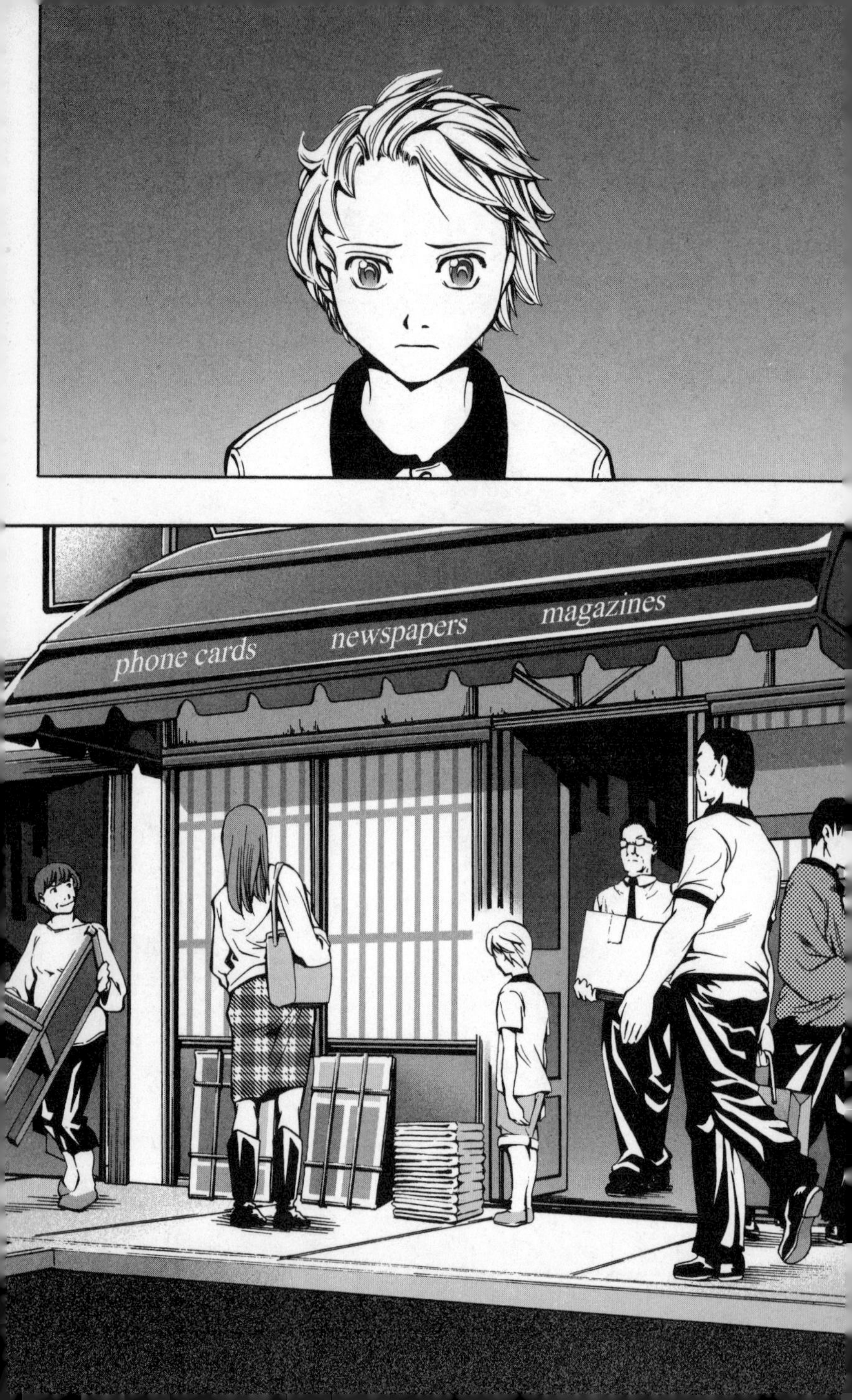
phone cards
newspapers
magazines

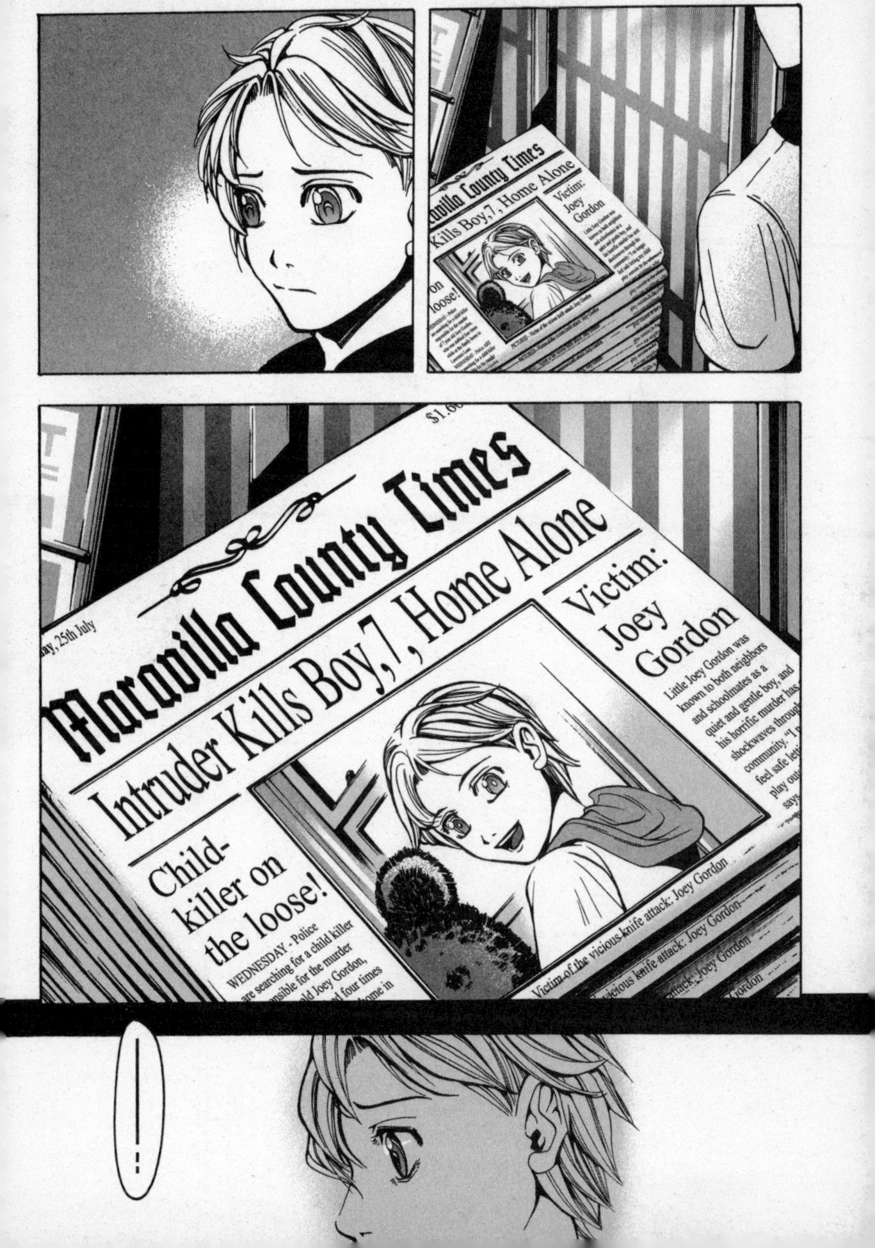
Maravilla County Times
Intruder Kills Boy,7, Home Alone
Victim: Joey Gordon
Little Joey Gordon was known to both neighbors and schoolmates as a quiet and gentle boy, and his horrific murder has
Child-killer on the loose!
WEDNESDAY - Police are searching for a child killer
Victim of the vicious knife attack: Joey Gordon
!

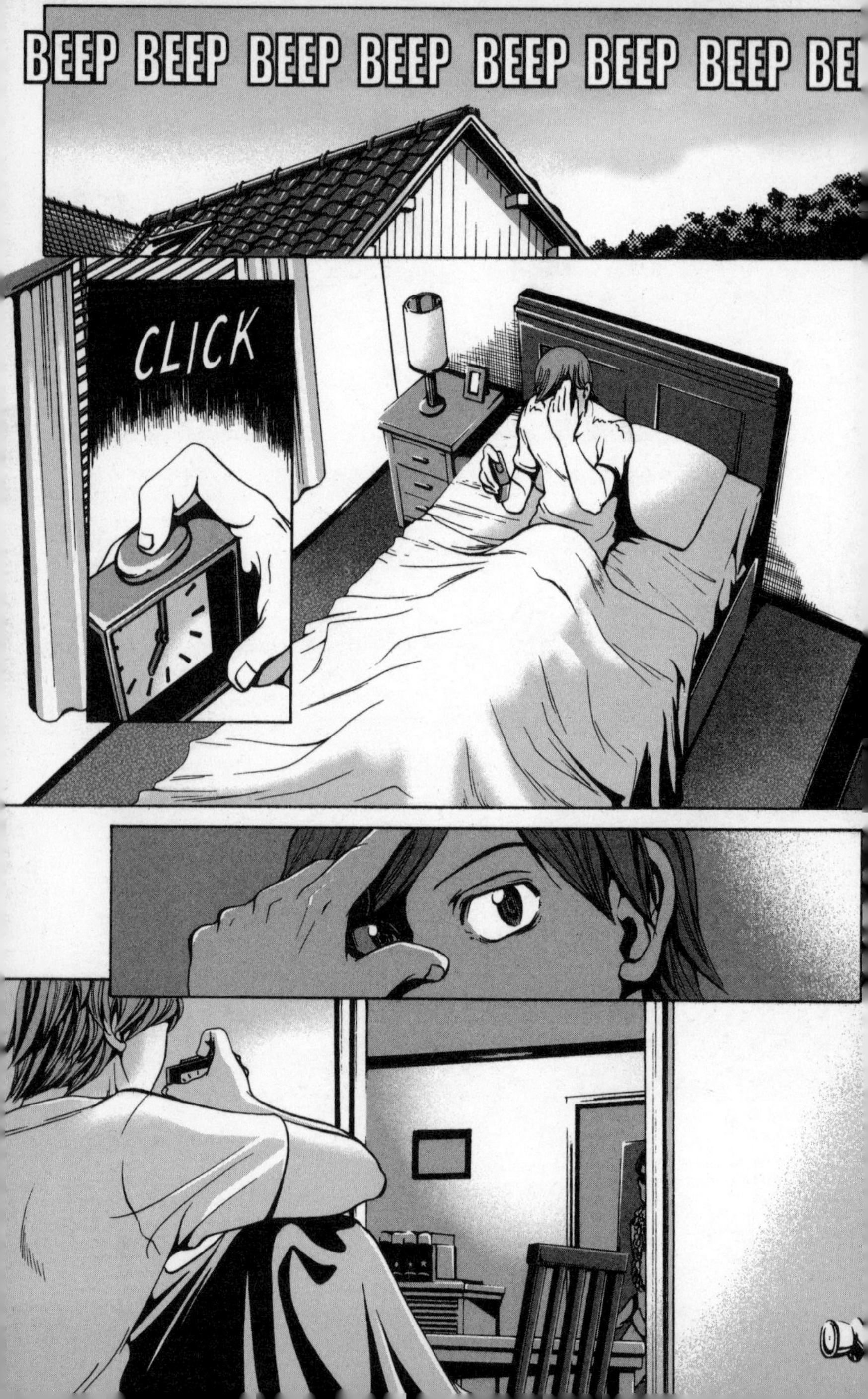
BEEP BEEP BEEP BEEP BEEP BEEP BEEP BE
CLICK

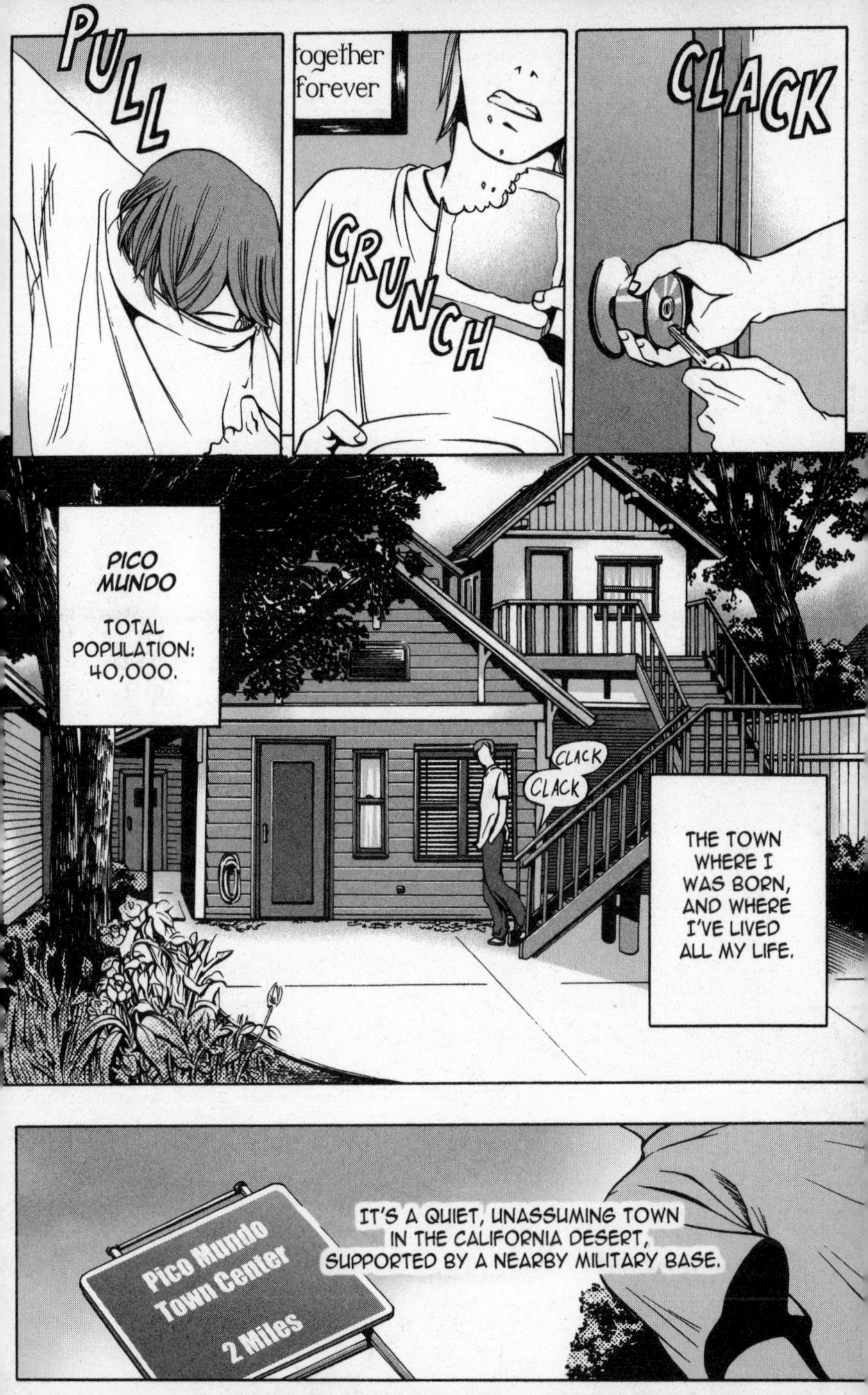
PULL
together
forever
CRUNCH
CLACK
PICO MUNDO
TOTAL POPULATION: 40,000.
CLACK
CLACK
THE TOWN WHERE I WAS BORN, AND WHERE I'VE LIVED ALL MY LIFE.
Pico Mundo
Town Center
2 Miles
IT'S A QUIET, UNASSUMING TOWN IN THE CALIFORNIA DESERT, SUPPORTED BY A NEARBY MILITARY BASE.

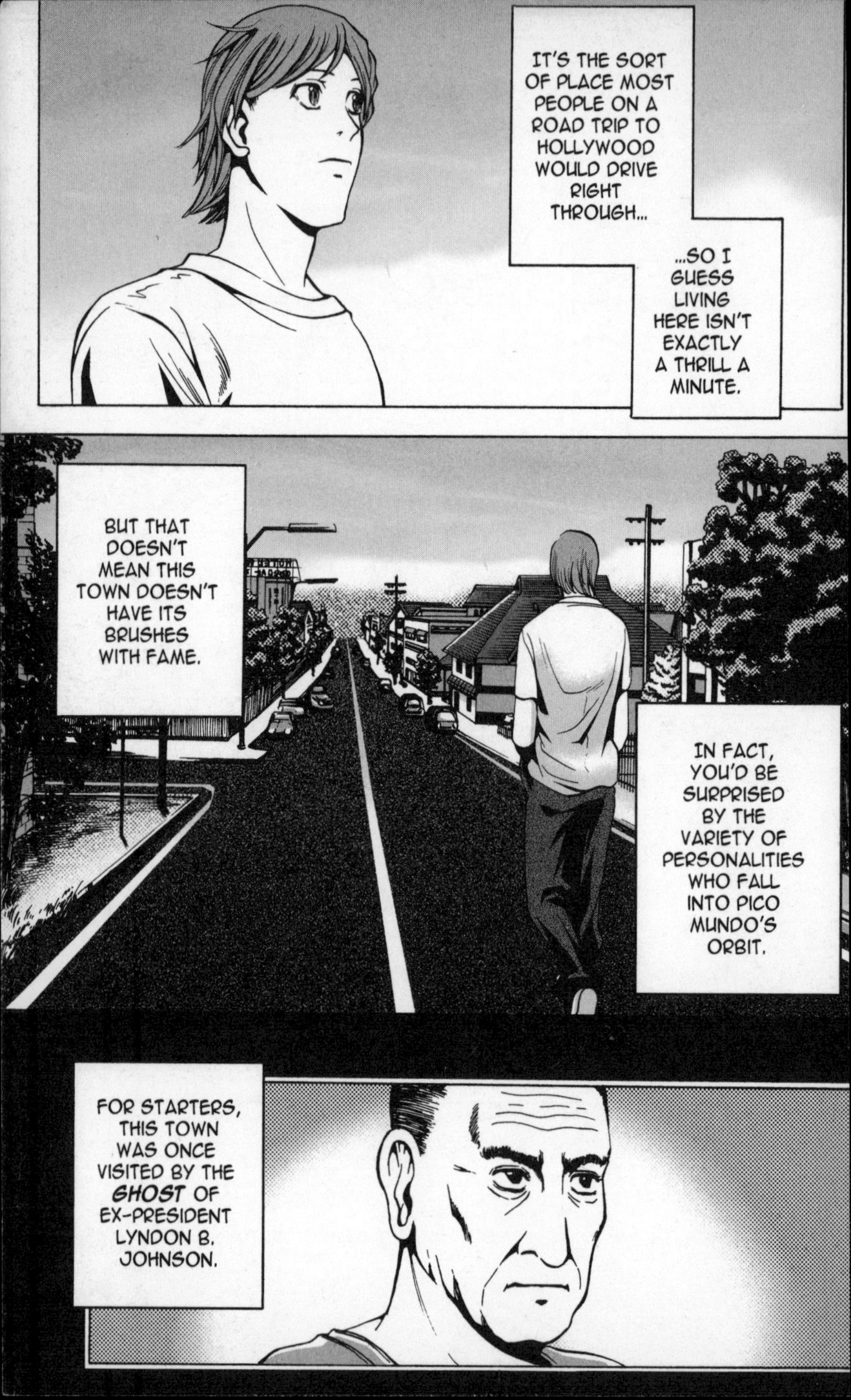
IT'S THE SORT OF PLACE MOST PEOPLE ON A ROAD TRIP TO HOLLYWOOD WOULD DRIVE RIGHT THROUGH...
...SO I GUESS LIVING HERE ISN'T EXACTLY A THRILL A MINUTE.
BUT THAT DOESN'T MEAN THIS TOWN DOESN'T HAVE ITS BRUSHES WITH FAME.
IN FACT, YOU'D BE SURPRISED BY THE VARIETY OF PERSONALITIES WHO FALL INTO PICO MUNDO'S ORBIT.
FOR STARTERS, THIS TOWN WAS ONCE VISITED BY THE GHOST OF EX-PRESIDENT LYNDON B. JOHNSON.

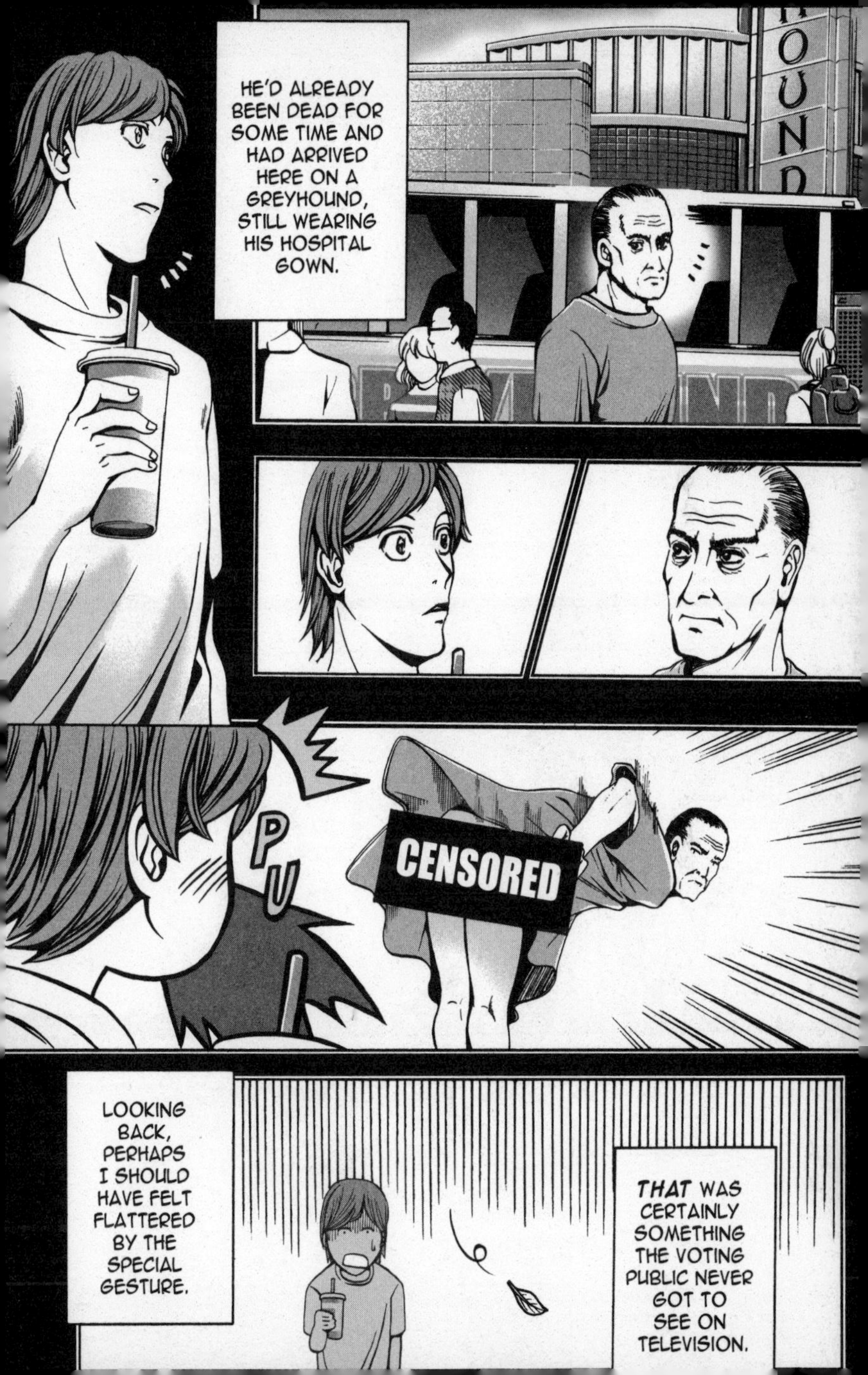
HE'D ALREADY BEEN DEAD FOR SOME TIME AND HAD ARRIVED HERE ON A GREYHOUND, STILL WEARING HIS HOSPITAL GOWN.
HOUND
PU
CENSORED
LOOKING BACK, PERHAPS I SHOULD HAVE FELT FLATTERED BY THE SPECIAL GESTURE.
THAT WAS CERTAINLY SOMETHING THE VOTING PUBLIC NEVER GOT TO SEE ON TELEVISION.

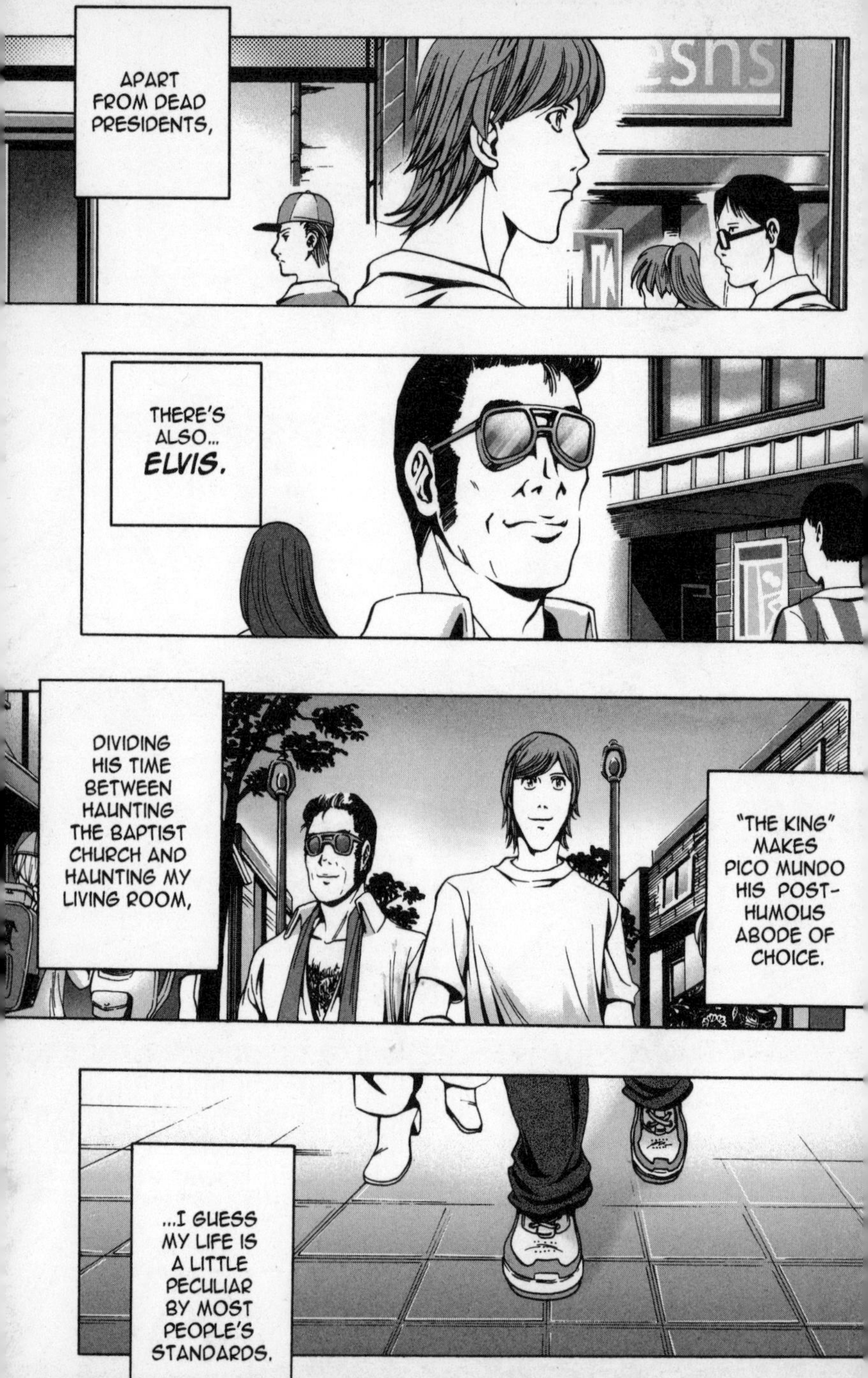
APART FROM DEAD PRESIDENTS,
esns
THERE'S ALSO... ELVIS.
DIVIDING HIS TIME BETWEEN HAUNTING THE BAPTIST CHURCH AND HAUNTING MY LIVING ROOM,
"THE KING" MAKES PICO MUNDO HIS POST-HUMOUS ABODE OF CHOICE.
...I GUESS MY LIFE IS A LITTLE PECULIAR BY MOST PEOPLE'S STANDARDS.

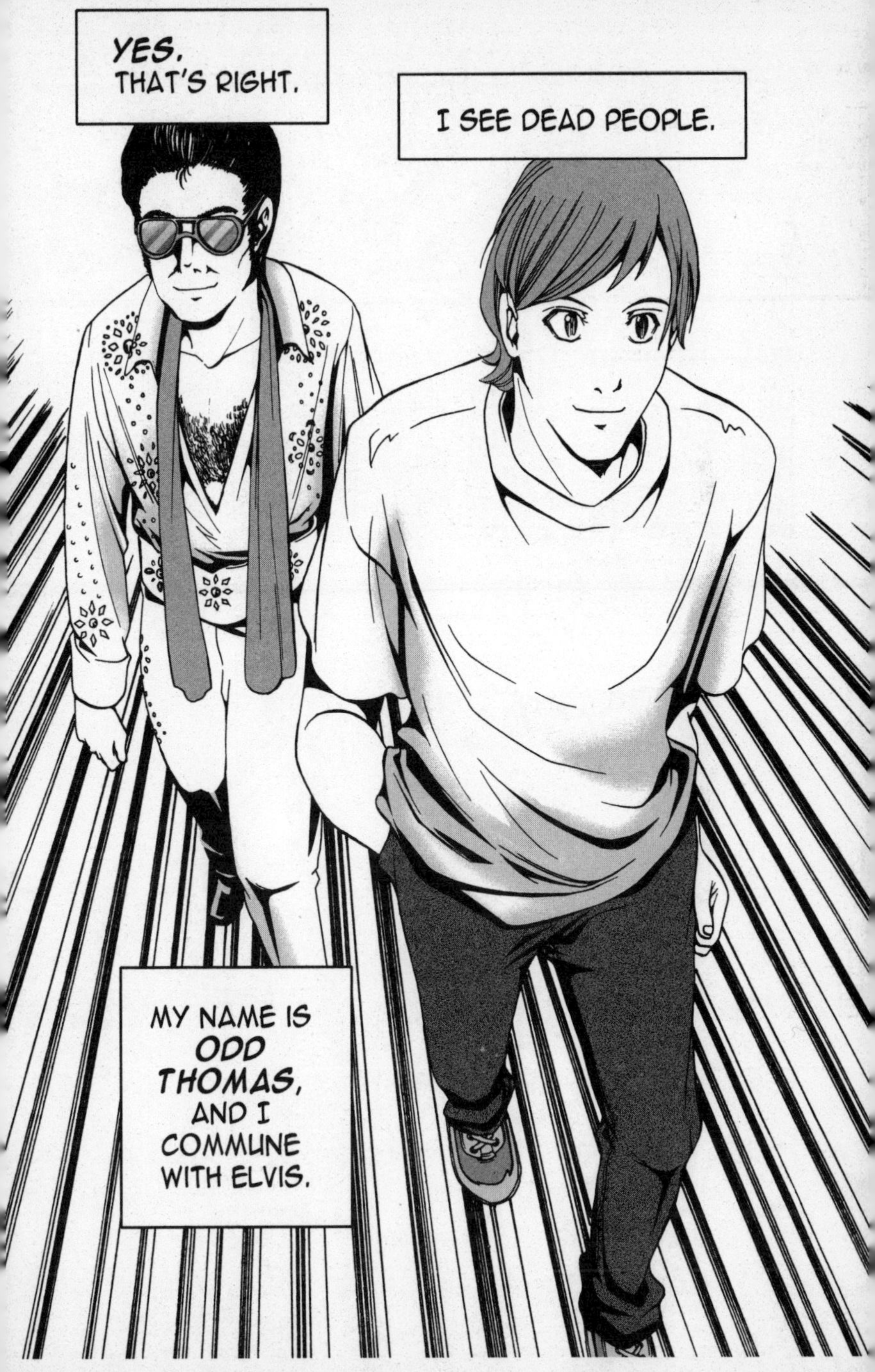
YES. THAT'S RIGHT.
I SEE DEAD PEOPLE.
MY NAME IS ODD THOMAS, AND I COMMUNE WITH ELVIS.

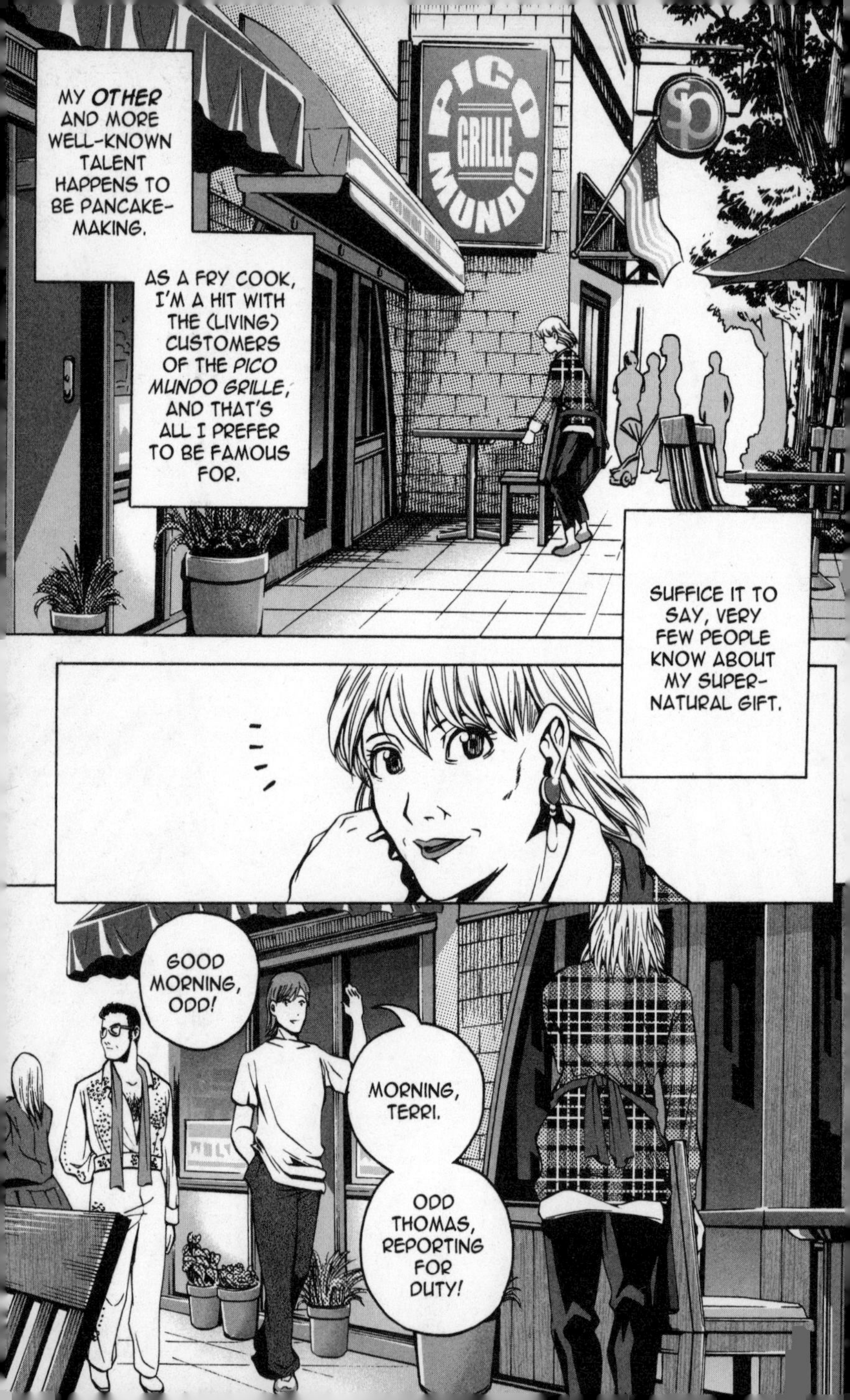
PICO GRILLE MUNDO
MY OTHER AND MORE WELL-KNOWN TALENT HAPPENS TO BE PANCAKE-MAKING.
AS A FRY COOK, I'M A HIT WITH THE (LIVING) CUSTOMERS OF THE PICO MUNDO GRILLE, AND THAT'S ALL I PREFER TO BE FAMOUS FOR.
SUFFICE IT TO SAY, VERY FEW PEOPLE KNOW ABOUT MY SUPER-NATURAL GIFT.
GOOD MORNING, ODD!
MORNING, TERRI.
ODD THOMAS, REPORTING FOR DUTY!

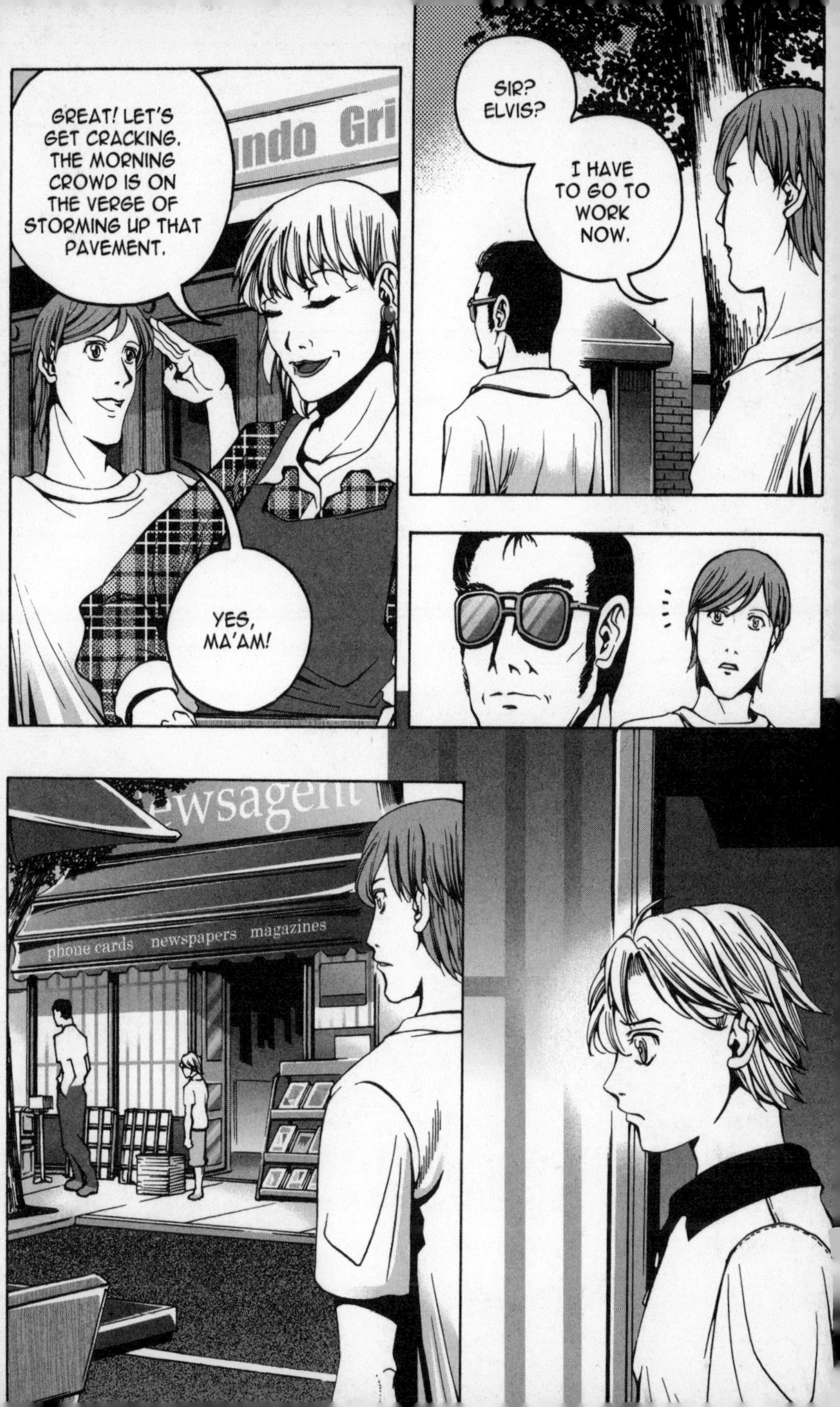
ndo Gri
GREAT! LET'S GET CRACKING. THE MORNING CROWD IS ON THE VERGE OF STORMING UP THAT PAVEMENT.
YES, MA'AM!
SIR? ELVIS?
I HAVE TO GO TO WORK NOW.
ewsagent
phone cards newspapers magazines

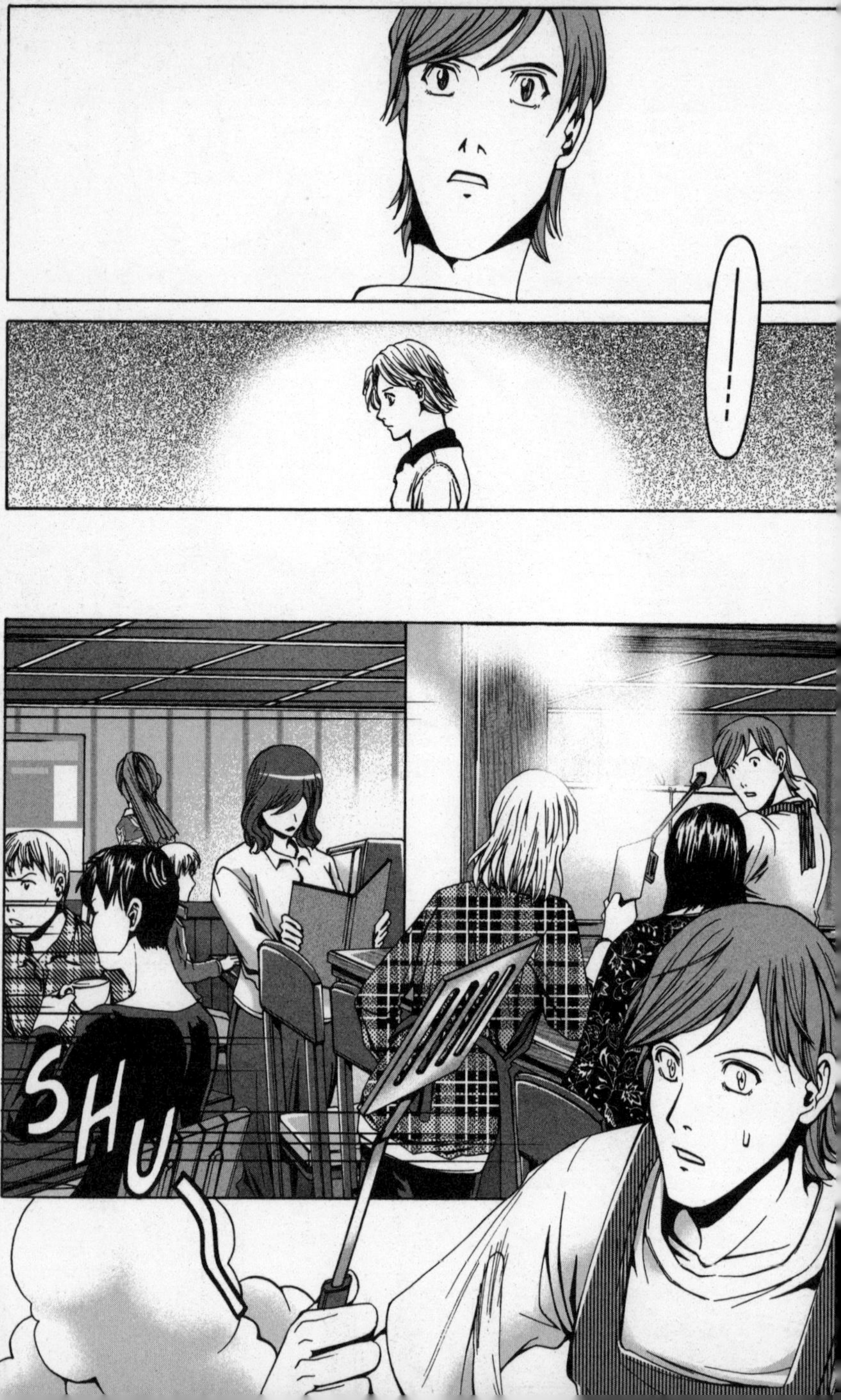
!
SHU

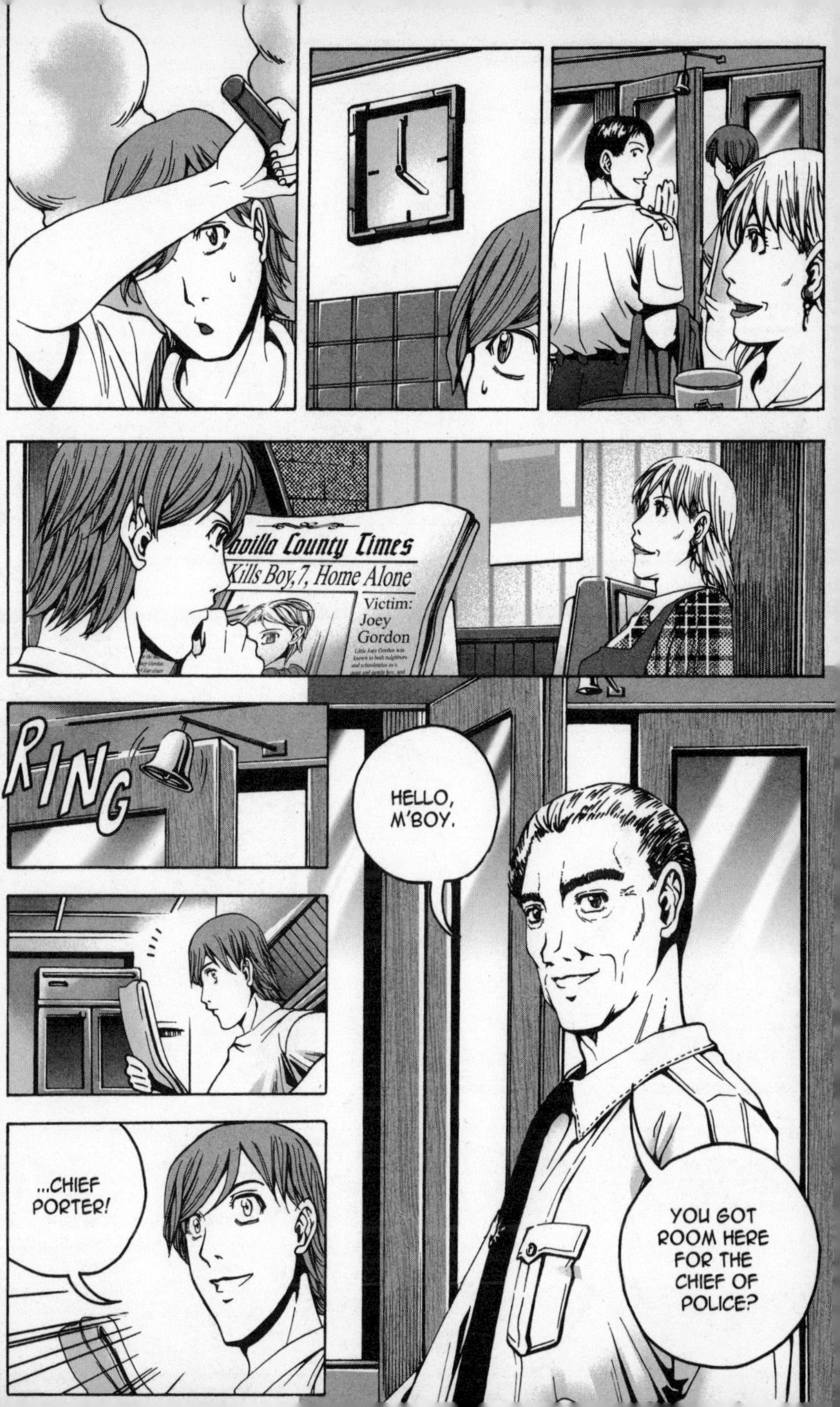

...villa County Times
Kills Boy, 7, Home Alone
Victim: Joey Gordon
RING
HELLO, M'BOY.
YOU GOT ROOM HERE FOR THE CHIEF OF POLICE?
...CHIEF PORTER!

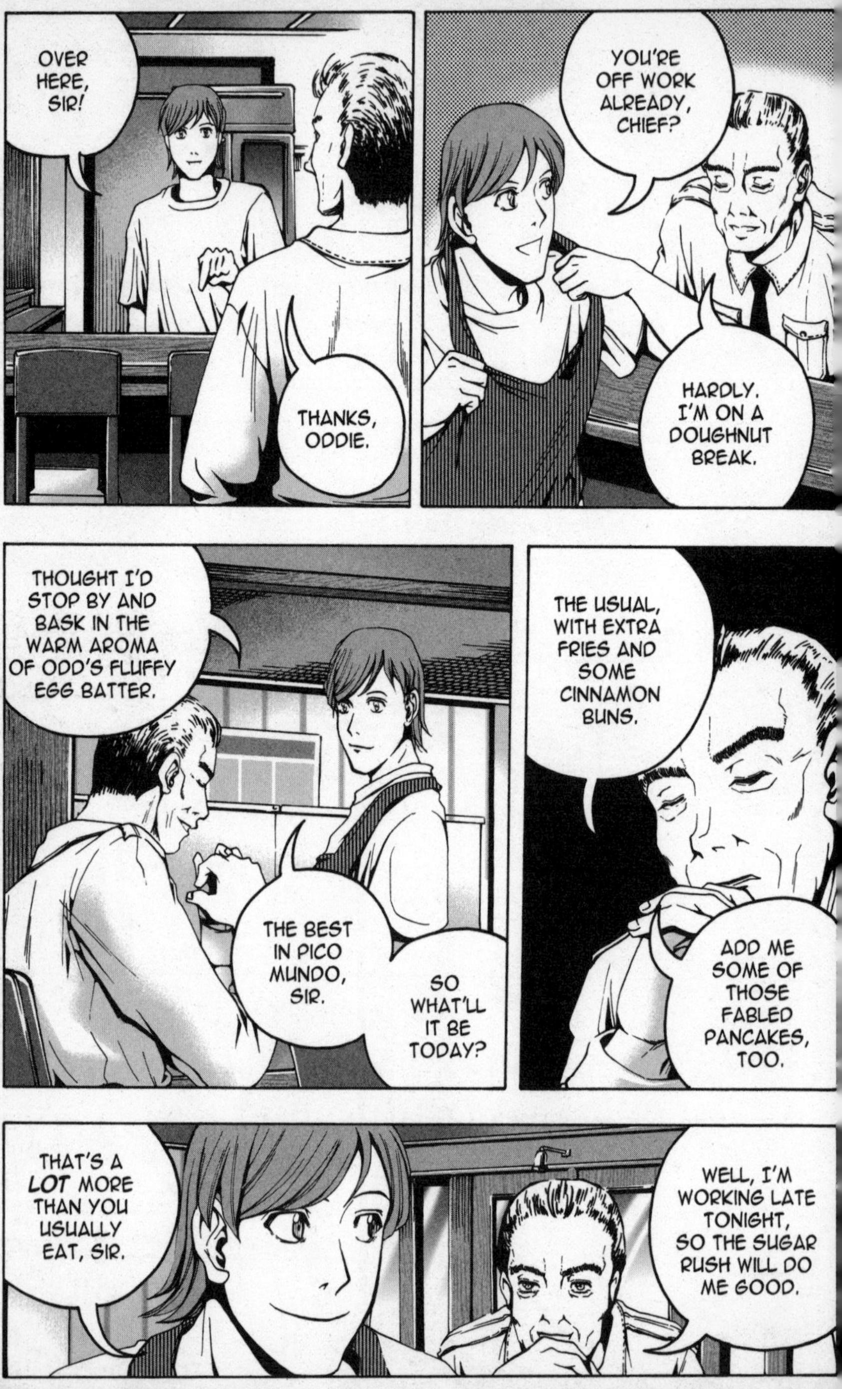
OVER HERE, SIR!
THANKS, ODDIE.
YOU'RE OFF WORK ALREADY, CHIEF?
HARDLY. I'M ON A DOUGHNUT BREAK.
THOUGHT I'D STOP BY AND BASK IN THE WARM AROMA OF ODD'S FLUFFY EGG BATTER.
THE BEST IN PICO MUNDO, SIR.
SO WHAT'LL IT BE TODAY?
THE USUAL, WITH EXTRA FRIES AND SOME CINNAMON BUNS.
ADD ME SOME OF THOSE FABLED PANCAKES, TOO.
THAT'S A *LOT* MORE THAN YOU USUALLY EAT, SIR.
WELL, I'M WORKING LATE TONIGHT, SO THE SUGAR RUSH WILL DO ME GOOD.

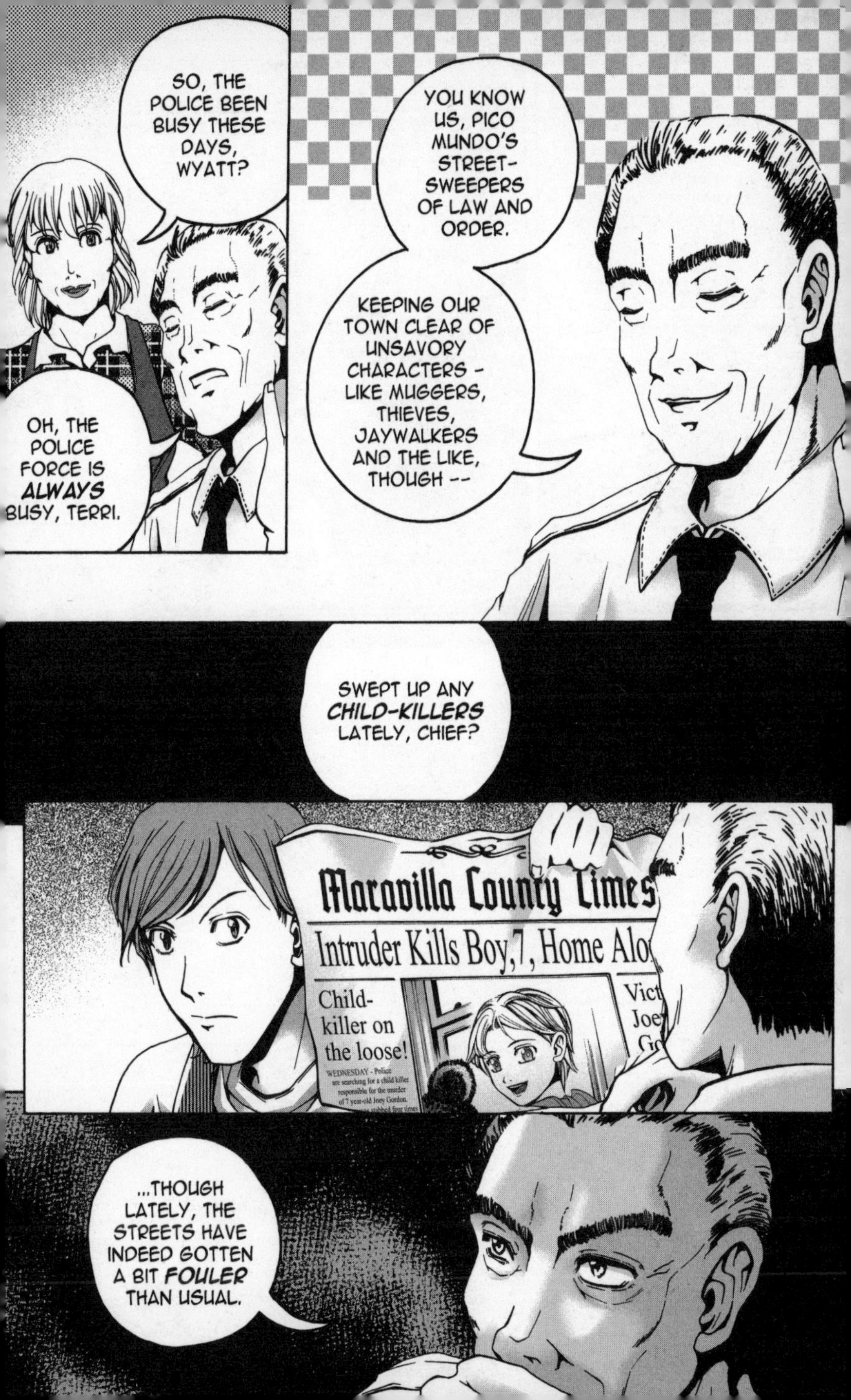
SO, THE POLICE BEEN BUSY THESE DAYS, WYATT?
OH, THE POLICE FORCE IS ALWAYS BUSY, TERRI.
YOU KNOW US, PICO MUNDO'S STREET-SWEEPERS OF LAW AND ORDER.
KEEPING OUR TOWN CLEAR OF UNSAVORY CHARACTERS - LIKE MUGGERS, THIEVES, JAYWALKERS AND THE LIKE, THOUGH --
SWEPT UP ANY CHILD-KILLERS LATELY, CHIEF?
Maravilla County Times
Intruder Kills Boy,7, Home Alo
Child-killer on the loose!
WEDNESDAY - Police are searching for a child killer responsible for the murder of 7 year-old Joey Gordon.
...THOUGH LATELY, THE STREETS HAVE INDEED GOTTEN A BIT FOULER THAN USUAL.

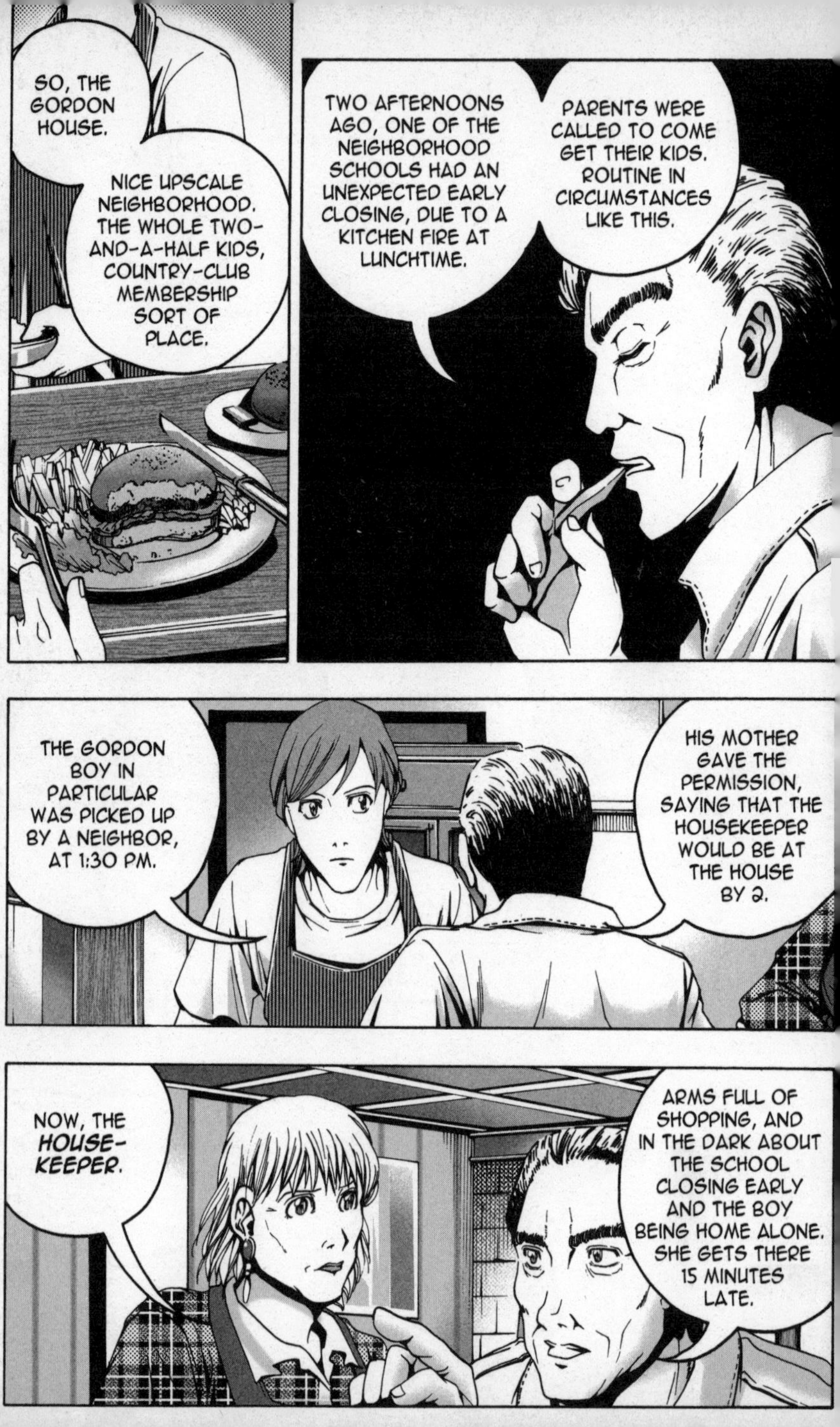
SO, THE GORDON HOUSE.
NICE UPSCALE NEIGHBORHOOD. THE WHOLE TWO-AND-A-HALF KIDS, COUNTRY-CLUB MEMBERSHIP SORT OF PLACE.
TWO AFTERNOONS AGO, ONE OF THE NEIGHBORHOOD SCHOOLS HAD AN UNEXPECTED EARLY CLOSING, DUE TO A KITCHEN FIRE AT LUNCHTIME.
PARENTS WERE CALLED TO COME GET THEIR KIDS. ROUTINE IN CIRCUMSTANCES LIKE THIS.
THE GORDON BOY IN PARTICULAR WAS PICKED UP BY A NEIGHBOR, AT 1:30 PM.
HIS MOTHER GAVE THE PERMISSION, SAYING THAT THE HOUSEKEEPER WOULD BE AT THE HOUSE BY 2.
NOW, THE *HOUSE-KEEPER*.
ARMS FULL OF SHOPPING, AND IN THE DARK ABOUT THE SCHOOL CLOSING EARLY AND THE BOY BEING HOME ALONE. SHE GETS THERE 15 MINUTES LATE.

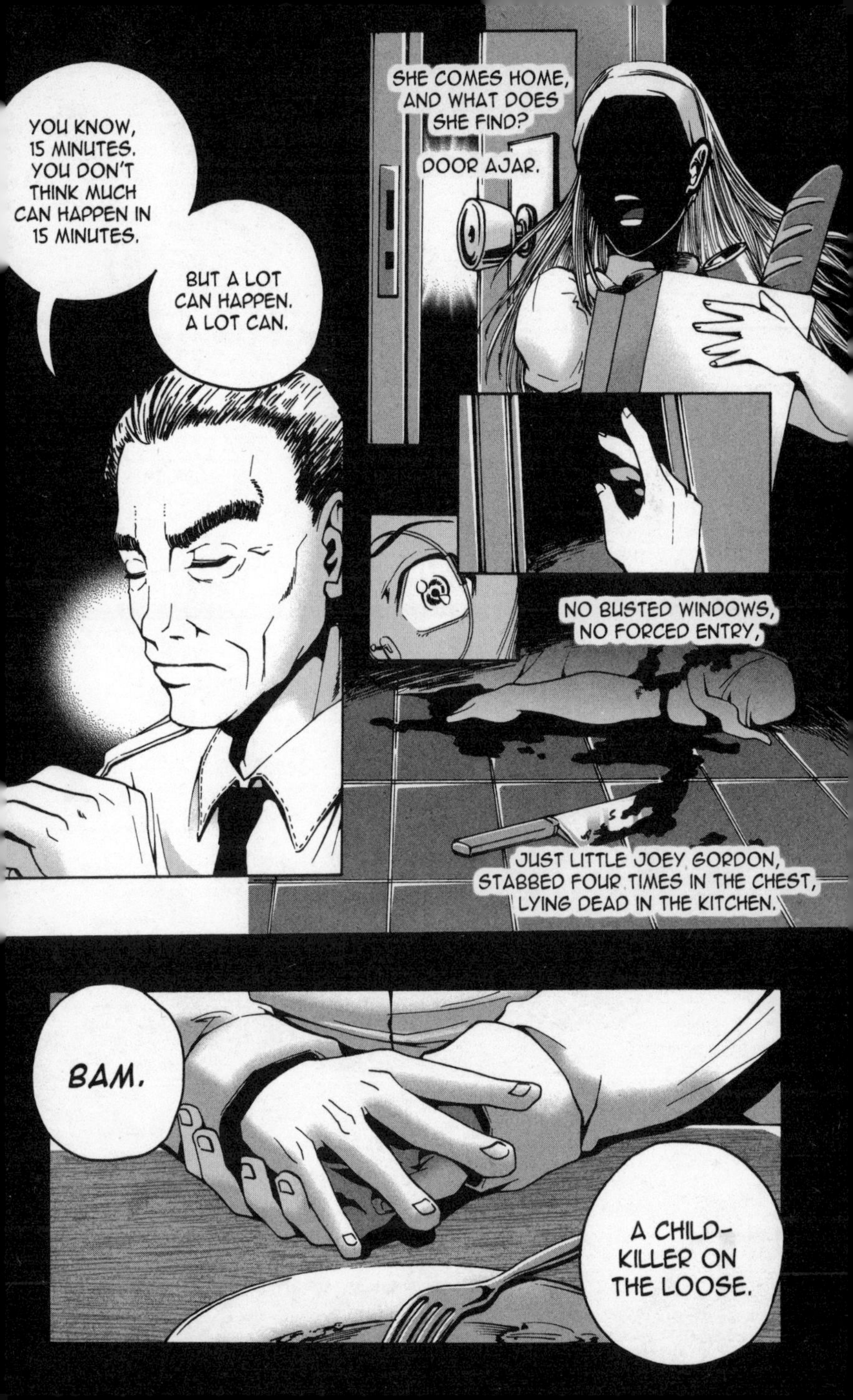
YOU KNOW, 15 MINUTES. YOU DON'T THINK MUCH CAN HAPPEN IN 15 MINUTES.
BUT A LOT CAN HAPPEN. A LOT CAN.
SHE COMES HOME, AND WHAT DOES SHE FIND?
DOOR AJAR.
NO BUSTED WINDOWS, NO FORCED ENTRY,
JUST LITTLE JOEY GORDON, STABBED FOUR TIMES IN THE CHEST, LYING DEAD IN THE KITCHEN.
BAM.
A CHILD-KILLER ON THE LOOSE.

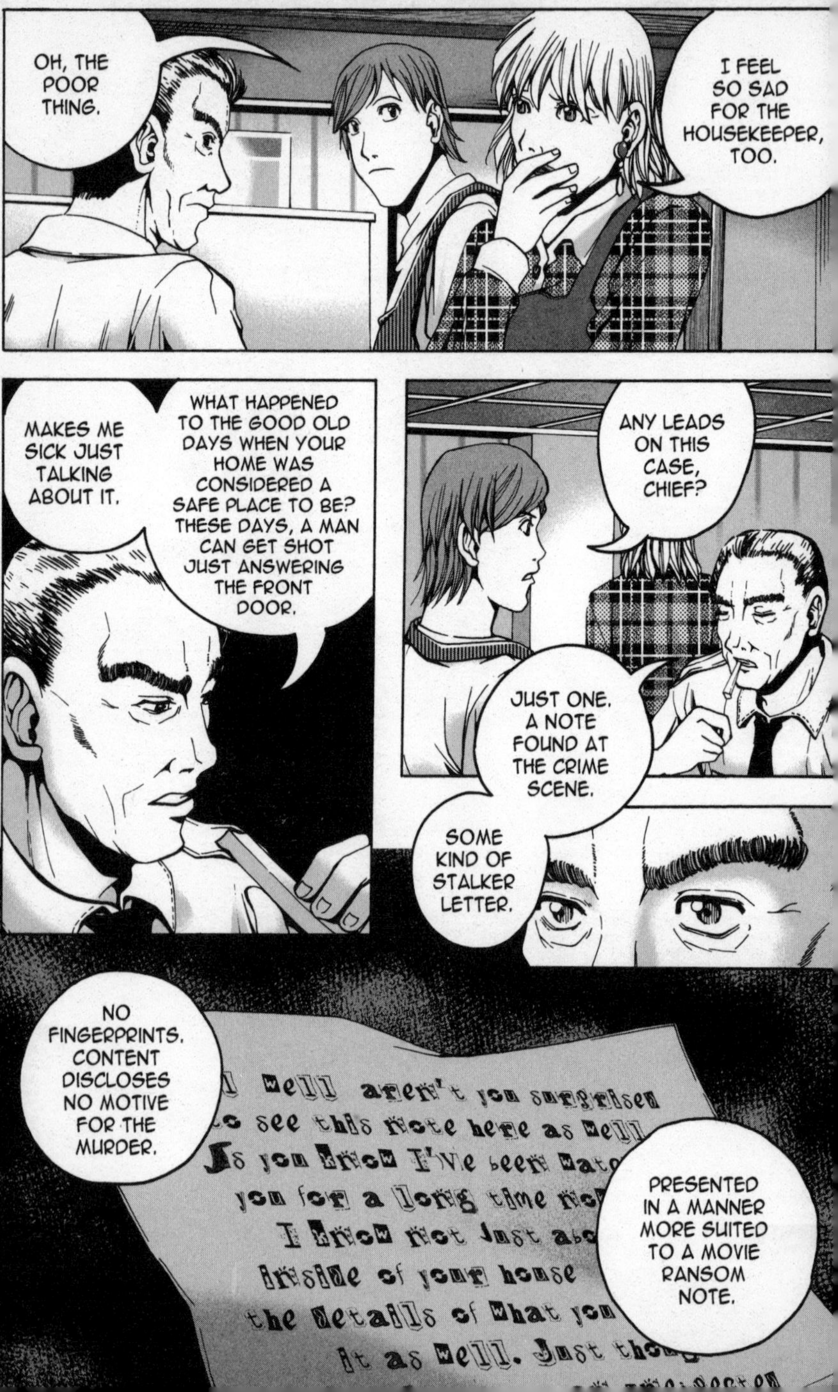
OH, THE POOR THING.
I FEEL SO SAD FOR THE HOUSEKEEPER, TOO.
MAKES ME SICK JUST TALKING ABOUT IT.
WHAT HAPPENED TO THE GOOD OLD DAYS WHEN YOUR HOME WAS CONSIDERED A SAFE PLACE TO BE? THESE DAYS, A MAN CAN GET SHOT JUST ANSWERING THE FRONT DOOR.
ANY LEADS ON THIS CASE, CHIEF?
JUST ONE. A NOTE FOUND AT THE CRIME SCENE.
SOME KIND OF STALKER LETTER.
NO FINGERPRINTS. CONTENT DISCLOSES NO MOTIVE FOR THE MURDER.
well aren't you surprised
to see this note here as well
As you know I've been
you for a long time
I know not just
inside of your house
the details of what you
it as well. Just
PRESENTED IN A MANNER MORE SUITED TO A MOVIE RANSOM NOTE.

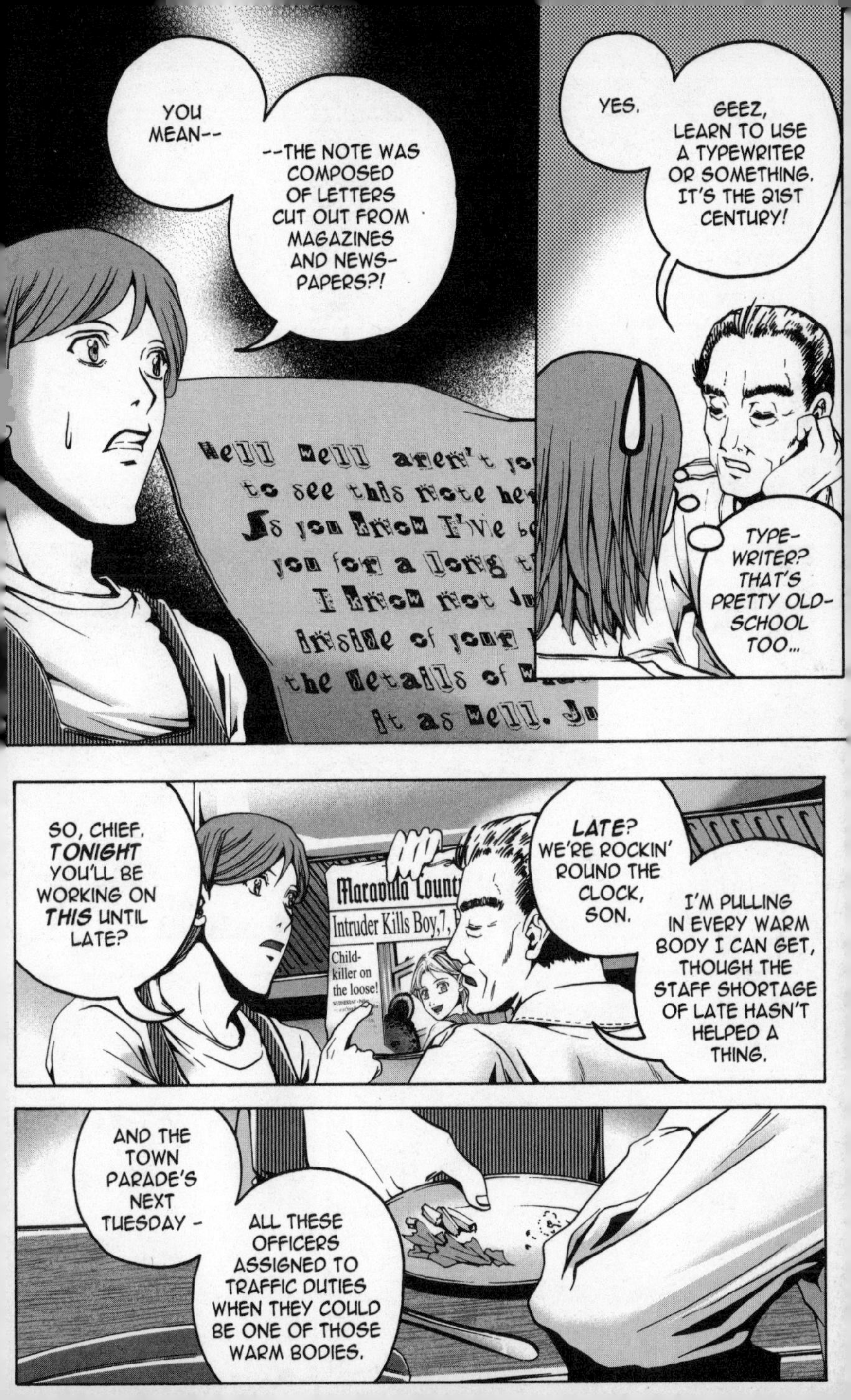
YOU MEAN--
--THE NOTE WAS COMPOSED OF LETTERS CUT OUT FROM MAGAZINES AND NEWS-PAPERS?!
YES.
GEEZ, LEARN TO USE A TYPEWRITER OR SOMETHING. IT'S THE 21ST CENTURY!
TYPE-WRITER? THAT'S PRETTY OLD-SCHOOL TOO...
SO, CHIEF. TONIGHT YOU'LL BE WORKING ON THIS UNTIL LATE?
LATE? WE'RE ROCKIN' ROUND THE CLOCK, SON.
I'M PULLING IN EVERY WARM BODY I CAN GET, THOUGH THE STAFF SHORTAGE OF LATE HASN'T HELPED A THING.
Intruder Kills Boy,7,
Child-killer on the loose!
AND THE TOWN PARADE'S NEXT TUESDAY -
ALL THESE OFFICERS ASSIGNED TO TRAFFIC DUTIES WHEN THEY COULD BE ONE OF THOSE WARM BODIES.

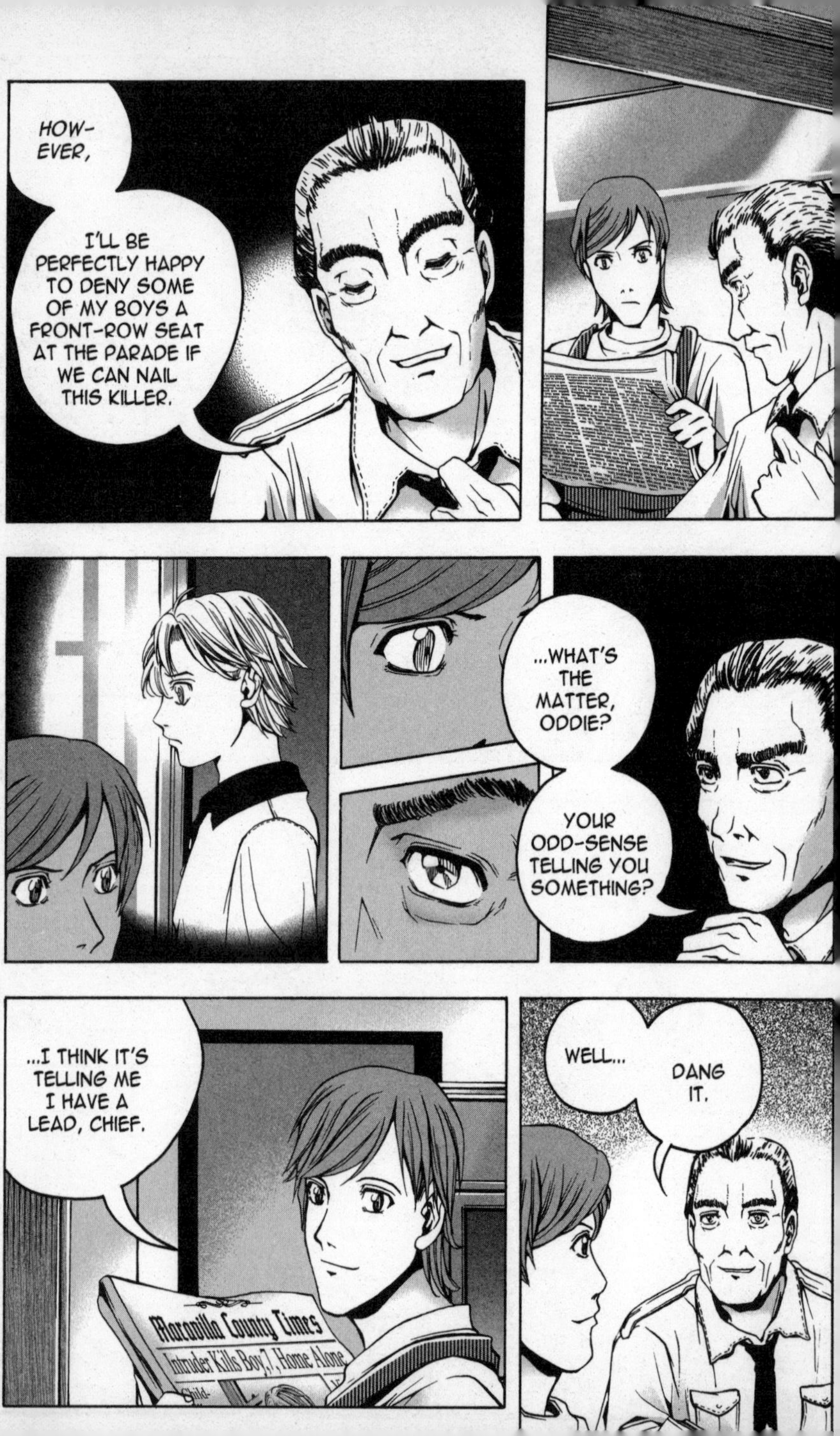
HOW-EVER,
I'LL BE PERFECTLY HAPPY TO DENY SOME OF MY BOYS A FRONT-ROW SEAT AT THE PARADE IF WE CAN NAIL THIS KILLER.
...WHAT'S THE MATTER, ODDIE?
YOUR ODD-SENSE TELLING YOU SOMETHING?
...I THINK IT'S TELLING ME I HAVE A LEAD, CHIEF.
Maravilla County Times
Intruder Kills Boy, 7, Home Alone
WELL...
DANG IT.

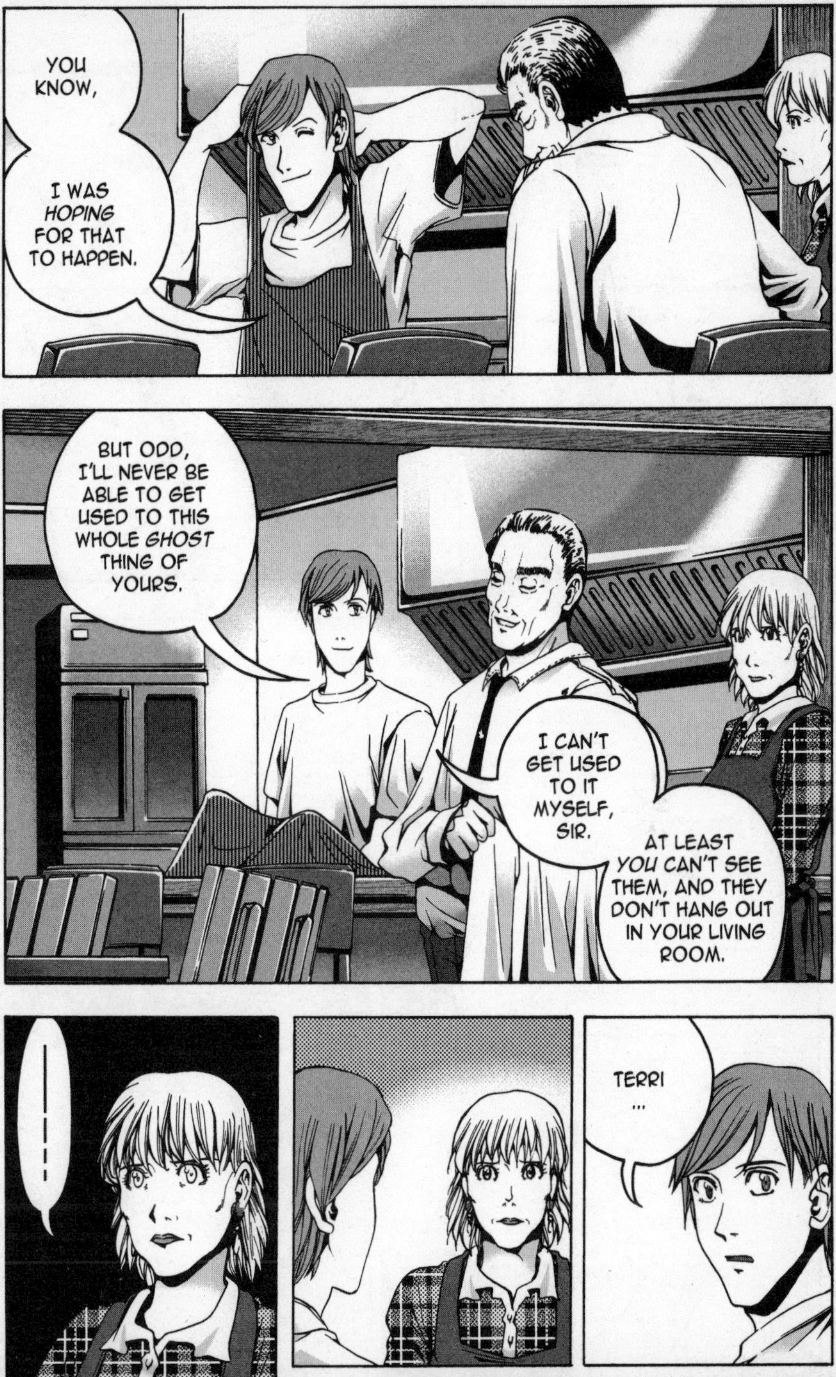
YOU KNOW,
I WAS *HOPING* FOR THAT TO HAPPEN.
BUT ODD, I'LL NEVER BE ABLE TO GET USED TO THIS WHOLE *GHOST* THING OF YOURS.
I CAN'T GET USED TO IT MYSELF, SIR.
AT LEAST *YOU* CAN'T SEE THEM, AND THEY DON'T HANG OUT IN YOUR LIVING ROOM.
- - -
TERRI ...

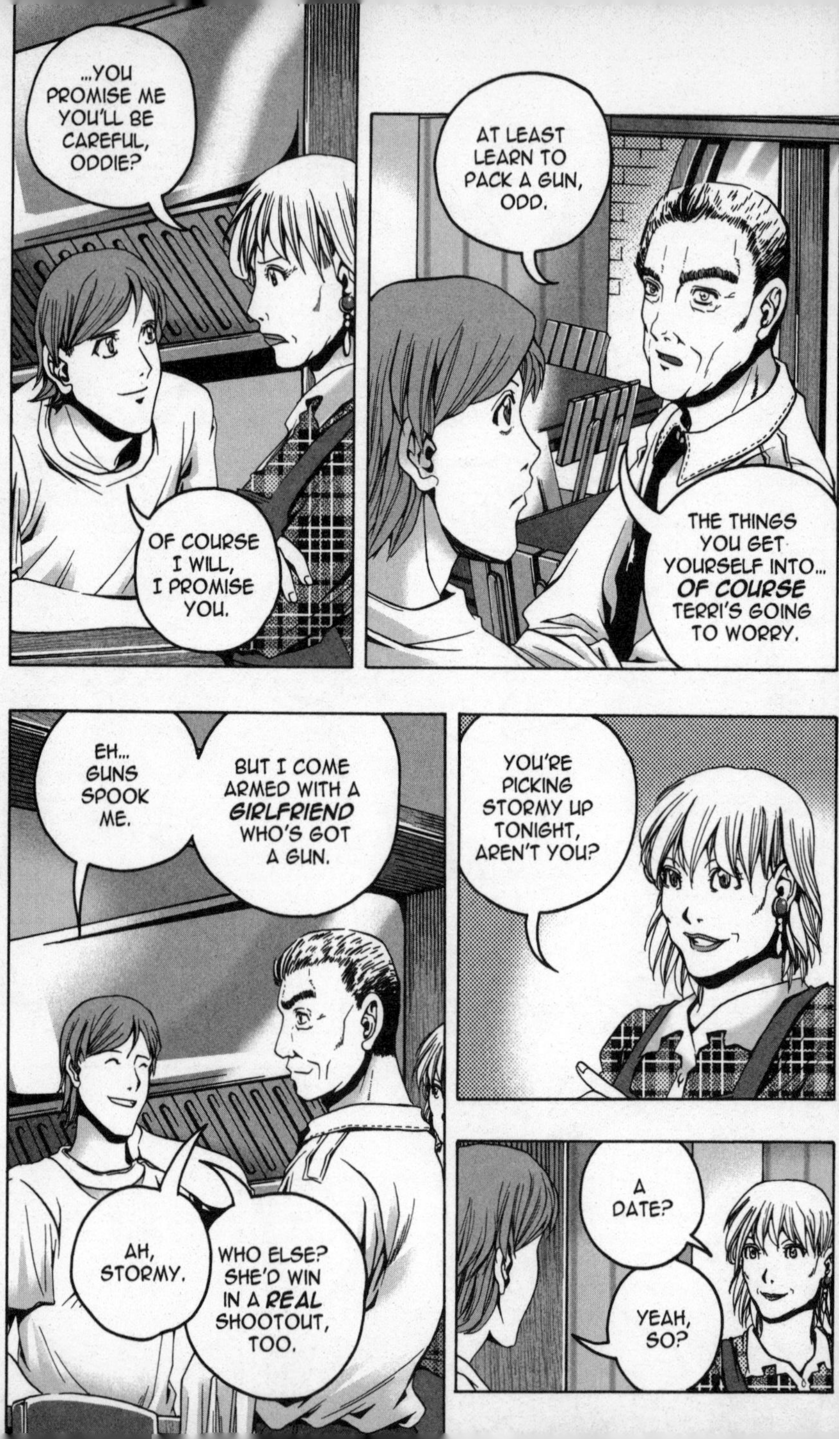
...YOU PROMISE ME YOU'LL BE CAREFUL, ODDIE?
OF COURSE I WILL, I PROMISE YOU.
AT LEAST LEARN TO PACK A GUN, ODD.
THE THINGS YOU GET YOURSELF INTO... OF COURSE TERRI'S GOING TO WORRY.
EH... GUNS SPOOK ME.
BUT I COME ARMED WITH A GIRLFRIEND WHO'S GOT A GUN.
AH, STORMY.
WHO ELSE? SHE'D WIN IN A REAL SHOOTOUT, TOO.
YOU'RE PICKING STORMY UP TONIGHT, AREN'T YOU?
A DATE?
YEAH, SO?

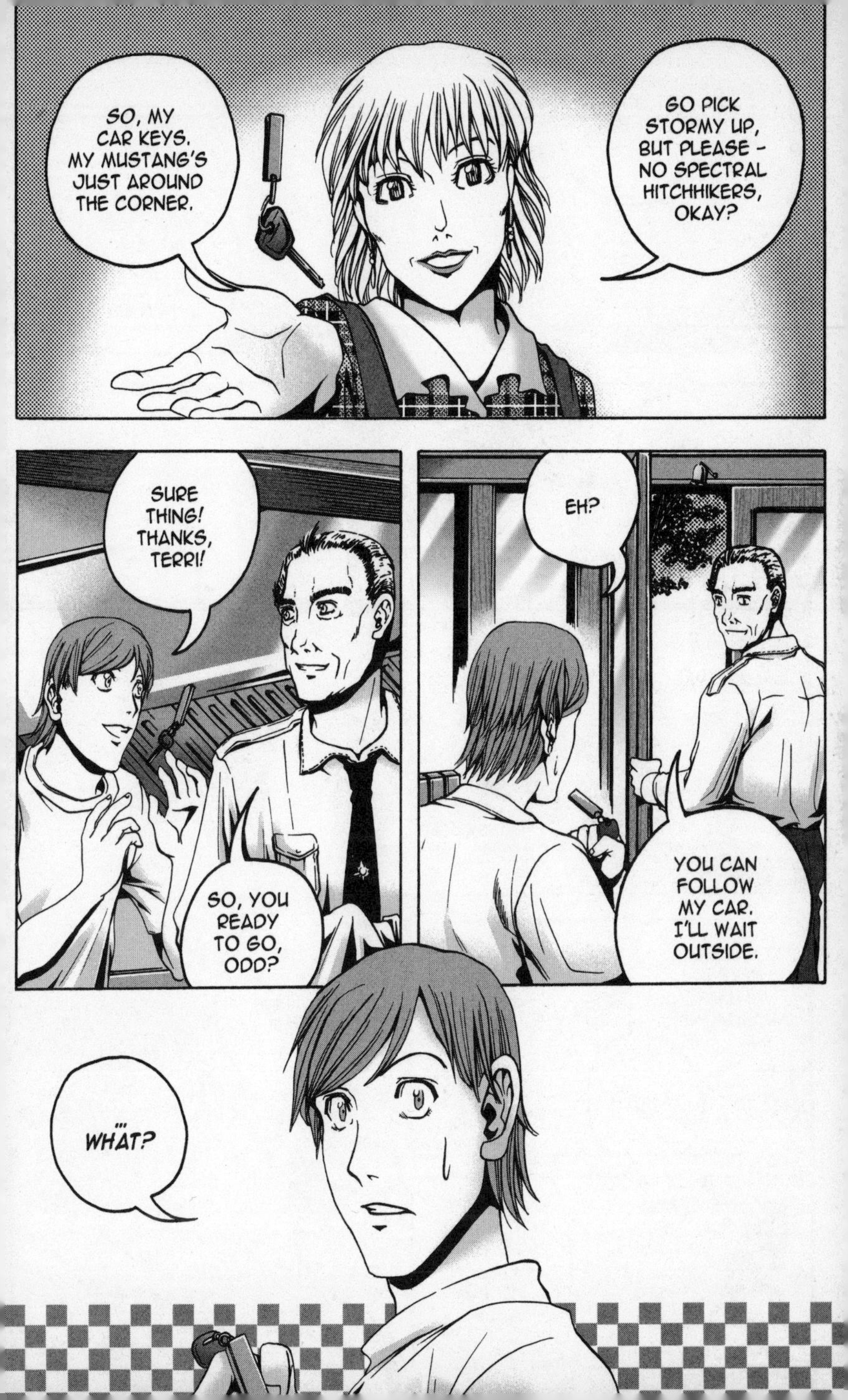
SO, MY CAR KEYS. MY MUSTANG'S JUST AROUND THE CORNER.
GO PICK STORMY UP, BUT PLEASE - NO SPECTRAL HITCHHIKERS, OKAY?
SURE THING! THANKS, TERRI!
SO, YOU READY TO GO, ODD?
EH?
YOU CAN FOLLOW MY CAR. I'LL WAIT OUTSIDE.
... WHAT?

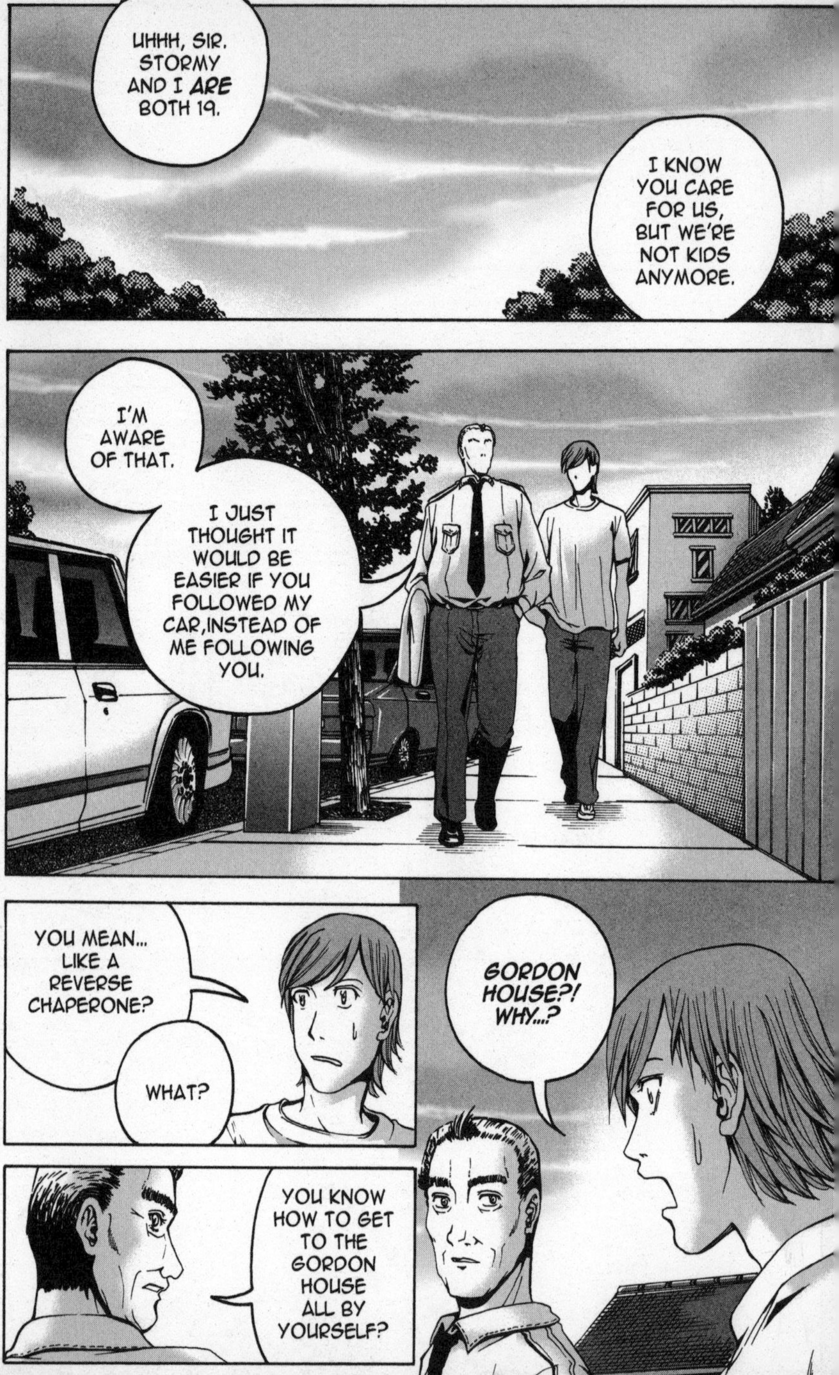
UHHH, SIR. STORMY AND I ARE BOTH 19.
I KNOW YOU CARE FOR US, BUT WE'RE NOT KIDS ANYMORE.
I'M AWARE OF THAT.
I JUST THOUGHT IT WOULD BE EASIER IF YOU FOLLOWED MY CAR,INSTEAD OF ME FOLLOWING YOU.
YOU MEAN... LIKE A REVERSE CHAPERONE?
WHAT?
GORDON HOUSE?! WHY...?
YOU KNOW HOW TO GET TO THE GORDON HOUSE ALL BY YOURSELF?

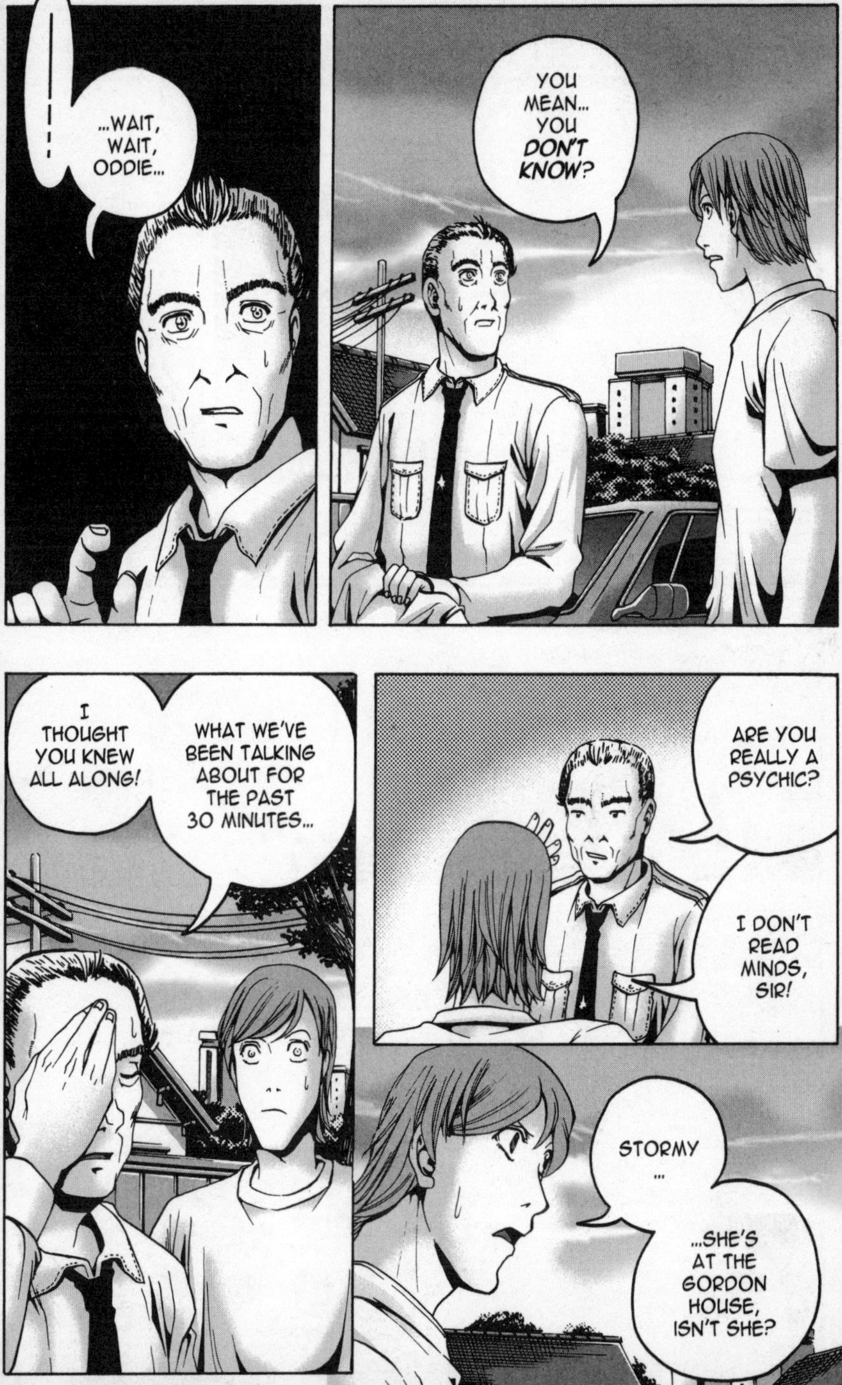
!
...WAIT, WAIT, ODDIE...
YOU MEAN... YOU DON'T KNOW?
I THOUGHT YOU KNEW ALL ALONG!
WHAT WE'VE BEEN TALKING ABOUT FOR THE PAST 30 MINUTES...
ARE YOU REALLY A PSYCHIC?
I DON'T READ MINDS, SIR!
STORMY ...
...SHE'S AT THE GORDON HOUSE, ISN'T SHE?

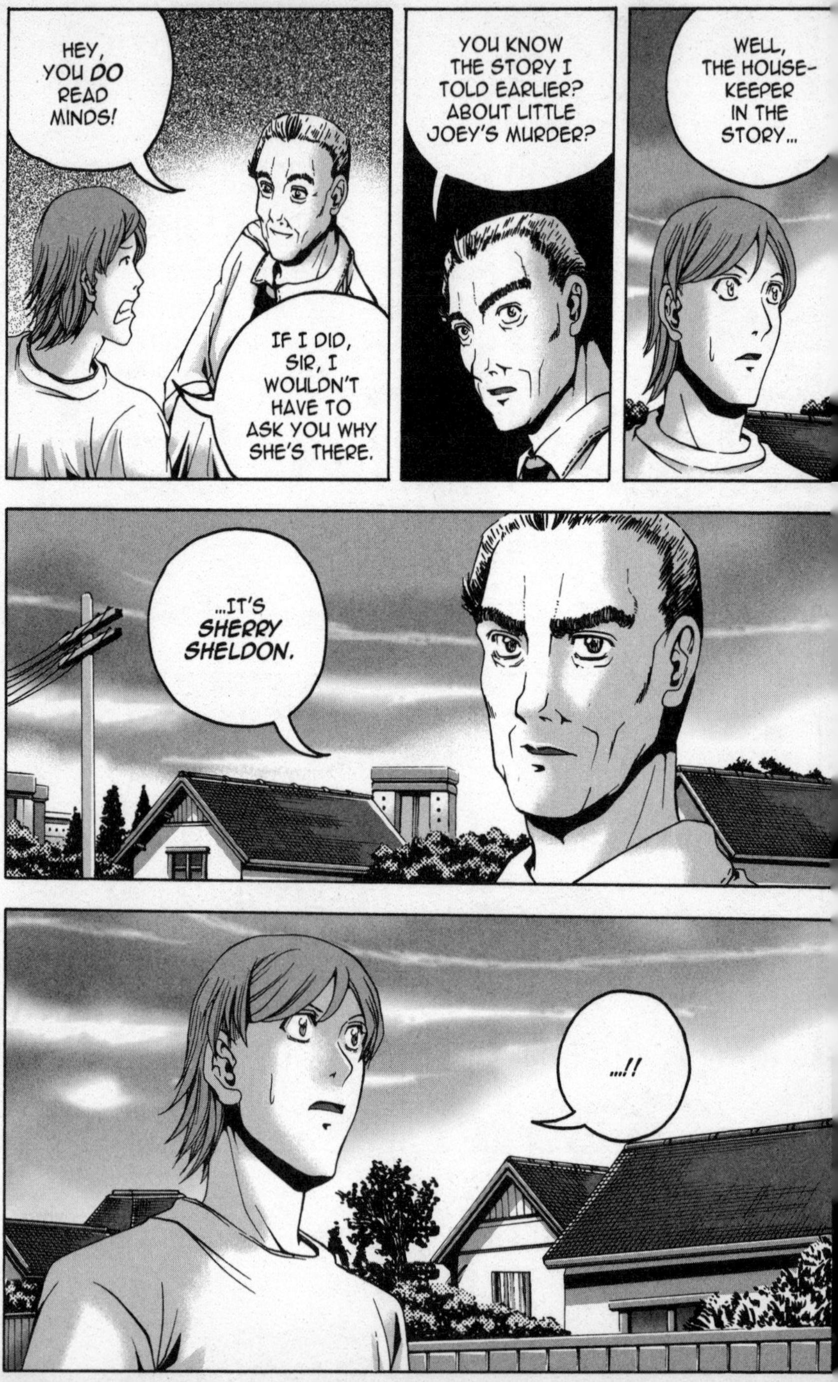
HEY, YOU DO READ MINDS!
IF I DID, SIR, I WOULDN'T HAVE TO ASK YOU WHY SHE'S THERE.
YOU KNOW THE STORY I TOLD EARLIER? ABOUT LITTLE JOEY'S MURDER?
WELL, THE HOUSE-KEEPER IN THE STORY...
...IT'S SHERRY SHELDON.
...!!

In Odd We Trust

Chapter 2

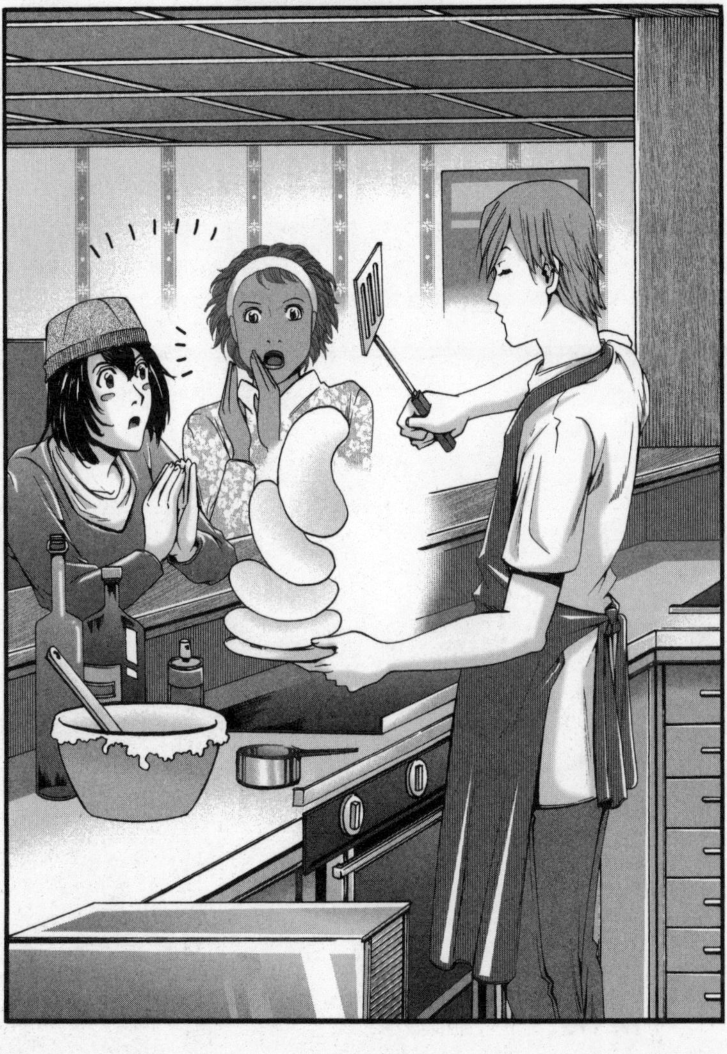

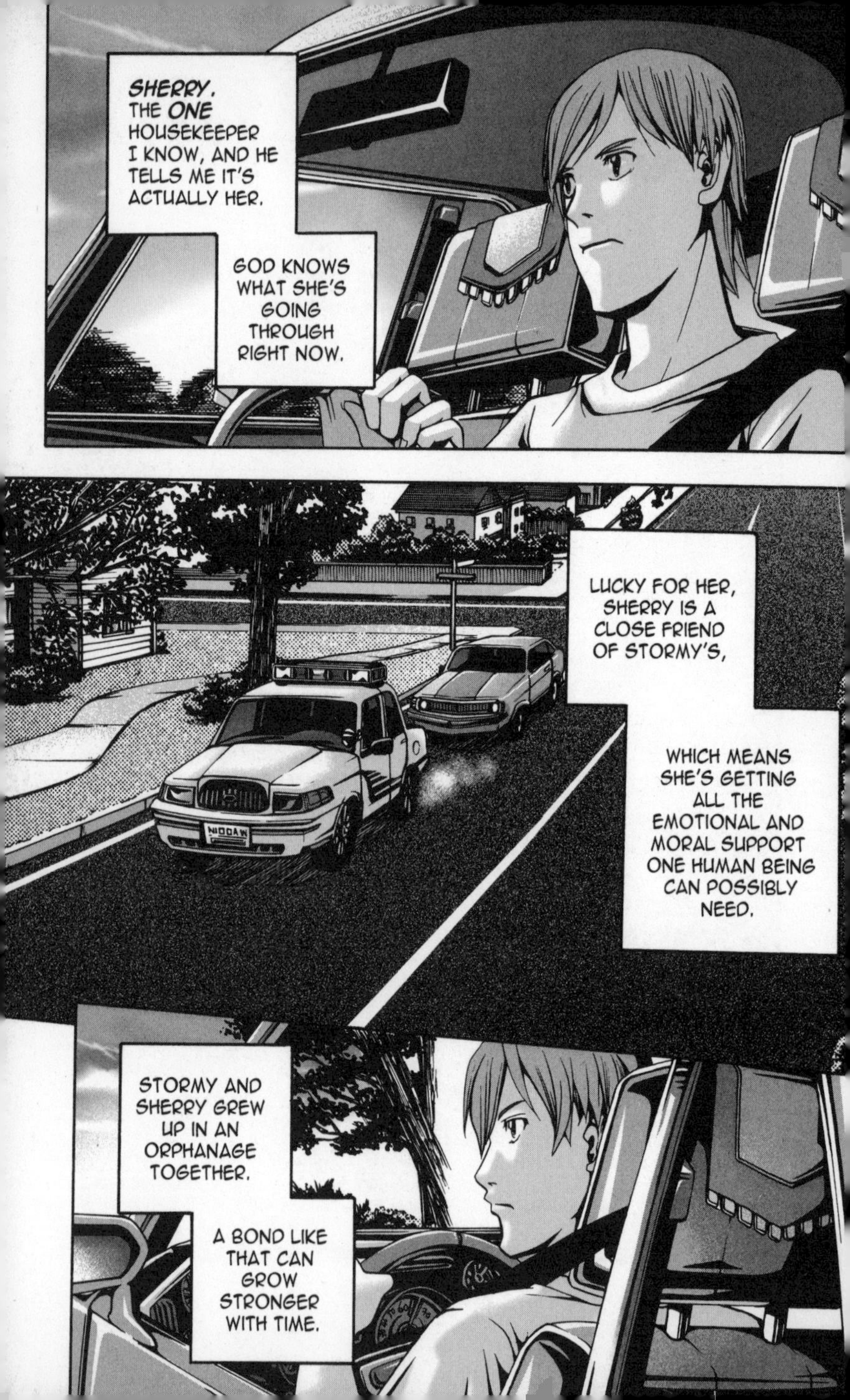
SHERRY. THE ONE HOUSEKEEPER I KNOW, AND HE TELLS ME IT'S ACTUALLY HER.
GOD KNOWS WHAT SHE'S GOING THROUGH RIGHT NOW.
LUCKY FOR HER, SHERRY IS A CLOSE FRIEND OF STORMY'S,
WHICH MEANS SHE'S GETTING ALL THE EMOTIONAL AND MORAL SUPPORT ONE HUMAN BEING CAN POSSIBLY NEED.
STORMY AND SHERRY GREW UP IN AN ORPHANAGE TOGETHER.
A BOND LIKE THAT CAN GROW STRONGER WITH TIME.

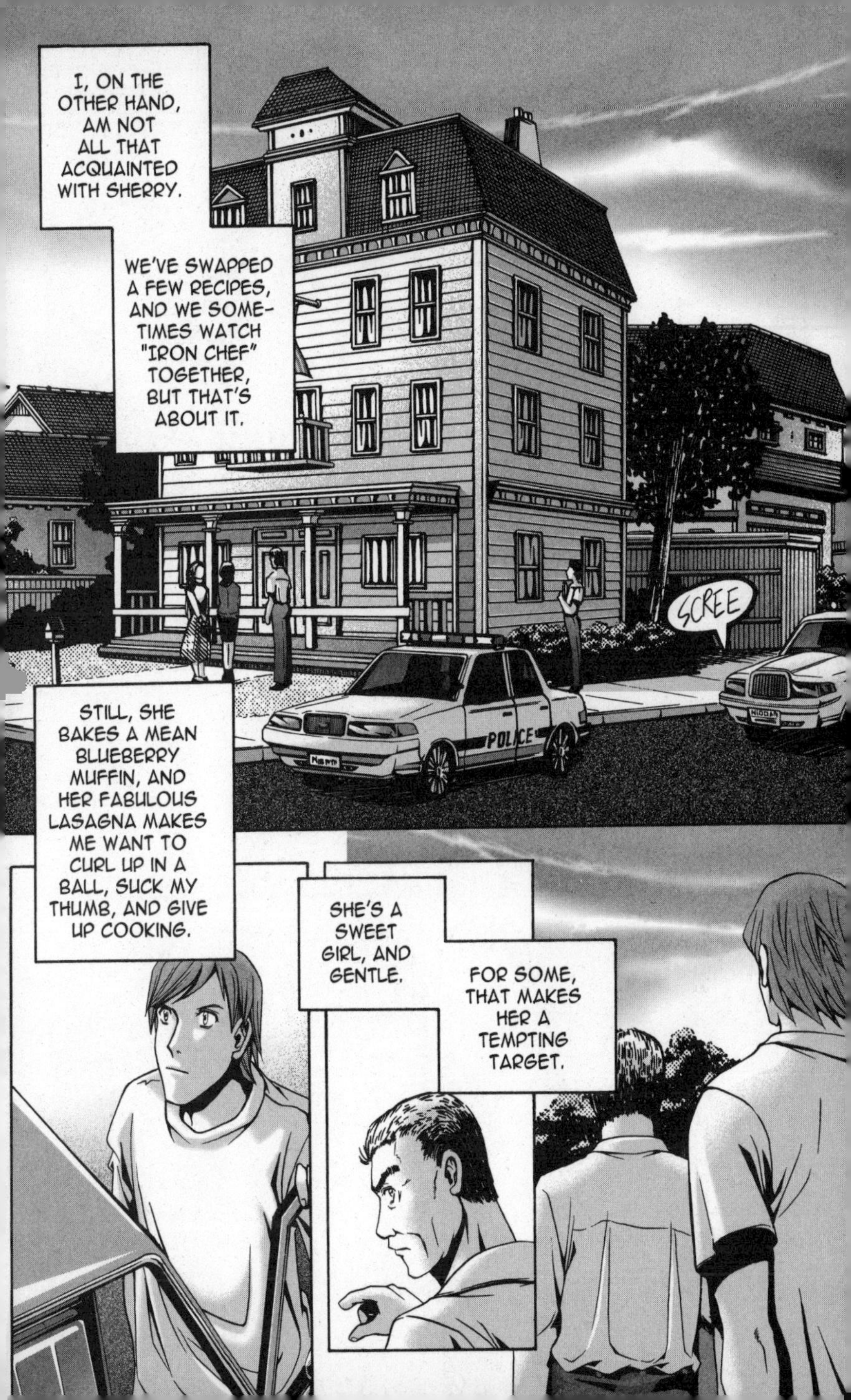
I, ON THE OTHER HAND, AM NOT ALL THAT ACQUAINTED WITH SHERRY.
WE'VE SWAPPED A FEW RECIPES, AND WE SOME-TIMES WATCH "IRON CHEF" TOGETHER, BUT THAT'S ABOUT IT.
SCREE
POLICE
STILL, SHE BAKES A MEAN BLUEBERRY MUFFIN, AND HER FABULOUS LASAGNA MAKES ME WANT TO CURL UP IN A BALL, SUCK MY THUMB, AND GIVE UP COOKING.
SHE'S A SWEET GIRL, AND GENTLE.
FOR SOME, THAT MAKES HER A TEMPTING TARGET.

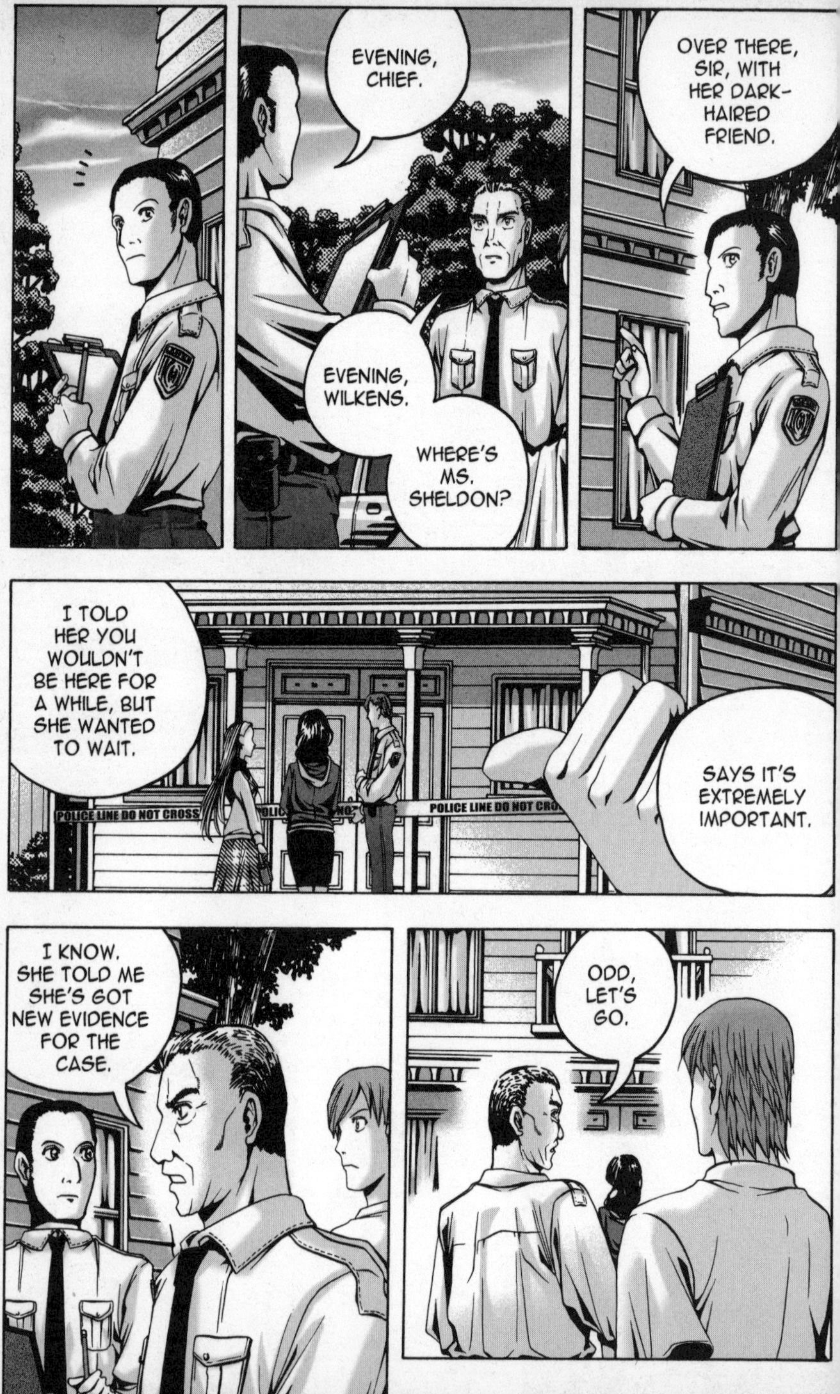

EVENING, CHIEF.
EVENING, WILKENS.
WHERE'S MS. SHELDON?
OVER THERE, SIR, WITH HER DARK-HAIRED FRIEND.
I TOLD HER YOU WOULDN'T BE HERE FOR A WHILE, BUT SHE WANTED TO WAIT.
POLICE LINE DO NOT CROSS
POLICE LINE DO NOT CROS
SAYS IT'S EXTREMELY IMPORTANT.
I KNOW. SHE TOLD ME SHE'S GOT NEW EVIDENCE FOR THE CASE.
ODD, LET'S GO.

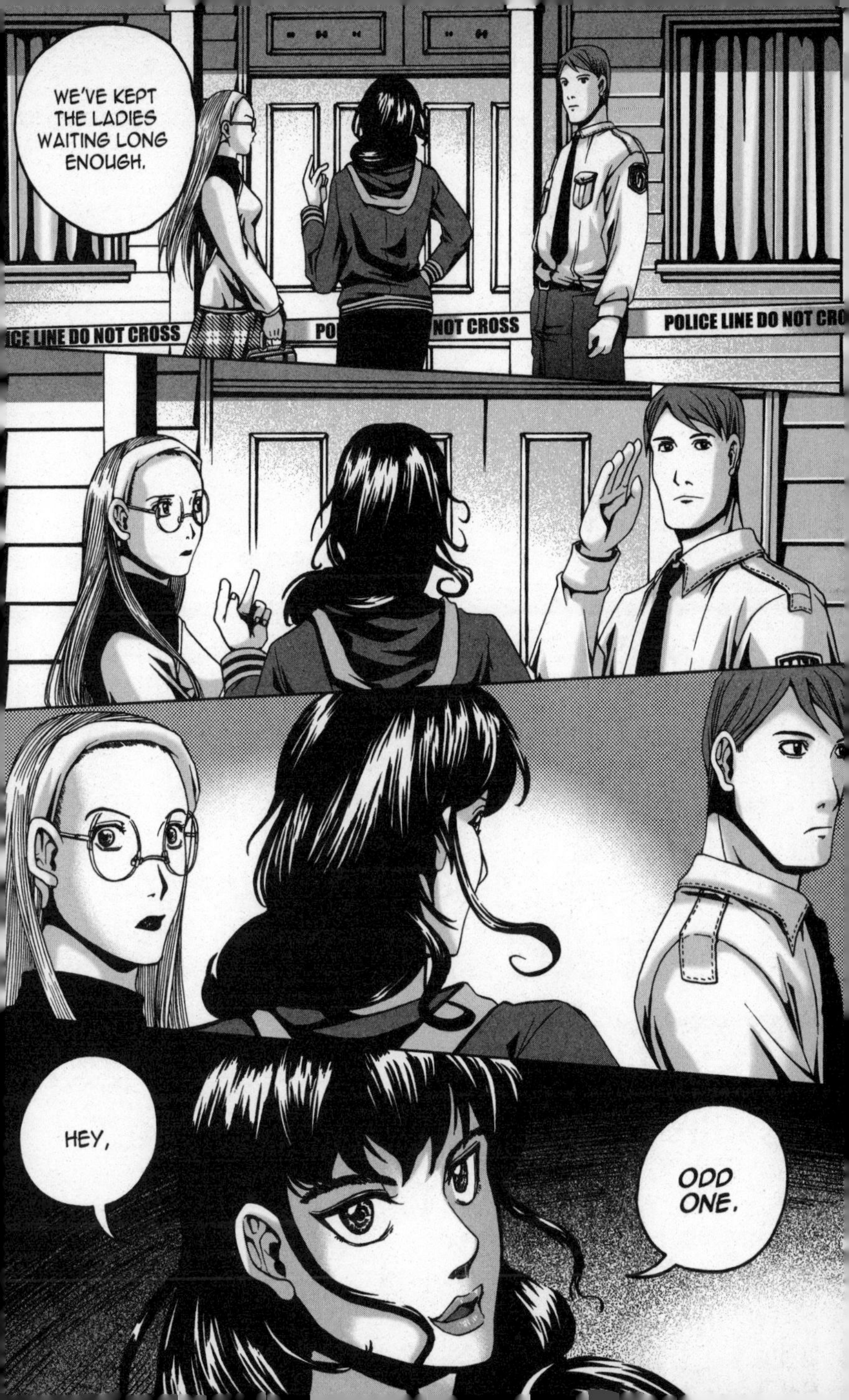
WE'VE KEPT THE LADIES WAITING LONG ENOUGH.
POLICE LINE DO NOT CROSS
HEY,
ODD ONE.

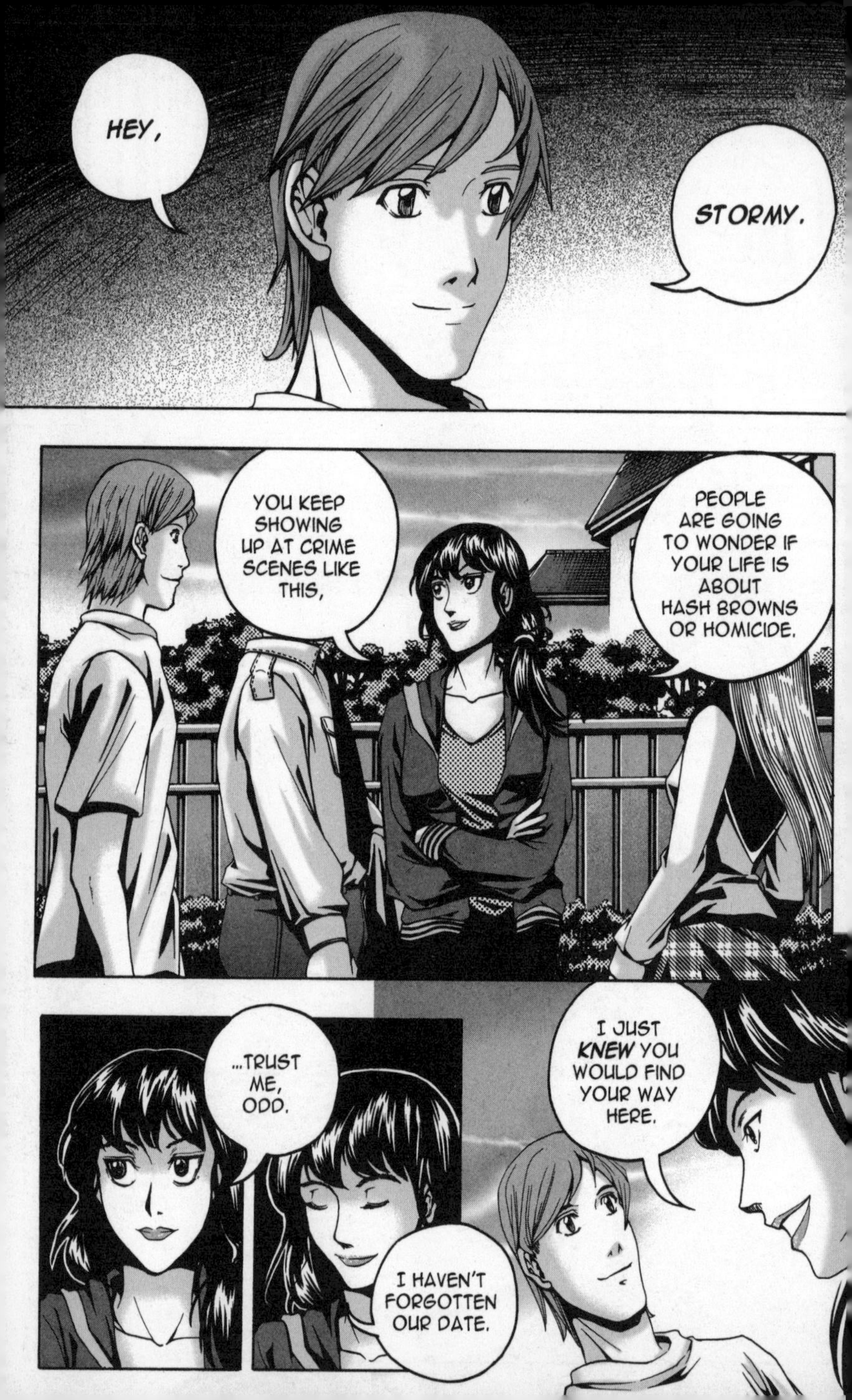
HEY,
STORMY.
YOU KEEP SHOWING UP AT CRIME SCENES LIKE THIS,
PEOPLE ARE GOING TO WONDER IF YOUR LIFE IS ABOUT HASH BROWNS OR HOMICIDE.
...TRUST ME, ODD.
I HAVEN'T FORGOTTEN OUR DATE.
I JUST *KNEW* YOU WOULD FIND YOUR WAY HERE.

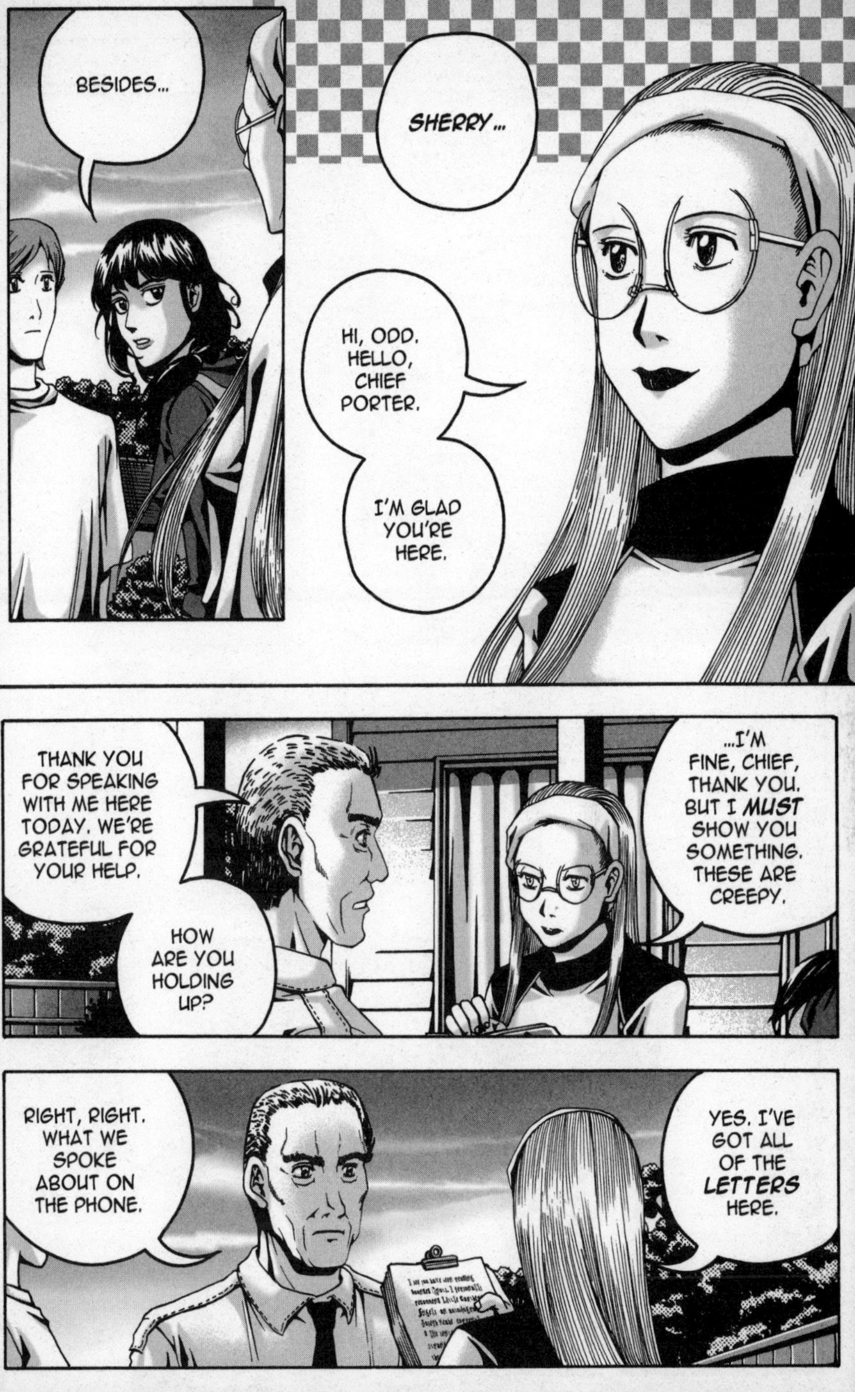
BESIDES...
SHERRY...
HI, ODD. HELLO, CHIEF PORTER.
I'M GLAD YOU'RE HERE.
THANK YOU FOR SPEAKING WITH ME HERE TODAY. WE'RE GRATEFUL FOR YOUR HELP.
HOW ARE YOU HOLDING UP?
...I'M FINE, CHIEF, THANK YOU. BUT I MUST SHOW YOU SOMETHING. THESE ARE CREEPY.
RIGHT, RIGHT. WHAT WE SPOKE ABOUT ON THE PHONE.
YES. I'VE GOT ALL OF THE LETTERS HERE.

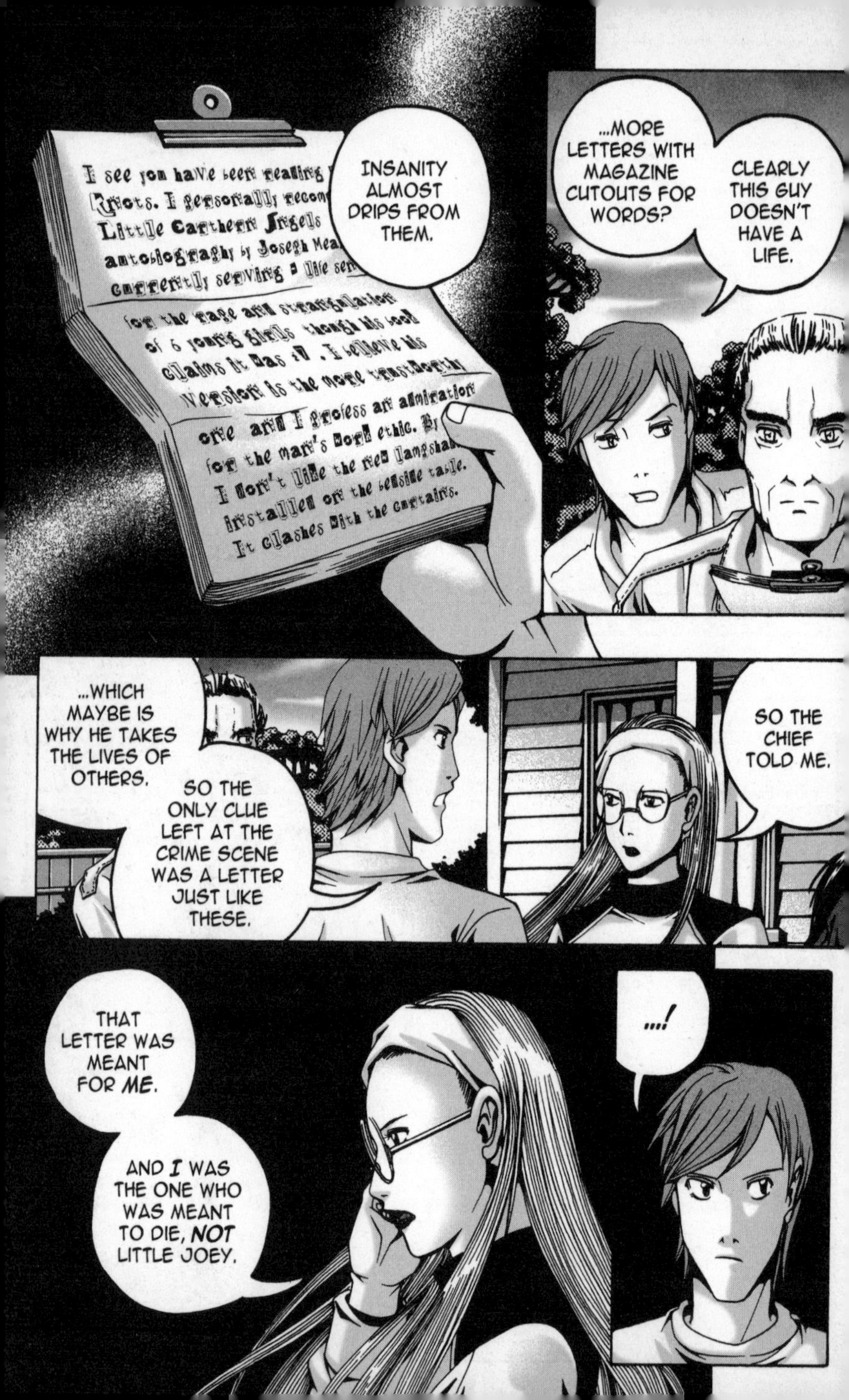

for the rape and strangulation
of 6 young girls though his book
claims it was 4. I believe his
version is the more trustworthy
one and I profess an admiration
for the man's work ethic.
I don't like the new lampshade
installed on the bedside table.
It clashes with the curtains.
INSANITY ALMOST DRIPS FROM THEM.
...MORE LETTERS WITH MAGAZINE CUTOUTS FOR WORDS?
CLEARLY THIS GUY DOESN'T HAVE A LIFE.
...WHICH MAYBE IS WHY HE TAKES THE LIVES OF OTHERS.
SO THE ONLY CLUE LEFT AT THE CRIME SCENE WAS A LETTER JUST LIKE THESE.
SO THE CHIEF TOLD ME.
THAT LETTER WAS MEANT FOR *ME*.
AND *I* WAS THE ONE WHO WAS MEANT TO DIE, ***NOT*** LITTLE JOEY.
...!

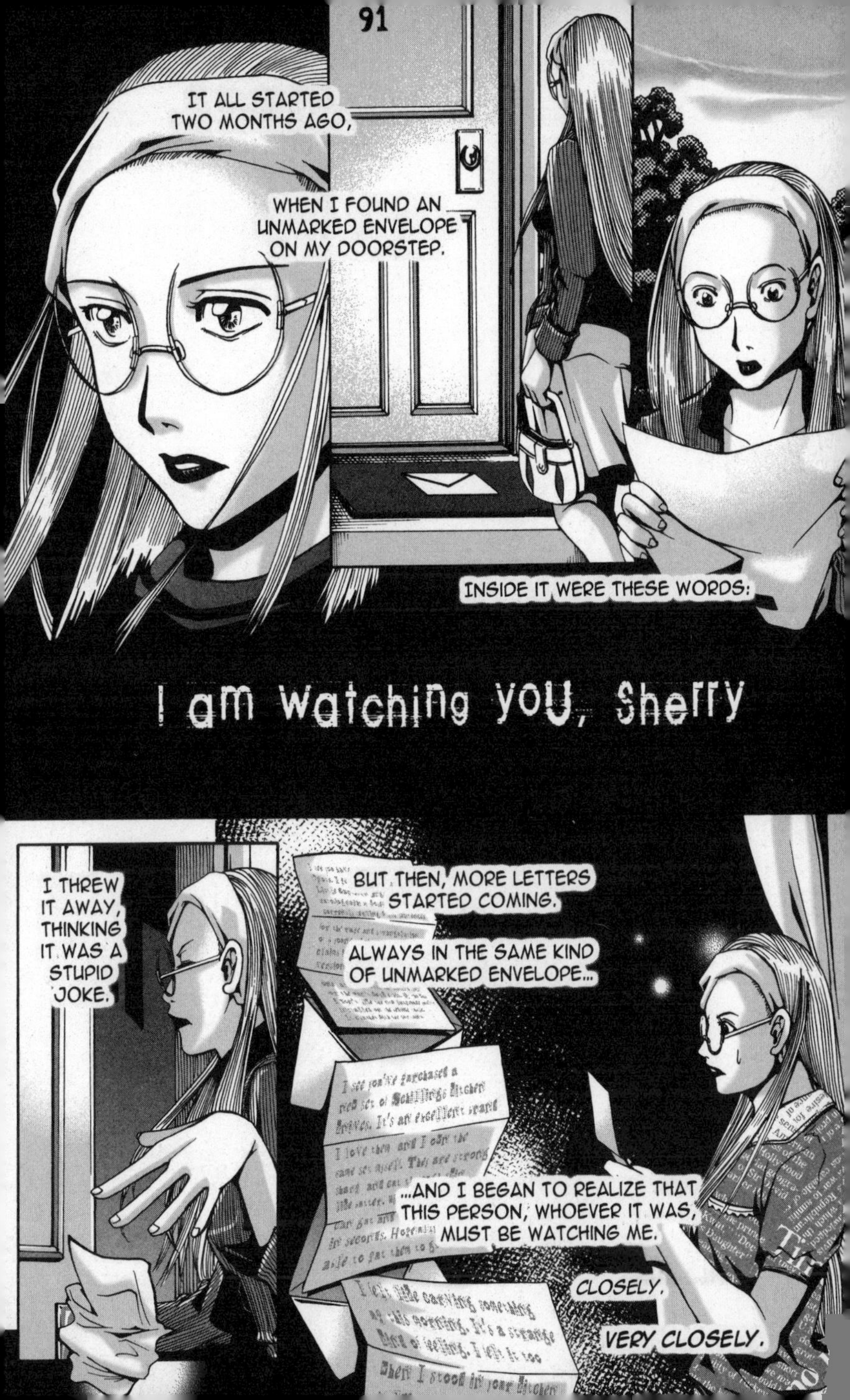
IT ALL STARTED TWO MONTHS AGO,
WHEN I FOUND AN UNMARKED ENVELOPE ON MY DOORSTEP.
INSIDE IT WERE THESE WORDS:
I am watching you, Sherry
I THREW IT AWAY, THINKING IT WAS A STUPID JOKE.
BUT THEN, MORE LETTERS STARTED COMING.
ALWAYS IN THE SAME KIND OF UNMARKED ENVELOPE...
...AND I BEGAN TO REALIZE THAT THIS PERSON, WHOEVER IT WAS, MUST BE WATCHING ME.
CLOSELY.
VERY CLOSELY.

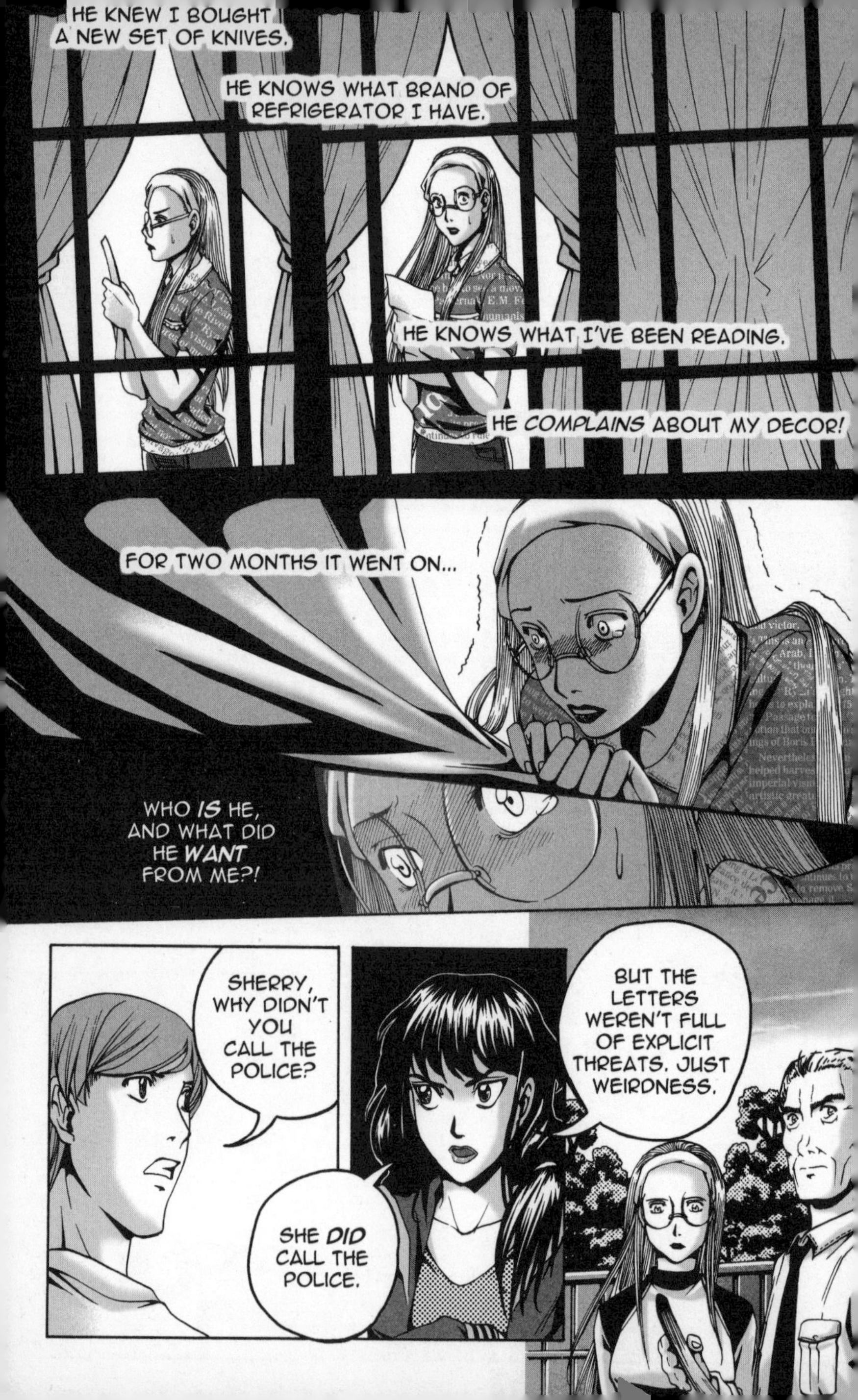
HE KNEW I BOUGHT A NEW SET OF KNIVES.
HE KNOWS WHAT BRAND OF REFRIGERATOR I HAVE.
HE KNOWS WHAT I'VE BEEN READING.
HE *COMPLAINS* ABOUT MY DECOR!
FOR TWO MONTHS IT WENT ON...
WHO *IS* HE, AND WHAT DID HE *WANT* FROM ME?!
SHERRY, WHY DIDN'T YOU CALL THE POLICE?
BUT THE LETTERS WEREN'T FULL OF EXPLICIT THREATS. JUST WEIRDNESS.
SHE *DID* CALL THE POLICE.

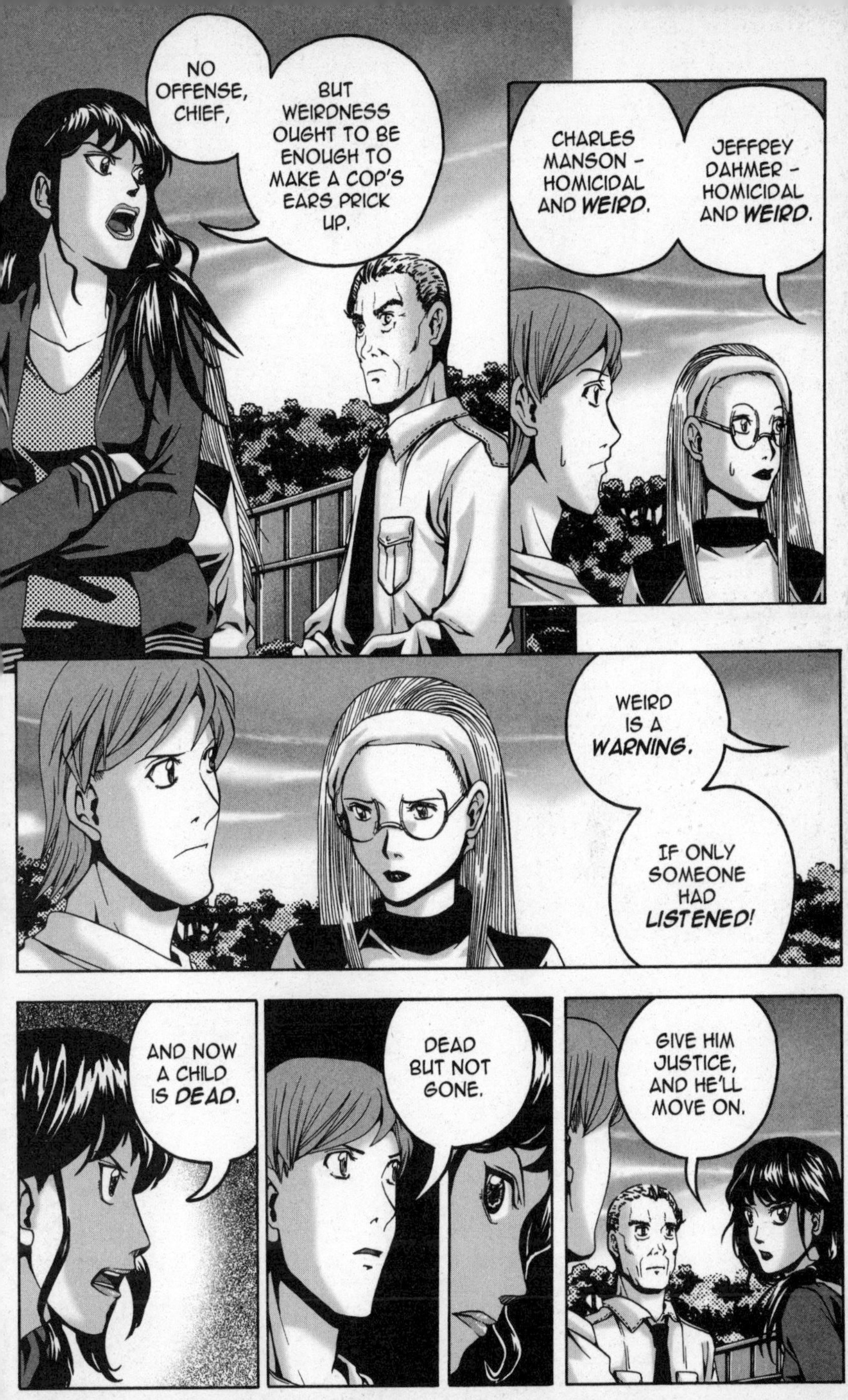
NO OFFENSE, CHIEF,
BUT WEIRDNESS OUGHT TO BE ENOUGH TO MAKE A COP'S EARS PRICK UP.
CHARLES MANSON - HOMICIDAL AND *WEIRD*.
JEFFREY DAHMER - HOMICIDAL AND *WEIRD*.
WEIRD IS A *WARNING*.
IF ONLY SOMEONE HAD *LISTENED*!
AND NOW A CHILD IS *DEAD*.
DEAD BUT NOT GONE.
GIVE HIM JUSTICE, AND HE'LL MOVE ON.

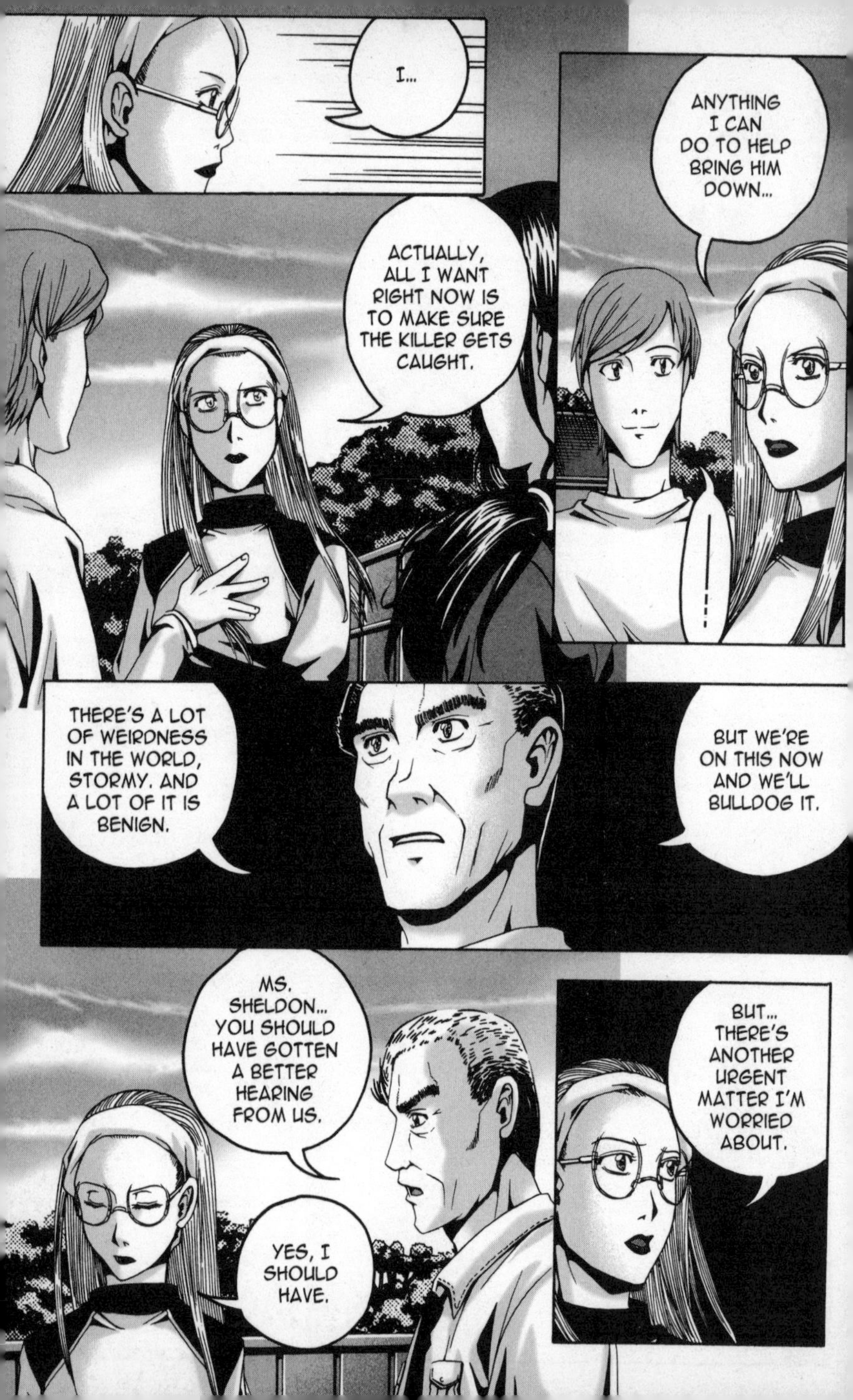
I...
ANYTHING I CAN DO TO HELP BRING HIM DOWN...
ACTUALLY, ALL I WANT RIGHT NOW IS TO MAKE SURE THE KILLER GETS CAUGHT.
THERE'S A LOT OF WEIRDNESS IN THE WORLD, STORMY. AND A LOT OF IT IS BENIGN.
BUT WE'RE ON THIS NOW AND WE'LL BULLDOG IT.
MS. SHELDON... YOU SHOULD HAVE GOTTEN A BETTER HEARING FROM US.
YES, I SHOULD HAVE.
BUT... THERE'S ANOTHER URGENT MATTER I'M WORRIED ABOUT.

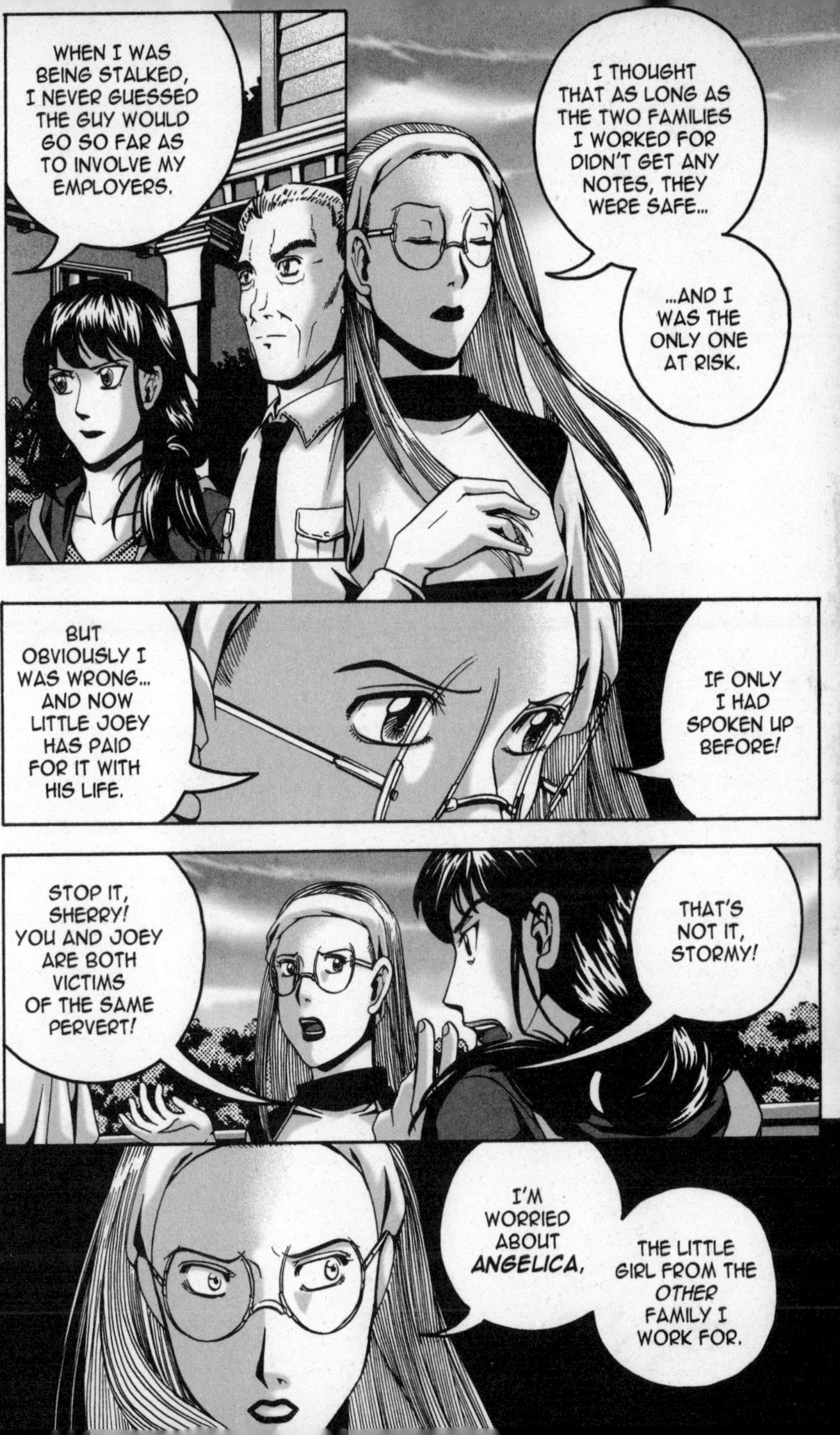
WHEN I WAS BEING STALKED, I NEVER GUESSED THE GUY WOULD GO SO FAR AS TO INVOLVE MY EMPLOYERS.
I THOUGHT THAT AS LONG AS THE TWO FAMILIES I WORKED FOR DIDN'T GET ANY NOTES, THEY WERE SAFE...
...AND I WAS THE ONLY ONE AT RISK.
BUT OBVIOUSLY I WAS WRONG... AND NOW LITTLE JOEY HAS PAID FOR IT WITH HIS LIFE.
IF ONLY I HAD SPOKEN UP BEFORE!
STOP IT, SHERRY! YOU AND JOEY ARE BOTH VICTIMS OF THE SAME PERVERT!
THAT'S NOT IT, STORMY!
I'M WORRIED ABOUT *ANGELICA*,
THE LITTLE GIRL FROM THE *OTHER* FAMILY I WORK FOR.

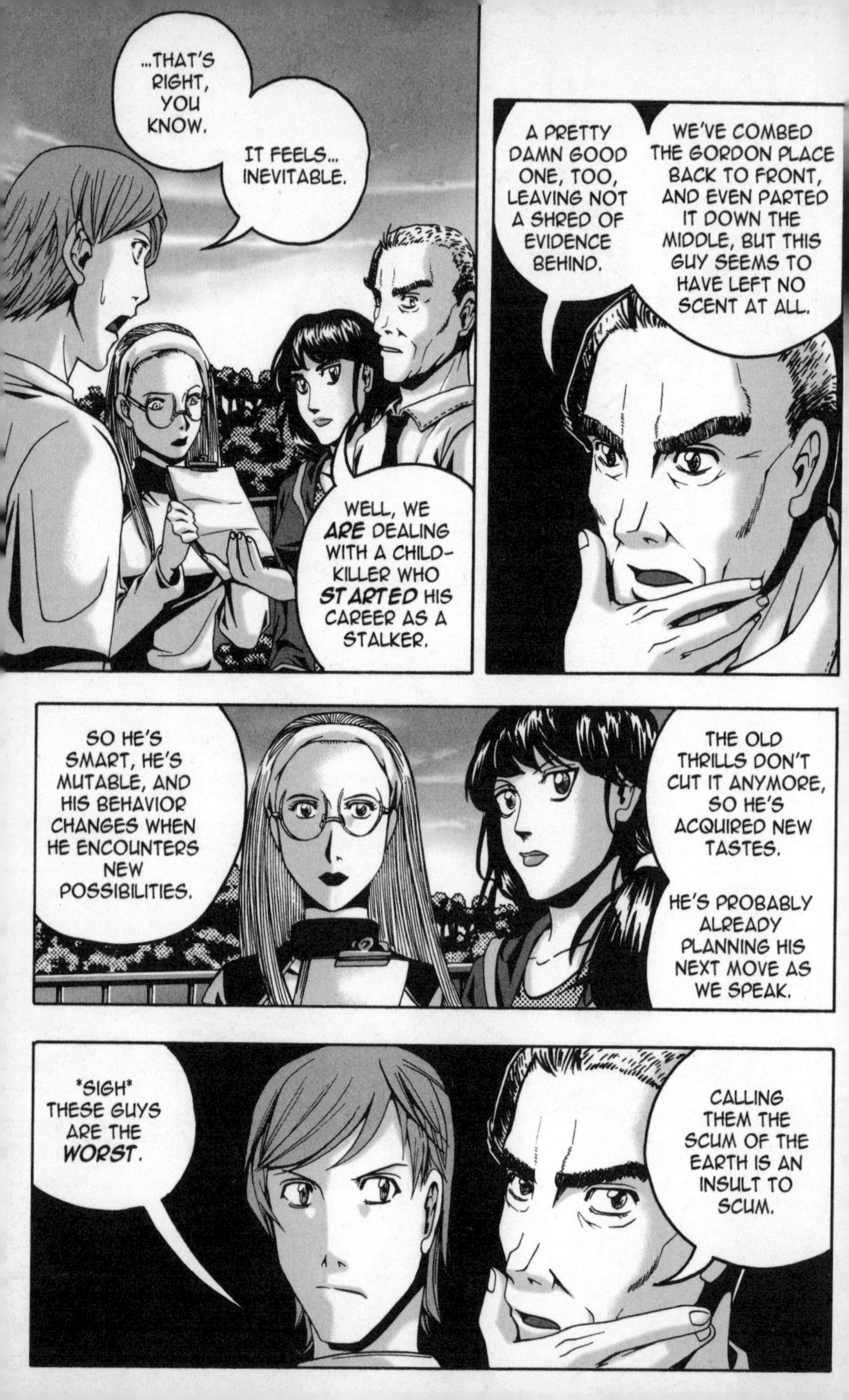
...THAT'S RIGHT, YOU KNOW.
IT FEELS... INEVITABLE.
WELL, WE ARE DEALING WITH A CHILD-KILLER WHO STARTED HIS CAREER AS A STALKER.
WE'VE COMBED THE GORDON PLACE BACK TO FRONT, AND EVEN PARTED IT DOWN THE MIDDLE, BUT THIS GUY SEEMS TO HAVE LEFT NO SCENT AT ALL.
A PRETTY DAMN GOOD ONE, TOO, LEAVING NOT A SHRED OF EVIDENCE BEHIND.
SO HE'S SMART, HE'S MUTABLE, AND HIS BEHAVIOR CHANGES WHEN HE ENCOUNTERS NEW POSSIBILITIES.
THE OLD THRILLS DON'T CUT IT ANYMORE, SO HE'S ACQUIRED NEW TASTES.
HE'S PROBABLY ALREADY PLANNING HIS NEXT MOVE AS WE SPEAK.
SIGH THESE GUYS ARE THE WORST.
CALLING THEM THE SCUM OF THE EARTH IS AN INSULT TO SCUM.

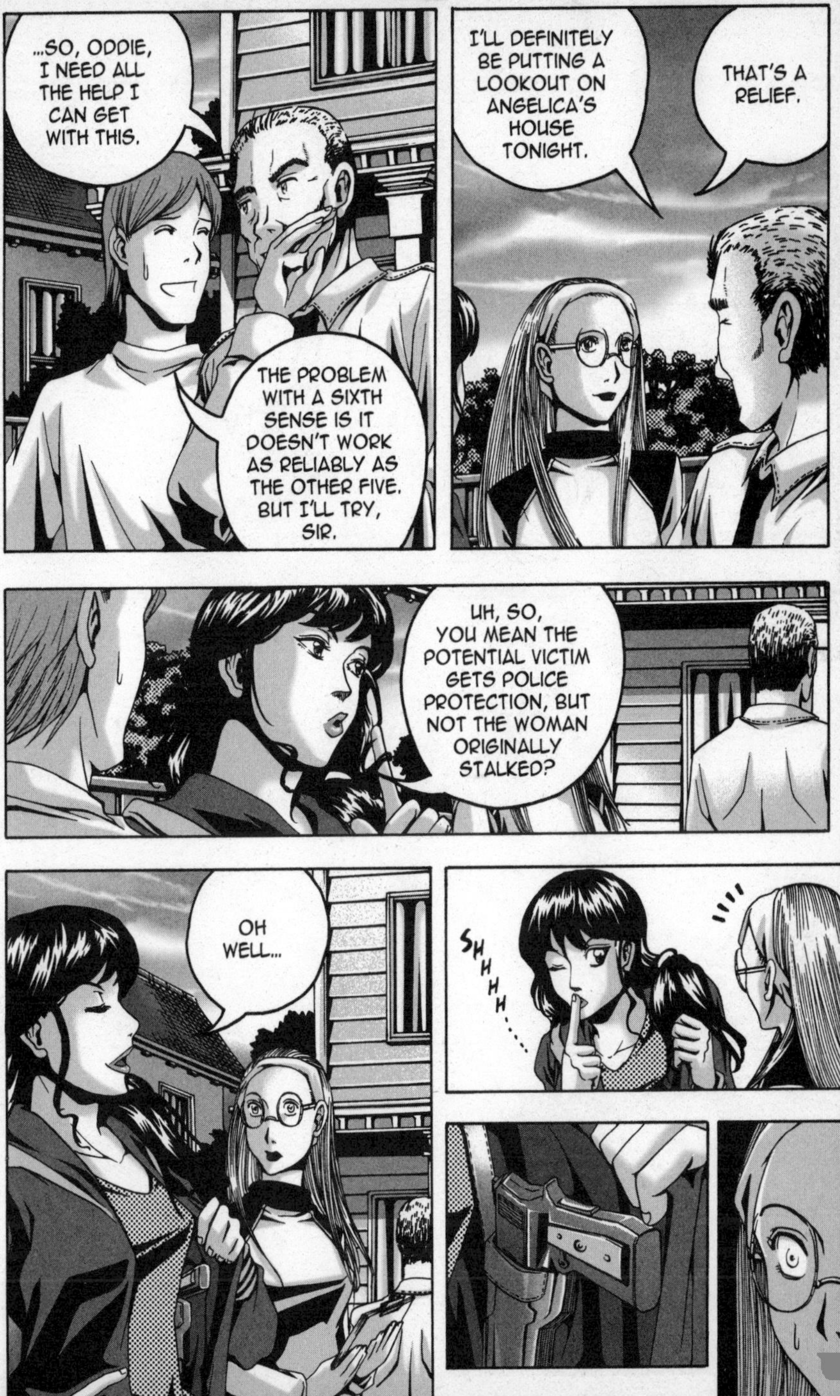
...SO, ODDIE, I NEED ALL THE HELP I CAN GET WITH THIS.
THE PROBLEM WITH A SIXTH SENSE IS IT DOESN'T WORK AS RELIABLY AS THE OTHER FIVE. BUT I'LL TRY, SIR.
THAT'S A RELIEF.
I'LL DEFINITELY BE PUTTING A LOOKOUT ON ANGELICA'S HOUSE TONIGHT.
UH, SO, YOU MEAN THE POTENTIAL VICTIM GETS POLICE PROTECTION, BUT NOT THE WOMAN ORIGINALLY STALKED?
OH WELL...
SHHHH...

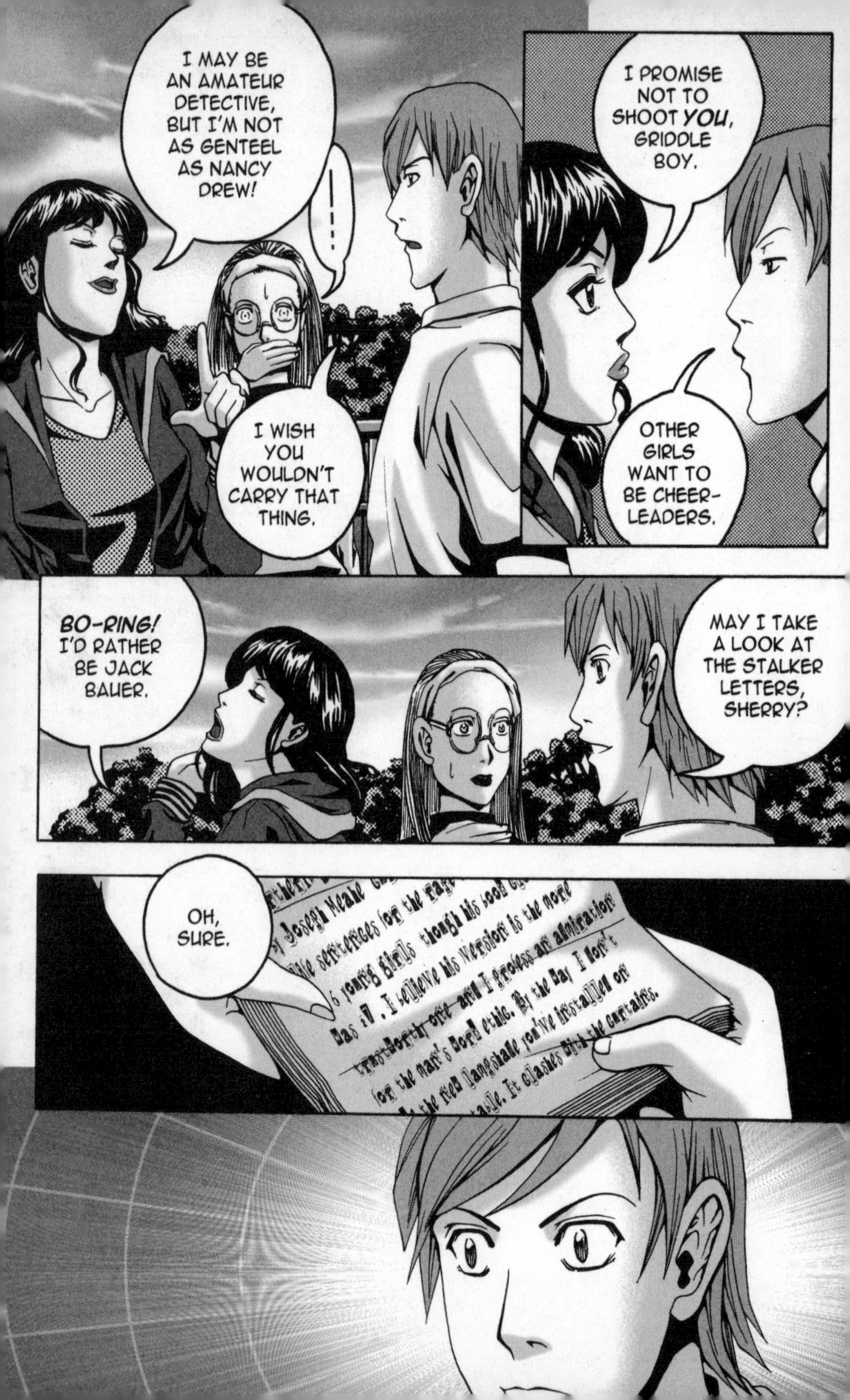
I MAY BE AN AMATEUR DETECTIVE, BUT I'M NOT AS GENTEEL AS NANCY DREW!
!!
I WISH YOU WOULDN'T CARRY THAT THING.
I PROMISE NOT TO SHOOT *YOU*, GRIDDLE BOY.
OTHER GIRLS WANT TO BE CHEER-LEADERS.
BO-RING! I'D RATHER BE JACK BAUER.
MAY I TAKE A LOOK AT THE STALKER LETTERS, SHERRY?
OH, SURE.

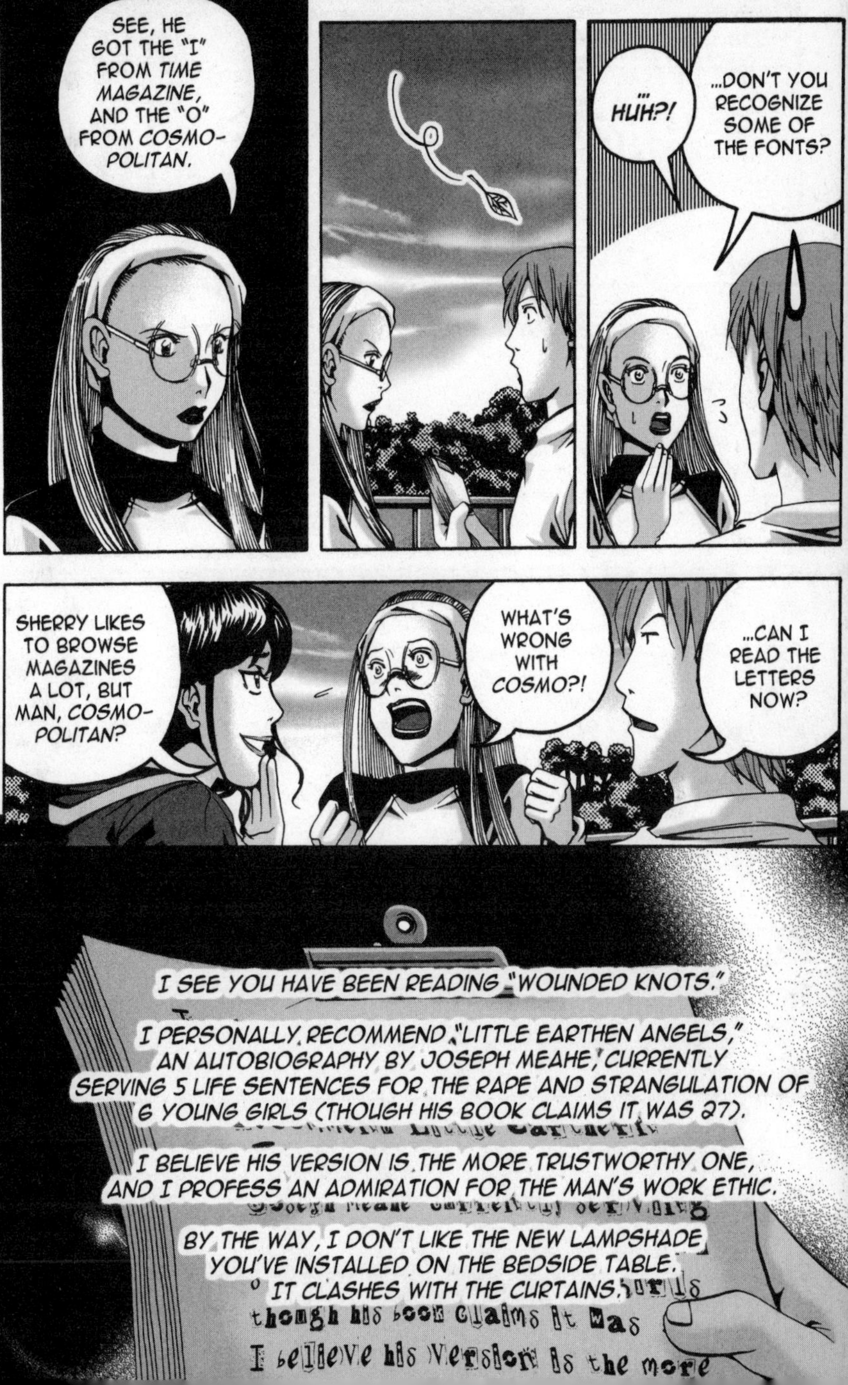
SEE, HE GOT THE "I" FROM TIME MAGAZINE, AND THE "O" FROM COSMO-POLITAN.
...HUH?!
...DON'T YOU RECOGNIZE SOME OF THE FONTS?
SHERRY LIKES TO BROWSE MAGAZINES A LOT, BUT MAN, COSMO-POLITAN?
WHAT'S WRONG WITH COSMO?!
...CAN I READ THE LETTERS NOW?
I SEE YOU HAVE BEEN READING "WOUNDED KNOTS."
I PERSONALLY RECOMMEND "LITTLE EARTHEN ANGELS," AN AUTOBIOGRAPHY BY JOSEPH MEAHE, CURRENTLY SERVING 5 LIFE SENTENCES FOR THE RAPE AND STRANGULATION OF 6 YOUNG GIRLS (THOUGH HIS BOOK CLAIMS IT WAS 27).
I BELIEVE HIS VERSION IS THE MORE TRUSTWORTHY ONE, AND I PROFESS AN ADMIRATION FOR THE MAN'S WORK ETHIC.
BY THE WAY, I DON'T LIKE THE NEW LAMPSHADE YOU'VE INSTALLED ON THE BEDSIDE TABLE. IT CLASHES WITH THE CURTAINS.

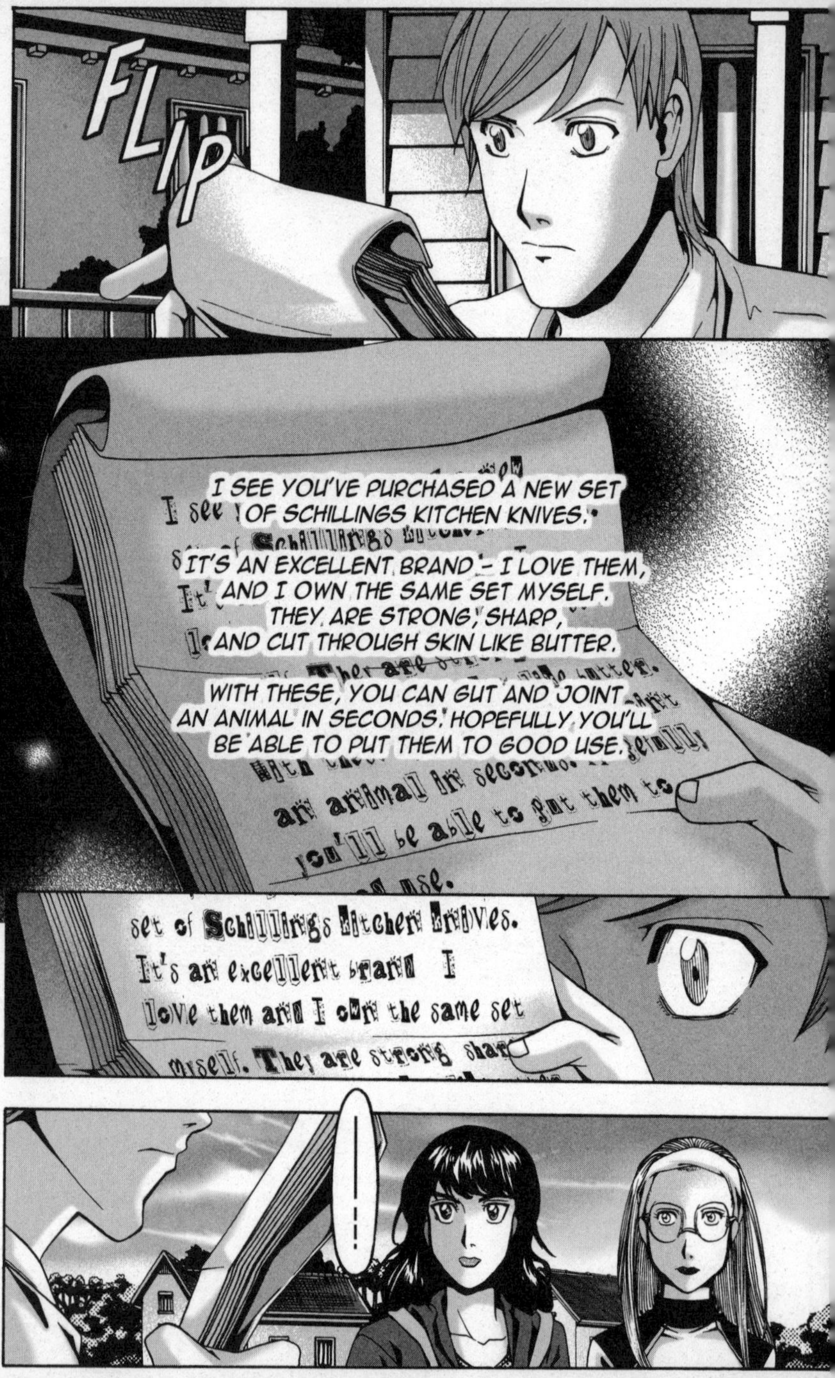
FLIP
I SEE YOU'VE PURCHASED A NEW SET OF SCHILLINGS KITCHEN KNIVES.
IT'S AN EXCELLENT BRAND - I LOVE THEM, AND I OWN THE SAME SET MYSELF. THEY ARE STRONG, SHARP, AND CUT THROUGH SKIN LIKE BUTTER.
WITH THESE, YOU CAN GUT AND JOINT AN ANIMAL IN SECONDS. HOPEFULLY YOU'LL BE ABLE TO PUT THEM TO GOOD USE.
set of Schillings kitchen knives.
It's an excellent brand I
love them and I own the same set
myself. They are strong shar
!

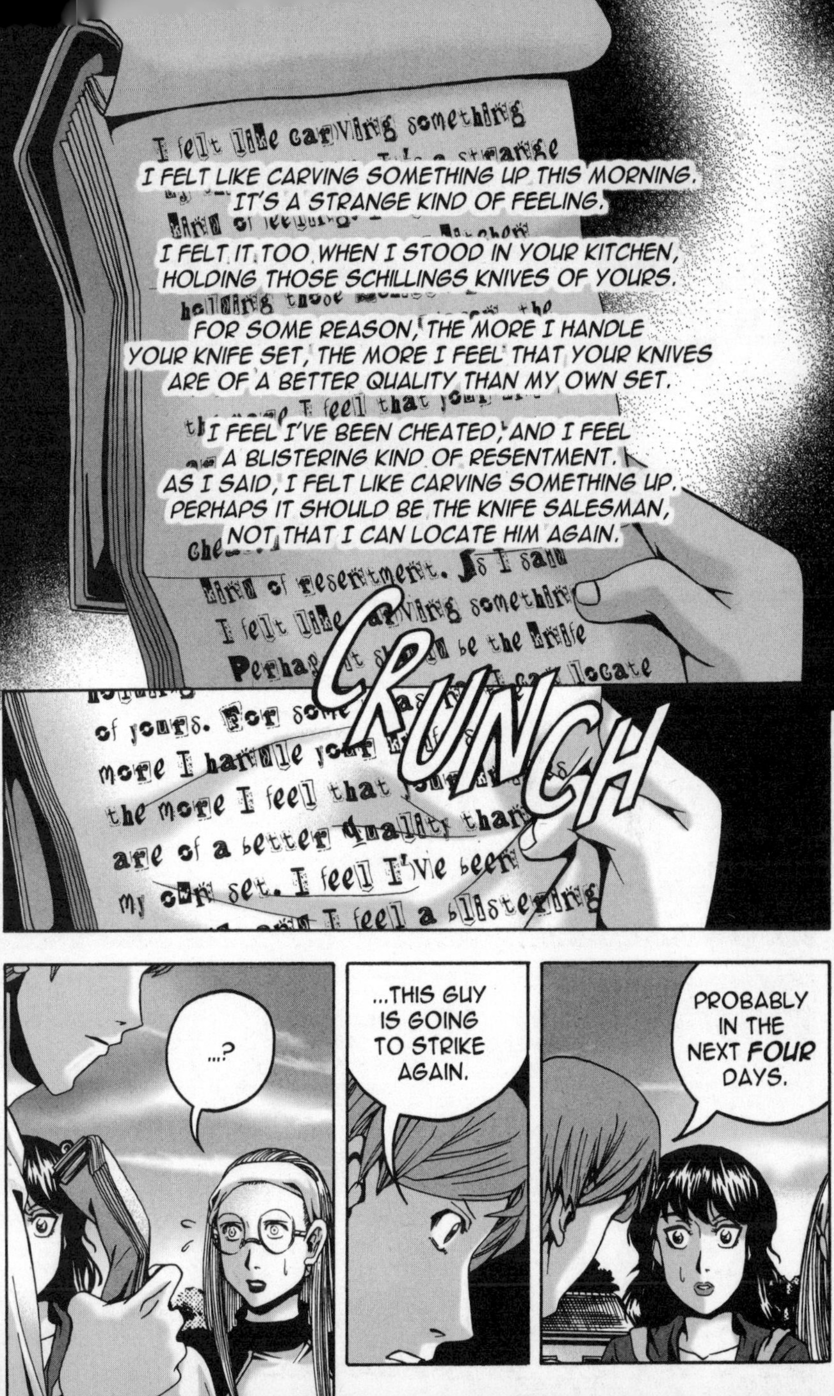

I FELT LIKE CARVING SOMETHING UP THIS MORNING. IT'S A STRANGE KIND OF FEELING.
I FELT IT TOO WHEN I STOOD IN YOUR KITCHEN, HOLDING THOSE SCHILLINGS KNIVES OF YOURS.
FOR SOME REASON, THE MORE I HANDLE YOUR KNIFE SET, THE MORE I FEEL THAT YOUR KNIVES ARE OF A BETTER QUALITY THAN MY OWN SET.
I FEEL I'VE BEEN CHEATED, AND I FEEL A BLISTERING KIND OF RESENTMENT. AS I SAID, I FELT LIKE CARVING SOMETHING UP. PERHAPS IT SHOULD BE THE KNIFE SALESMAN, NOT THAT I CAN LOCATE HIM AGAIN.
CRUNCH
...?
...THIS GUY IS GOING TO STRIKE AGAIN.
PROBABLY IN THE NEXT FOUR DAYS.

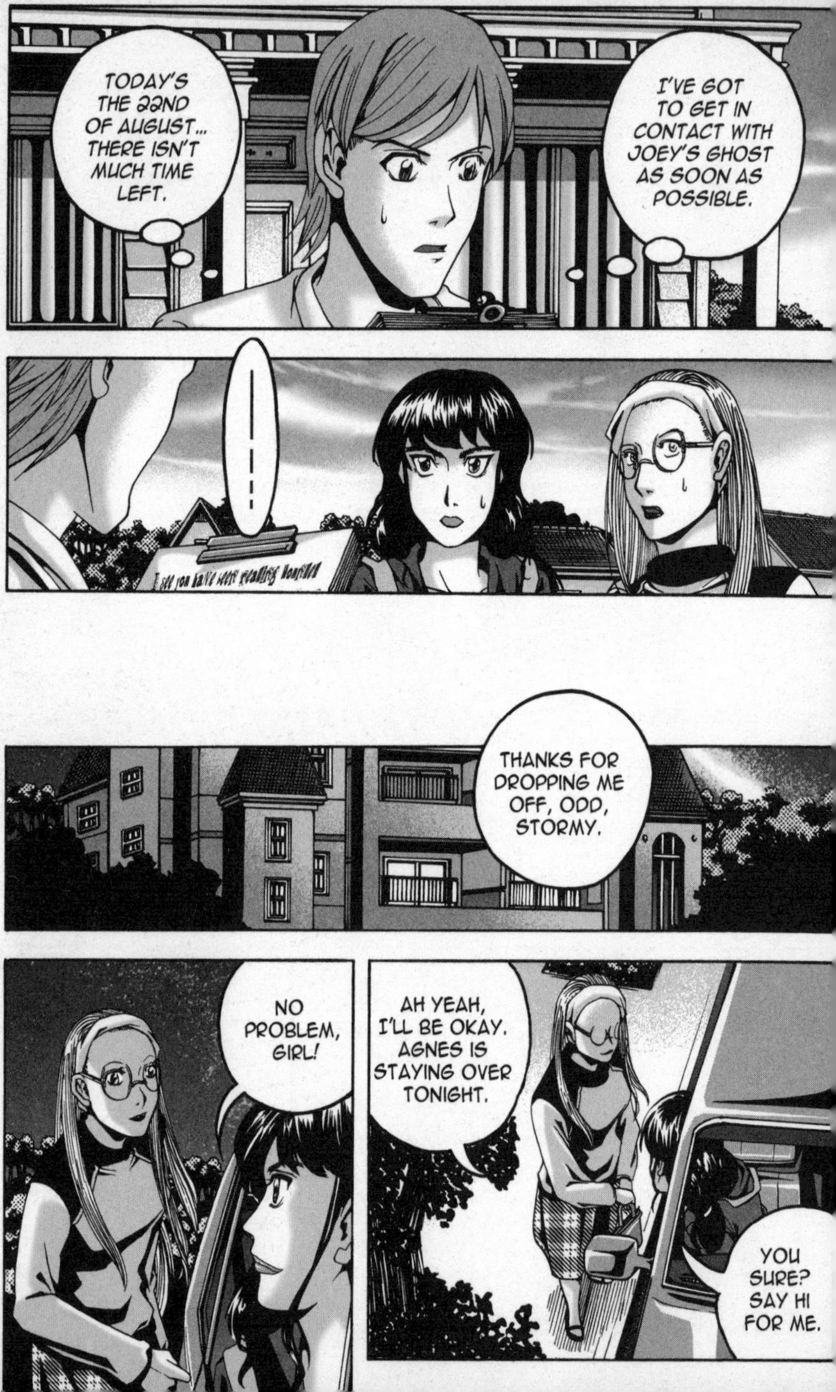
TODAY'S THE 22ND OF AUGUST... THERE ISN'T MUCH TIME LEFT.
I'VE GOT TO GET IN CONTACT WITH JOEY'S GHOST AS SOON AS POSSIBLE.
!
THANKS FOR DROPPING ME OFF, ODD, STORMY.
NO PROBLEM, GIRL!
AH YEAH, I'LL BE OKAY. AGNES IS STAYING OVER TONIGHT.
YOU SURE? SAY HI FOR ME.

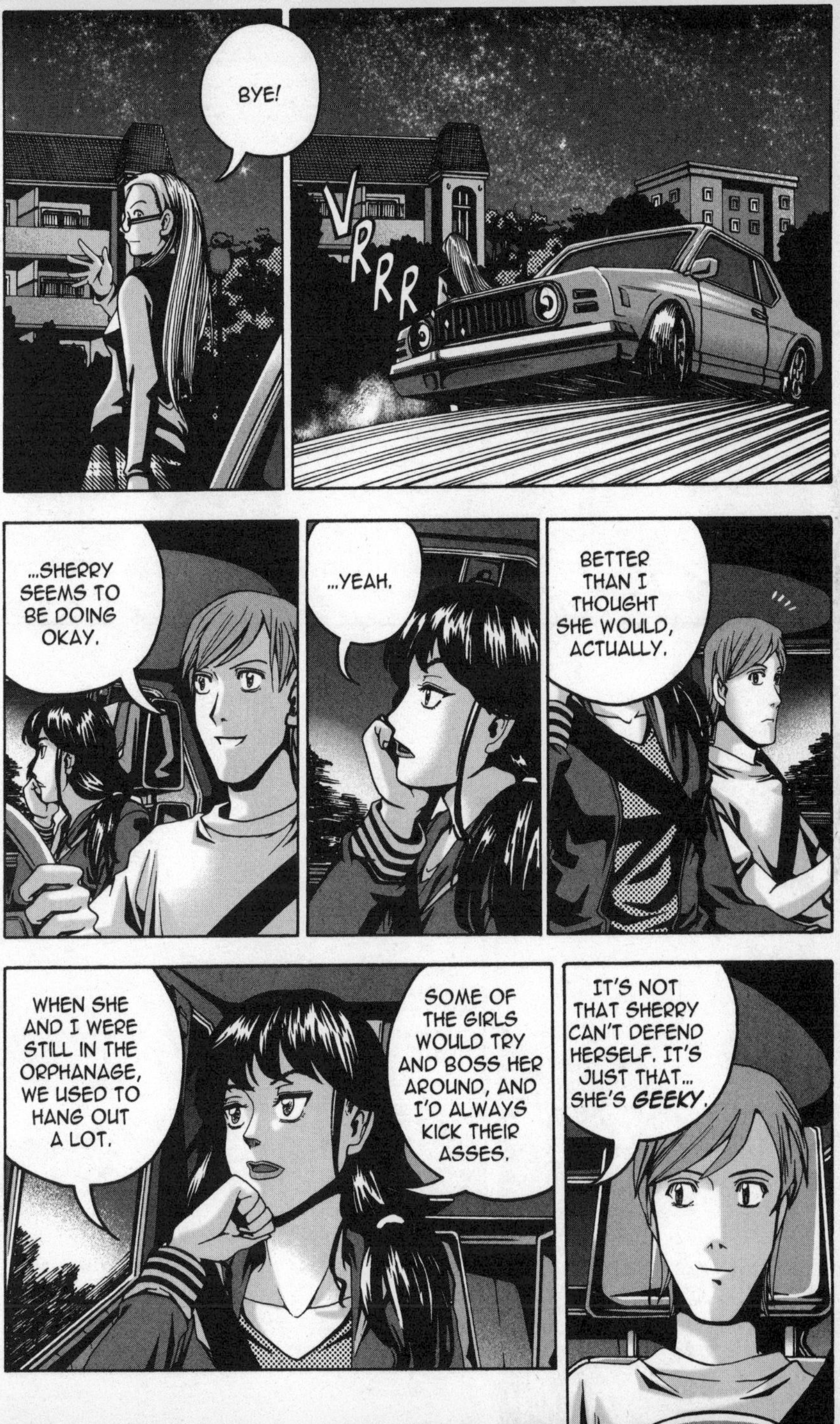

BYE!
VRRRR
...SHERRY SEEMS TO BE DOING OKAY.
...YEAH.
BETTER THAN I THOUGHT SHE WOULD, ACTUALLY.
WHEN SHE AND I WERE STILL IN THE ORPHANAGE, WE USED TO HANG OUT A LOT.
SOME OF THE GIRLS WOULD TRY AND BOSS HER AROUND, AND I'D ALWAYS KICK THEIR ASSES.
IT'S NOT THAT SHERRY CAN'T DEFEND HERSELF. IT'S JUST THAT... SHE'S *GEEKY*.

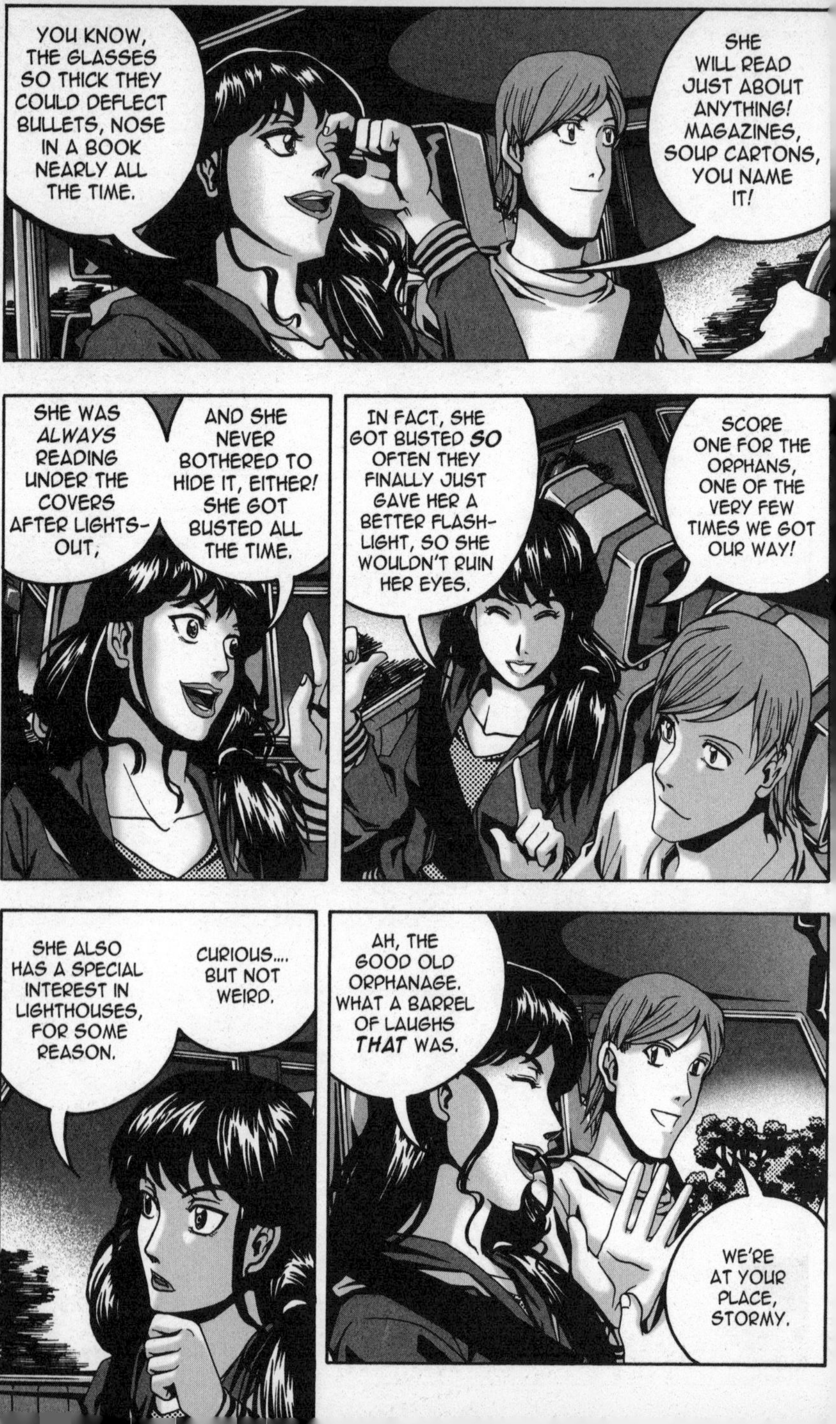
YOU KNOW, THE GLASSES SO THICK THEY COULD DEFLECT BULLETS, NOSE IN A BOOK NEARLY ALL THE TIME.
SHE WILL READ JUST ABOUT ANYTHING! MAGAZINES, SOUP CARTONS, YOU NAME IT!
SHE WAS ALWAYS READING UNDER THE COVERS AFTER LIGHTS-OUT,
AND SHE NEVER BOTHERED TO HIDE IT, EITHER! SHE GOT BUSTED ALL THE TIME.
IN FACT, SHE GOT BUSTED SO OFTEN THEY FINALLY JUST GAVE HER A BETTER FLASH-LIGHT, SO SHE WOULDN'T RUIN HER EYES.
SCORE ONE FOR THE ORPHANS, ONE OF THE VERY FEW TIMES WE GOT OUR WAY!
SHE ALSO HAS A SPECIAL INTEREST IN LIGHTHOUSES, FOR SOME REASON.
CURIOUS.... BUT NOT WEIRD.
AH, THE GOOD OLD ORPHANAGE. WHAT A BARREL OF LAUGHS THAT WAS.
WE'RE AT YOUR PLACE, STORMY.

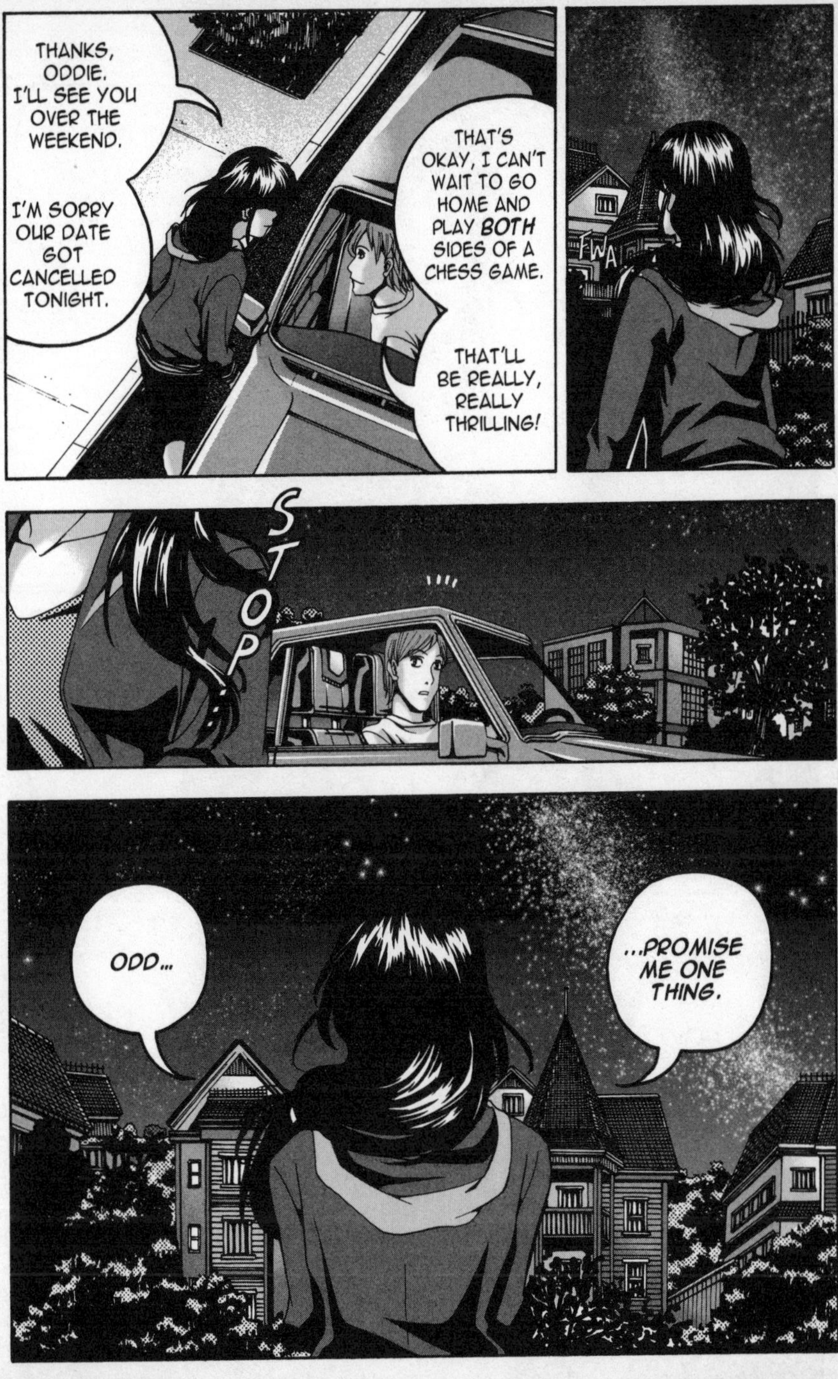
THANKS, ODDIE. I'LL SEE YOU OVER THE WEEKEND.
I'M SORRY OUR DATE GOT CANCELLED TONIGHT.
THAT'S OKAY, I CAN'T WAIT TO GO HOME AND PLAY BOTH SIDES OF A CHESS GAME.
THAT'LL BE REALLY, REALLY THRILLING!
FWA
STOP
ODD...
...PROMISE ME ONE THING.

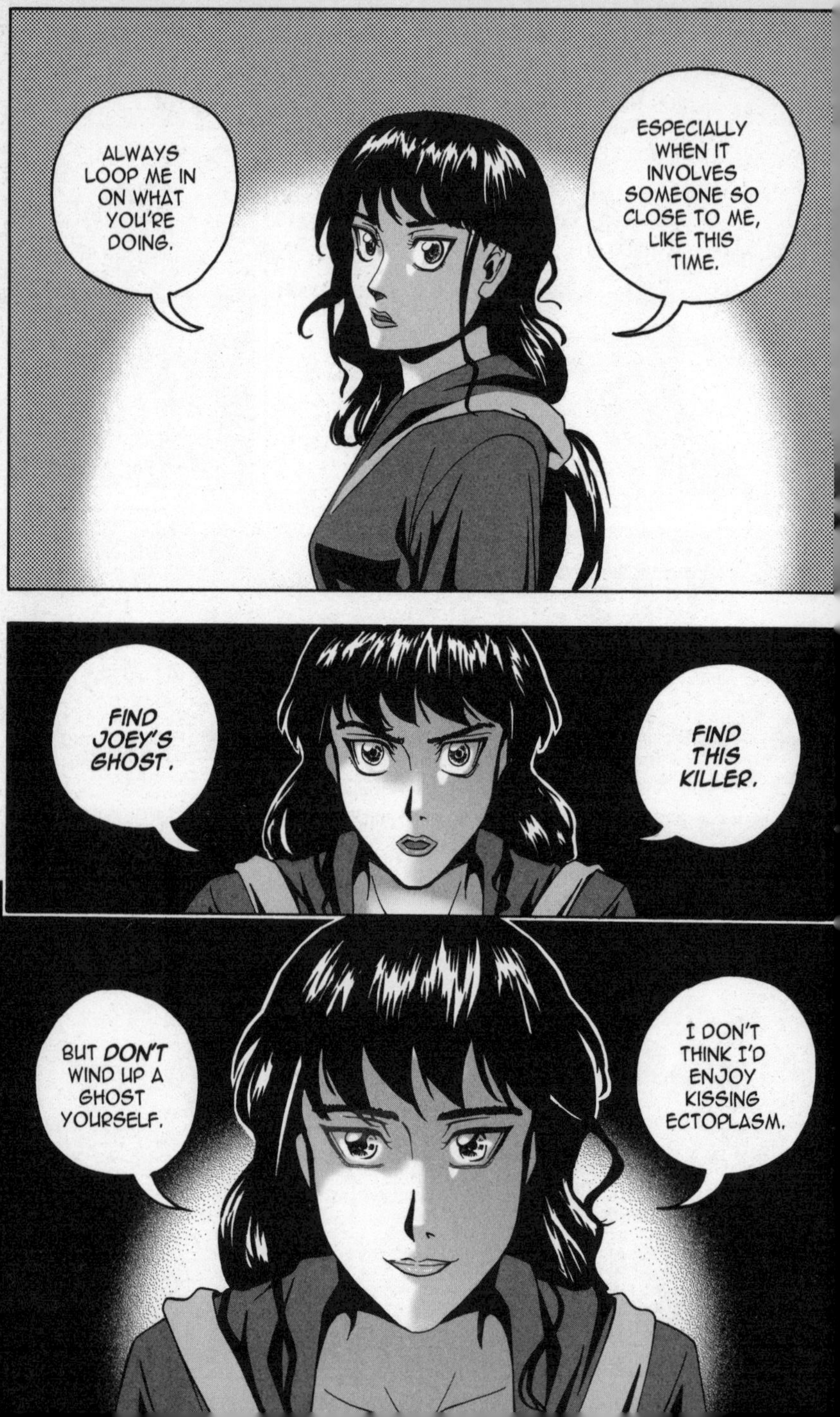
ALWAYS LOOP ME IN ON WHAT YOU'RE DOING.
ESPECIALLY WHEN IT INVOLVES SOMEONE SO CLOSE TO ME, LIKE THIS TIME.
FIND JOEY'S GHOST.
FIND THIS KILLER.
BUT DON'T WIND UP A GHOST YOURSELF.
I DON'T THINK I'D ENJOY KISSING ECTOPLASM.

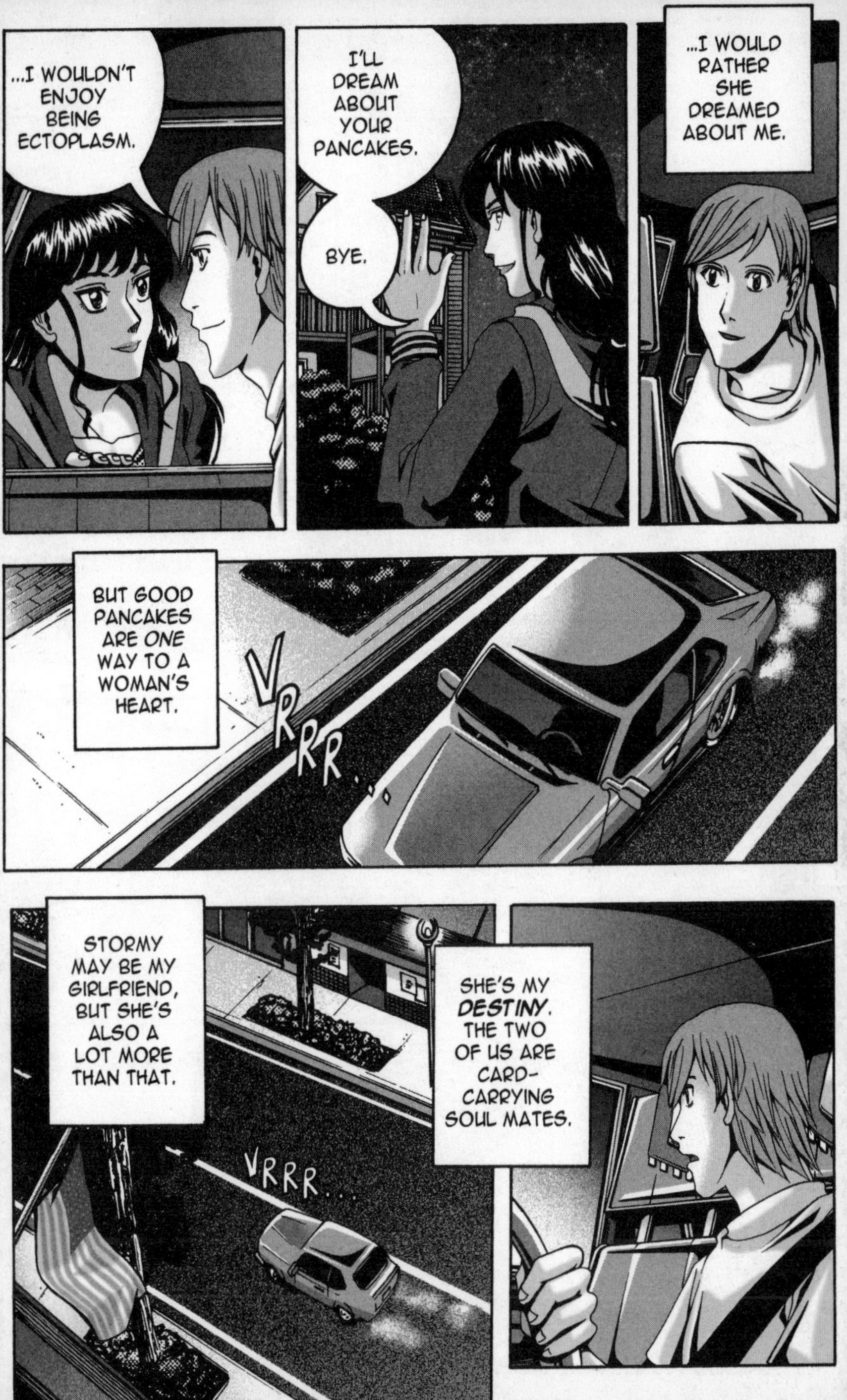
...I WOULDN'T ENJOY BEING ECTOPLASM.
I'LL DREAM ABOUT YOUR PANCAKES.
BYE.
...I WOULD RATHER SHE DREAMED ABOUT ME.
BUT GOOD PANCAKES ARE *ONE* WAY TO A WOMAN'S HEART.
VRRR...
STORMY MAY BE MY GIRLFRIEND, BUT SHE'S ALSO A LOT MORE THAN THAT.
VRRR...
SHE'S MY ***DESTINY***. THE TWO OF US ARE CARD-CARRYING SOUL MATES.

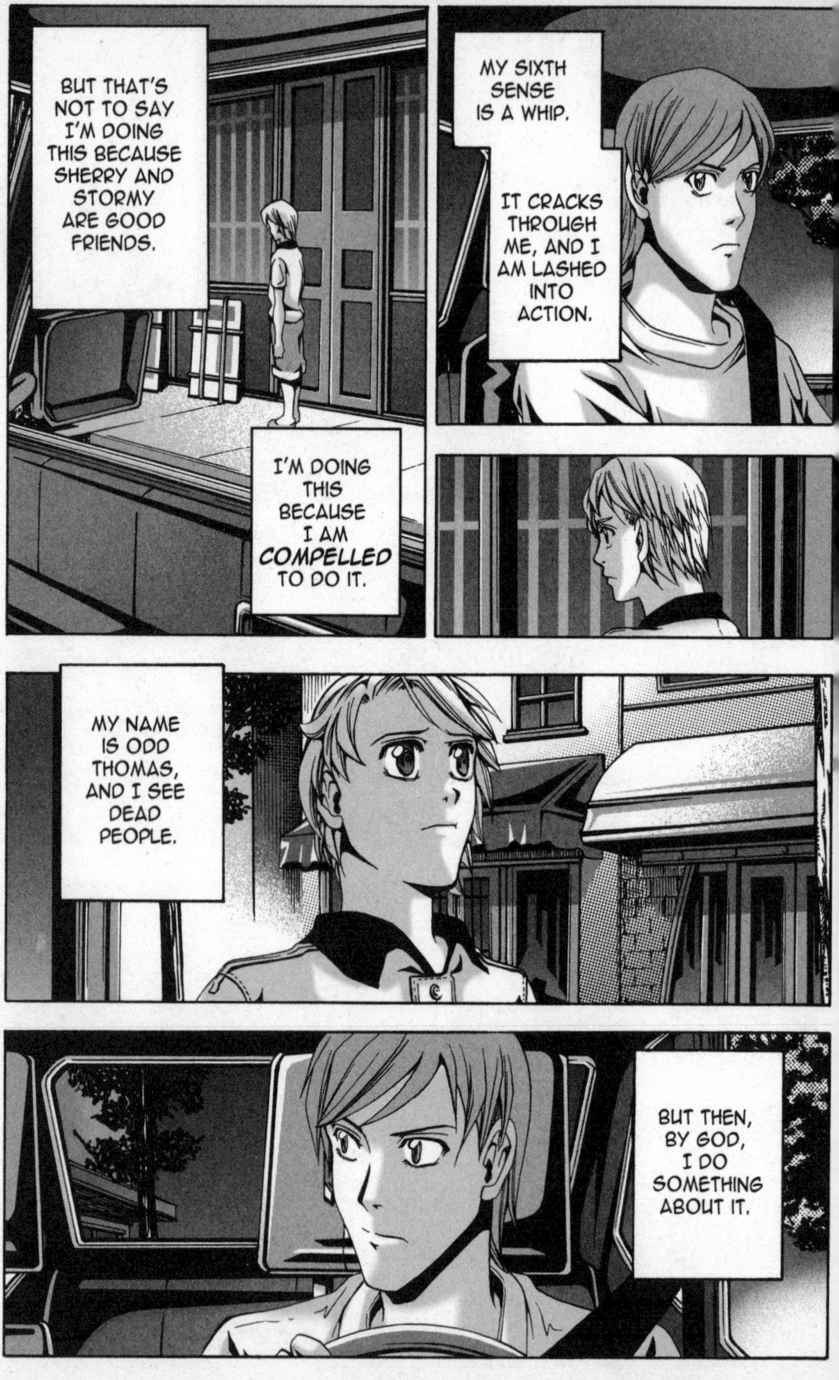
BUT THAT'S NOT TO SAY I'M DOING THIS BECAUSE SHERRY AND STORMY ARE GOOD FRIENDS.
I'M DOING THIS BECAUSE I AM *COMPELLED* TO DO IT.
MY SIXTH SENSE IS A WHIP.
IT CRACKS THROUGH ME, AND I AM LASHED INTO ACTION.
MY NAME IS ODD THOMAS, AND I SEE DEAD PEOPLE.
BUT THEN, BY GOD, I DO SOMETHING ABOUT IT.

In Odd We Trust

Chapter 3

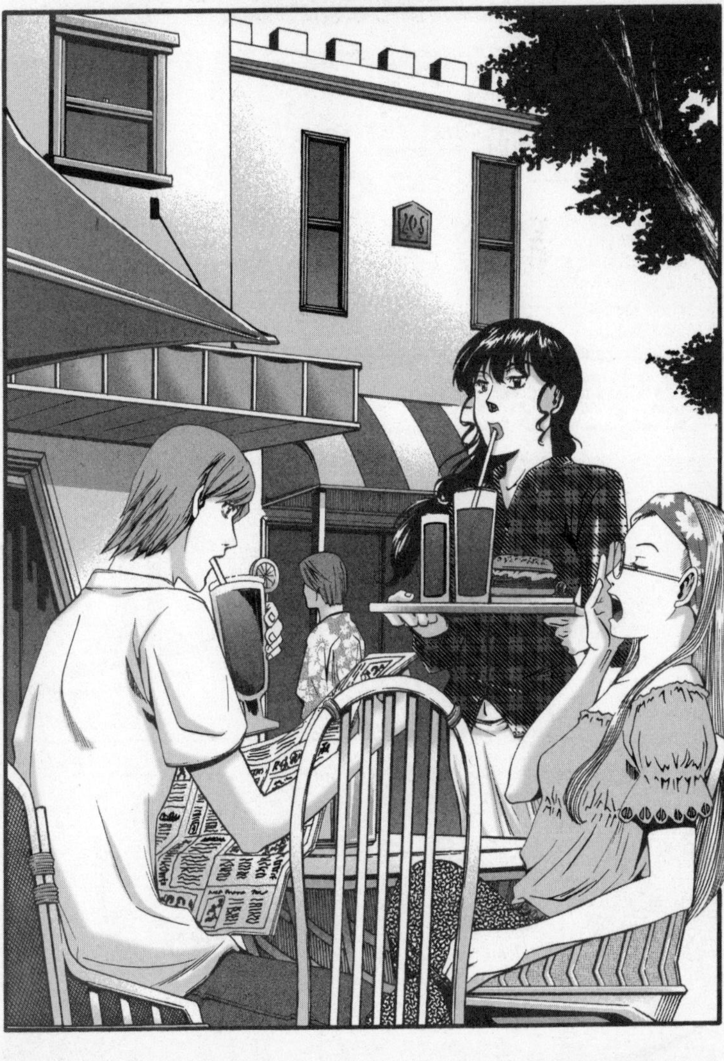

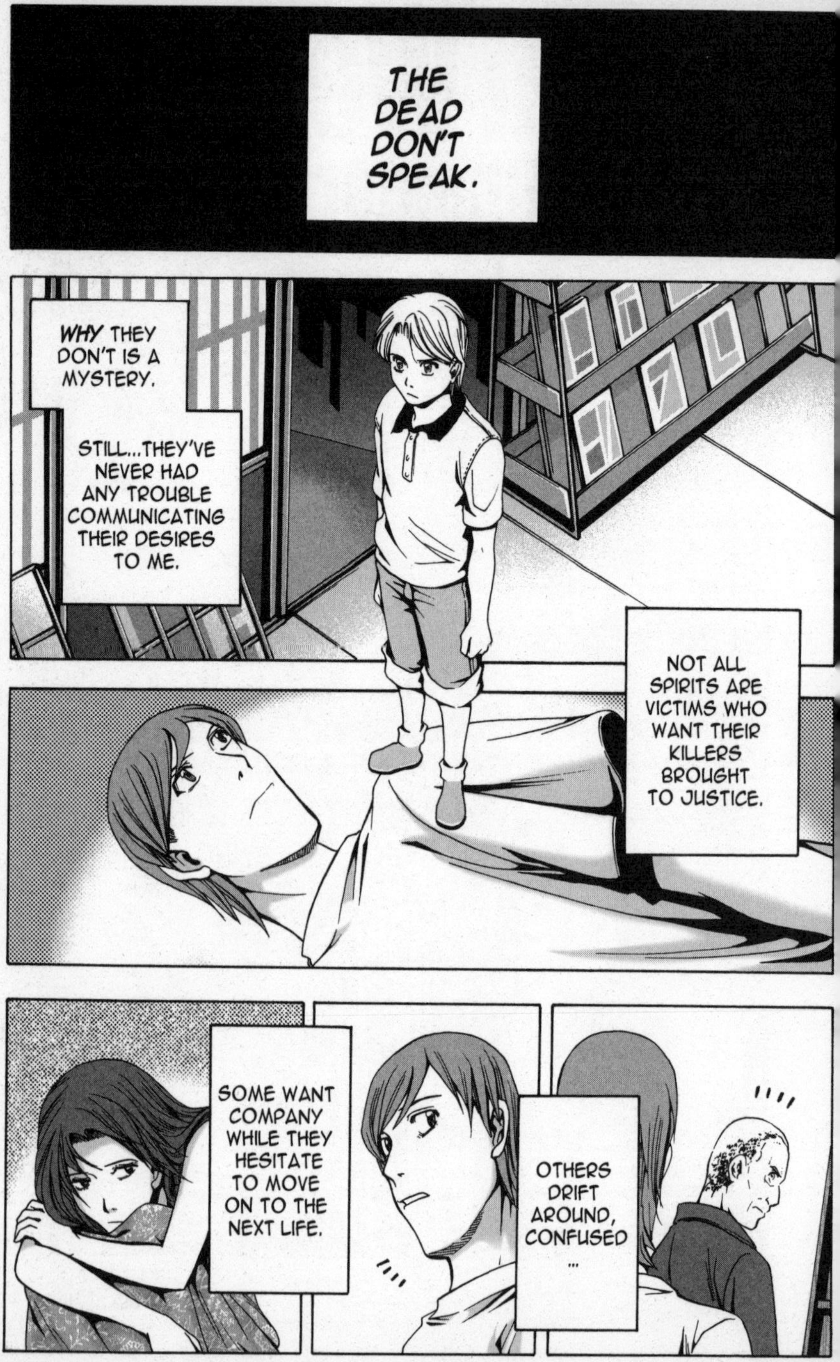
THE DEAD DON'T SPEAK.
WHY THEY DON'T IS A MYSTERY.
STILL...THEY'VE NEVER HAD ANY TROUBLE COMMUNICATING THEIR DESIRES TO ME.
NOT ALL SPIRITS ARE VICTIMS WHO WANT THEIR KILLERS BROUGHT TO JUSTICE.
SOME WANT COMPANY WHILE THEY HESITATE TO MOVE ON TO THE NEXT LIFE.
OTHERS DRIFT AROUND, CONFUSED
...

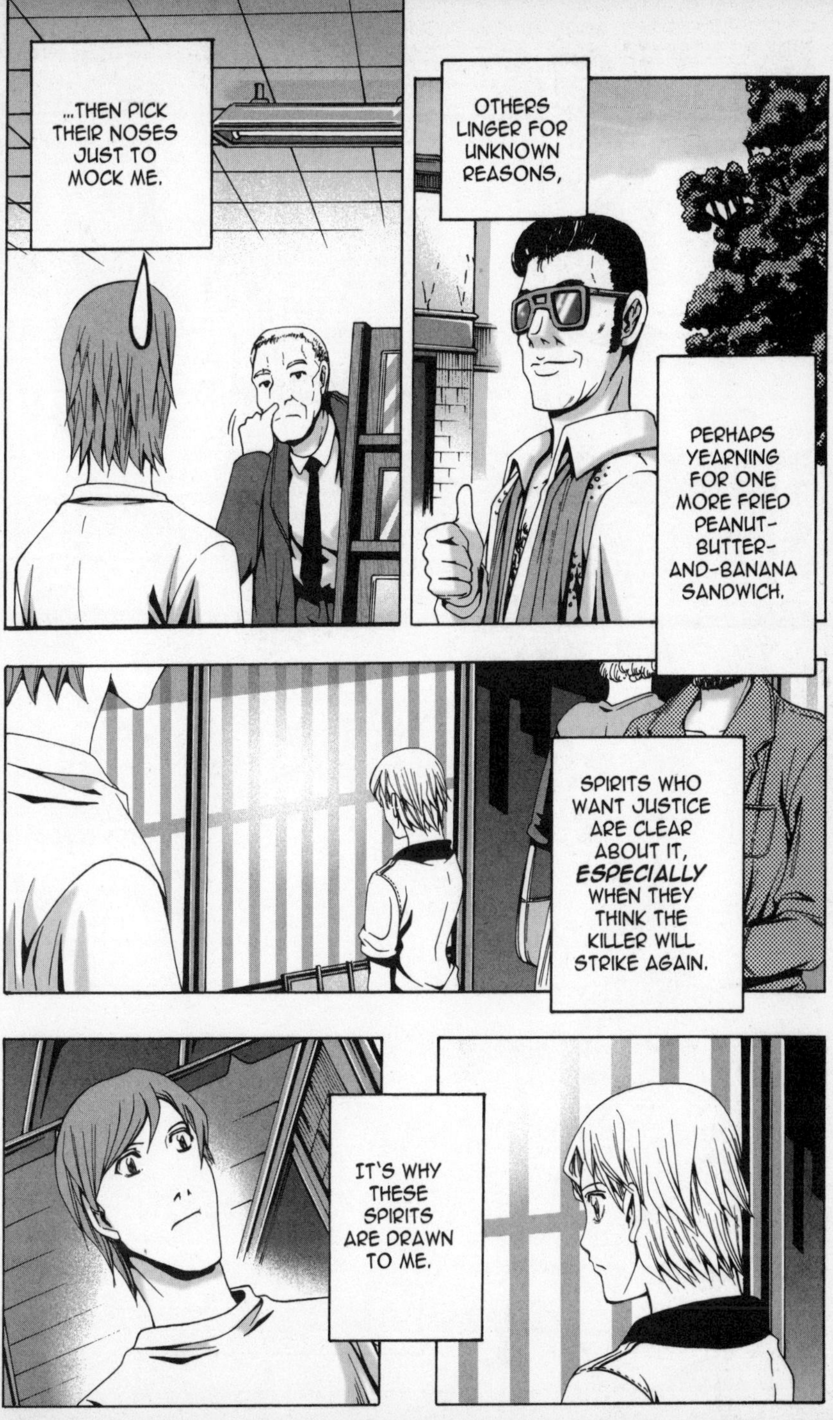
...THEN PICK THEIR NOSES JUST TO MOCK ME.
OTHERS LINGER FOR UNKNOWN REASONS,
PERHAPS YEARNING FOR ONE MORE FRIED PEANUT-BUTTER-AND-BANANA SANDWICH.
SPIRITS WHO WANT JUSTICE ARE CLEAR ABOUT IT, ESPECIALLY WHEN THEY THINK THE KILLER WILL STRIKE AGAIN.
IT'S WHY THESE SPIRITS ARE DRAWN TO ME.

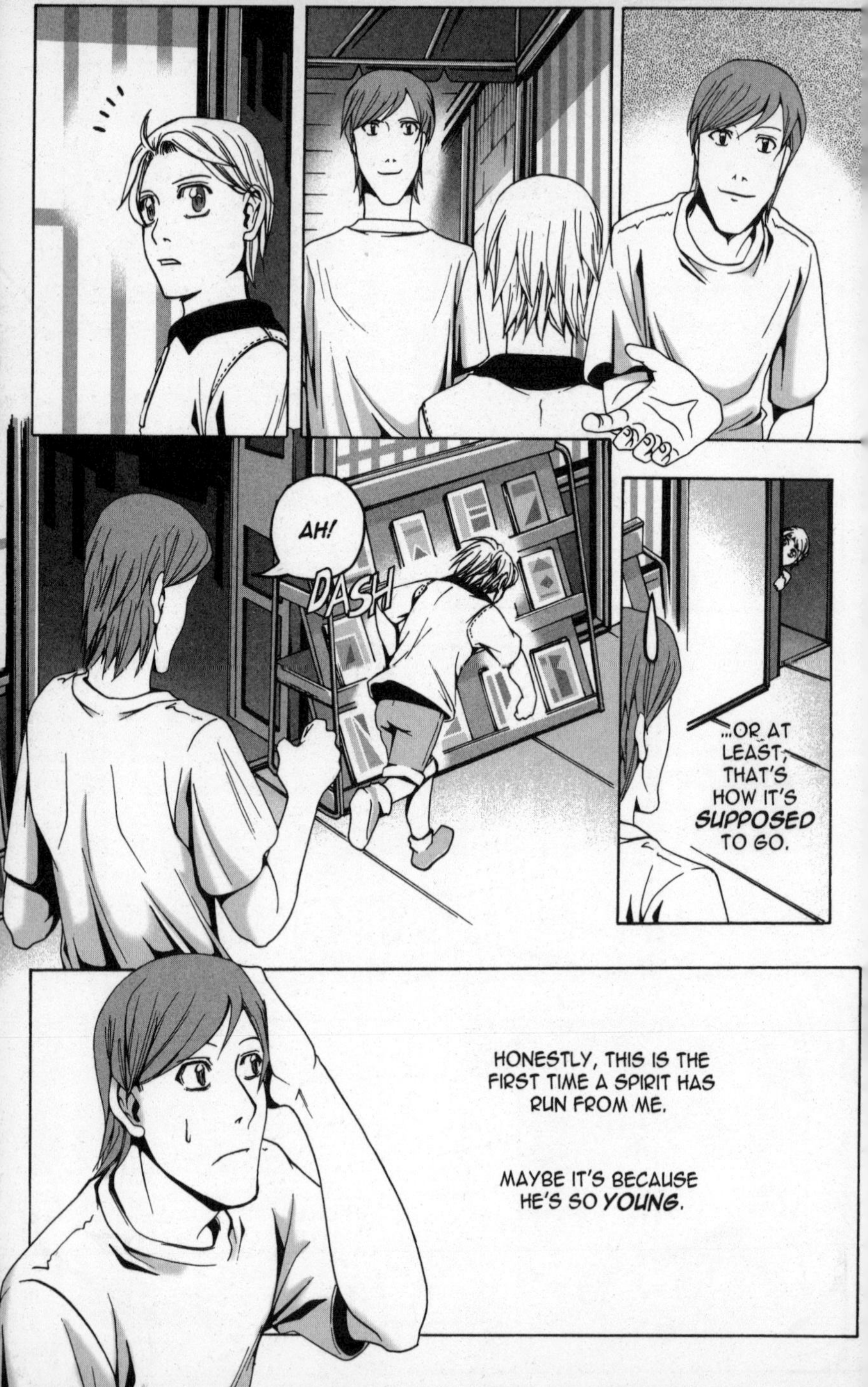
AH!
DASH
...OR AT LEAST, THAT'S HOW IT'S SUPPOSED TO GO.
HONESTLY, THIS IS THE FIRST TIME A SPIRIT HAS RUN FROM ME.
MAYBE IT'S BECAUSE HE'S SO YOUNG.

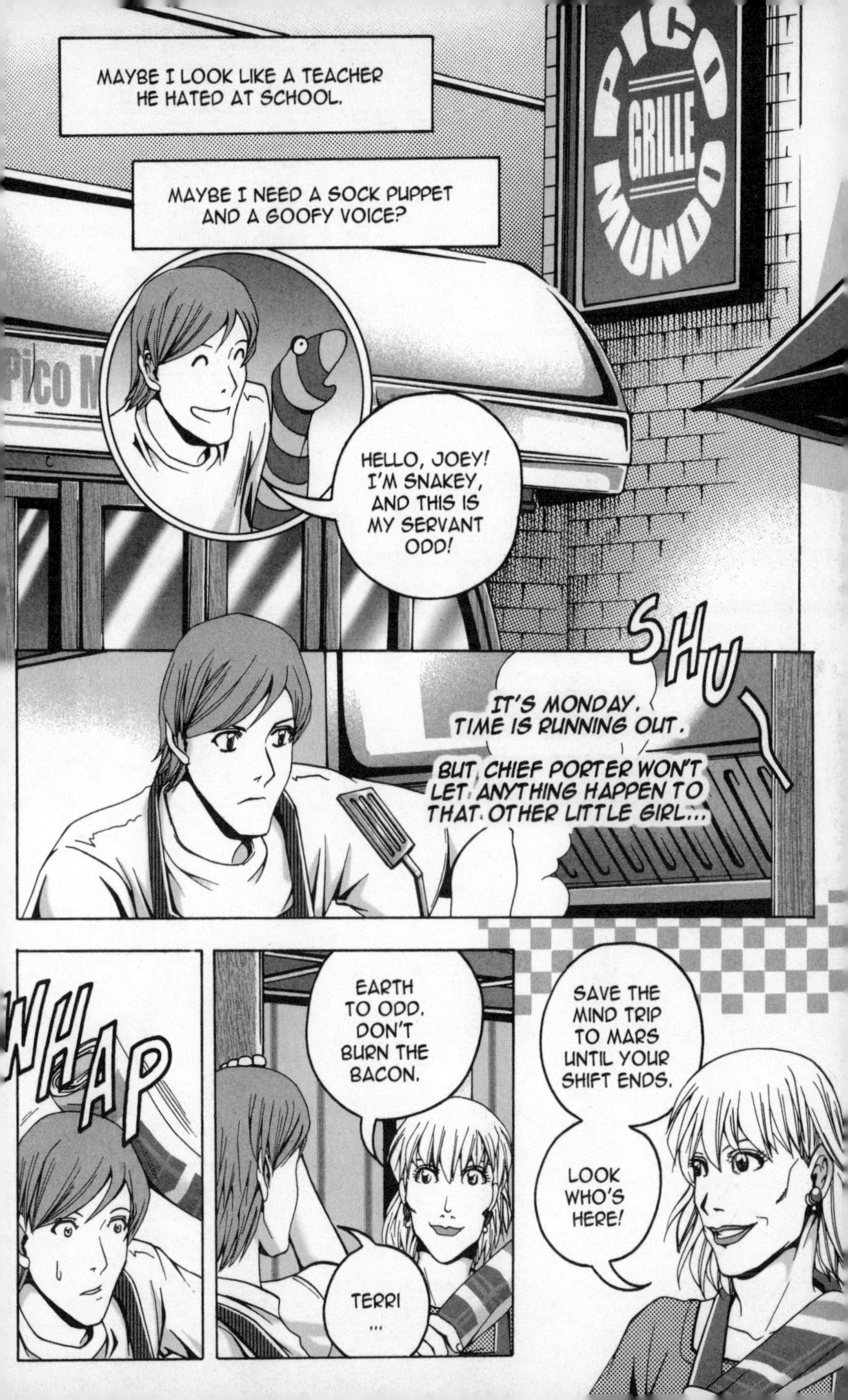
MAYBE I LOOK LIKE A TEACHER HE HATED AT SCHOOL.
MAYBE I NEED A SOCK PUPPET AND A GOOFY VOICE?
PICO MUNDO GRILLE
HELLO, JOEY! I'M SNAKEY, AND THIS IS MY SERVANT ODD!
SHU
IT'S MONDAY. TIME IS RUNNING OUT.
BUT CHIEF PORTER WON'T LET ANYTHING HAPPEN TO THAT OTHER LITTLE GIRL...
WHAP
EARTH TO ODD. DON'T BURN THE BACON.
SAVE THE MIND TRIP TO MARS UNTIL YOUR SHIFT ENDS.
LOOK WHO'S HERE!
TERRI ...

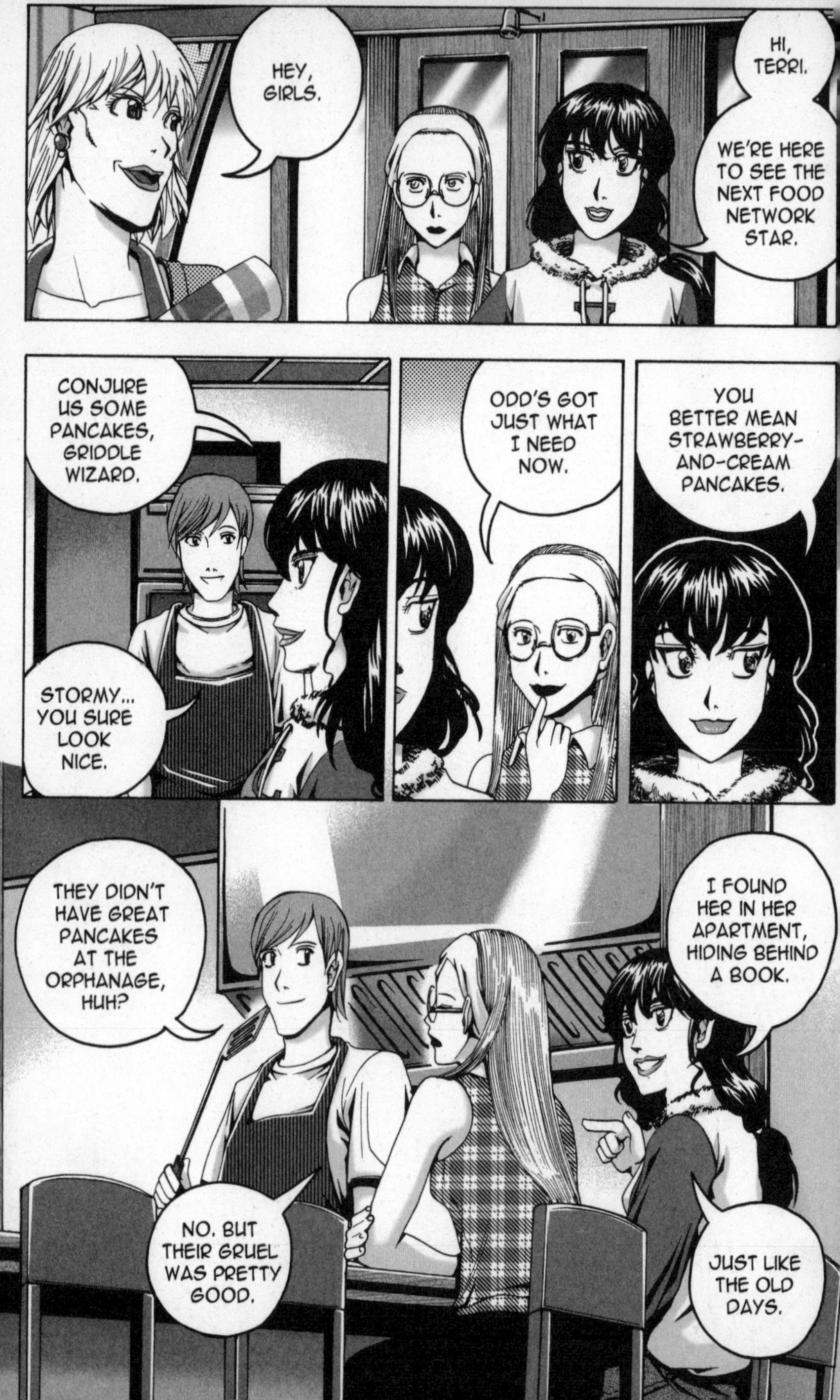
HEY, GIRLS.
HI, TERRI.
WE'RE HERE TO SEE THE NEXT FOOD NETWORK STAR.
CONJURE US SOME PANCAKES, GRIDDLE WIZARD.
STORMY... YOU SURE LOOK NICE.
ODD'S GOT JUST WHAT I NEED NOW.
YOU BETTER MEAN STRAWBERRY-AND-CREAM PANCAKES.
THEY DIDN'T HAVE GREAT PANCAKES AT THE ORPHANAGE, HUH?
I FOUND HER IN HER APARTMENT, HIDING BEHIND A BOOK.
NO. BUT THEIR GRUEL WAS PRETTY GOOD.
JUST LIKE THE OLD DAYS.

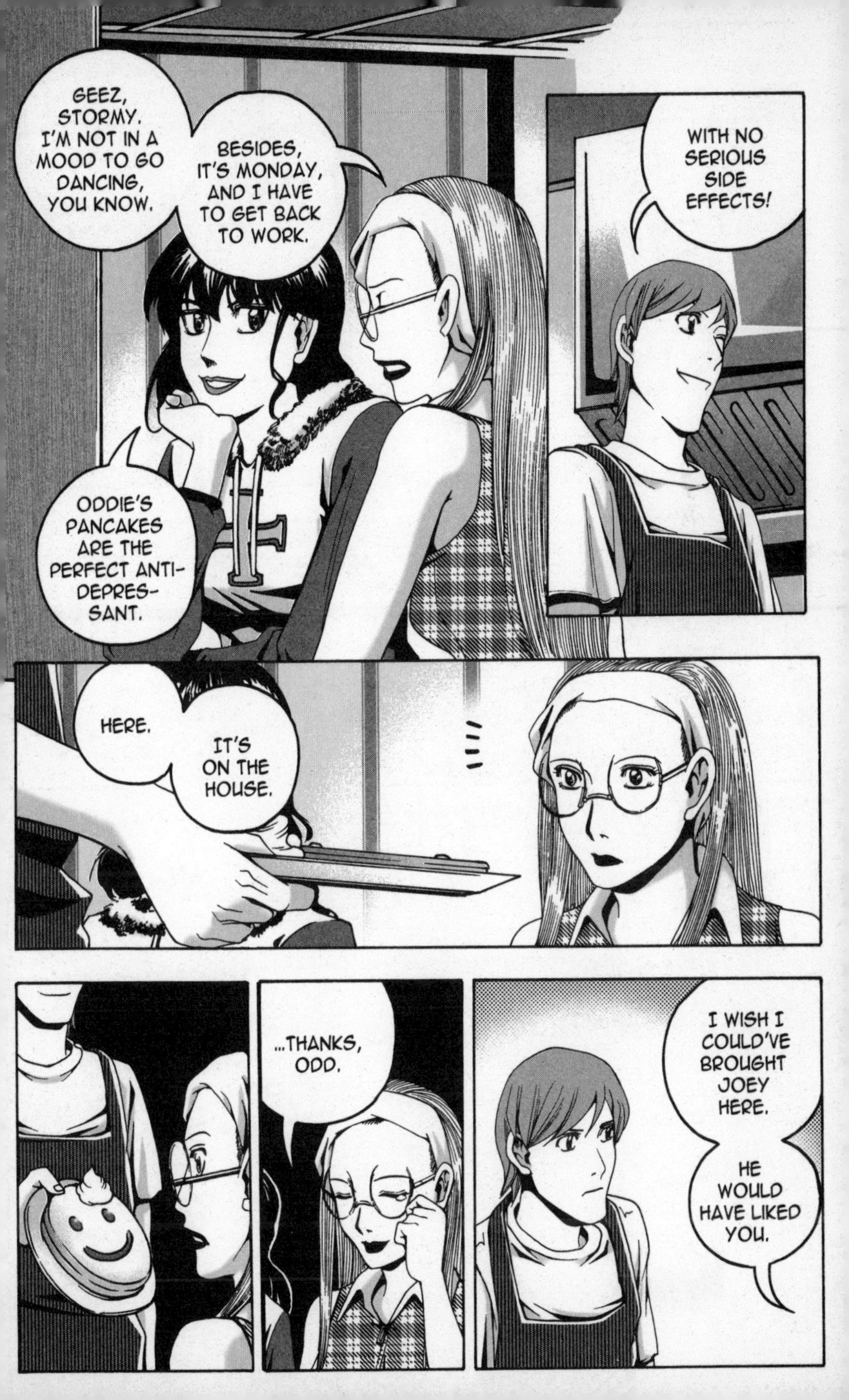
GEEZ, STORMY. I'M NOT IN A MOOD TO GO DANCING, YOU KNOW.
BESIDES, IT'S MONDAY, AND I HAVE TO GET BACK TO WORK.
ODDIE'S PANCAKES ARE THE PERFECT ANTI-DEPRES-SANT.
WITH NO SERIOUS SIDE EFFECTS!
HERE.
IT'S ON THE HOUSE.
...THANKS, ODD.
I WISH I COULD'VE BROUGHT JOEY HERE.
HE WOULD HAVE LIKED YOU.

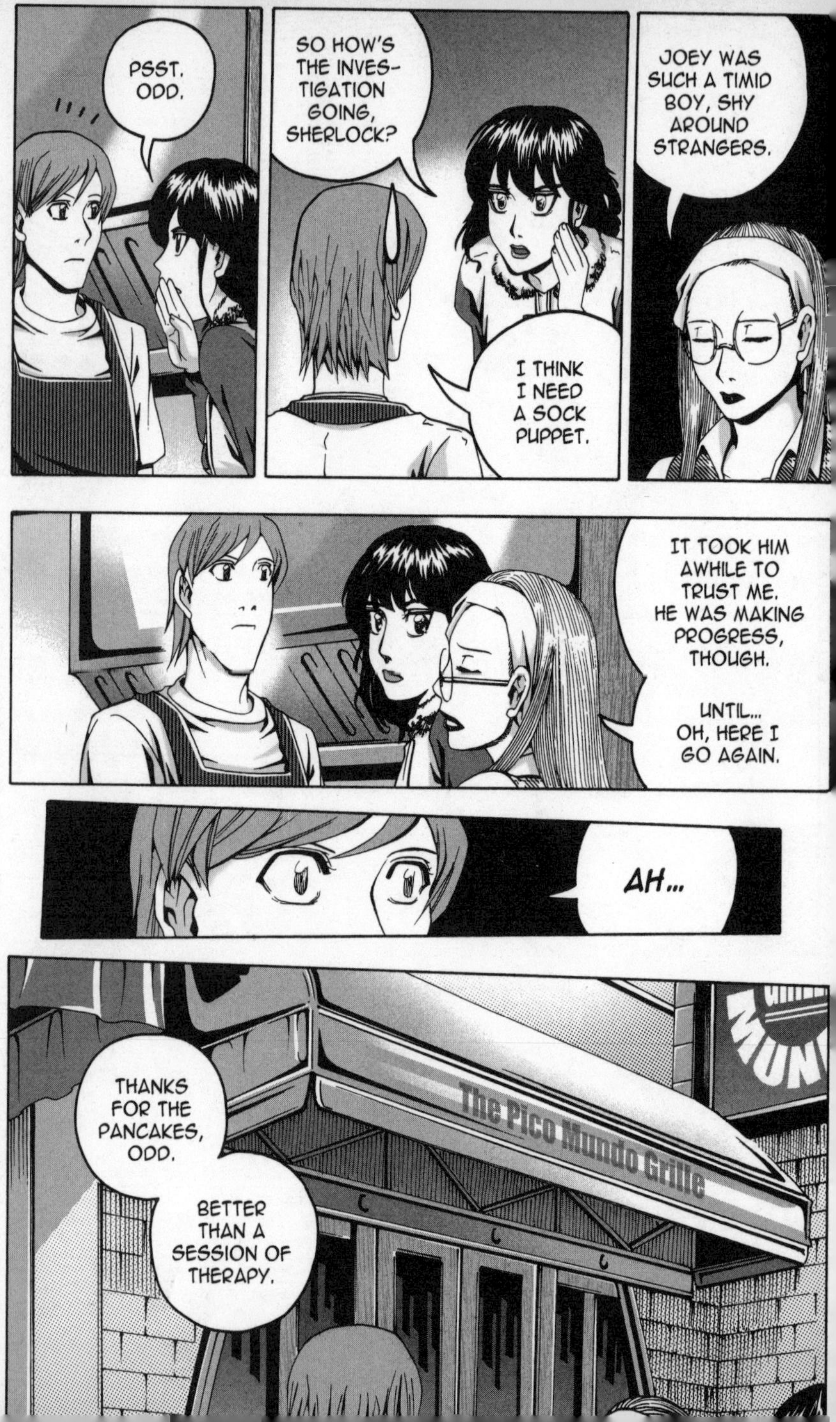
PSST. ODD.
SO HOW'S THE INVESTIGATION GOING, SHERLOCK?
I THINK I NEED A SOCK PUPPET.
JOEY WAS SUCH A TIMID BOY, SHY AROUND STRANGERS.
IT TOOK HIM AWHILE TO TRUST ME. HE WAS MAKING PROGRESS, THOUGH.
UNTIL... OH, HERE I GO AGAIN.
AH...
The Pico Mundo Grille
THANKS FOR THE PANCAKES, ODD.
BETTER THAN A SESSION OF THERAPY.

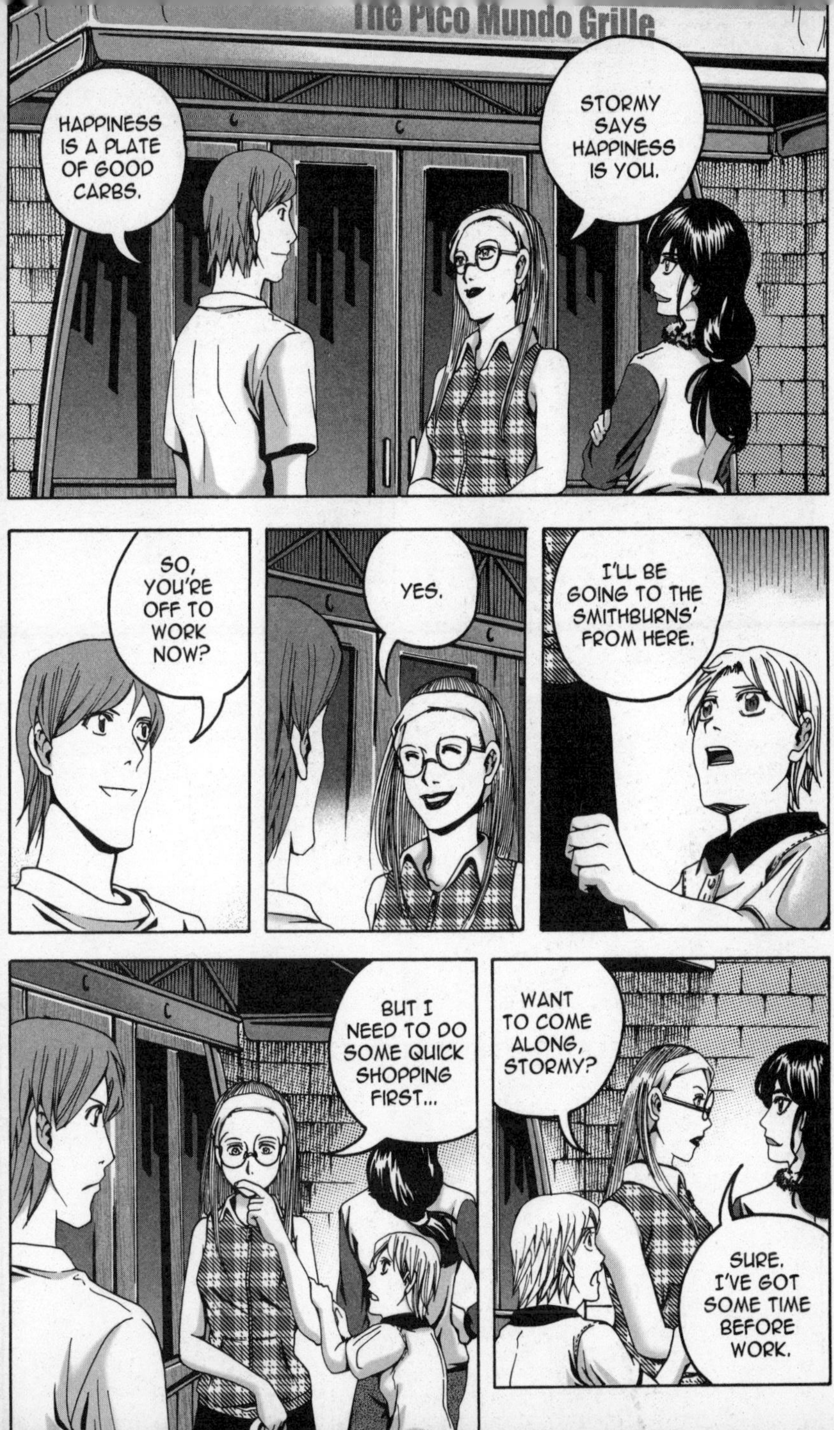
The Pico Mundo Grille
HAPPINESS IS A PLATE OF GOOD CARBS.
STORMY SAYS HAPPINESS IS YOU.
SO, YOU'RE OFF TO WORK NOW?
YES.
I'LL BE GOING TO THE SMITHBURNS' FROM HERE.
BUT I NEED TO DO SOME QUICK SHOPPING FIRST...
WANT TO COME ALONG, STORMY?
SURE. I'VE GOT SOME TIME BEFORE WORK.

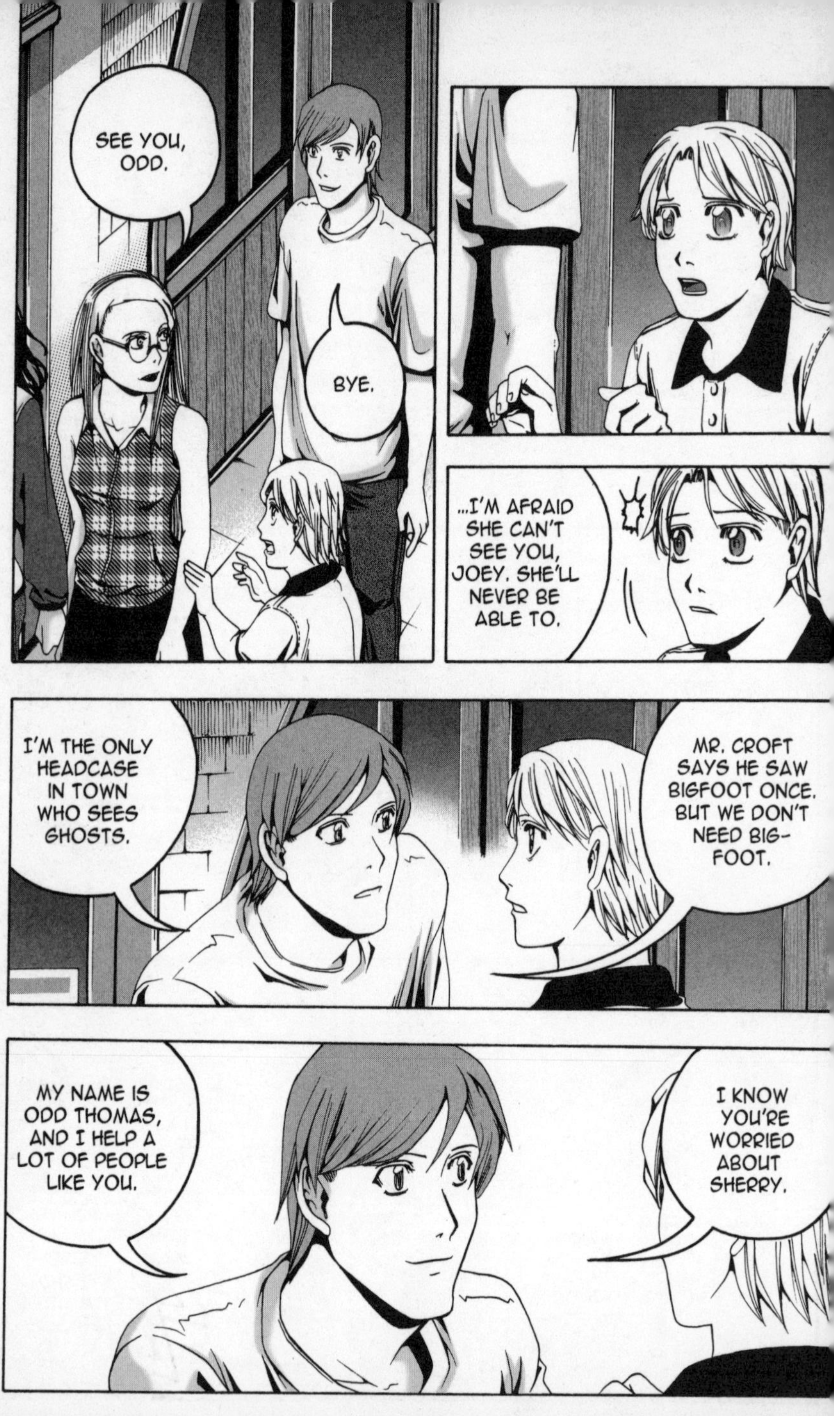
SEE YOU, ODD.
BYE.
...I'M AFRAID SHE CAN'T SEE YOU, JOEY. SHE'LL NEVER BE ABLE TO.
I'M THE ONLY HEADCASE IN TOWN WHO SEES GHOSTS.
MR. CROFT SAYS HE SAW BIGFOOT ONCE. BUT WE DON'T NEED BIG-FOOT.
MY NAME IS ODD THOMAS, AND I HELP A LOT OF PEOPLE LIKE YOU.
I KNOW YOU'RE WORRIED ABOUT SHERRY.

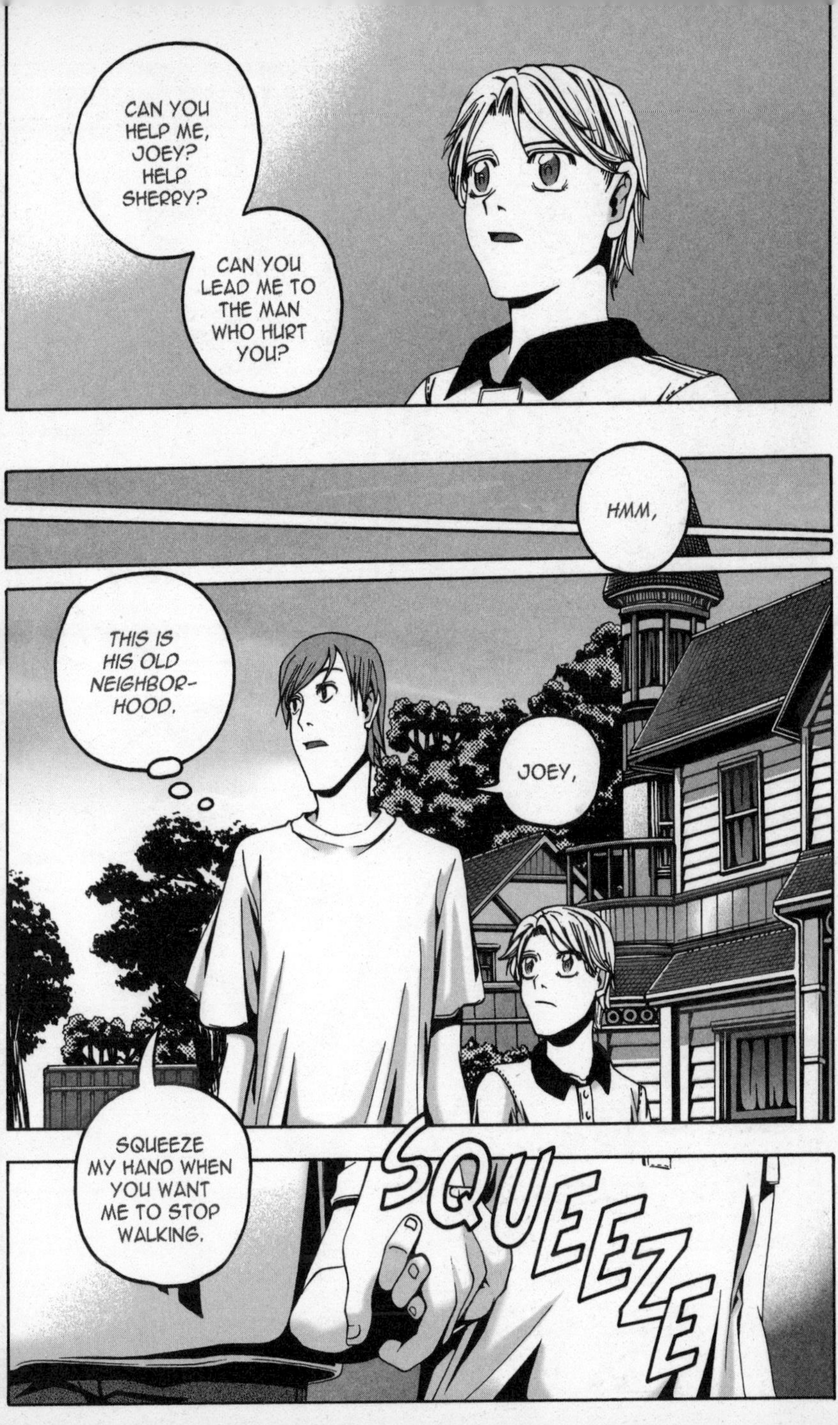
CAN YOU HELP ME, JOEY? HELP SHERRY?
CAN YOU LEAD ME TO THE MAN WHO HURT YOU?
HMM,
THIS IS HIS OLD NEIGHBOR-HOOD.
JOEY,
SQUEEZE MY HAND WHEN YOU WANT ME TO STOP WALKING.
SQUEEZE

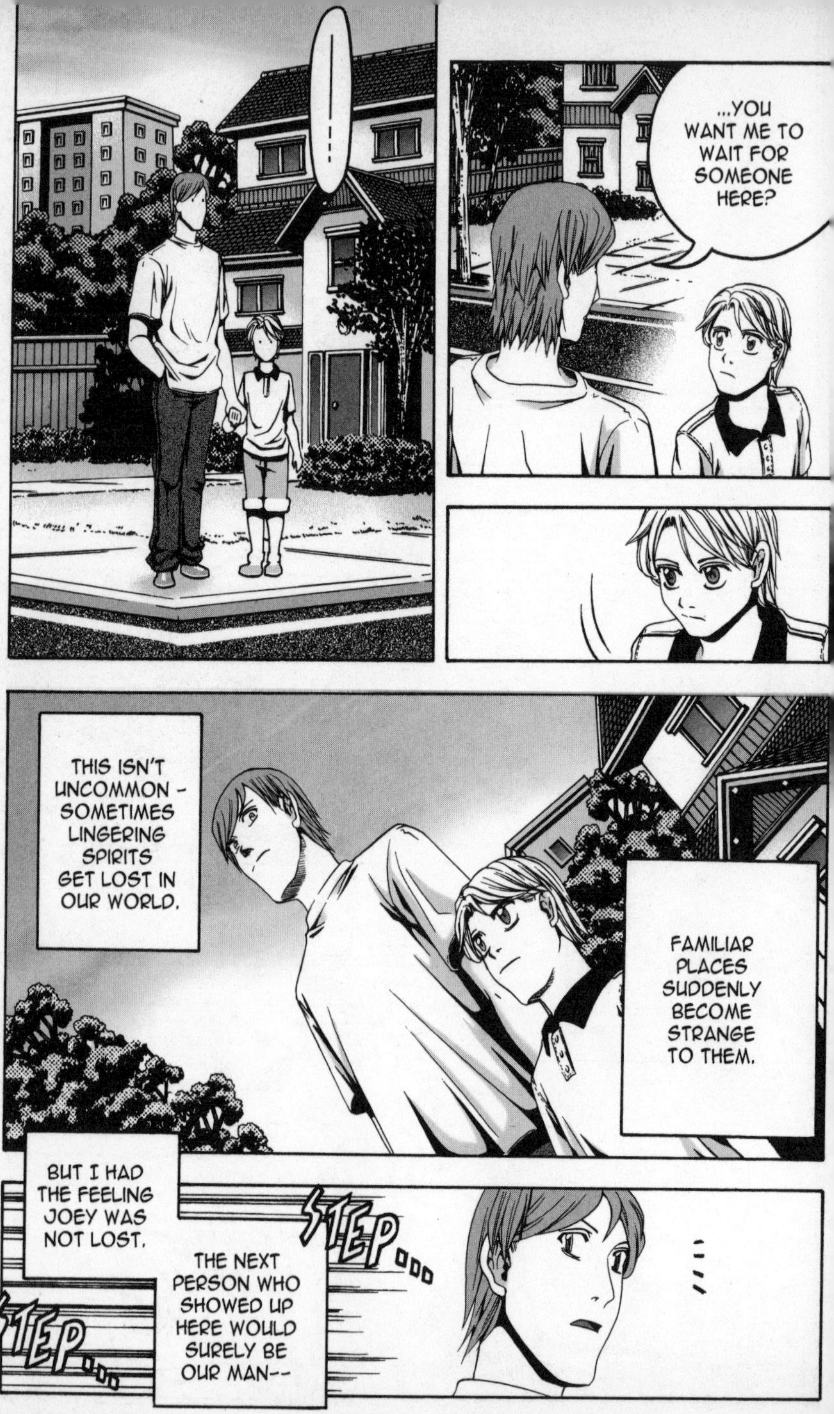
!
...YOU WANT ME TO WAIT FOR SOMEONE HERE?
THIS ISN'T UNCOMMON - SOMETIMES LINGERING SPIRITS GET LOST IN OUR WORLD.
FAMILIAR PLACES SUDDENLY BECOME STRANGE TO THEM.
BUT I HAD THE FEELING JOEY WAS NOT LOST.
THE NEXT PERSON WHO SHOWED UP HERE WOULD SURELY BE OUR MAN--
STEP...
STEP...
...

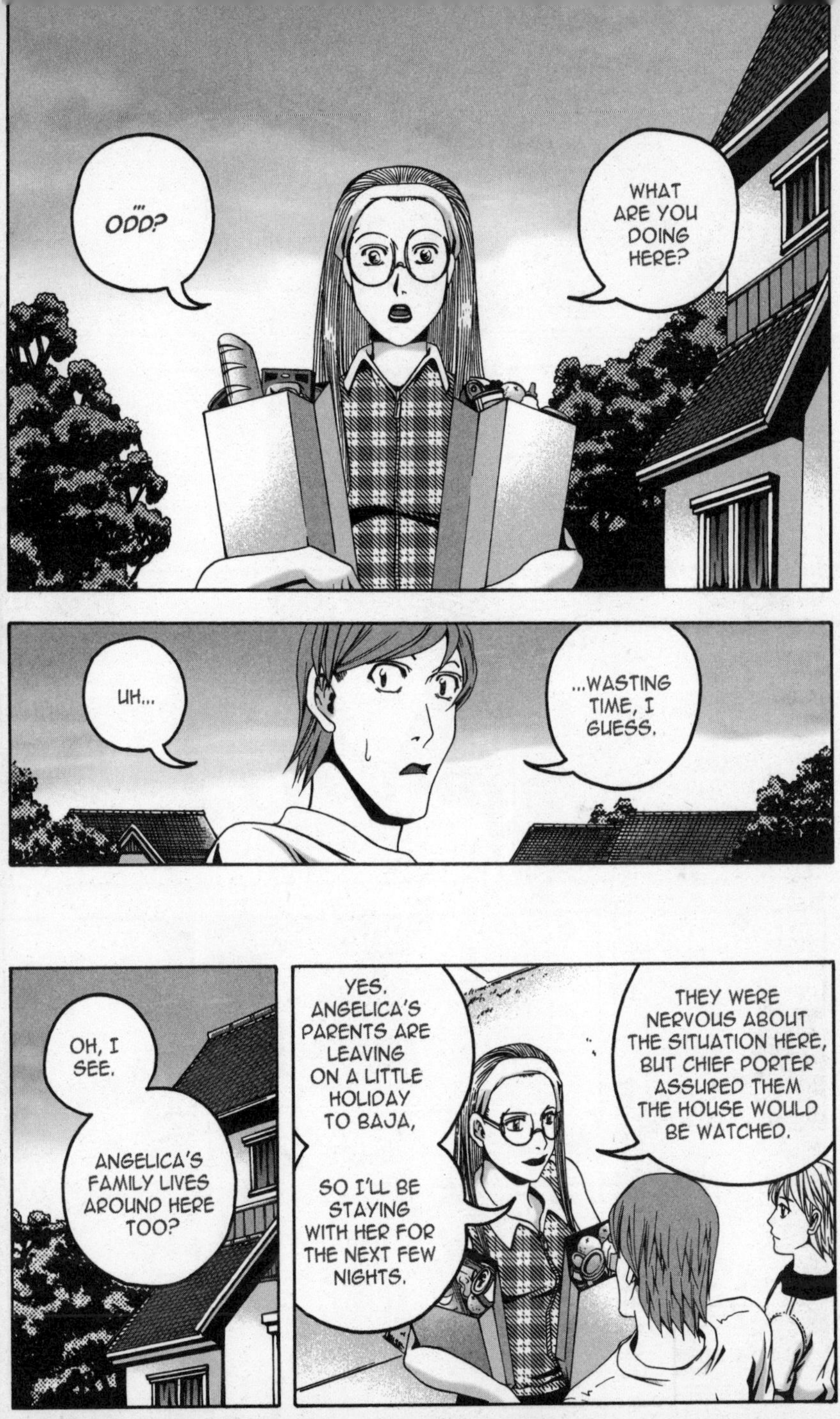
...ODD?
WHAT ARE YOU DOING HERE?
UH...
...WASTING TIME, I GUESS.
OH, I SEE.
ANGELICA'S FAMILY LIVES AROUND HERE TOO?
YES. ANGELICA'S PARENTS ARE LEAVING ON A LITTLE HOLIDAY TO BAJA,
SO I'LL BE STAYING WITH HER FOR THE NEXT FEW NIGHTS.
THEY WERE NERVOUS ABOUT THE SITUATION HERE, BUT CHIEF PORTER ASSURED THEM THE HOUSE WOULD BE WATCHED.

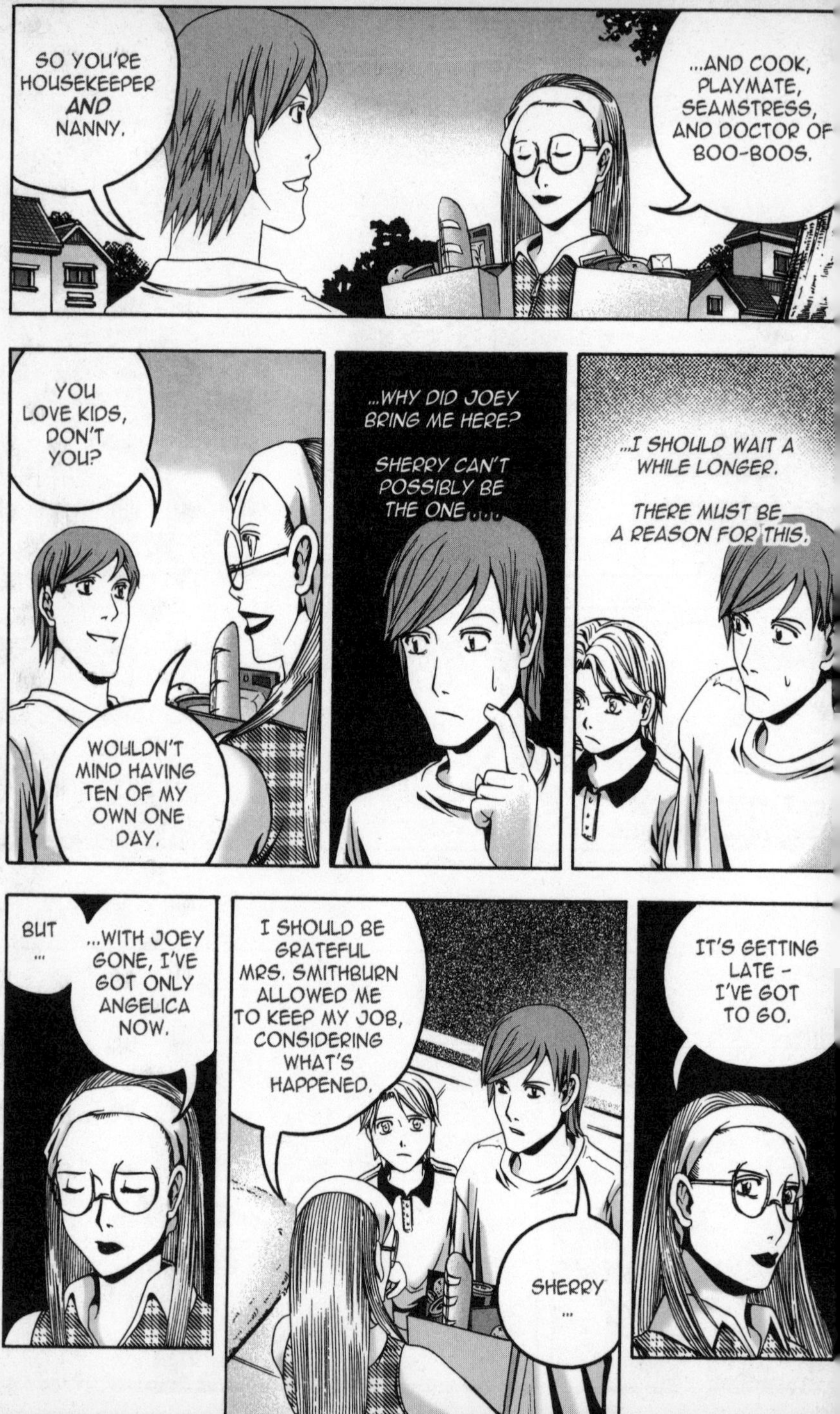
SO YOU'RE HOUSEKEEPER AND NANNY.
...AND COOK, PLAYMATE, SEAMSTRESS, AND DOCTOR OF BOO-BOOS.
YOU LOVE KIDS, DON'T YOU?
WOULDN'T MIND HAVING TEN OF MY OWN ONE DAY.
...WHY DID JOEY BRING ME HERE?
SHERRY CAN'T POSSIBLY BE THE ONE...
...I SHOULD WAIT A WHILE LONGER.
THERE MUST BE A REASON FOR THIS.
BUT ...
...WITH JOEY GONE, I'VE GOT ONLY ANGELICA NOW.
I SHOULD BE GRATEFUL MRS. SMITHBURN ALLOWED ME TO KEEP MY JOB, CONSIDERING WHAT'S HAPPENED.
SHERRY ...
IT'S GETTING LATE - I'VE GOT TO GO.

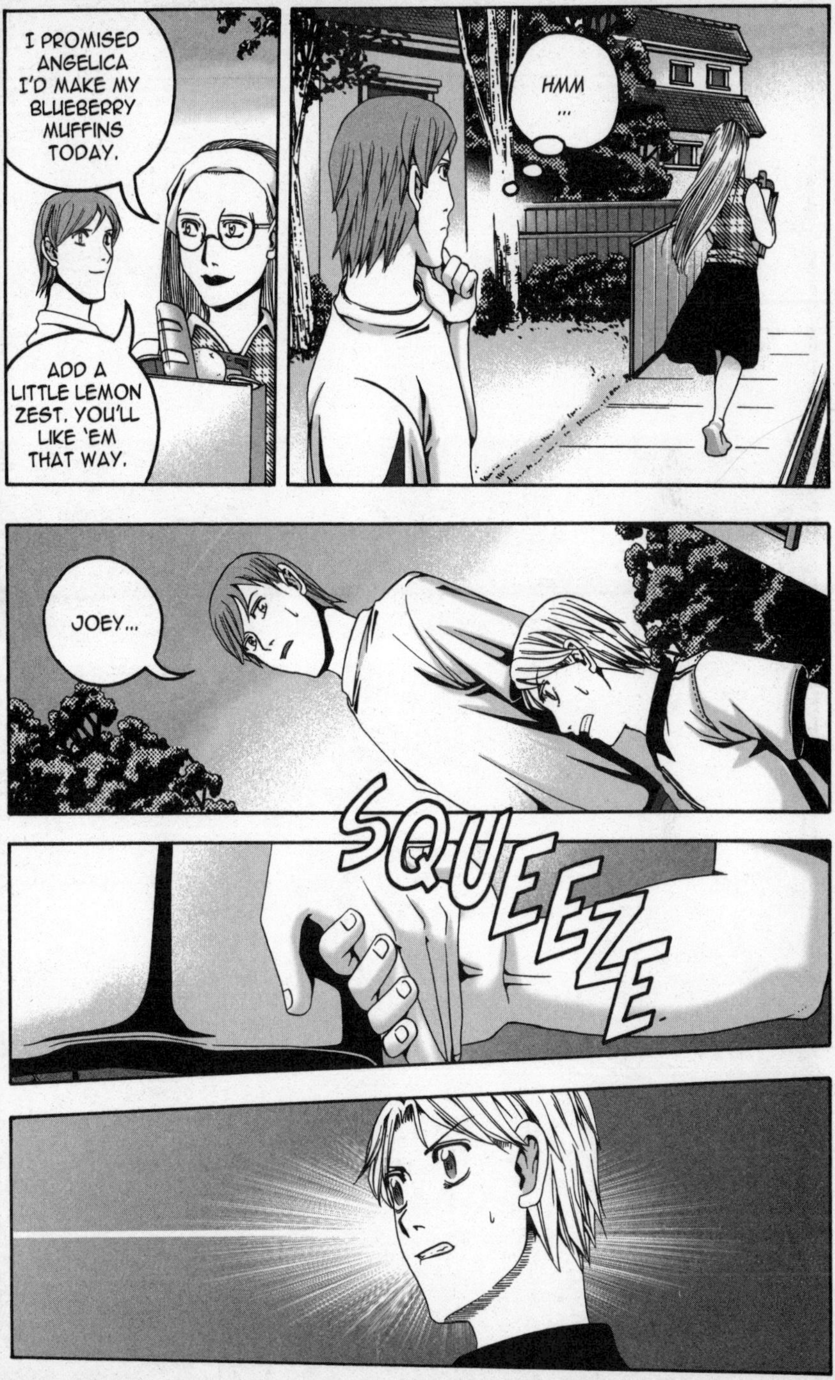
I PROMISED ANGELICA I'D MAKE MY BLUEBERRY MUFFINS TODAY.
ADD A LITTLE LEMON ZEST. YOU'LL LIKE 'EM THAT WAY.
HMM ...
JOEY...
SQUEEZE

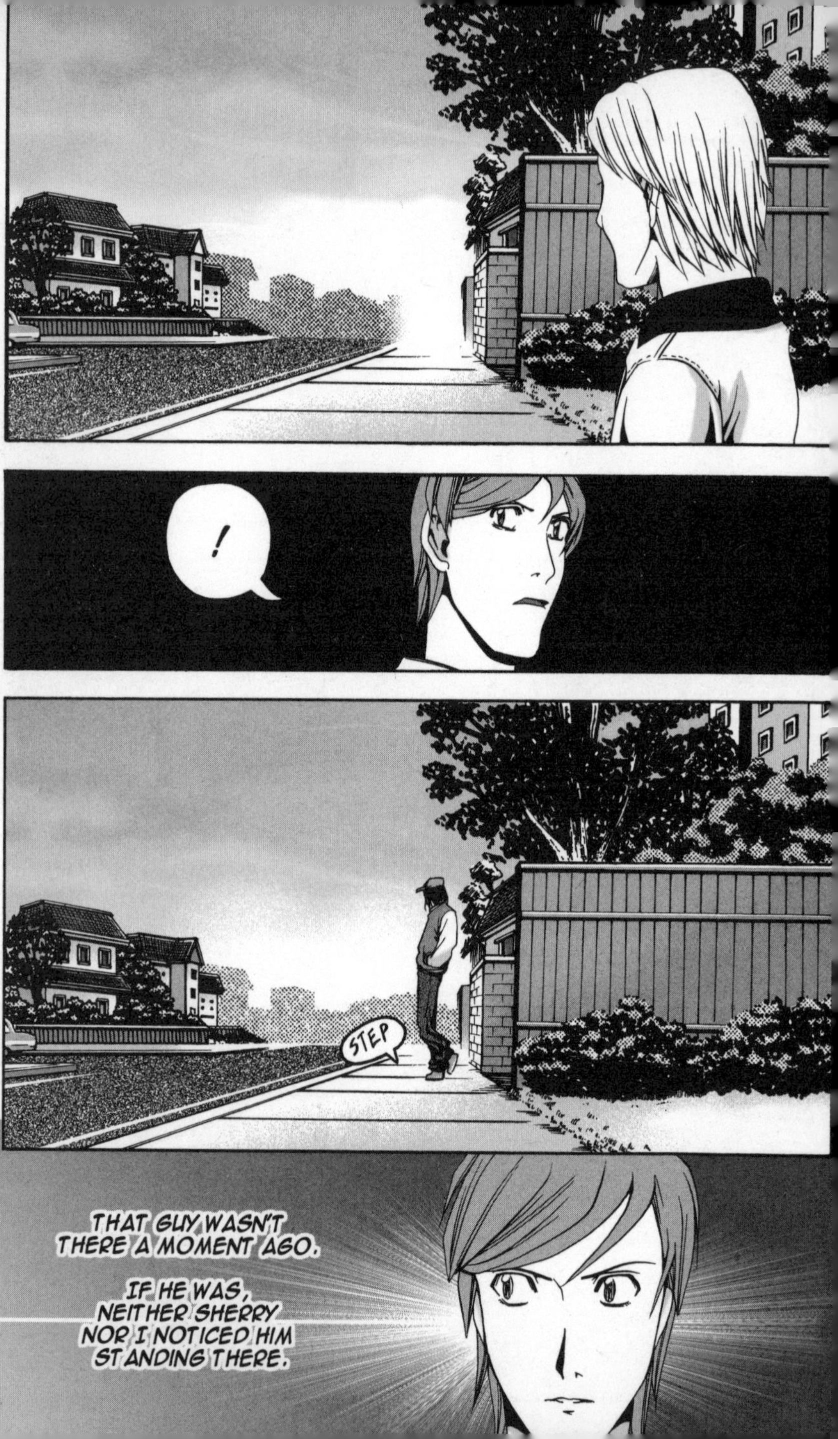
!
STEP
THAT GUY WASN'T THERE A MOMENT AGO.
IF HE WAS, NEITHER SHERRY NOR I NOTICED HIM STANDING THERE.

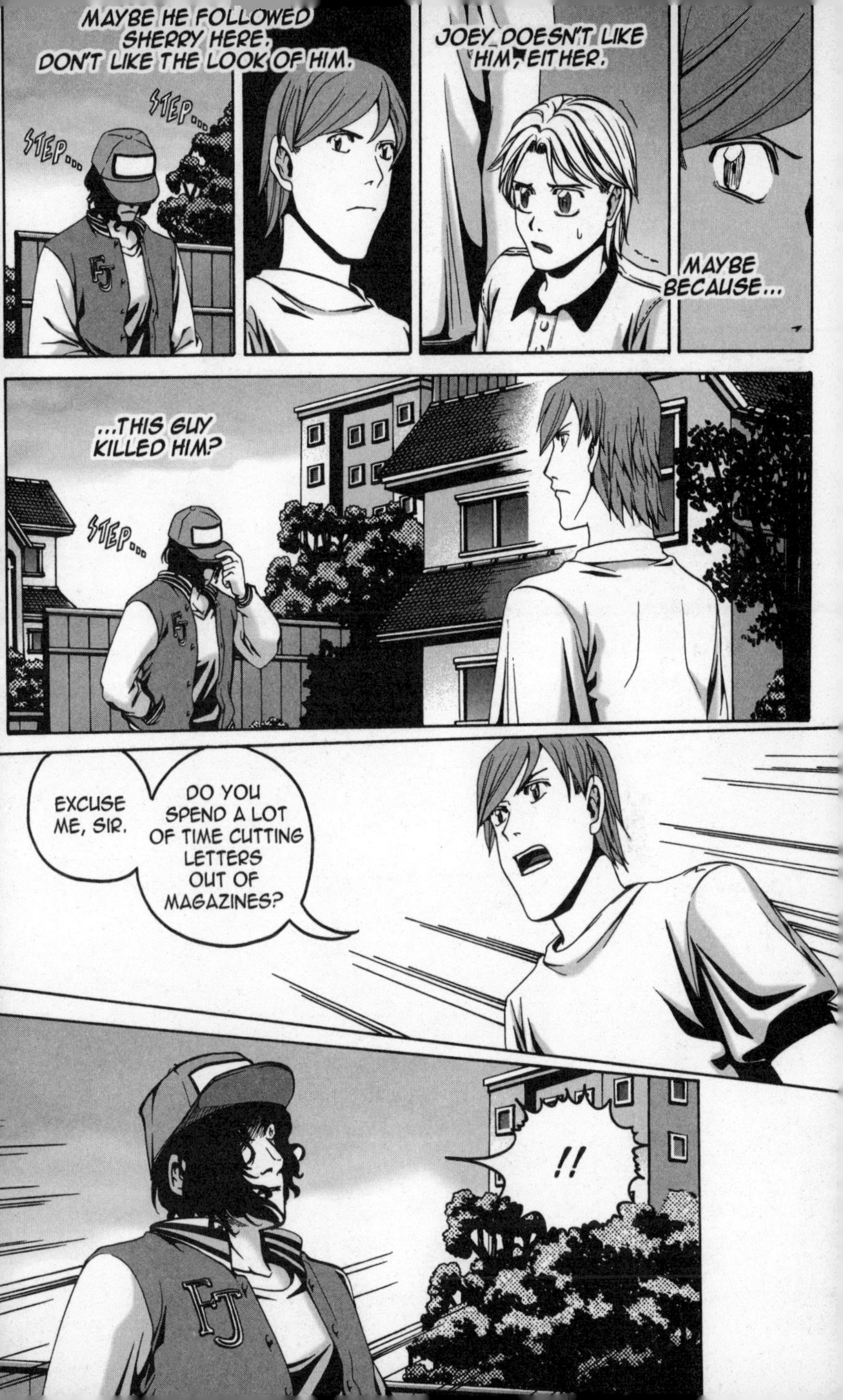
MAYBE HE FOLLOWED SHERRY HERE. DON'T LIKE THE LOOK OF HIM.
STEP...
STEP...
JOEY DOESN'T LIKE HIM, EITHER.
MAYBE BECAUSE...
...THIS GUY KILLED HIM?
STEP...
EXCUSE ME, SIR.
DO YOU SPEND A LOT OF TIME CUTTING LETTERS OUT OF MAGAZINES?
!!

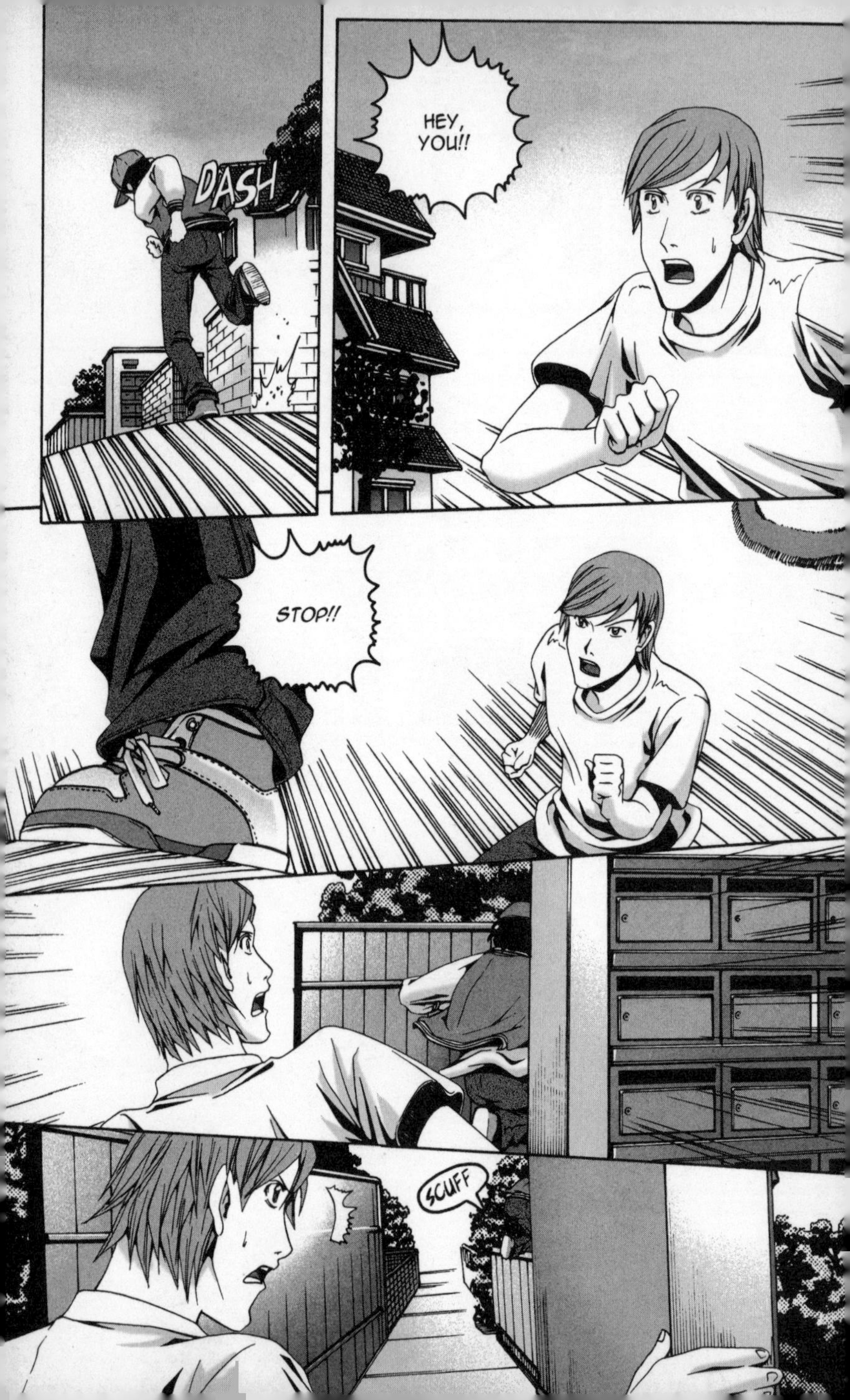
HEY, YOU!!
DASH
STOP!!
SCUFF

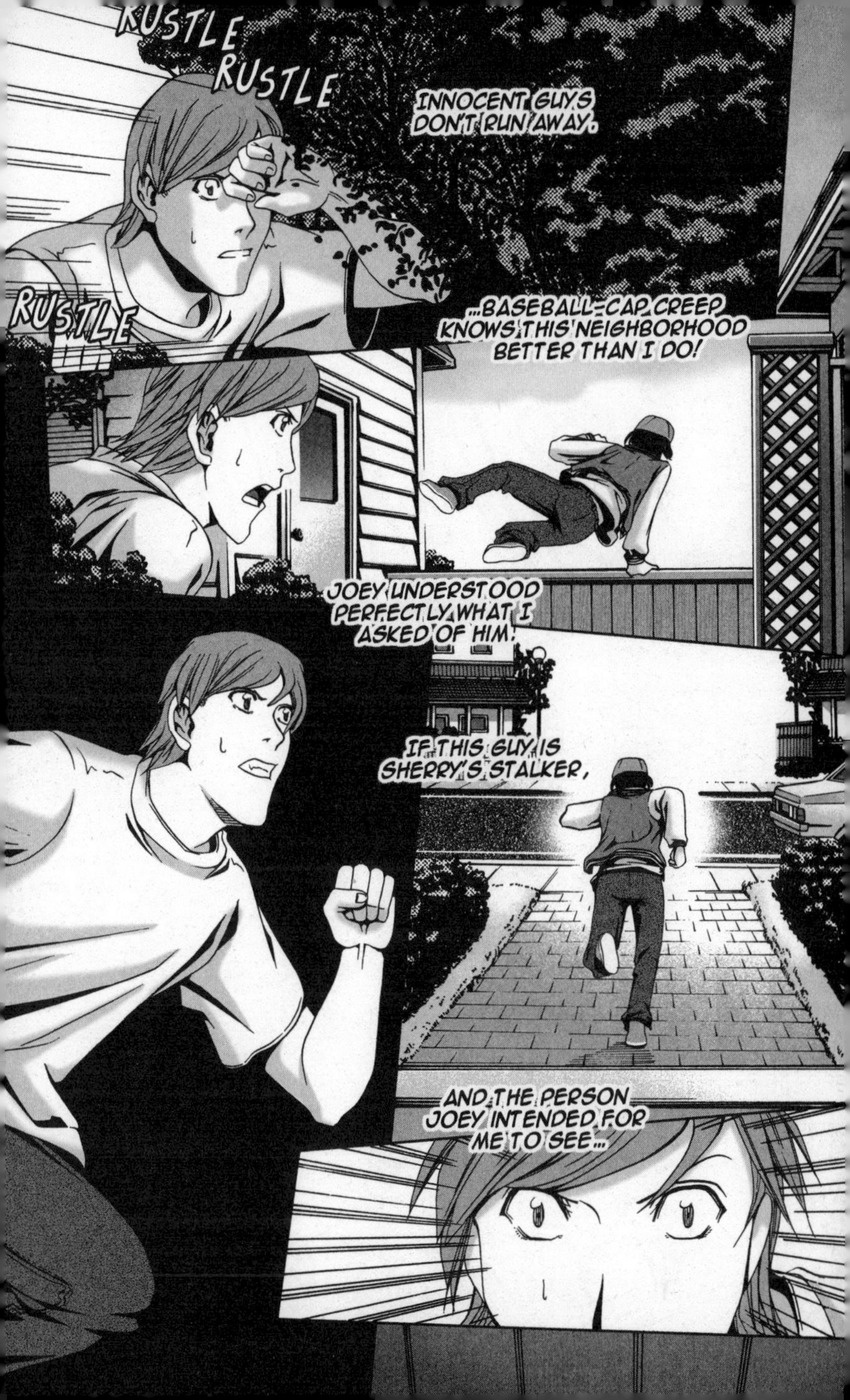
RUSTLE
RUSTLE
RUSTLE
INNOCENT GUYS DON'T RUN AWAY.
...BASEBALL-CAP CREEP KNOWS THIS NEIGHBORHOOD BETTER THAN I DO!
JOEY UNDERSTOOD PERFECTLY WHAT I ASKED OF HIM.
IF THIS GUY IS SHERRY'S STALKER,
AND THE PERSON JOEY INTENDED FOR ME TO SEE...

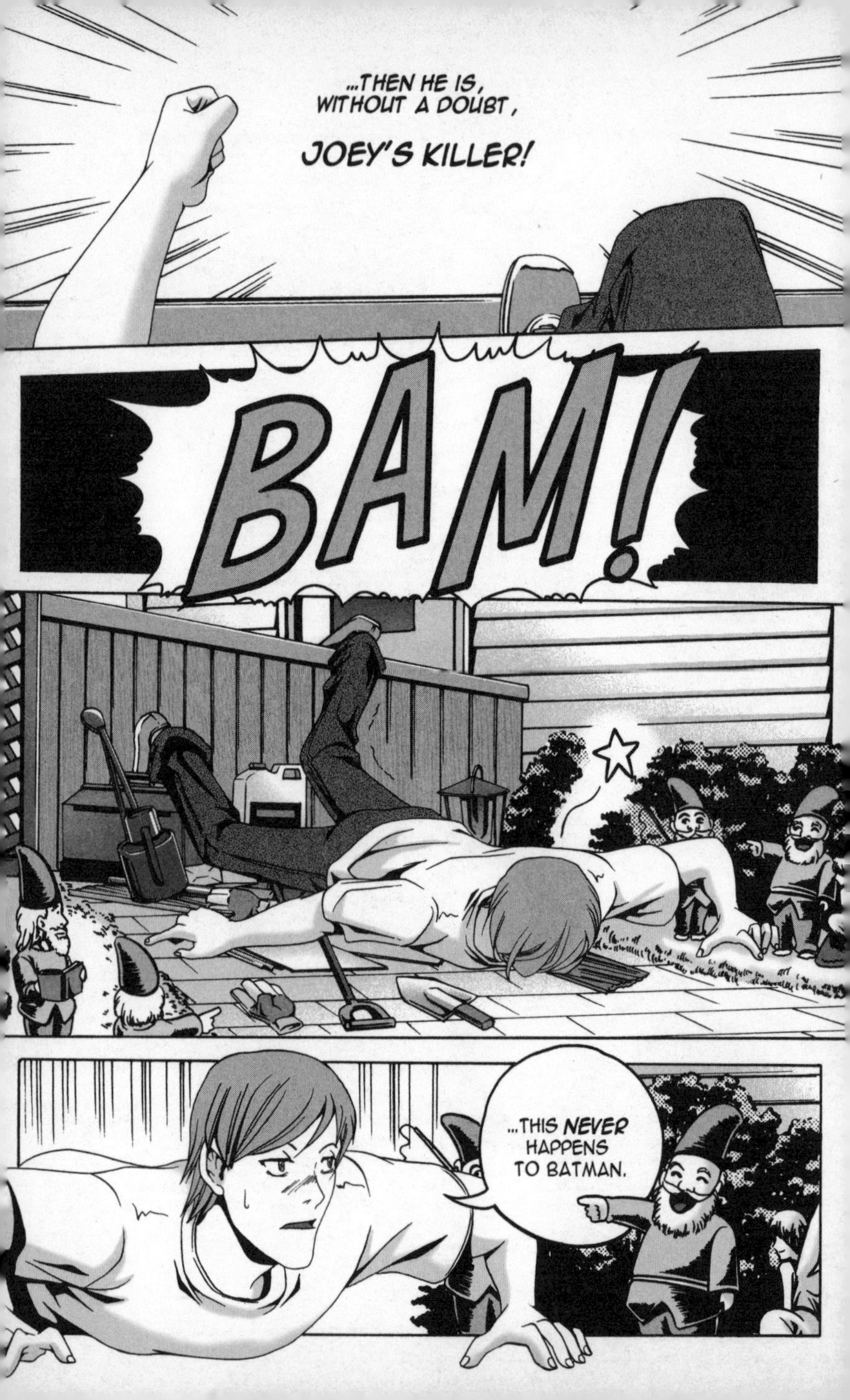
...THEN HE IS, WITHOUT A DOUBT,
JOEY'S KILLER!
BAM!
...THIS NEVER HAPPENS TO BATMAN.

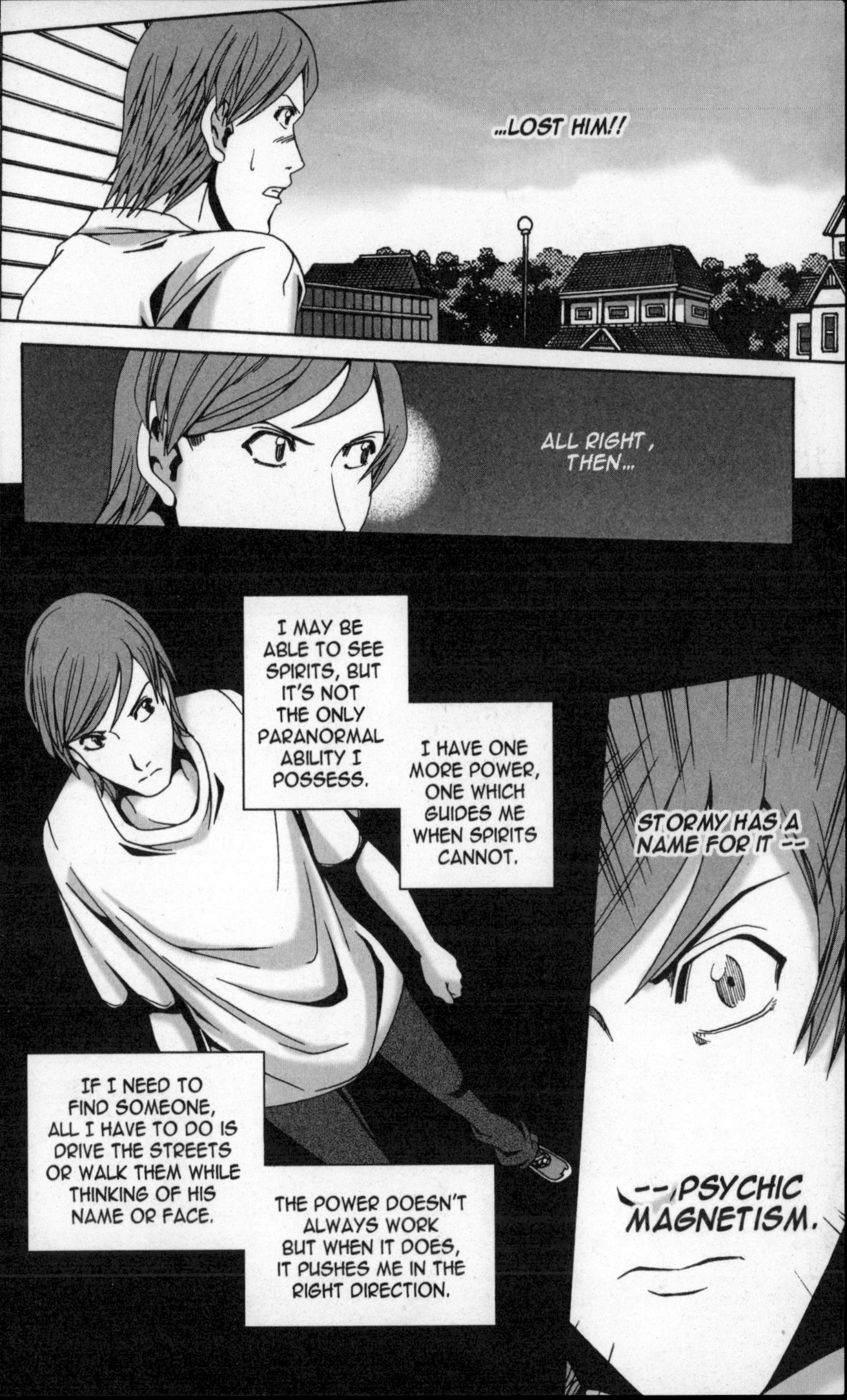
...LOST HIM!!
ALL RIGHT, THEN...
I MAY BE ABLE TO SEE SPIRITS, BUT IT'S NOT THE ONLY PARANORMAL ABILITY I POSSESS.
I HAVE ONE MORE POWER, ONE WHICH GUIDES ME WHEN SPIRITS CANNOT.
IF I NEED TO FIND SOMEONE, ALL I HAVE TO DO IS DRIVE THE STREETS OR WALK THEM WHILE THINKING OF HIS NAME OR FACE.
THE POWER DOESN'T ALWAYS WORK BUT WHEN IT DOES, IT PUSHES ME IN THE RIGHT DIRECTION.
STORMY HAS A NAME FOR IT --
--PSYCHIC MAGNETISM.

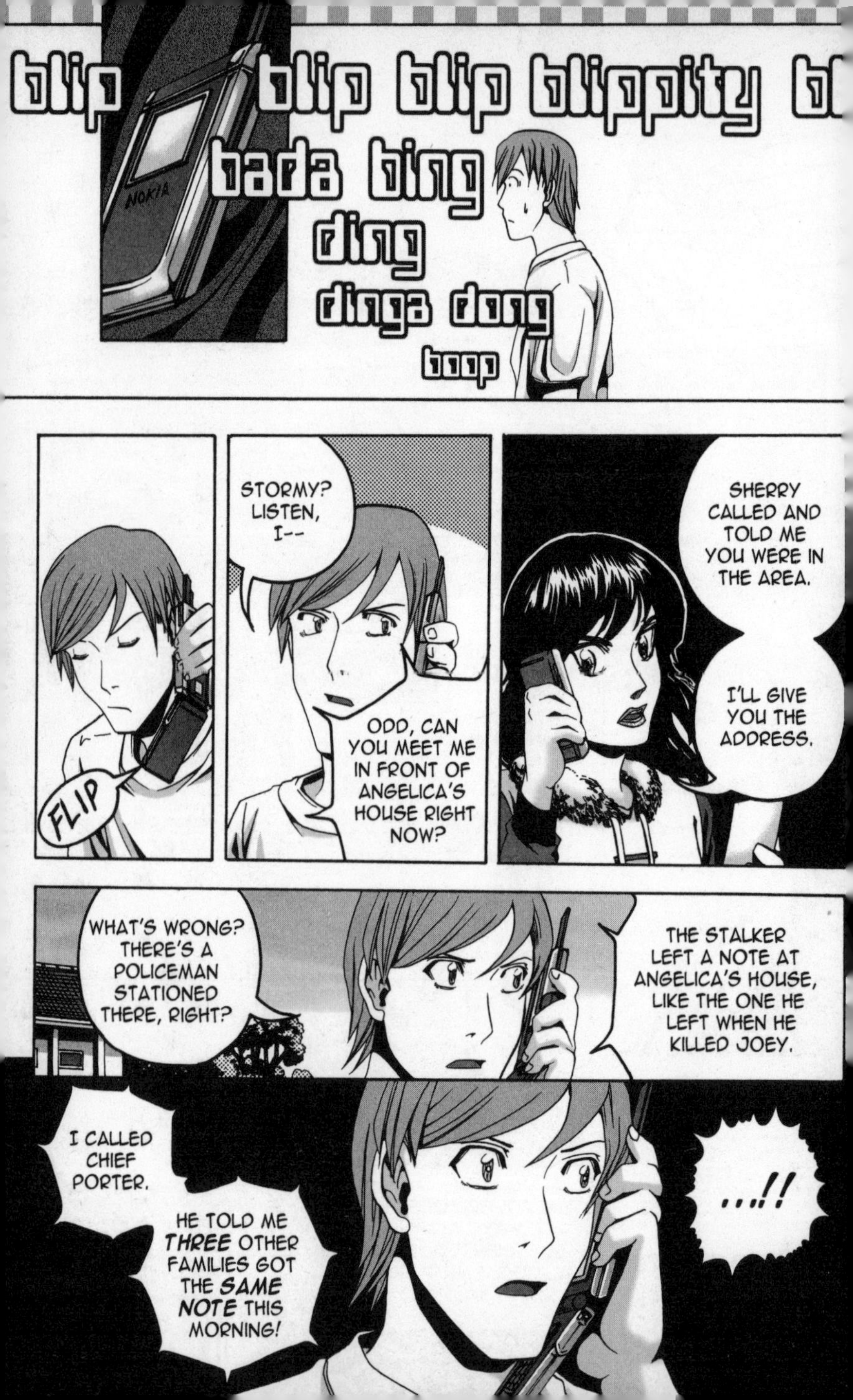
blip blip blip blippity bl
bada bing
ding
dinga dong
boop
FLIP
STORMY? LISTEN, I--
ODD, CAN YOU MEET ME IN FRONT OF ANGELICA'S HOUSE RIGHT NOW?
SHERRY CALLED AND TOLD ME YOU WERE IN THE AREA.
I'LL GIVE YOU THE ADDRESS.
WHAT'S WRONG? THERE'S A POLICEMAN STATIONED THERE, RIGHT?
THE STALKER LEFT A NOTE AT ANGELICA'S HOUSE, LIKE THE ONE HE LEFT WHEN HE KILLED JOEY.
I CALLED CHIEF PORTER.
HE TOLD ME THREE OTHER FAMILIES GOT THE SAME NOTE THIS MORNING!
...!!

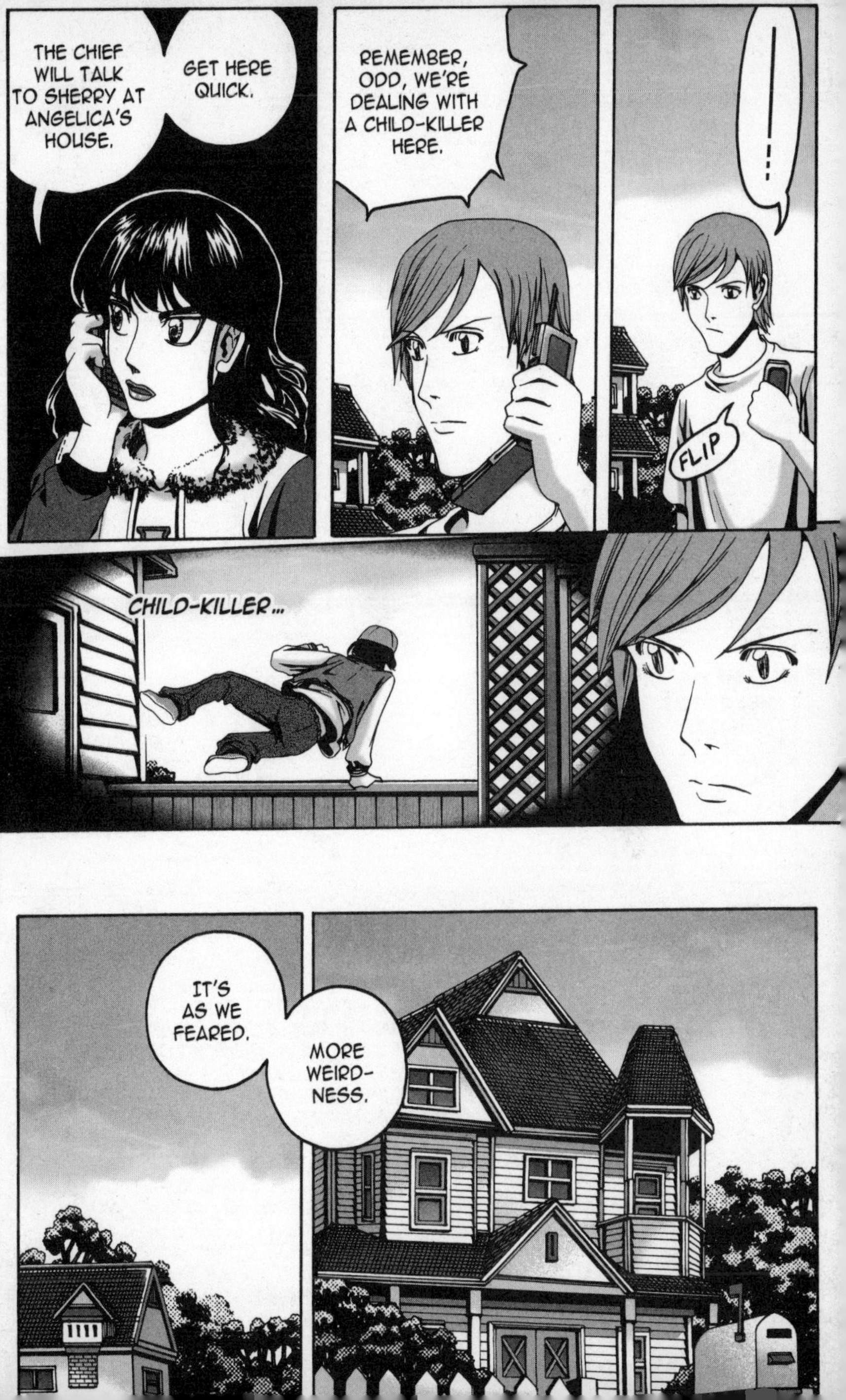

THE CHIEF WILL TALK TO SHERRY AT ANGELICA'S HOUSE.
GET HERE QUICK.
REMEMBER, ODD, WE'RE DEALING WITH A CHILD-KILLER HERE.
!
FLIP
CHILD-KILLER...
IT'S AS WE FEARED.
MORE WEIRD-NESS.

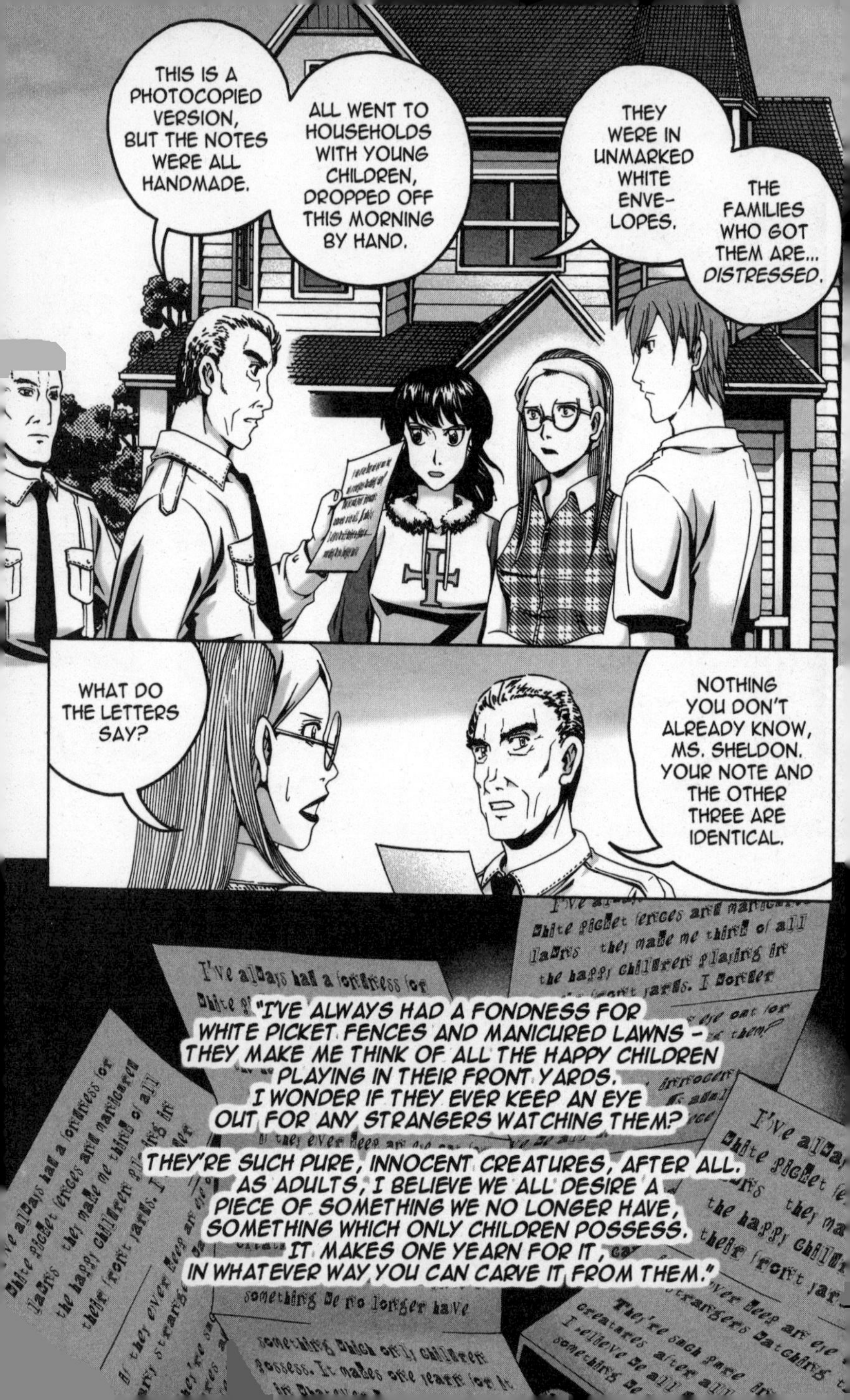
THIS IS A PHOTOCOPIED VERSION, BUT THE NOTES WERE ALL HANDMADE.
ALL WENT TO HOUSEHOLDS WITH YOUNG CHILDREN, DROPPED OFF THIS MORNING BY HAND.
THEY WERE IN UNMARKED WHITE ENVE-LOPES.
THE FAMILIES WHO GOT THEM ARE... DISTRESSED.
WHAT DO THE LETTERS SAY?
NOTHING YOU DON'T ALREADY KNOW, MS. SHELDON. YOUR NOTE AND THE OTHER THREE ARE IDENTICAL.
"I'VE ALWAYS HAD A FONDNESS FOR WHITE PICKET FENCES AND MANICURED LAWNS – THEY MAKE ME THINK OF ALL THE HAPPY CHILDREN PLAYING IN THEIR FRONT YARDS. I WONDER IF THEY EVER KEEP AN EYE OUT FOR ANY STRANGERS WATCHING THEM?
THEY'RE SUCH PURE, INNOCENT CREATURES, AFTER ALL. AS ADULTS, I BELIEVE WE ALL DESIRE A PIECE OF SOMETHING WE NO LONGER HAVE, SOMETHING WHICH ONLY CHILDREN POSSESS. IT MAKES ONE YEARN FOR IT, IN WHATEVER WAY YOU CAN CARVE IT FROM THEM."

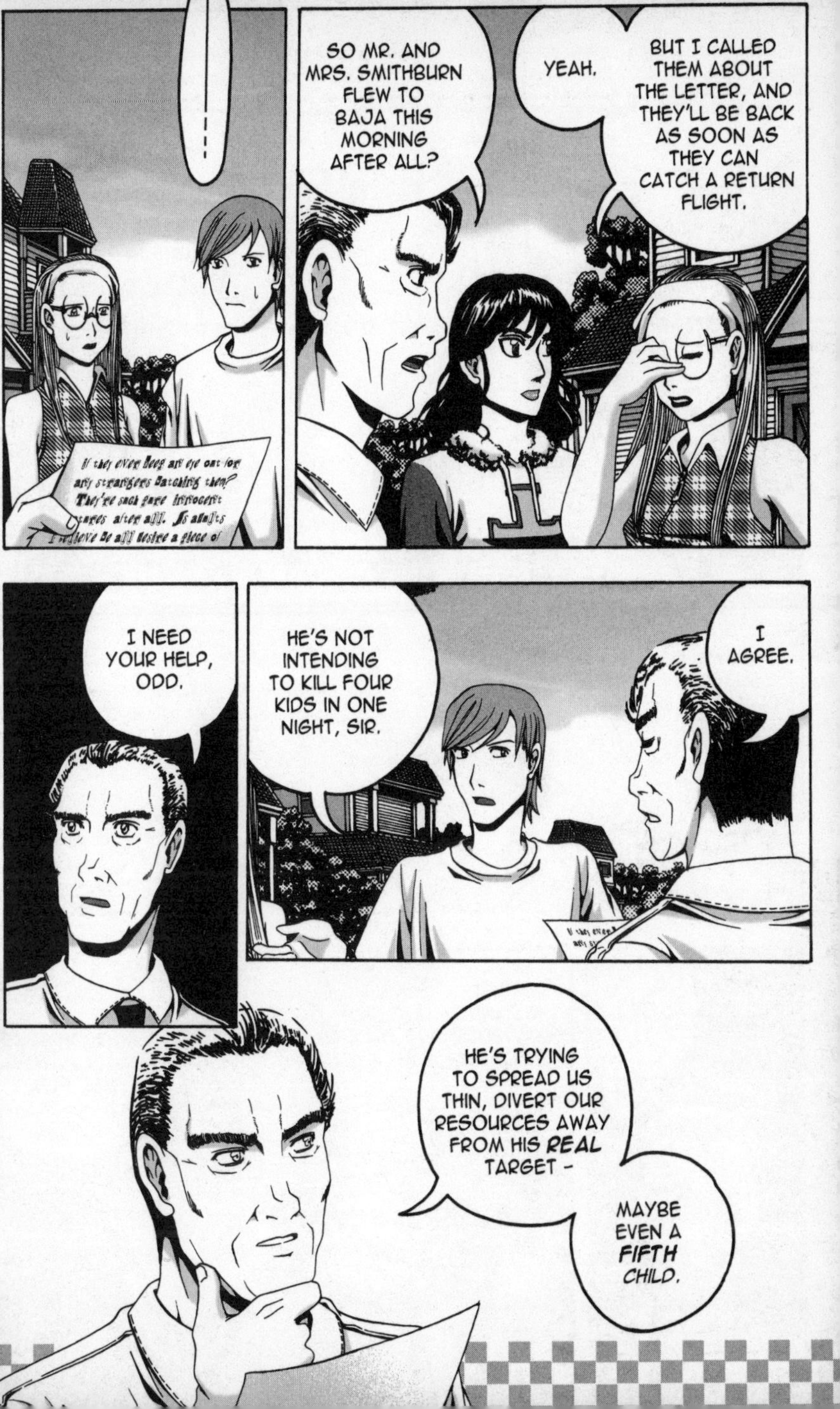
SO MR. AND MRS. SMITHBURN FLEW TO BAJA THIS MORNING AFTER ALL?
YEAH.
BUT I CALLED THEM ABOUT THE LETTER, AND THEY'LL BE BACK AS SOON AS THEY CAN CATCH A RETURN FLIGHT.
I NEED YOUR HELP, ODD.
HE'S NOT INTENDING TO KILL FOUR KIDS IN ONE NIGHT, SIR.
I AGREE.
HE'S TRYING TO SPREAD US THIN, DIVERT OUR RESOURCES AWAY FROM HIS REAL TARGET -
MAYBE EVEN A FIFTH CHILD.

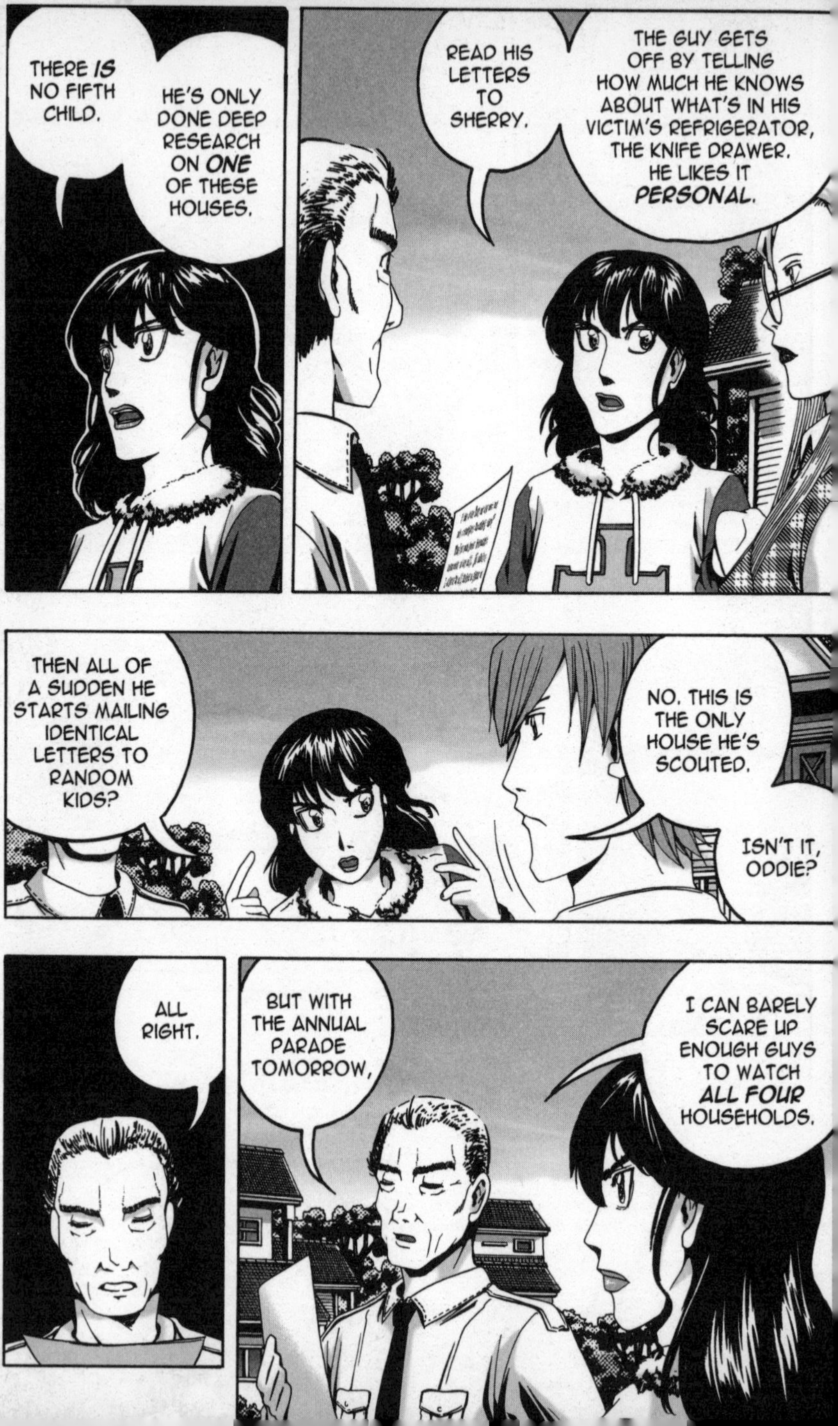
THERE IS NO FIFTH CHILD.
HE'S ONLY DONE DEEP RESEARCH ON ONE OF THESE HOUSES.
READ HIS LETTERS TO SHERRY.
THE GUY GETS OFF BY TELLING HOW MUCH HE KNOWS ABOUT WHAT'S IN HIS VICTIM'S REFRIGERATOR, THE KNIFE DRAWER. HE LIKES IT PERSONAL.
THEN ALL OF A SUDDEN HE STARTS MAILING IDENTICAL LETTERS TO RANDOM KIDS?
NO. THIS IS THE ONLY HOUSE HE'S SCOUTED.
ISN'T IT, ODDIE?
ALL RIGHT.
BUT WITH THE ANNUAL PARADE TOMORROW,
I CAN BARELY SCARE UP ENOUGH GUYS TO WATCH ALL FOUR HOUSEHOLDS.

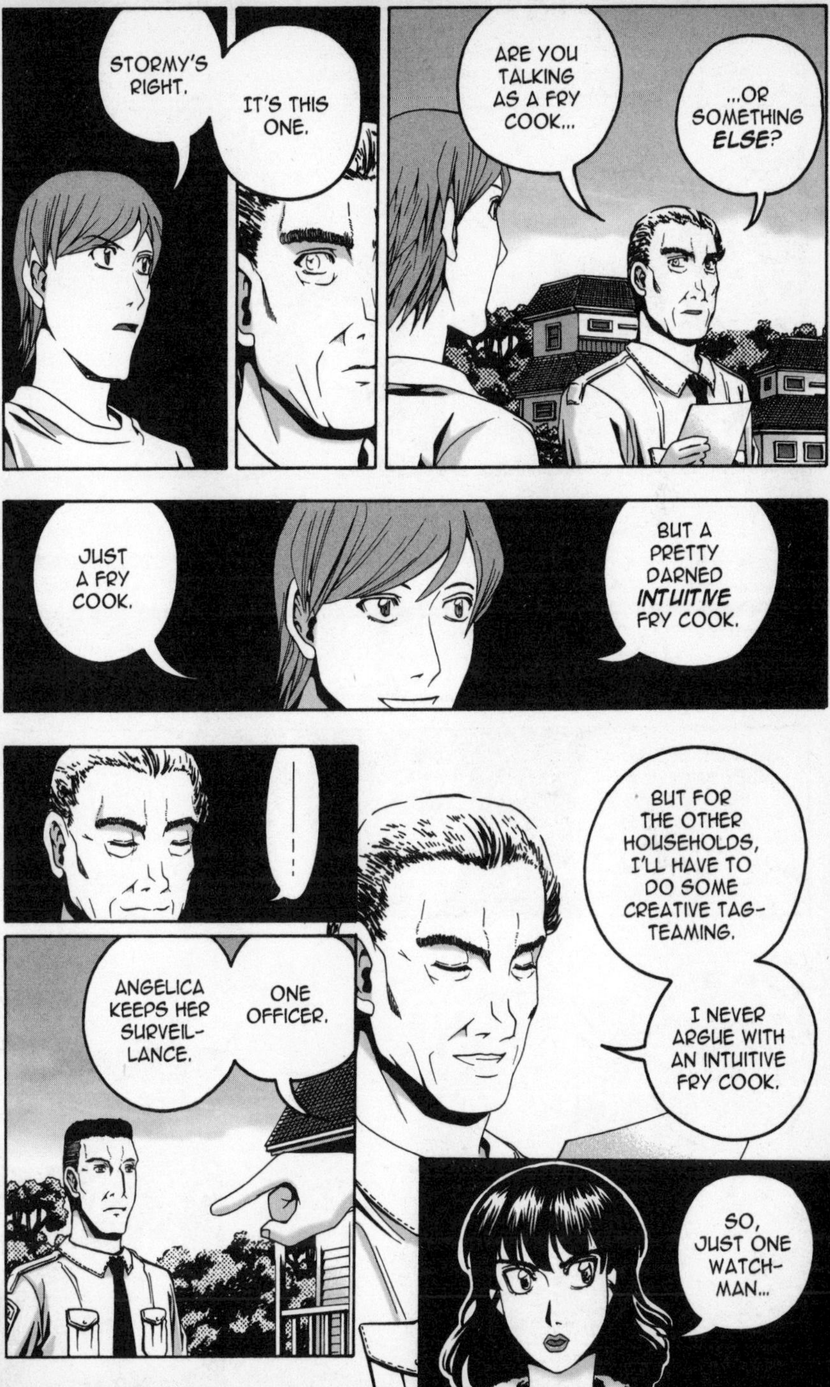
STORMY'S RIGHT.
IT'S THIS ONE.
ARE YOU TALKING AS A FRY COOK...
...OR SOMETHING ELSE?
JUST A FRY COOK.
BUT A PRETTY DARNED INTUITIVE FRY COOK.
...!
BUT FOR THE OTHER HOUSEHOLDS, I'LL HAVE TO DO SOME CREATIVE TAG-TEAMING.
I NEVER ARGUE WITH AN INTUITIVE FRY COOK.
ONE OFFICER.
ANGELICA KEEPS HER SURVEIL-LANCE.
SO, JUST ONE WATCH-MAN...

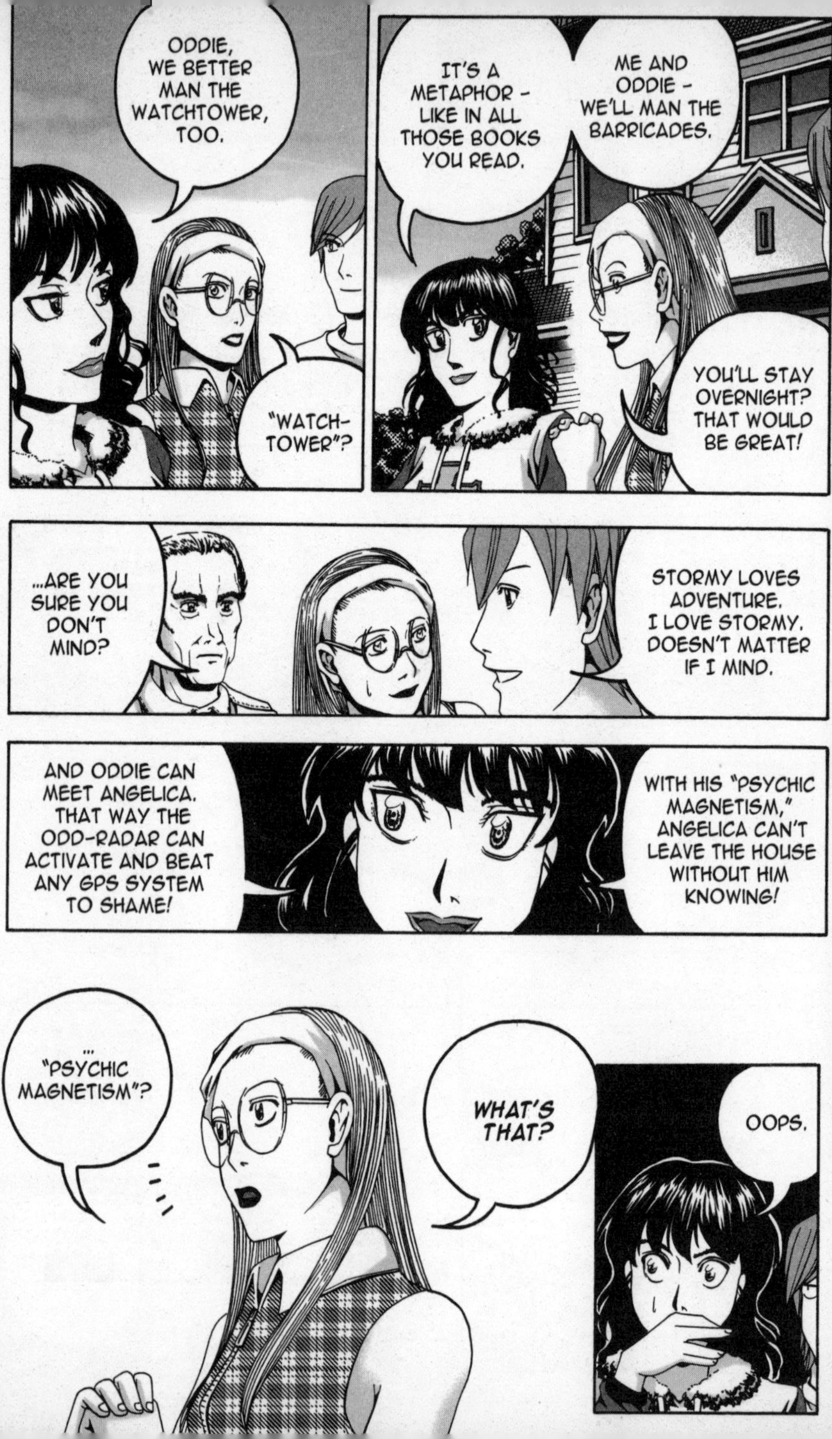
ODDIE, WE BETTER MAN THE WATCHTOWER, TOO.
"WATCH-TOWER"?
IT'S A METAPHOR - LIKE IN ALL THOSE BOOKS YOU READ.
ME AND ODDIE - WE'LL MAN THE BARRICADES.
YOU'LL STAY OVERNIGHT? THAT WOULD BE GREAT!
...ARE YOU SURE YOU DON'T MIND?
STORMY LOVES ADVENTURE. I LOVE STORMY. DOESN'T MATTER IF I MIND.
AND ODDIE CAN MEET ANGELICA. THAT WAY THE ODD-RADAR CAN ACTIVATE AND BEAT ANY GPS SYSTEM TO SHAME!
WITH HIS "PSYCHIC MAGNETISM," ANGELICA CAN'T LEAVE THE HOUSE WITHOUT HIM KNOWING!
... "PSYCHIC MAGNETISM"?
WHAT'S THAT?
OOPS.

In Odd We Trust

Chapter 4

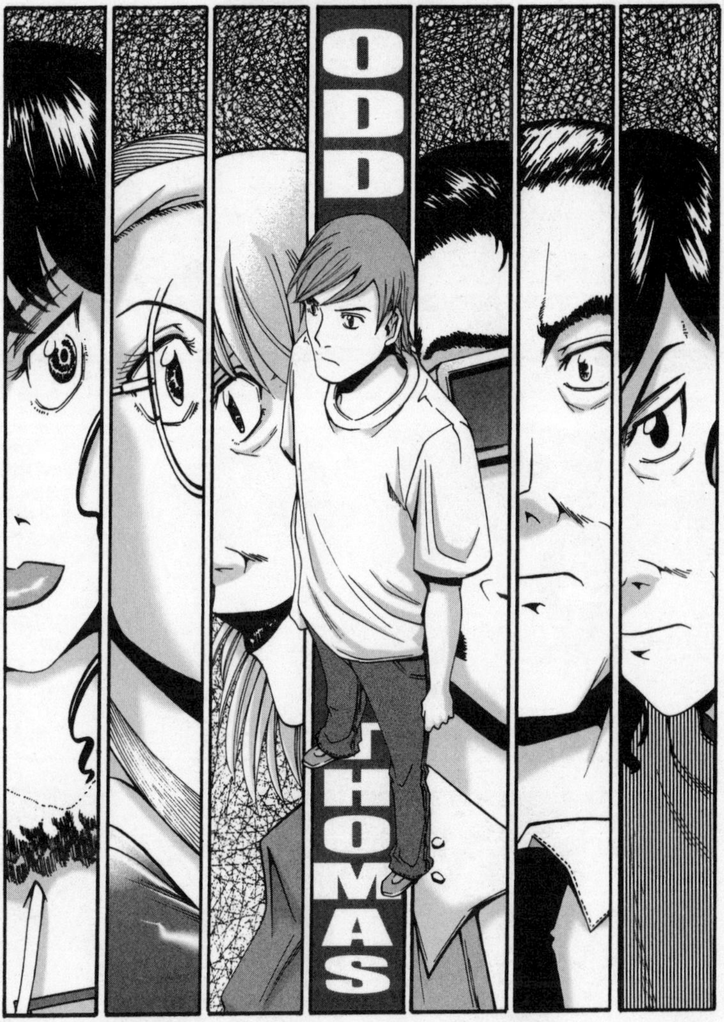
ODD
THOMAS

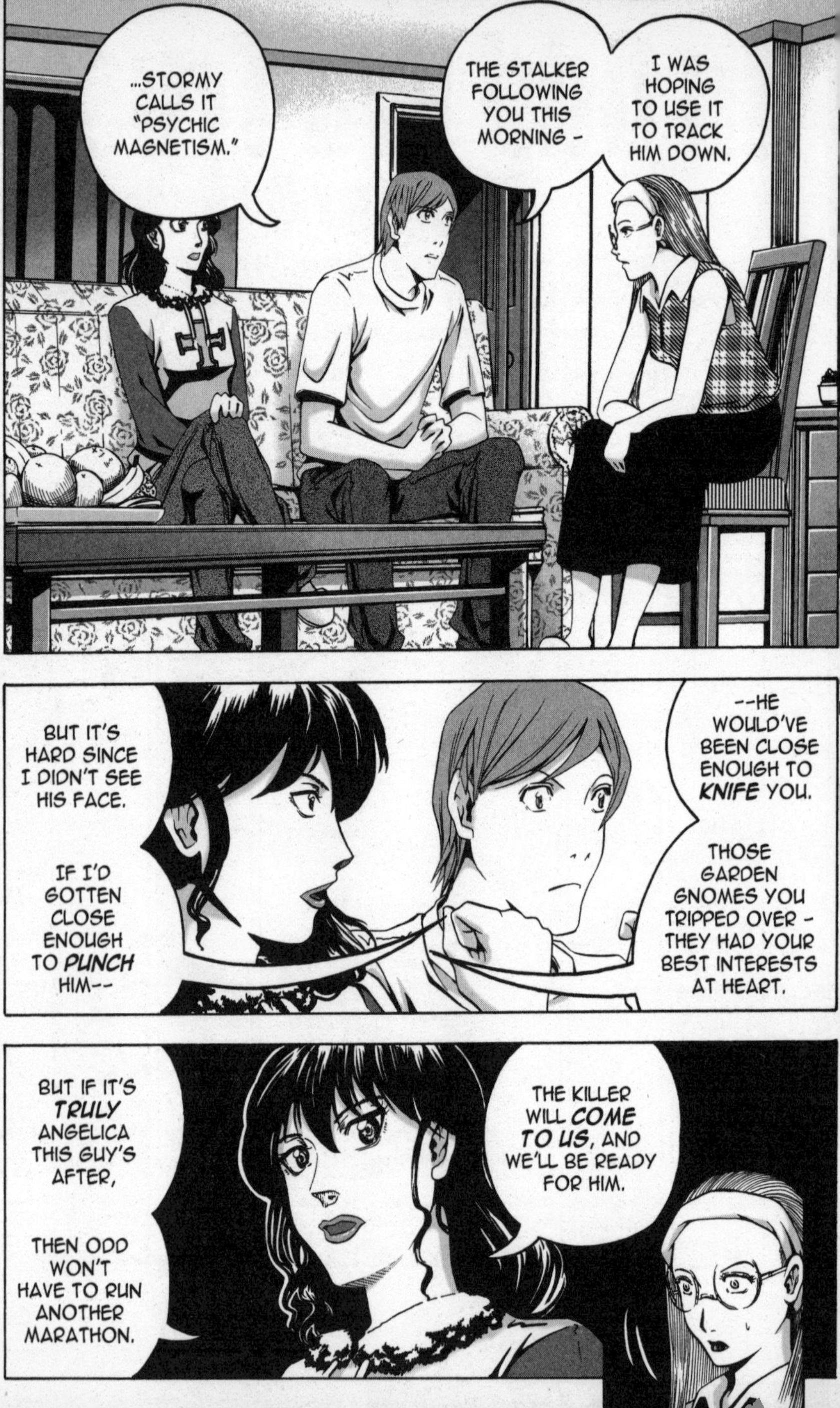
...STORMY CALLS IT "PSYCHIC MAGNETISM."
THE STALKER FOLLOWING YOU THIS MORNING -
I WAS HOPING TO USE IT TO TRACK HIM DOWN.
BUT IT'S HARD SINCE I DIDN'T SEE HIS FACE.
IF I'D GOTTEN CLOSE ENOUGH TO PUNCH HIM--
--HE WOULD'VE BEEN CLOSE ENOUGH TO KNIFE YOU.
THOSE GARDEN GNOMES YOU TRIPPED OVER - THEY HAD YOUR BEST INTERESTS AT HEART.
BUT IF IT'S TRULY ANGELICA THIS GUY'S AFTER,
THEN ODD WON'T HAVE TO RUN ANOTHER MARATHON.
THE KILLER WILL COME TO US, AND WE'LL BE READY FOR HIM.

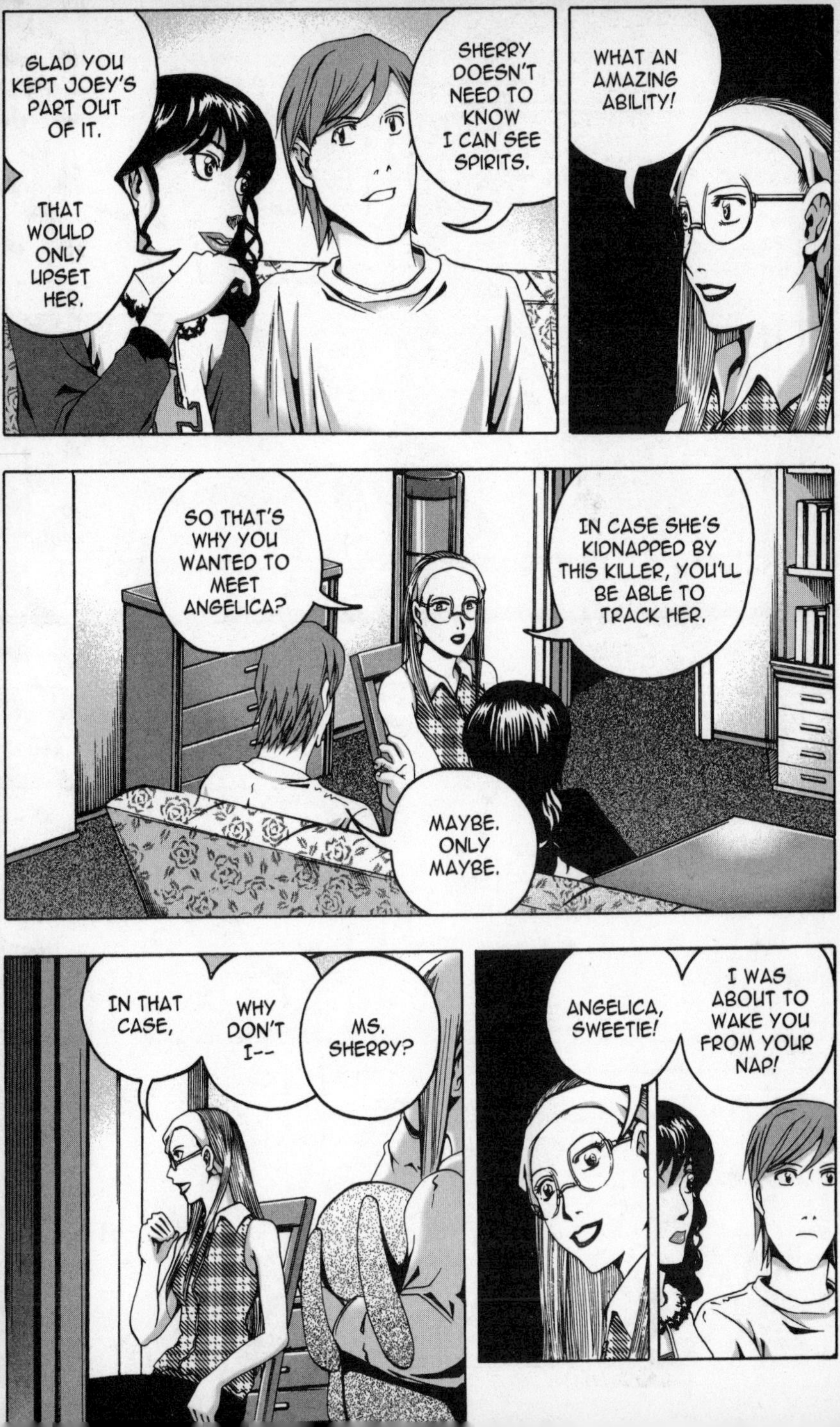
GLAD YOU KEPT JOEY'S PART OUT OF IT.
THAT WOULD ONLY UPSET HER.
SHERRY DOESN'T NEED TO KNOW I CAN SEE SPIRITS.
WHAT AN AMAZING ABILITY!
SO THAT'S WHY YOU WANTED TO MEET ANGELICA?
IN CASE SHE'S KIDNAPPED BY THIS KILLER, YOU'LL BE ABLE TO TRACK HER.
MAYBE. ONLY MAYBE.
IN THAT CASE,
WHY DON'T I--
MS. SHERRY?
ANGELICA, SWEETIE!
I WAS ABOUT TO WAKE YOU FROM YOUR NAP!

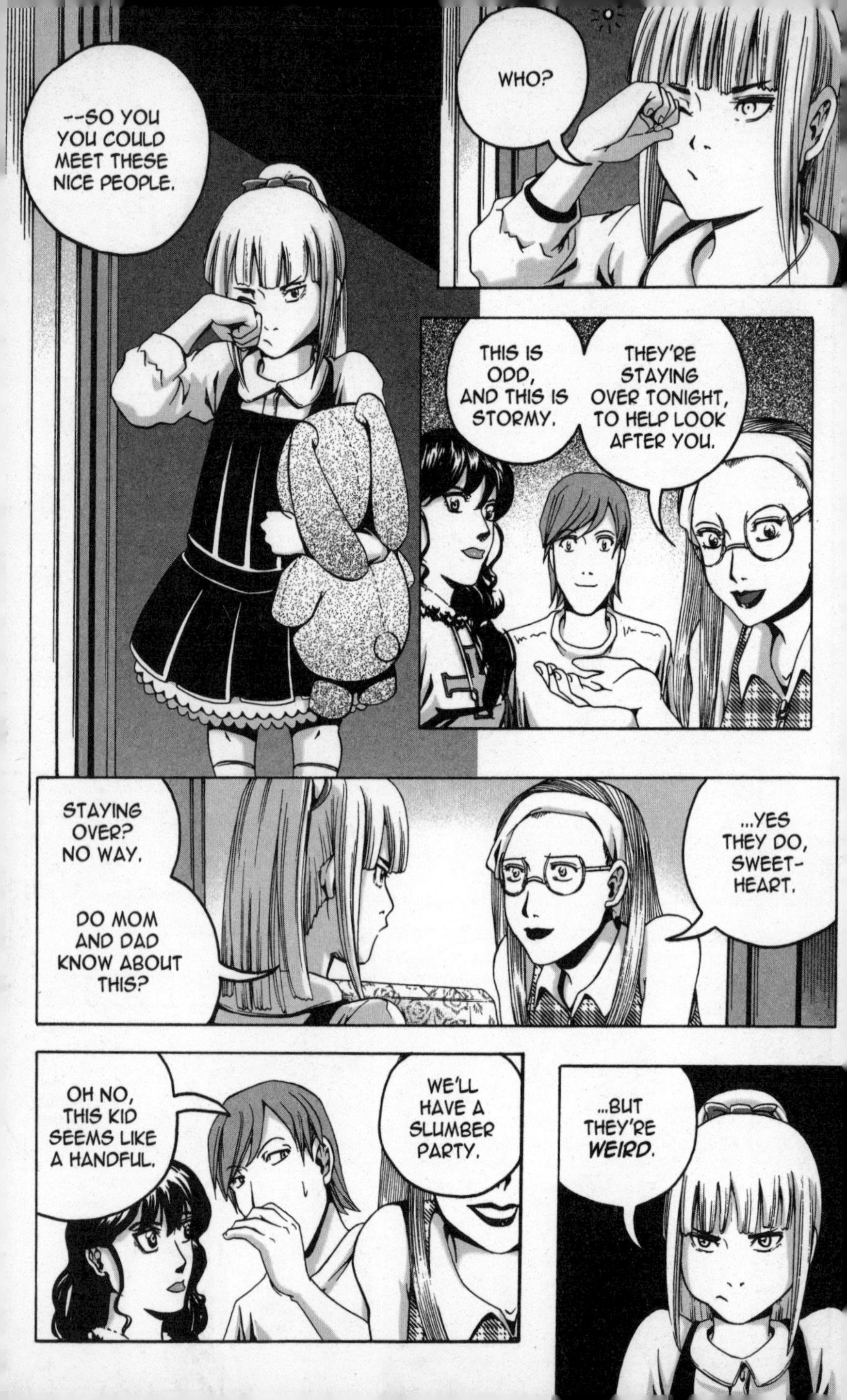
--SO YOU YOU COULD MEET THESE NICE PEOPLE.
WHO?
THIS IS ODD, AND THIS IS STORMY.
THEY'RE STAYING OVER TONIGHT, TO HELP LOOK AFTER YOU.
STAYING OVER? NO WAY.
DO MOM AND DAD KNOW ABOUT THIS?
...YES THEY DO, SWEET-HEART.
OH NO, THIS KID SEEMS LIKE A HANDFUL.
WE'LL HAVE A SLUMBER PARTY.
...BUT THEY'RE *WEIRD*.

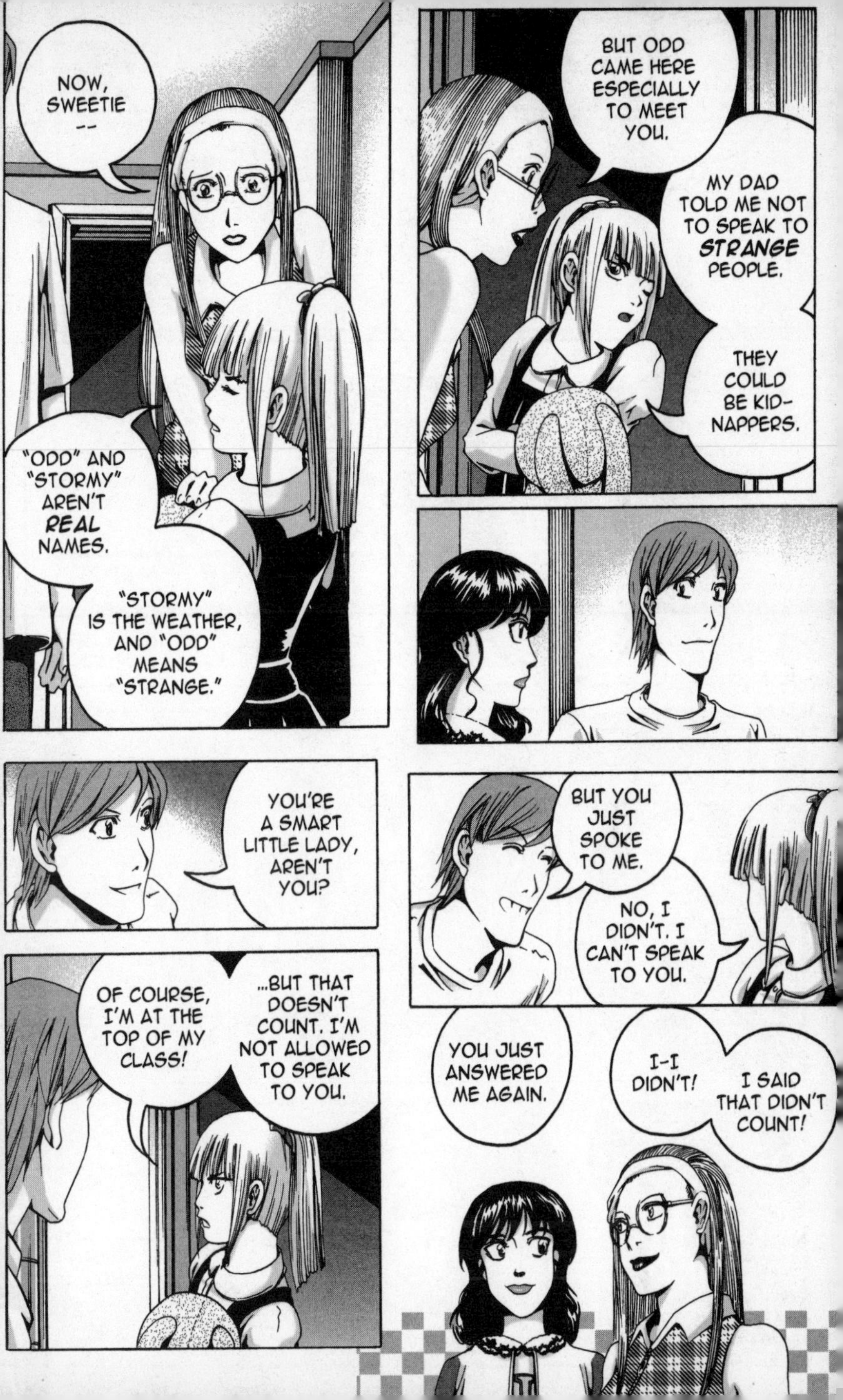
NOW, SWEETIE --
"ODD" AND "STORMY" AREN'T REAL NAMES.
"STORMY" IS THE WEATHER, AND "ODD" MEANS "STRANGE."
BUT ODD CAME HERE ESPECIALLY TO MEET YOU.
MY DAD TOLD ME NOT TO SPEAK TO STRANGE PEOPLE.
THEY COULD BE KID-NAPPERS.
YOU'RE A SMART LITTLE LADY, AREN'T YOU?
OF COURSE, I'M AT THE TOP OF MY CLASS!
...BUT THAT DOESN'T COUNT. I'M NOT ALLOWED TO SPEAK TO YOU.
BUT YOU JUST SPOKE TO ME.
NO, I DIDN'T. I CAN'T SPEAK TO YOU.
YOU JUST ANSWERED ME AGAIN.
I-I DIDN'T!
I SAID THAT DIDN'T COUNT!

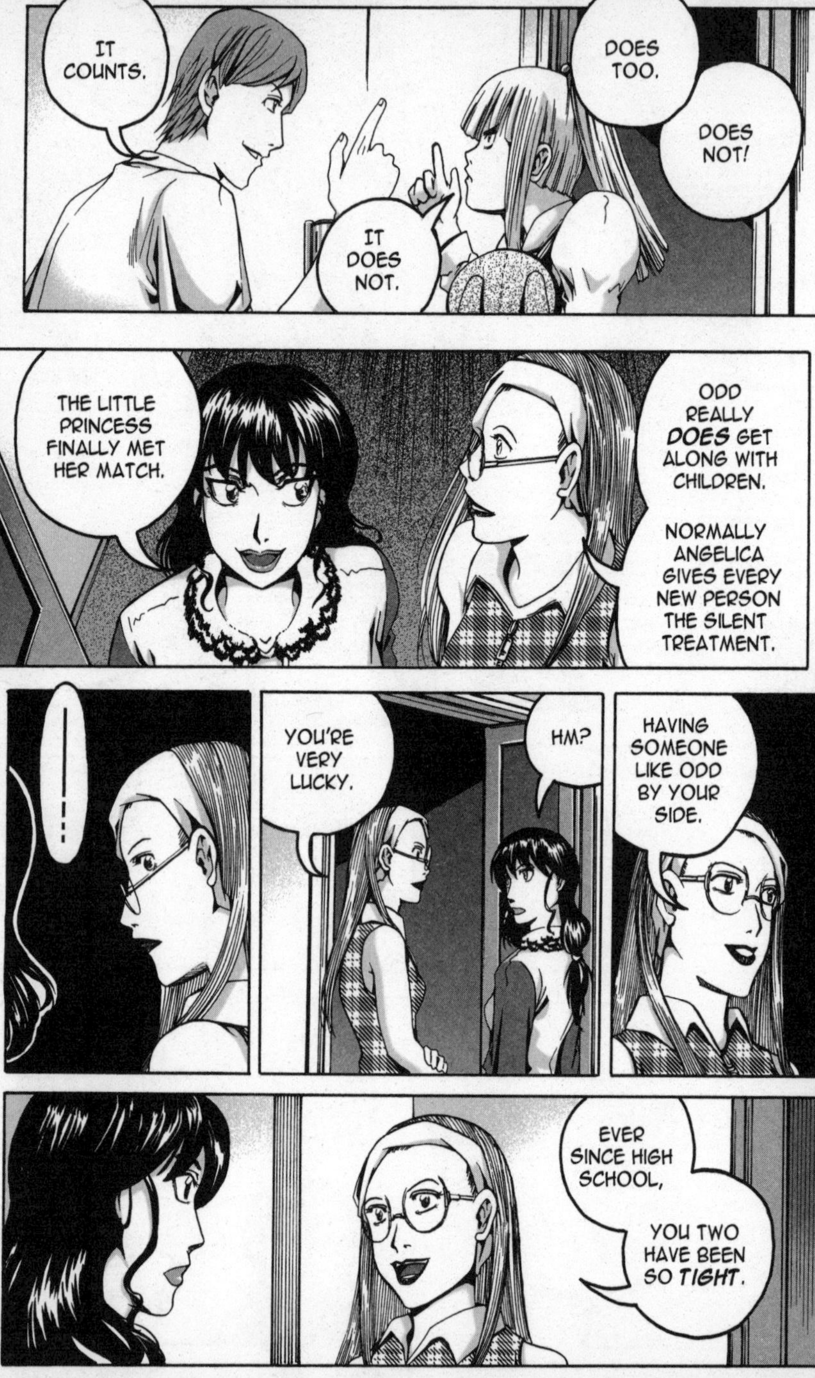
IT COUNTS.
DOES TOO.
DOES NOT!
IT DOES NOT.
THE LITTLE PRINCESS FINALLY MET HER MATCH.
ODD REALLY DOES GET ALONG WITH CHILDREN.
NORMALLY ANGELICA GIVES EVERY NEW PERSON THE SILENT TREATMENT.
!
YOU'RE VERY LUCKY.
HM?
HAVING SOMEONE LIKE ODD BY YOUR SIDE.
EVER SINCE HIGH SCHOOL,
YOU TWO HAVE BEEN SO TIGHT.

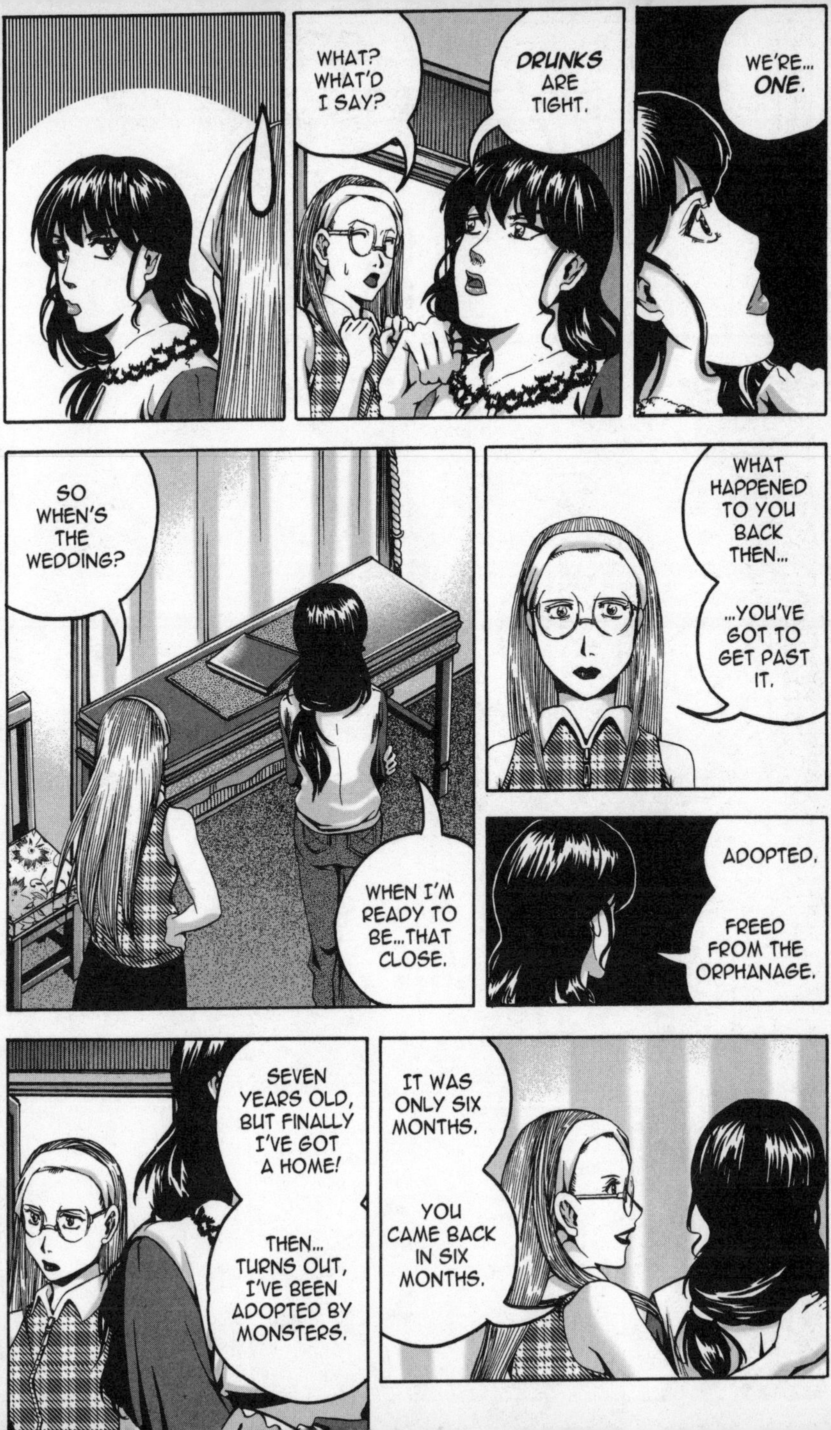
WHAT? WHAT'D I SAY?
DRUNKS ARE TIGHT.
WE'RE... ONE.
SO WHEN'S THE WEDDING?
WHEN I'M READY TO BE...THAT CLOSE.
WHAT HAPPENED TO YOU BACK THEN...
...YOU'VE GOT TO GET PAST IT.
ADOPTED.
FREED FROM THE ORPHANAGE.
SEVEN YEARS OLD, BUT FINALLY I'VE GOT A HOME!
THEN... TURNS OUT, I'VE BEEN ADOPTED BY MONSTERS.
IT WAS ONLY SIX MONTHS.
YOU CAME BACK IN SIX MONTHS.

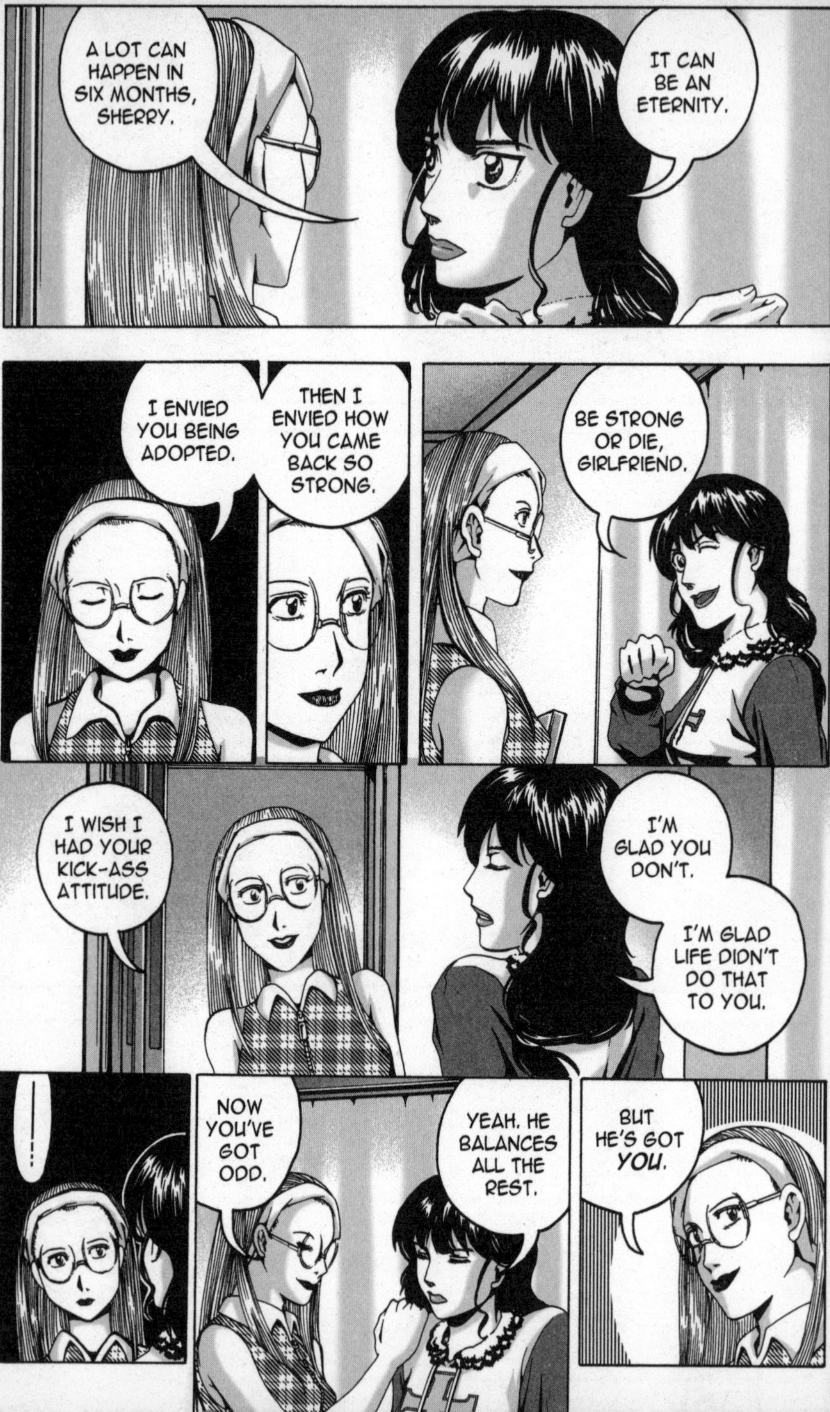
A LOT CAN HAPPEN IN SIX MONTHS, SHERRY.
IT CAN BE AN ETERNITY.
I ENVIED YOU BEING ADOPTED.
THEN I ENVIED HOW YOU CAME BACK SO STRONG.
BE STRONG OR DIE, GIRLFRIEND.
I WISH I HAD YOUR KICK-ASS ATTITUDE.
I'M GLAD YOU DON'T.
I'M GLAD LIFE DIDN'T DO THAT TO YOU.
!
NOW YOU'VE GOT ODD.
YEAH. HE BALANCES ALL THE REST.
BUT HE'S GOT *YOU*.

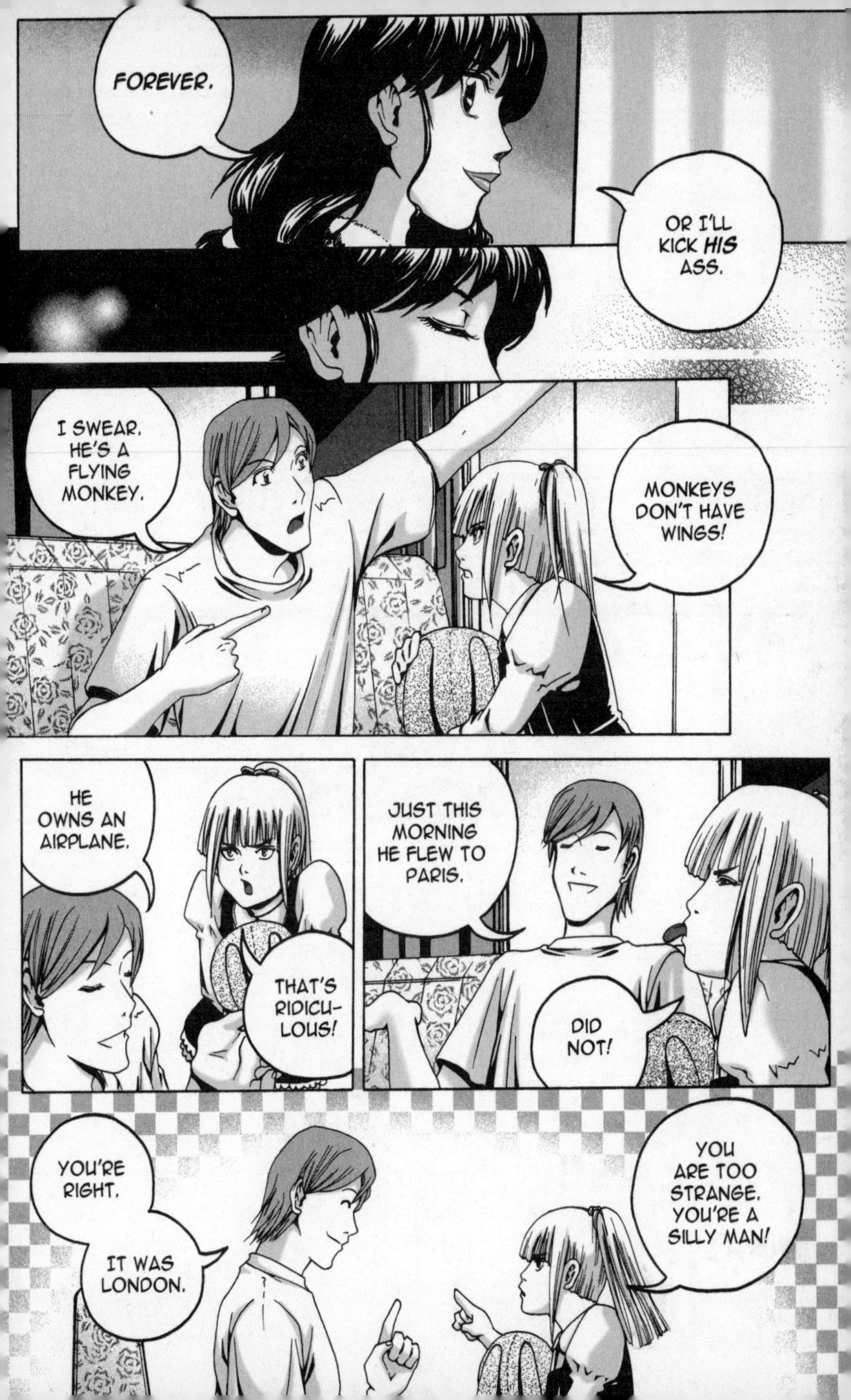
FOREVER.
OR I'LL KICK HIS ASS.
I SWEAR. HE'S A FLYING MONKEY.
MONKEYS DON'T HAVE WINGS!
HE OWNS AN AIRPLANE.
THAT'S RIDICU-LOUS!
JUST THIS MORNING HE FLEW TO PARIS.
DID NOT!
YOU'RE RIGHT.
IT WAS LONDON.
YOU ARE TOO STRANGE. YOU'RE A SILLY MAN!

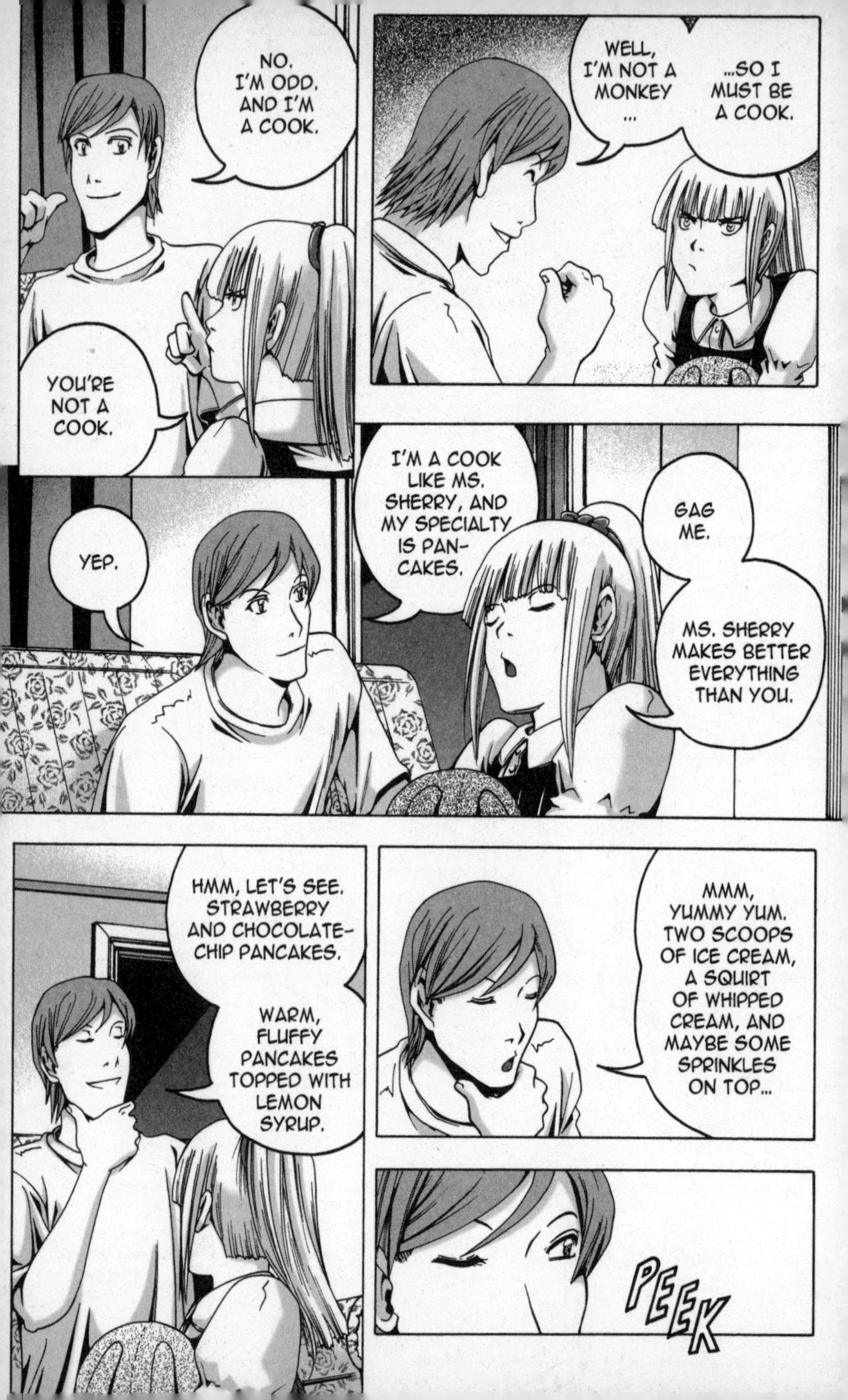

YOU'RE NOT A COOK.
NO. I'M ODD. AND I'M A COOK.
WELL, I'M NOT A MONKEY ...
...SO I MUST BE A COOK.
YEP.
I'M A COOK LIKE MS. SHERRY, AND MY SPECIALTY IS PAN-CAKES.
GAG ME.
MS. SHERRY MAKES BETTER EVERYTHING THAN YOU.
HMM, LET'S SEE. STRAWBERRY AND CHOCOLATE-CHIP PANCAKES.
WARM, FLUFFY PANCAKES TOPPED WITH LEMON SYRUP.
MMM, YUMMY YUM. TWO SCOOPS OF ICE CREAM, A SQUIRT OF WHIPPED CREAM, AND MAYBE SOME SPRINKLES ON TOP...
PEEK

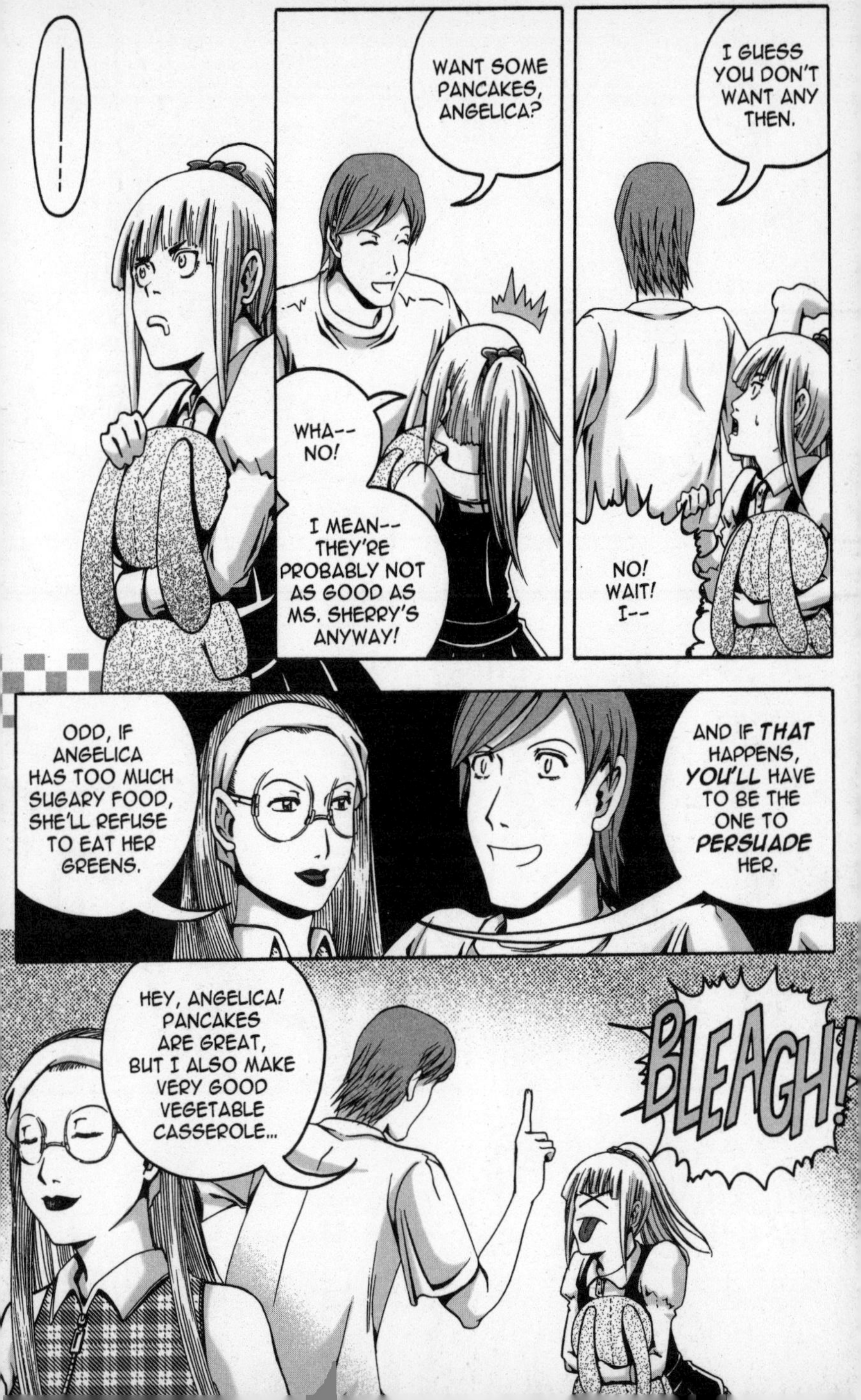
...!
WANT SOME PANCAKES, ANGELICA?
WHA-- NO!
I MEAN-- THEY'RE PROBABLY NOT AS GOOD AS MS. SHERRY'S ANYWAY!
I GUESS YOU DON'T WANT ANY THEN.
NO! WAIT! I--
ODD, IF ANGELICA HAS TOO MUCH SUGARY FOOD, SHE'LL REFUSE TO EAT HER GREENS.
AND IF THAT HAPPENS, YOU'LL HAVE TO BE THE ONE TO PERSUADE HER.
HEY, ANGELICA! PANCAKES ARE GREAT, BUT I ALSO MAKE VERY GOOD VEGETABLE CASSEROLE...
BLEAGH!

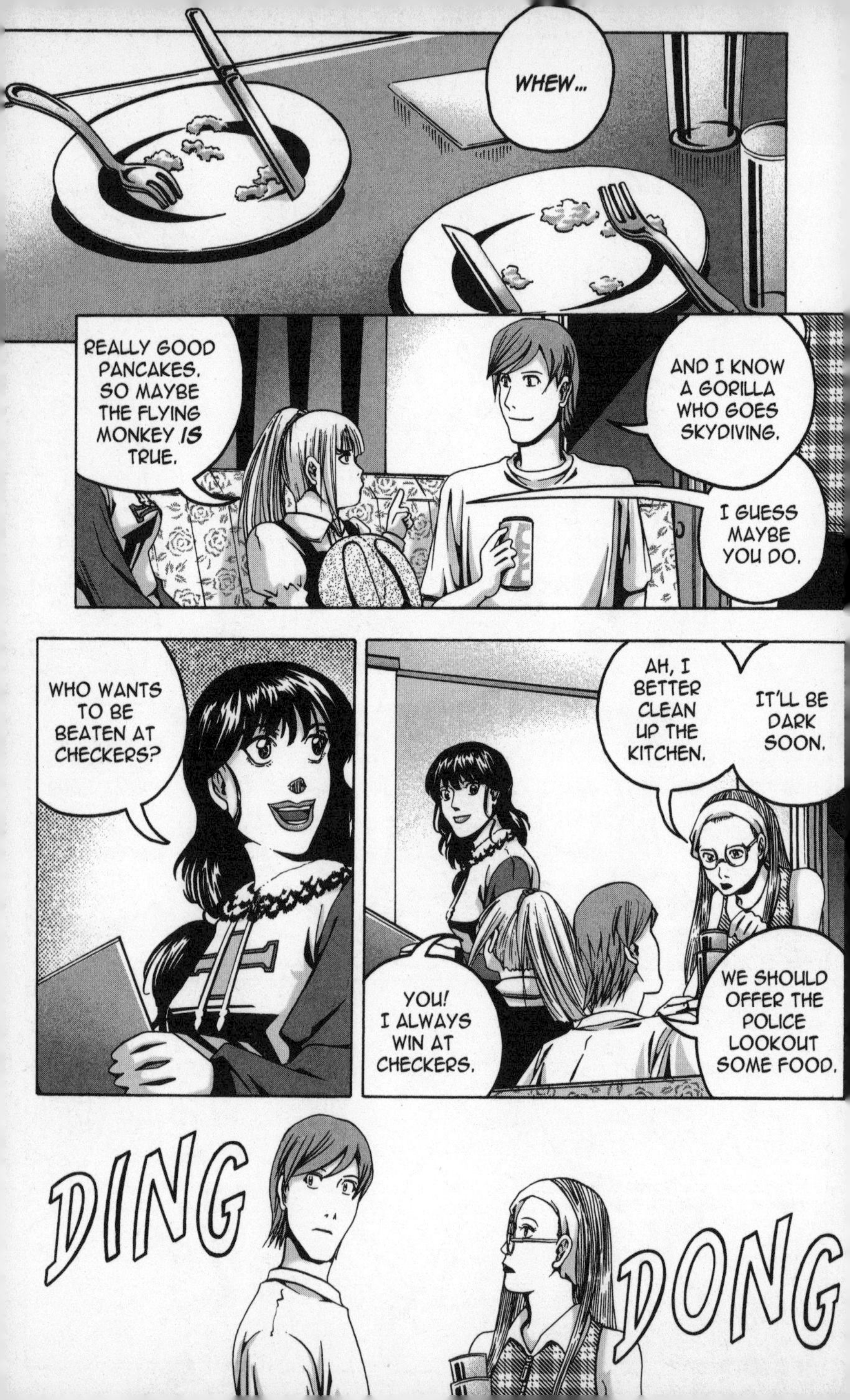
WHEW...
REALLY GOOD PANCAKES. SO MAYBE THE FLYING MONKEY IS TRUE.
AND I KNOW A GORILLA WHO GOES SKYDIVING.
I GUESS MAYBE YOU DO.
WHO WANTS TO BE BEATEN AT CHECKERS?
YOU! I ALWAYS WIN AT CHECKERS.
AH, I BETTER CLEAN UP THE KITCHEN.
IT'LL BE DARK SOON.
WE SHOULD OFFER THE POLICE LOOKOUT SOME FOOD.
DING
DONG

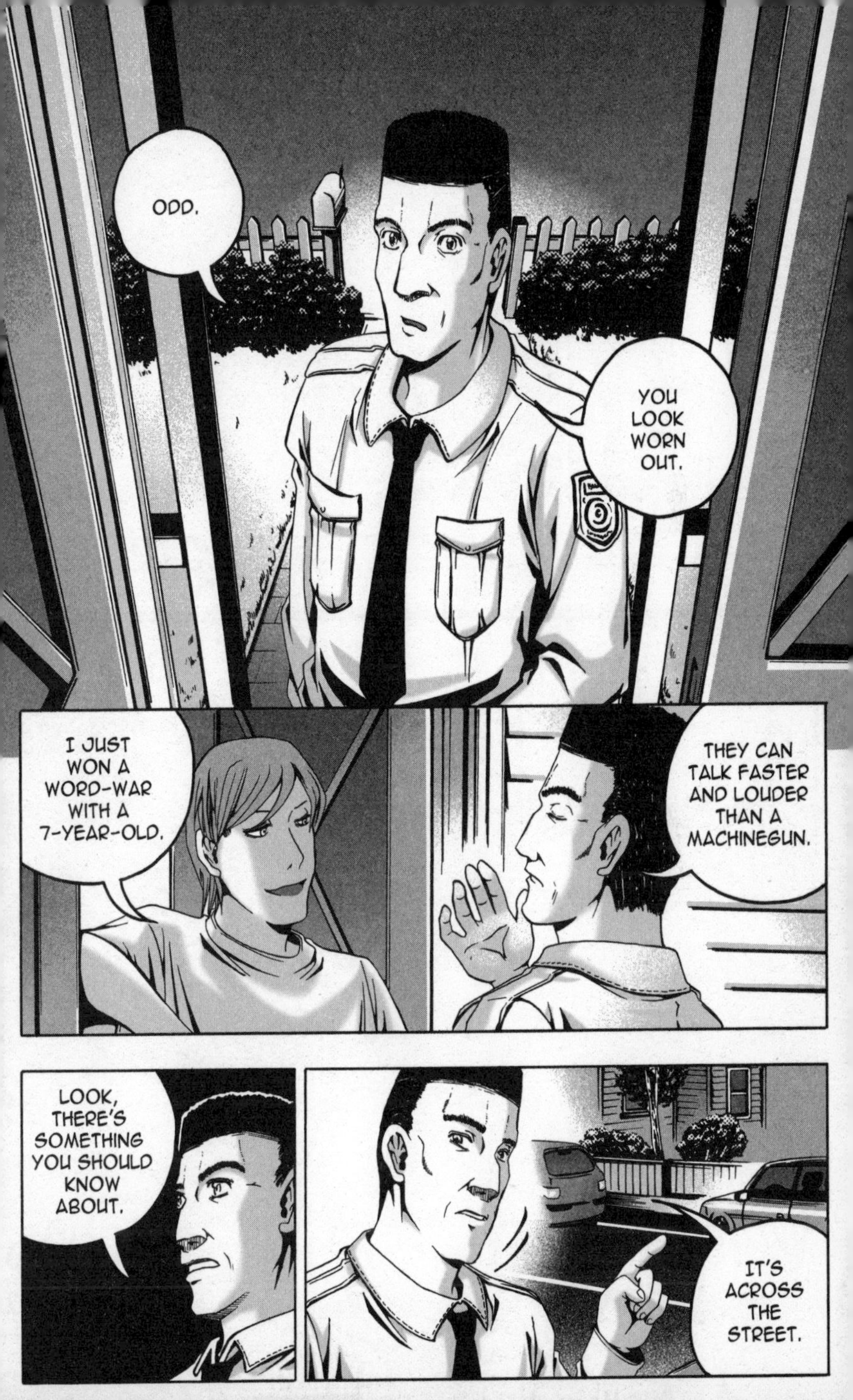
ODD.
YOU LOOK WORN OUT.
I JUST WON A WORD-WAR WITH A 7-YEAR-OLD.
THEY CAN TALK FASTER AND LOUDER THAN A MACHINEGUN.
LOOK, THERE'S SOMETHING YOU SHOULD KNOW ABOUT.
IT'S ACROSS THE STREET.

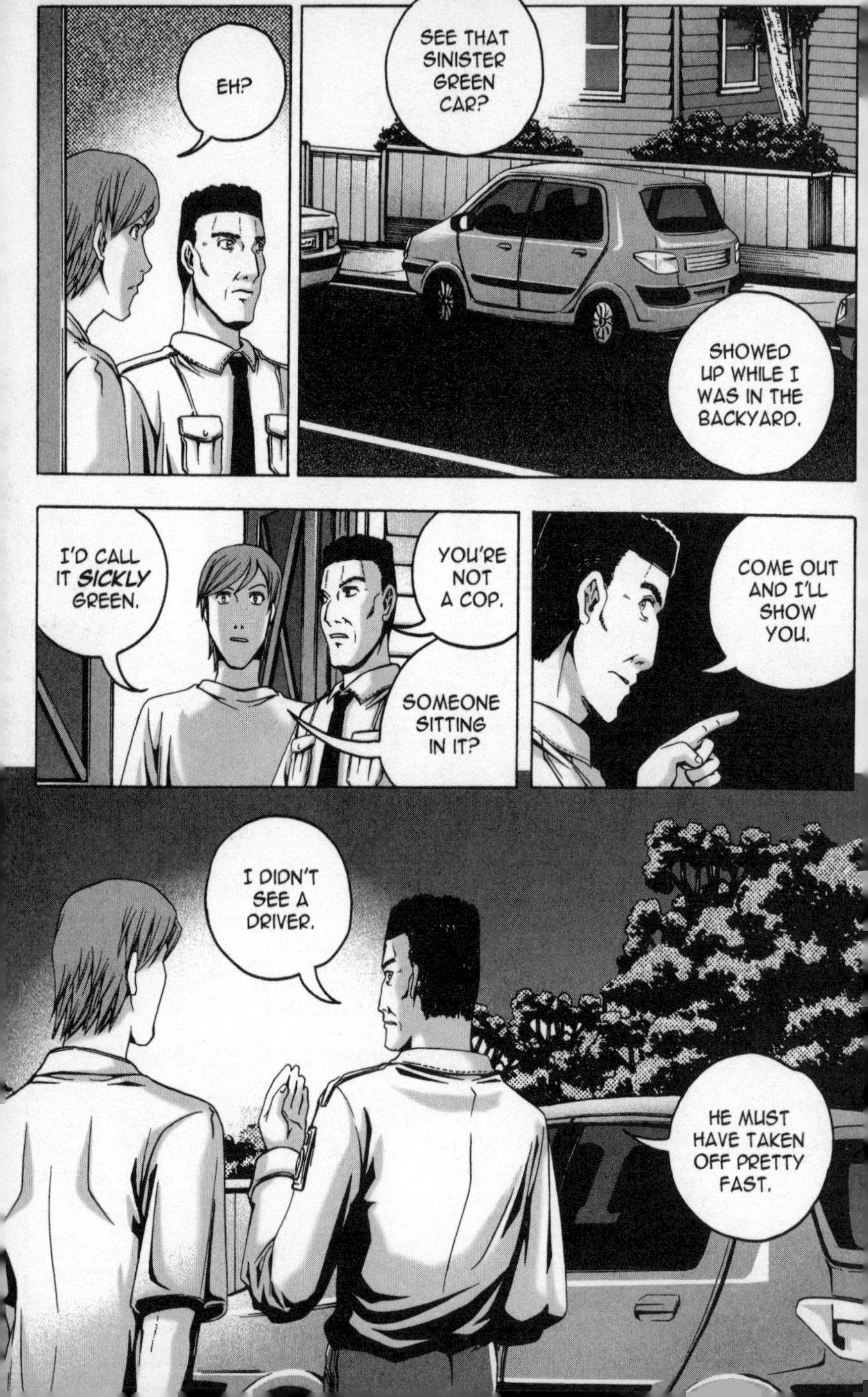
EH?
SEE THAT SINISTER GREEN CAR?
SHOWED UP WHILE I WAS IN THE BACKYARD.
I'D CALL IT *SICKLY* GREEN.
YOU'RE NOT A COP.
SOMEONE SITTING IN IT?
COME OUT AND I'LL SHOW YOU.
I DIDN'T SEE A DRIVER.
HE MUST HAVE TAKEN OFF PRETTY FAST.

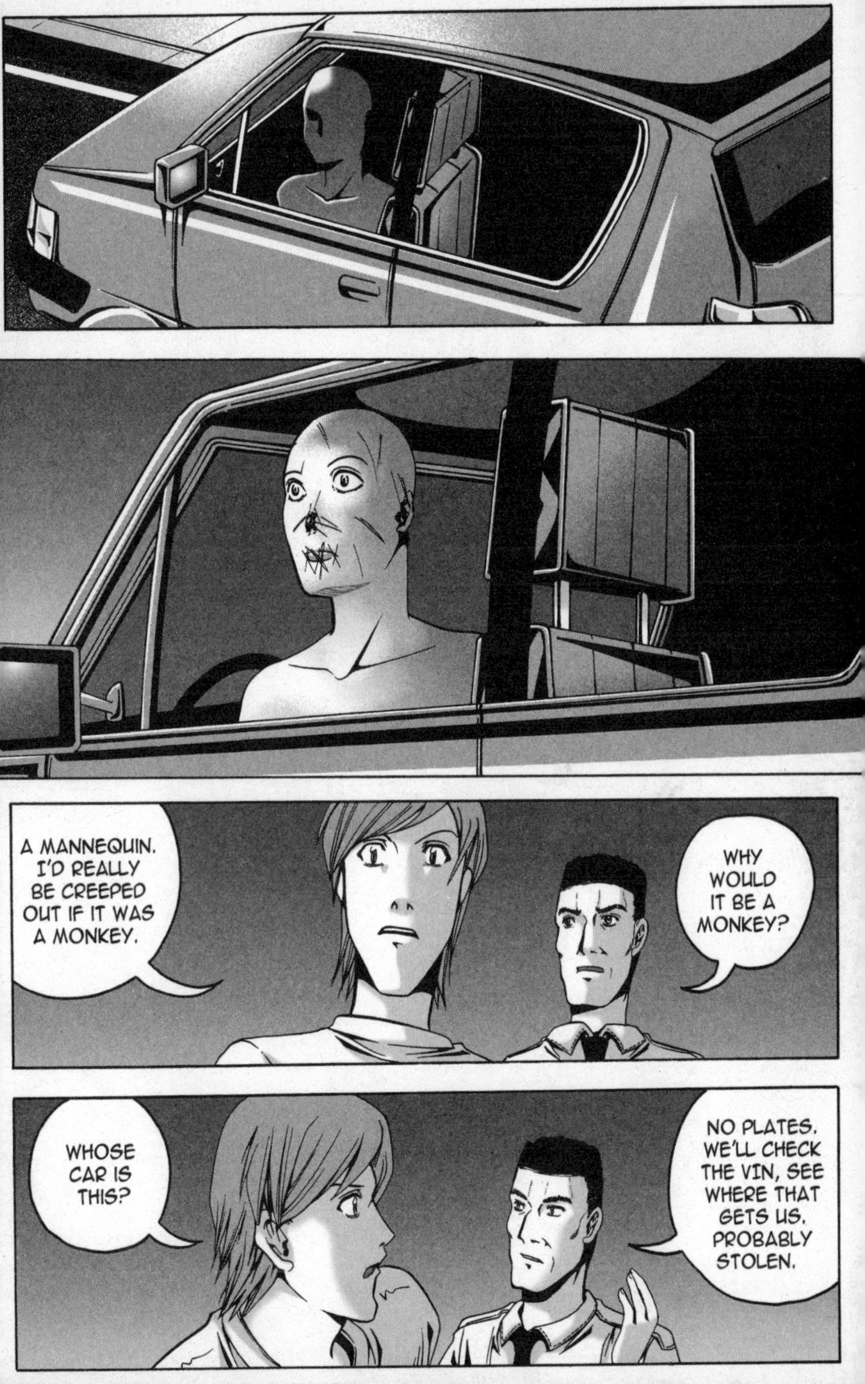
A MANNEQUIN. I'D REALLY BE CREEPED OUT IF IT WAS A MONKEY.
WHY WOULD IT BE A MONKEY?
WHOSE CAR IS THIS?
NO PLATES. WE'LL CHECK THE VIN, SEE WHERE THAT GETS US. PROBABLY STOLEN.

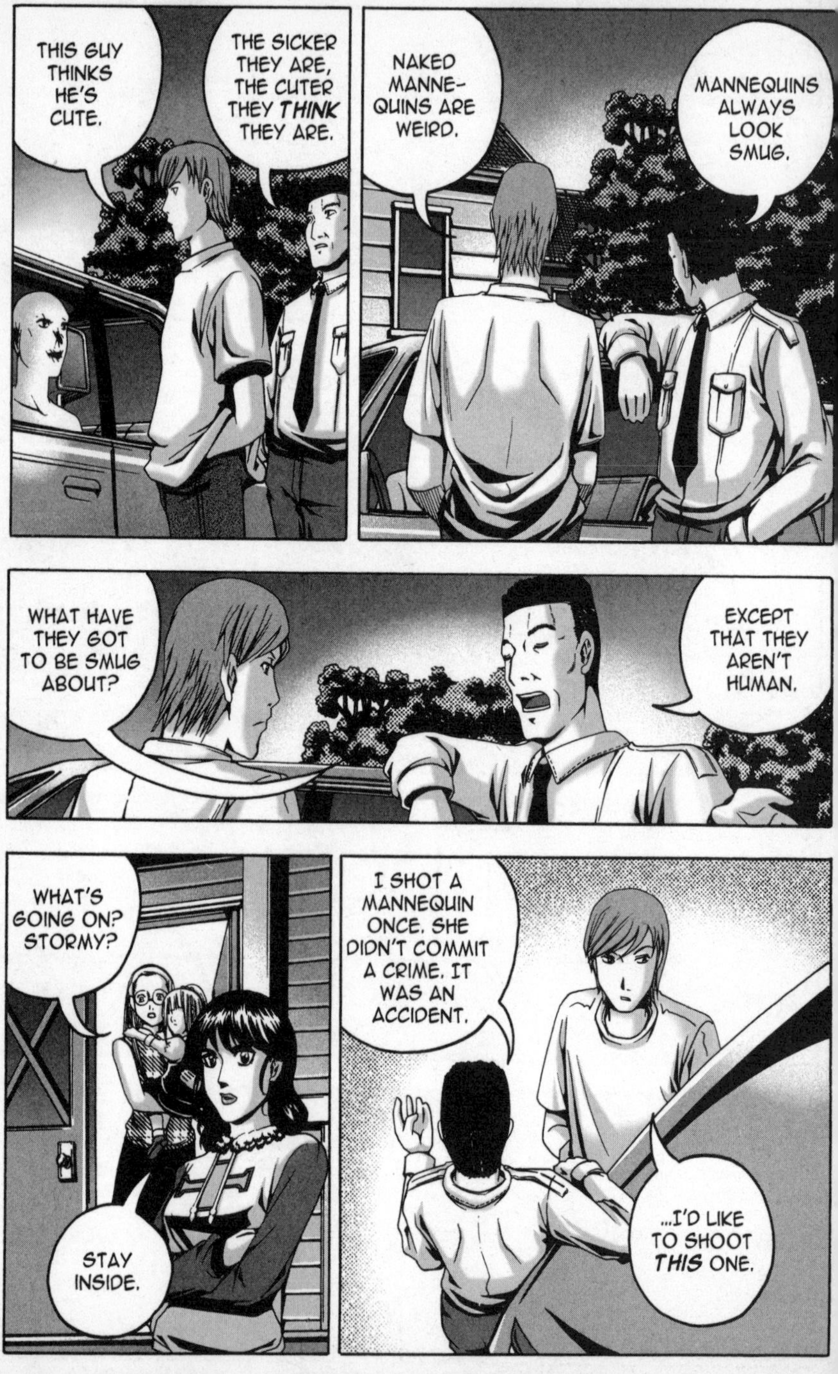

THIS GUY THINKS HE'S CUTE.
THE SICKER THEY ARE, THE CUTER THEY *THINK* THEY ARE.
NAKED MANNE-QUINS ARE WEIRD.
MANNEQUINS ALWAYS LOOK SMUG.
WHAT HAVE THEY GOT TO BE SMUG ABOUT?
EXCEPT THAT THEY AREN'T HUMAN.
WHAT'S GOING ON? STORMY?
STAY INSIDE.
I SHOT A MANNEQUIN ONCE. SHE DIDN'T COMMIT A CRIME. IT WAS AN ACCIDENT.
...I'D LIKE TO SHOOT *THIS* ONE.

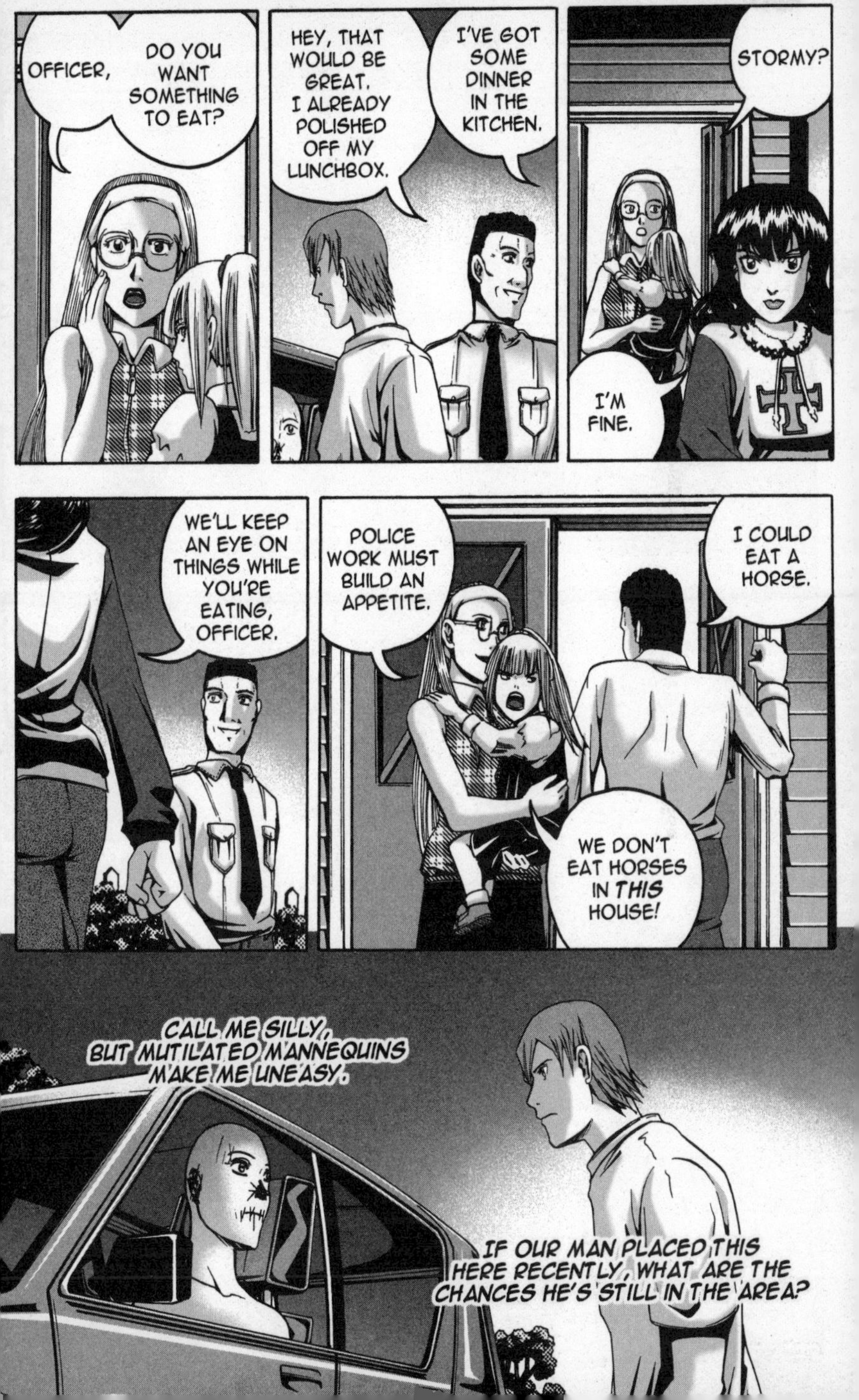
OFFICER,
DO YOU WANT SOMETHING TO EAT?
HEY, THAT WOULD BE GREAT. I ALREADY POLISHED OFF MY LUNCHBOX.
I'VE GOT SOME DINNER IN THE KITCHEN.
STORMY?
I'M FINE.
WE'LL KEEP AN EYE ON THINGS WHILE YOU'RE EATING, OFFICER.
POLICE WORK MUST BUILD AN APPETITE.
I COULD EAT A HORSE.
WE DON'T EAT HORSES IN *THIS* HOUSE!
CALL ME SILLY, BUT MUTILATED MANNEQUINS MAKE ME UNEASY.
IF OUR MAN PLACED THIS HERE RECENTLY, WHAT ARE THE CHANCES HE'S STILL IN THE AREA?

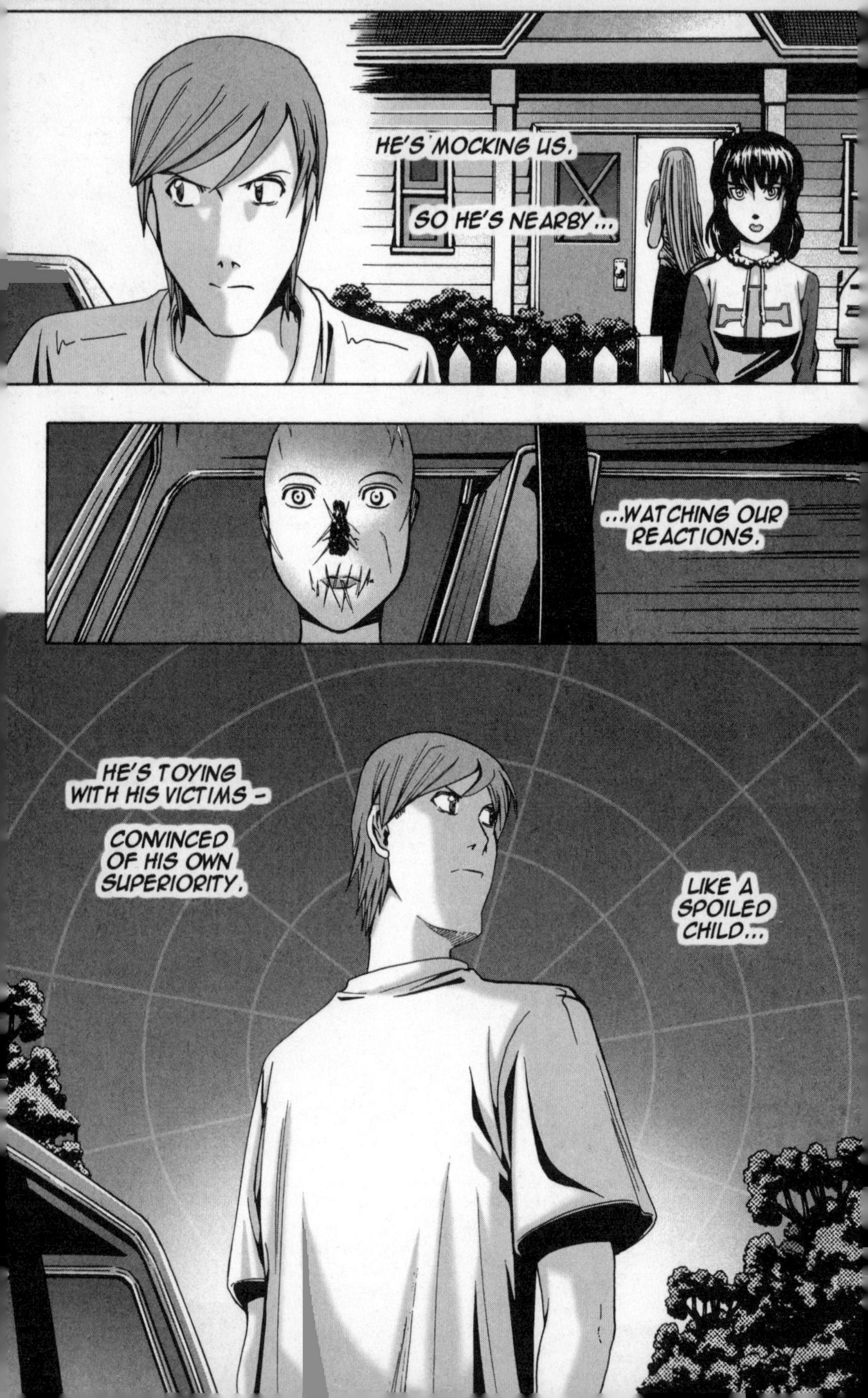
HE'S MOCKING US.
SO HE'S NEARBY...
...WATCHING OUR REACTIONS.
HE'S TOYING WITH HIS VICTIMS -
CONVINCED OF HIS OWN SUPERIORITY.
LIKE A SPOILED CHILD...

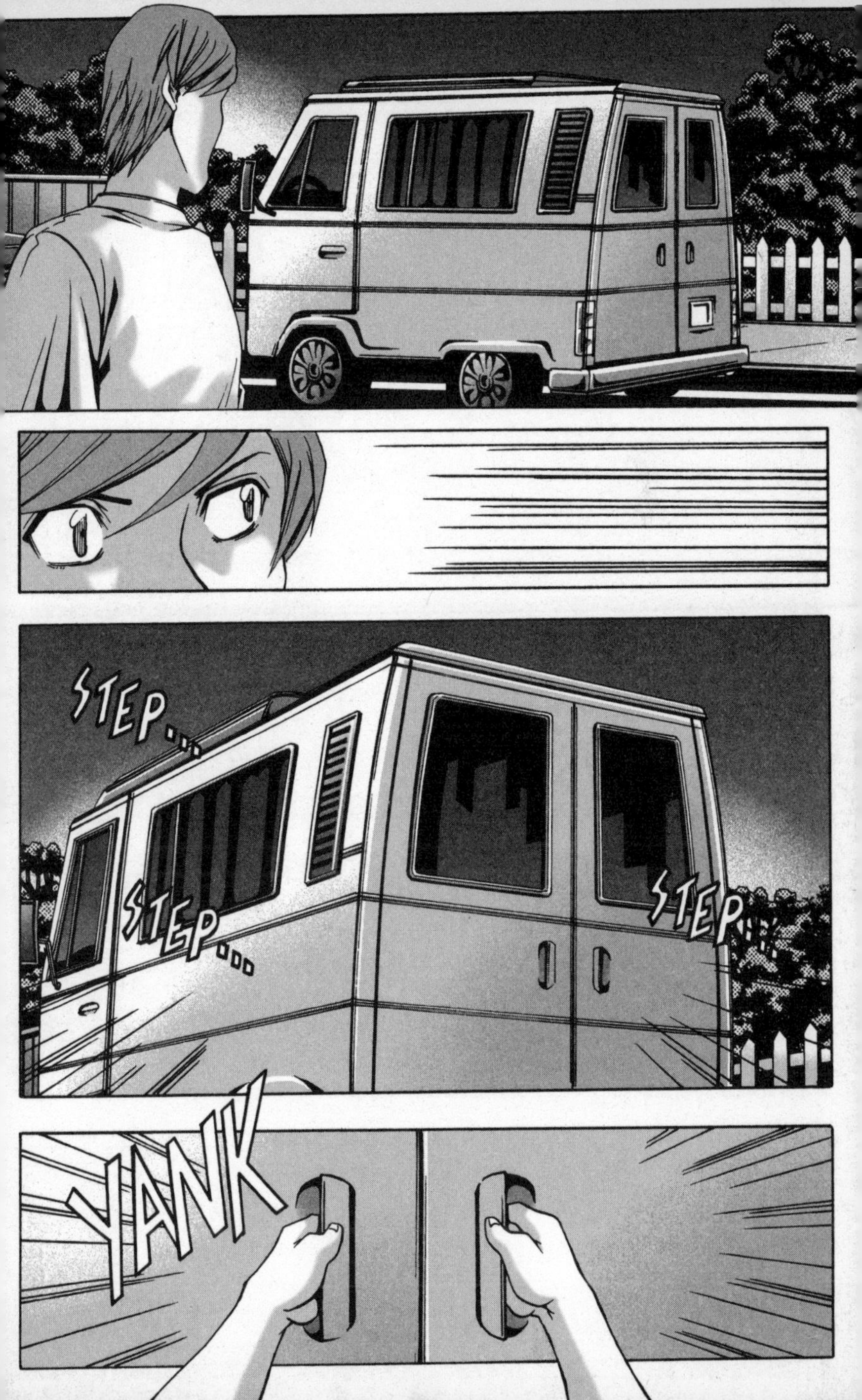
STEP...
STEP...
STEP...
YANK

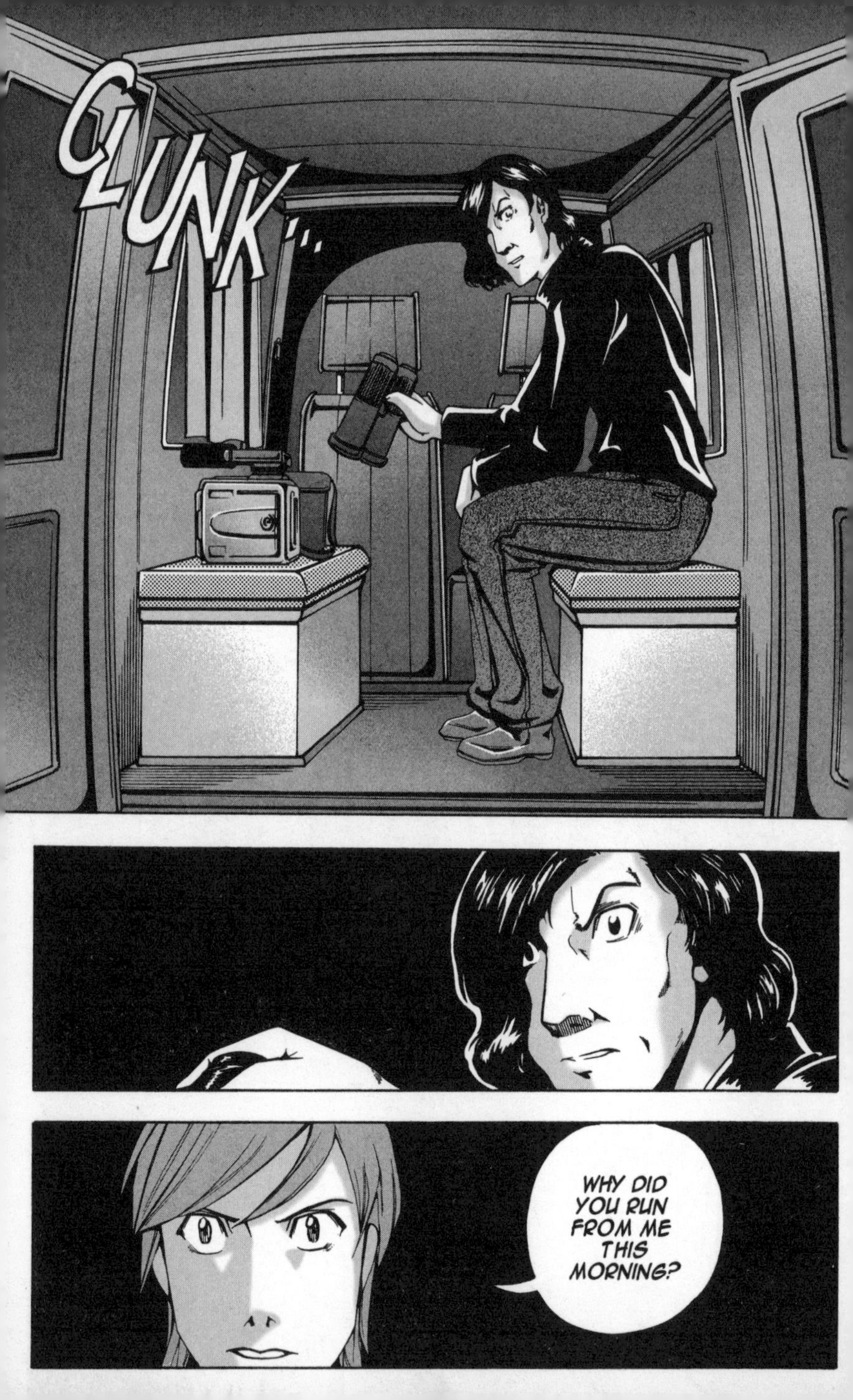
CLUNK...
WHY DID YOU RUN FROM ME THIS MORNING?

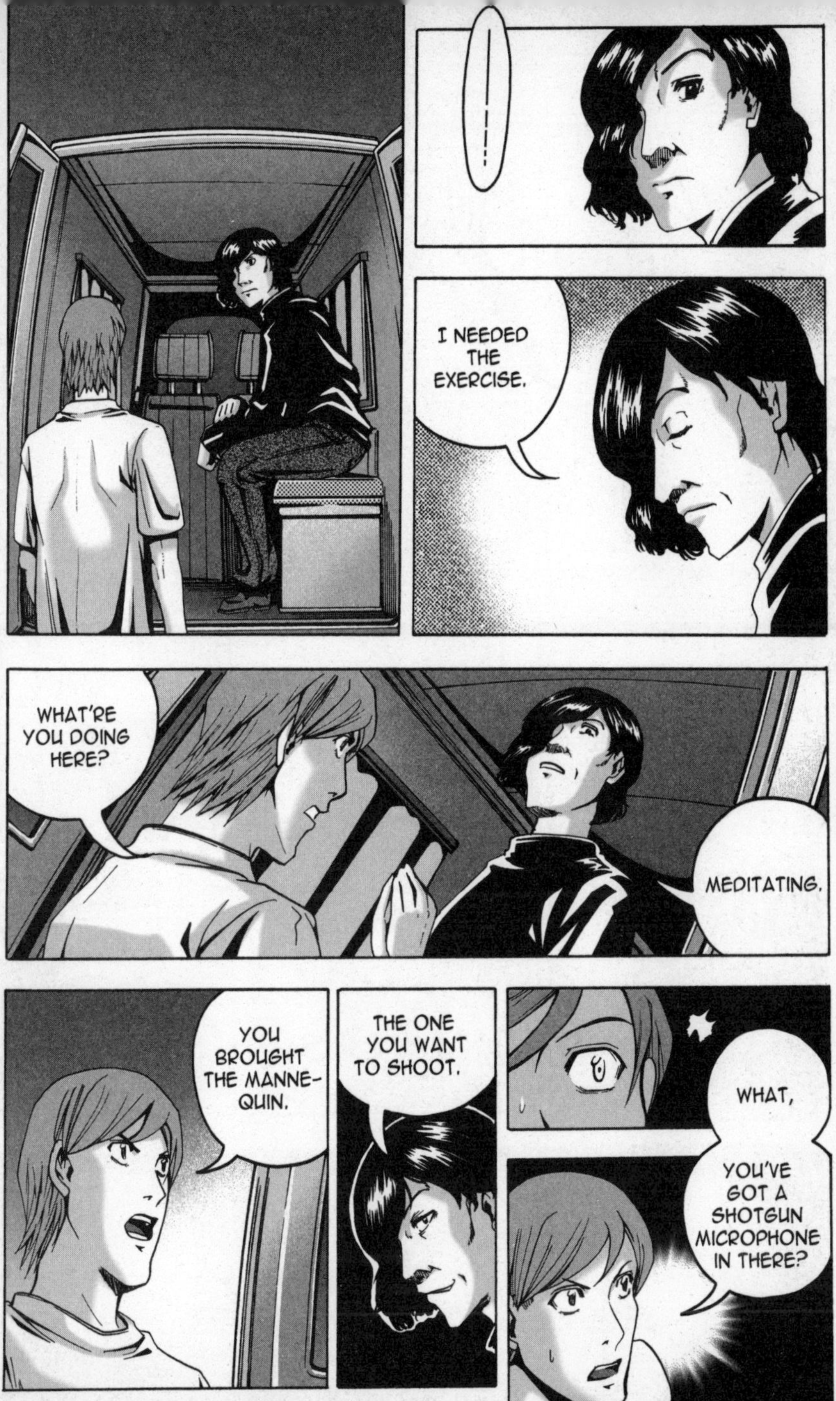
!
I NEEDED THE EXERCISE.
WHAT'RE YOU DOING HERE?
MEDITATING.
YOU BROUGHT THE MANNE-QUIN.
THE ONE YOU WANT TO SHOOT.
WHAT,
YOU'VE GOT A SHOTGUN MICROPHONE IN THERE?

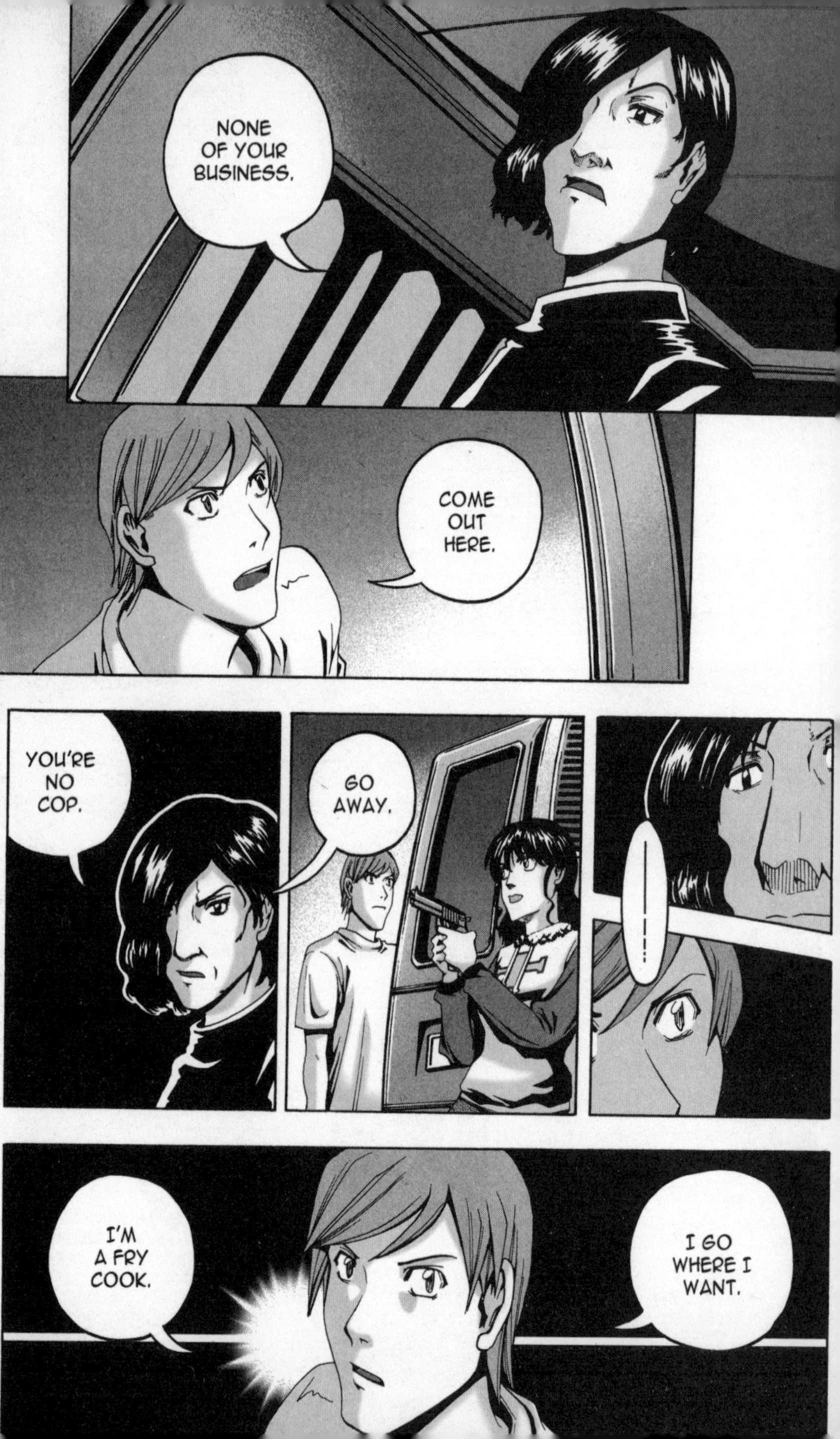
NONE OF YOUR BUSINESS.
COME OUT HERE.
YOU'RE NO COP.
GO AWAY.
......
I'M A FRY COOK.
I GO WHERE I WANT.

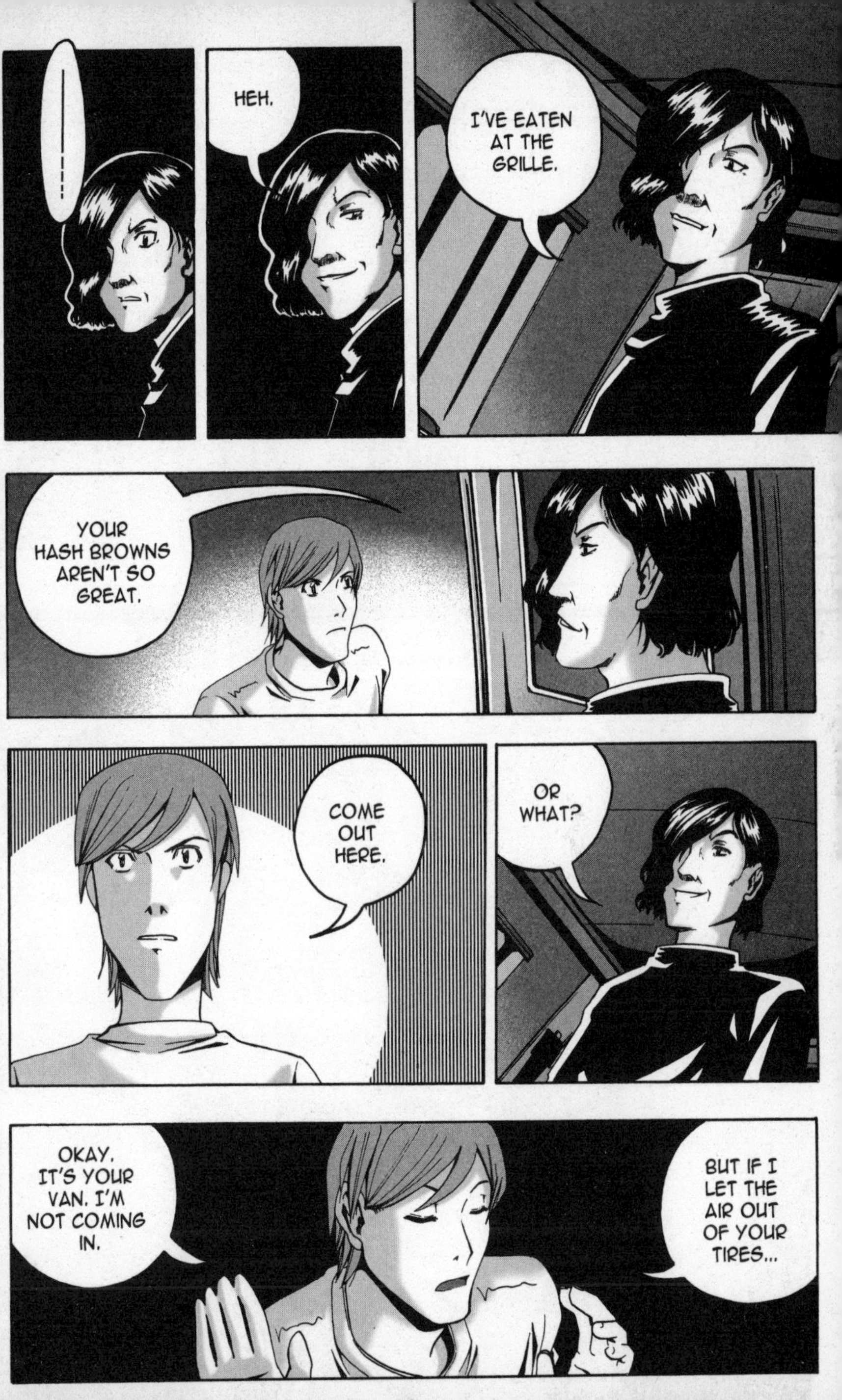
!
HEH.
I'VE EATEN AT THE GRILLE.
YOUR HASH BROWNS AREN'T SO GREAT.
COME OUT HERE.
OR WHAT?
OKAY. IT'S YOUR VAN. I'M NOT COMING IN.
BUT IF I LET THE AIR OUT OF YOUR TIRES...

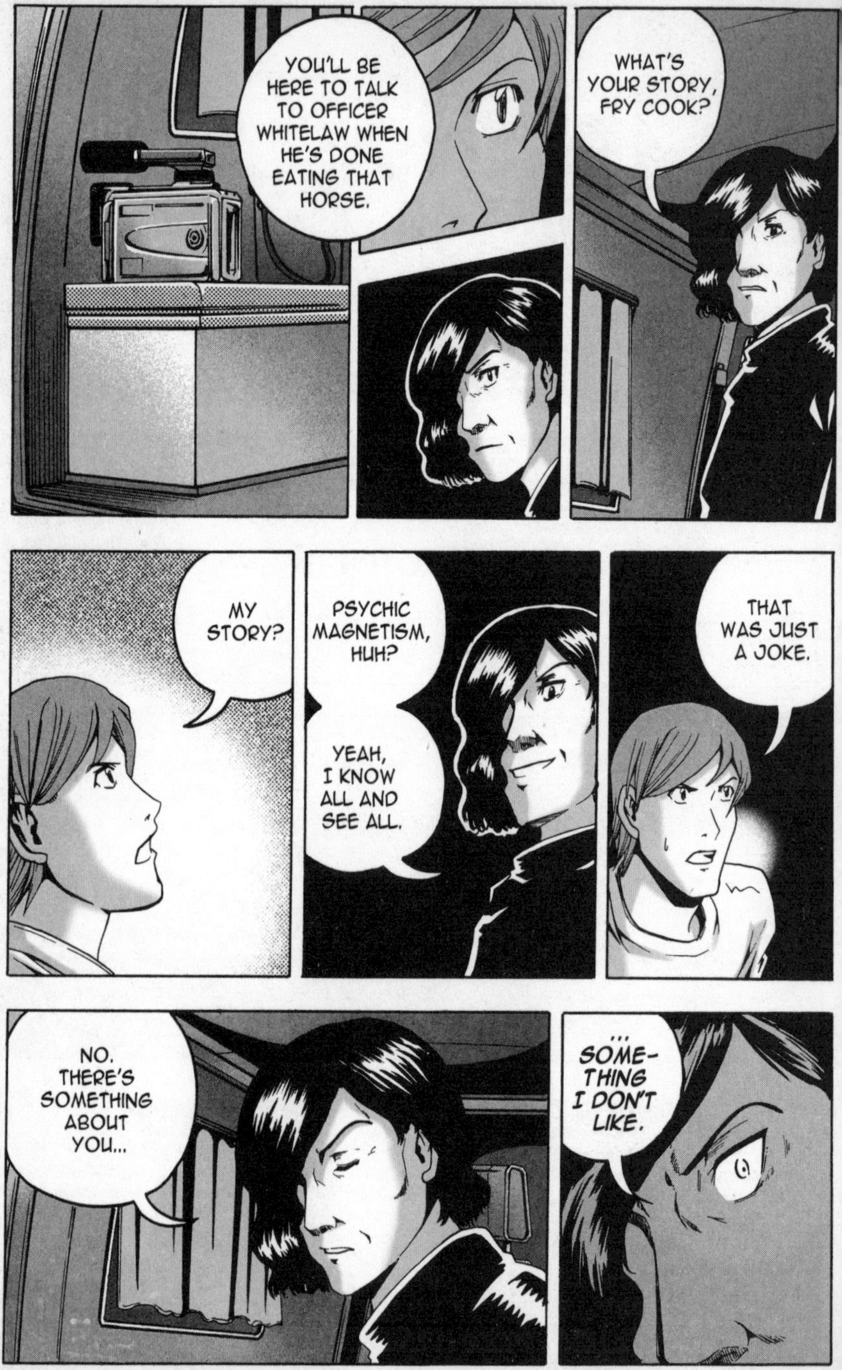
YOU'LL BE HERE TO TALK TO OFFICER WHITELAW WHEN HE'S DONE EATING THAT HORSE.
WHAT'S YOUR STORY, FRY COOK?
MY STORY?
PSYCHIC MAGNETISM, HUH?
YEAH, I KNOW ALL AND SEE ALL.
THAT WAS JUST A JOKE.
NO. THERE'S SOMETHING ABOUT YOU...
...SOME-THING I DON'T LIKE.

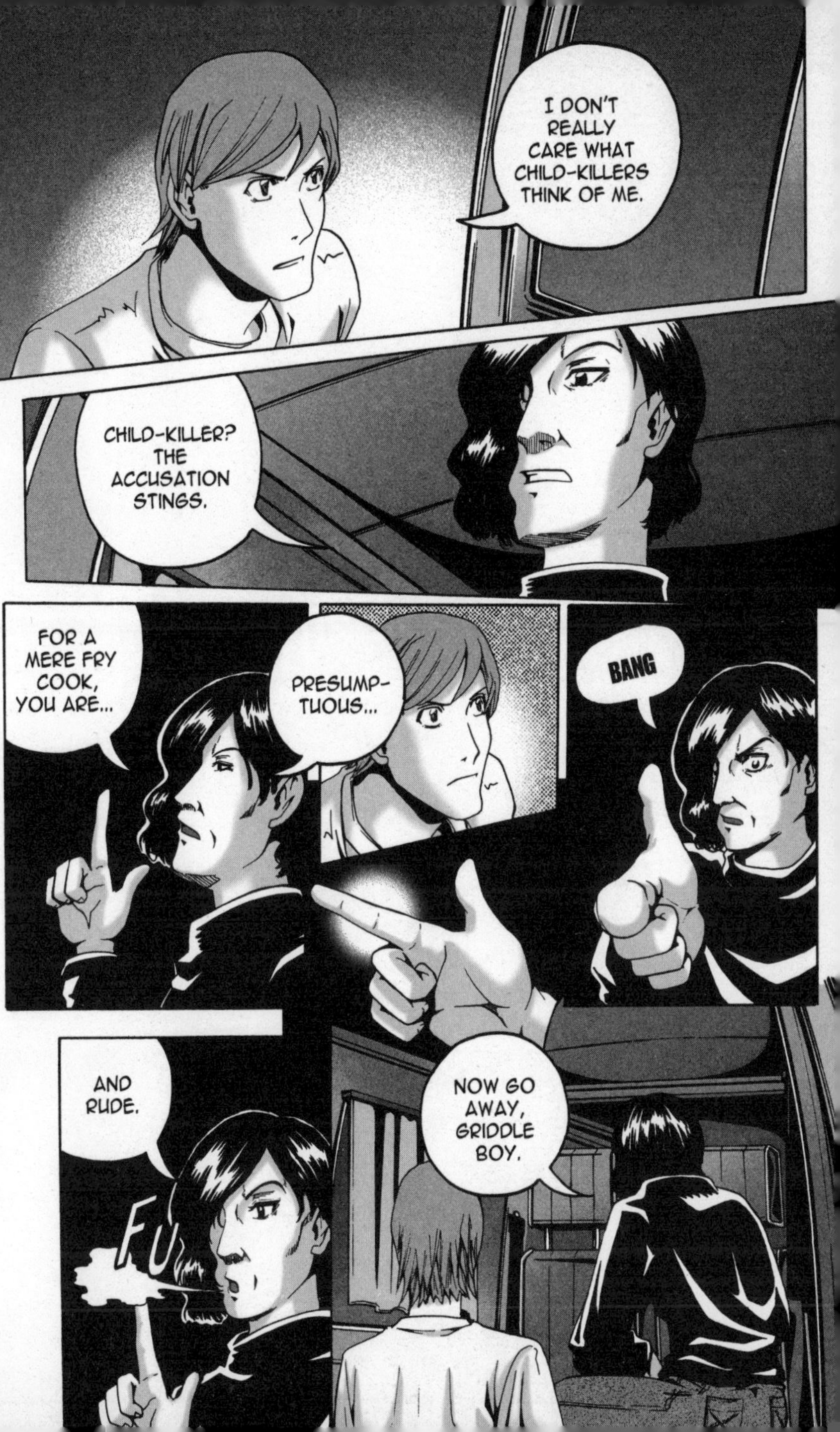
I DON'T REALLY CARE WHAT CHILD-KILLERS THINK OF ME.
CHILD-KILLER? THE ACCUSATION STINGS.
FOR A MERE FRY COOK, YOU ARE...
PRESUMPTUOUS...
BANG
AND RUDE.
FU
NOW GO AWAY, GRIDDLE BOY.

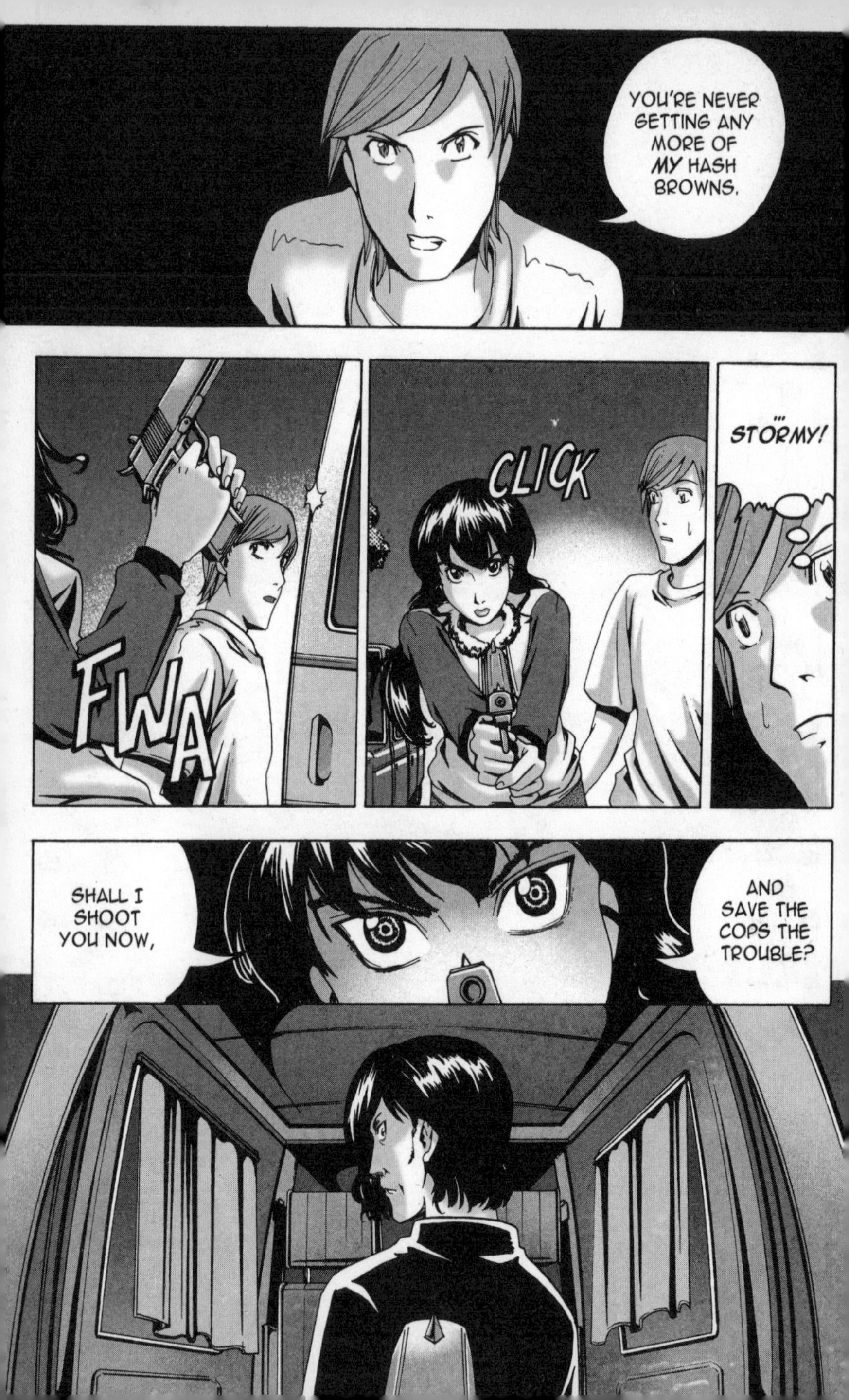
YOU'RE NEVER GETTING ANY MORE OF MY HASH BROWNS.
FWA
CLICK
...STORMY!
SHALL I SHOOT YOU NOW,
AND SAVE THE COPS THE TROUBLE?

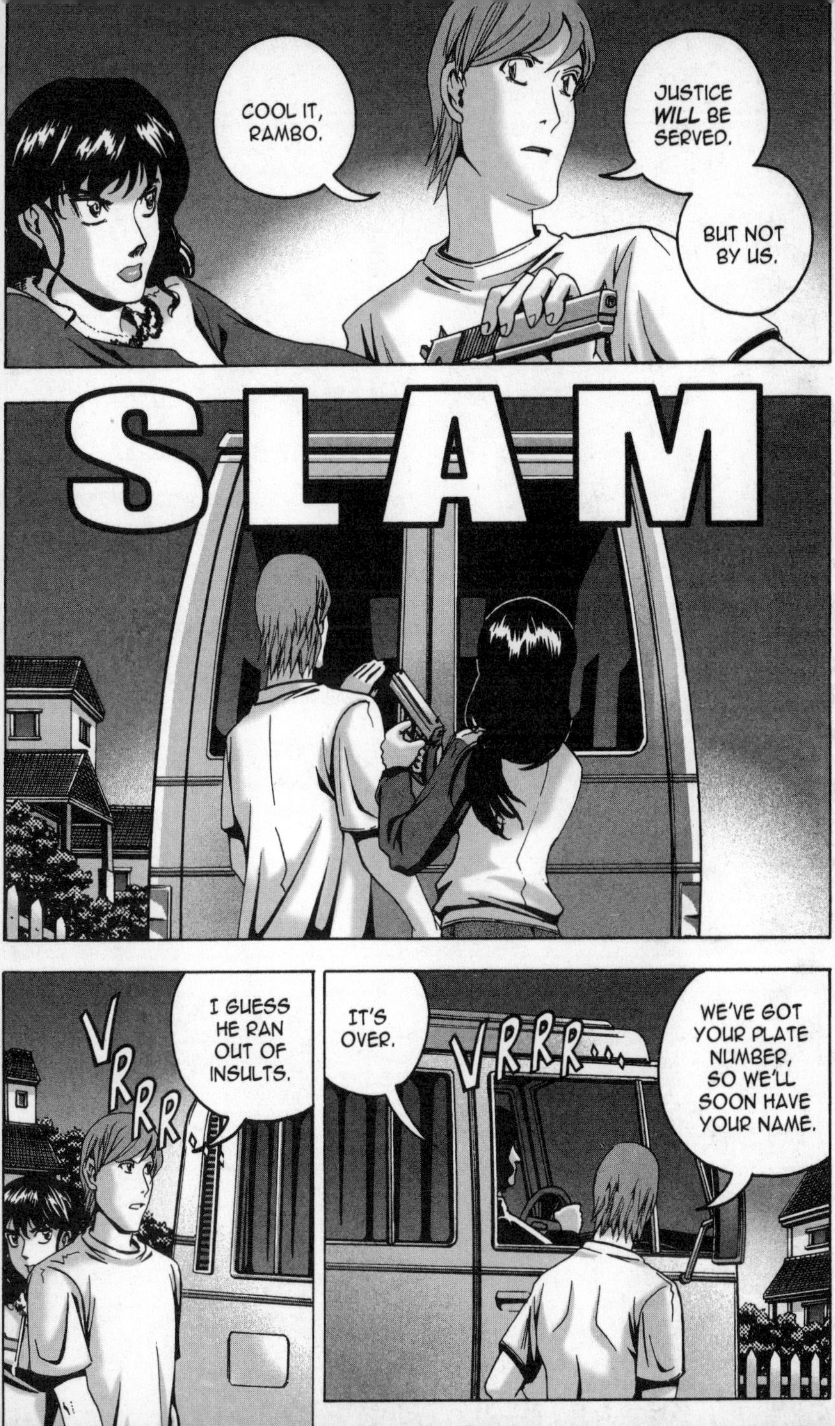

COOL IT, RAMBO.
JUSTICE WILL BE SERVED.
BUT NOT BY US.
SLAM
I GUESS HE RAN OUT OF INSULTS.
VRRR...
IT'S OVER.
VRRR...
WE'VE GOT YOUR PLATE NUMBER, SO WE'LL SOON HAVE YOUR NAME.

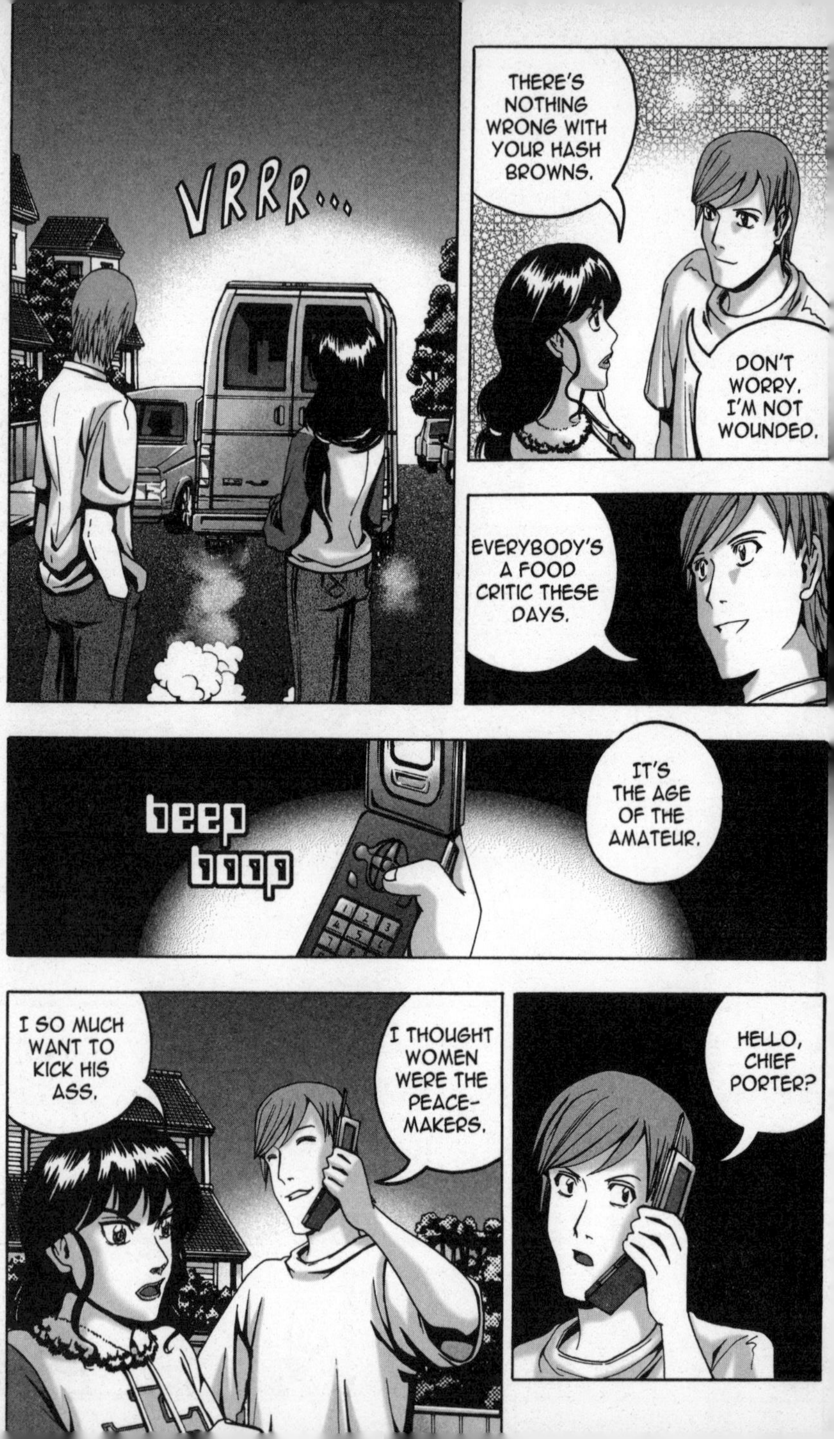
VRRR...
THERE'S NOTHING WRONG WITH YOUR HASH BROWNS.
DON'T WORRY. I'M NOT WOUNDED.
EVERYBODY'S A FOOD CRITIC THESE DAYS.
beep boop
IT'S THE AGE OF THE AMATEUR.
I SO MUCH WANT TO KICK HIS ASS.
I THOUGHT WOMEN WERE THE PEACE-MAKERS.
HELLO, CHIEF PORTER?

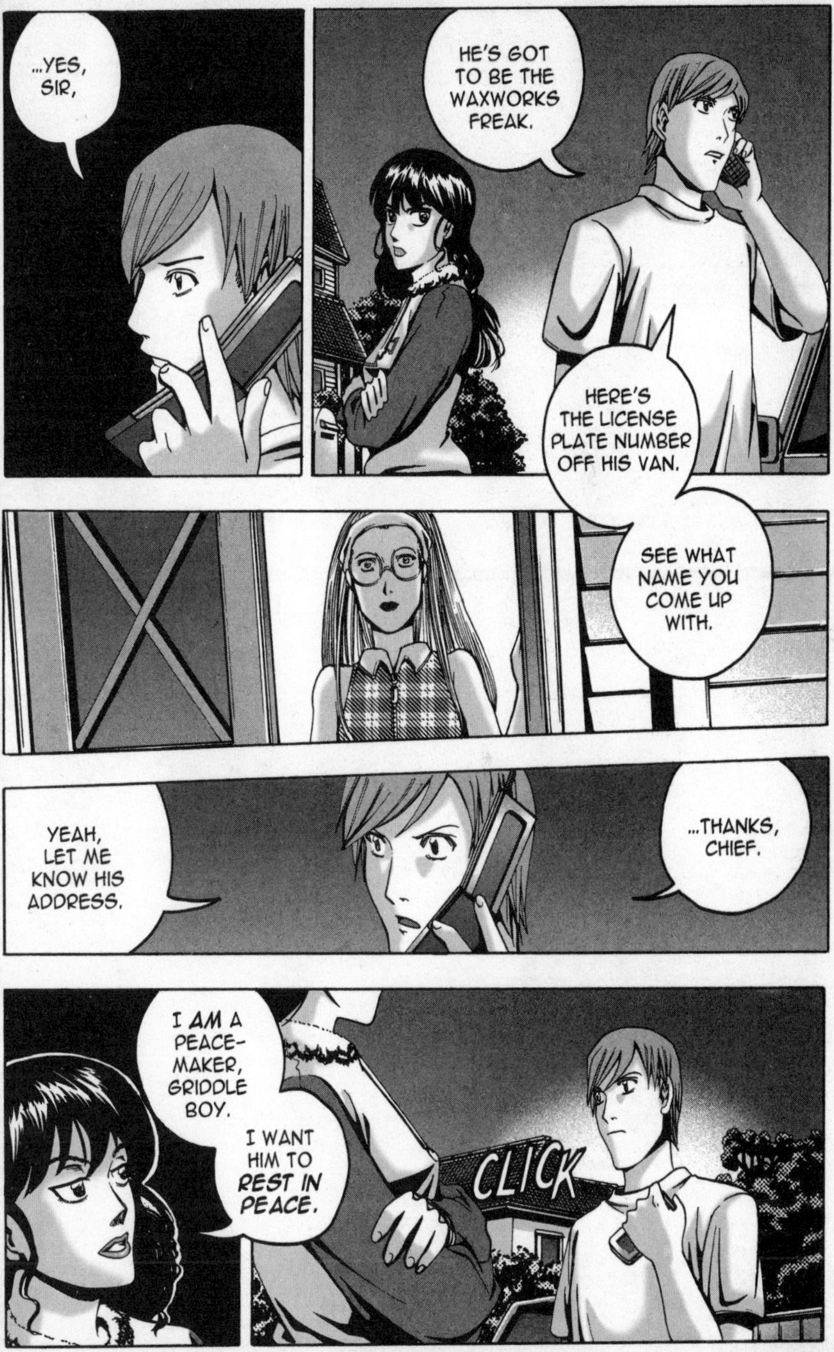

...YES, SIR,
HE'S GOT TO BE THE WAXWORKS FREAK.
HERE'S THE LICENSE PLATE NUMBER OFF HIS VAN.
SEE WHAT NAME YOU COME UP WITH.
YEAH, LET ME KNOW HIS ADDRESS.
...THANKS, CHIEF.
I AM A PEACE-MAKER, GRIDDLE BOY.
I WANT HIM TO REST IN PEACE.
CLICK

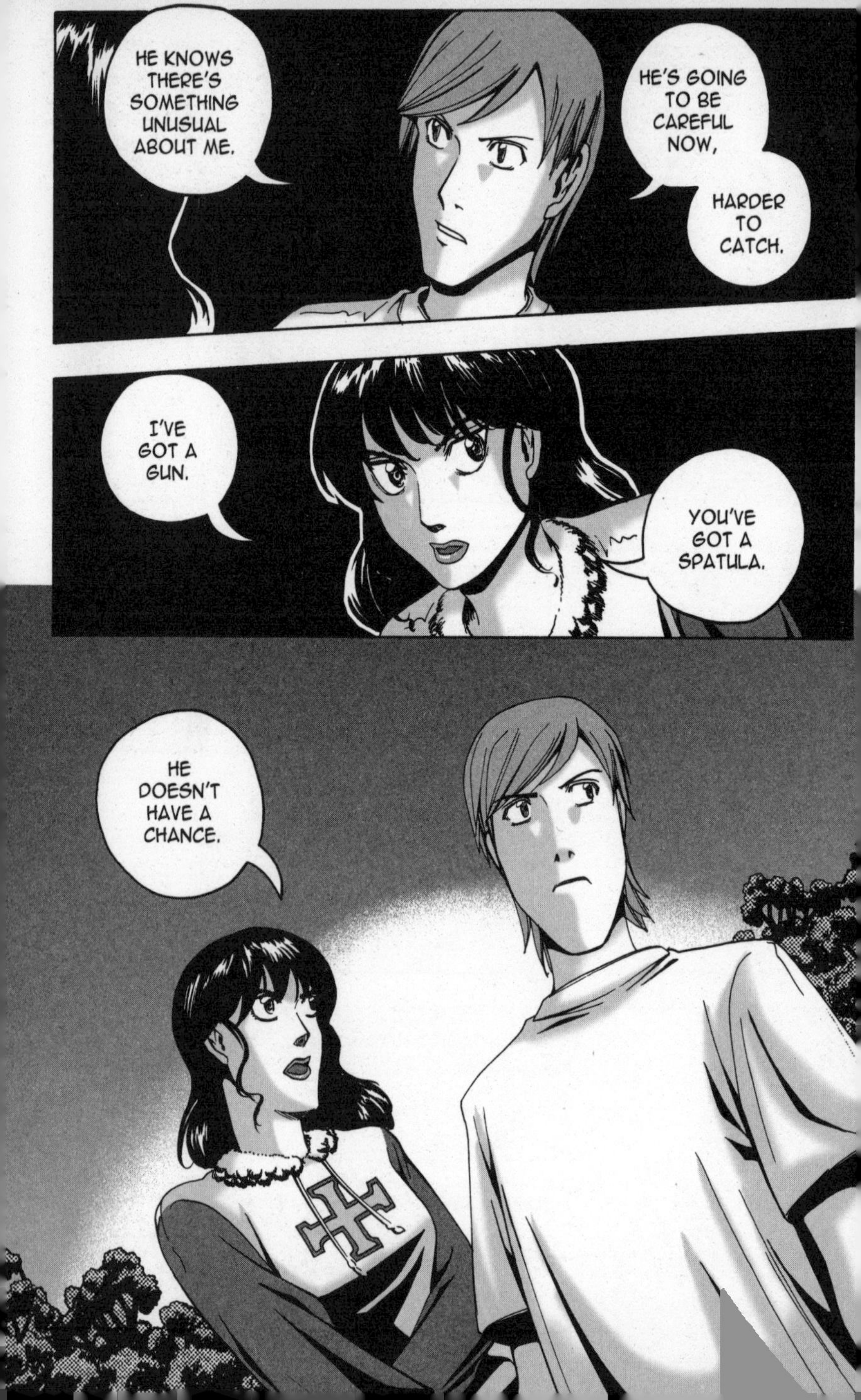
HE KNOWS THERE'S SOMETHING UNUSUAL ABOUT ME.
HE'S GOING TO BE CAREFUL NOW,
HARDER TO CATCH.
I'VE GOT A GUN.
YOU'VE GOT A SPATULA.
HE DOESN'T HAVE A CHANCE.

In Odd We Trust

Chapter 5

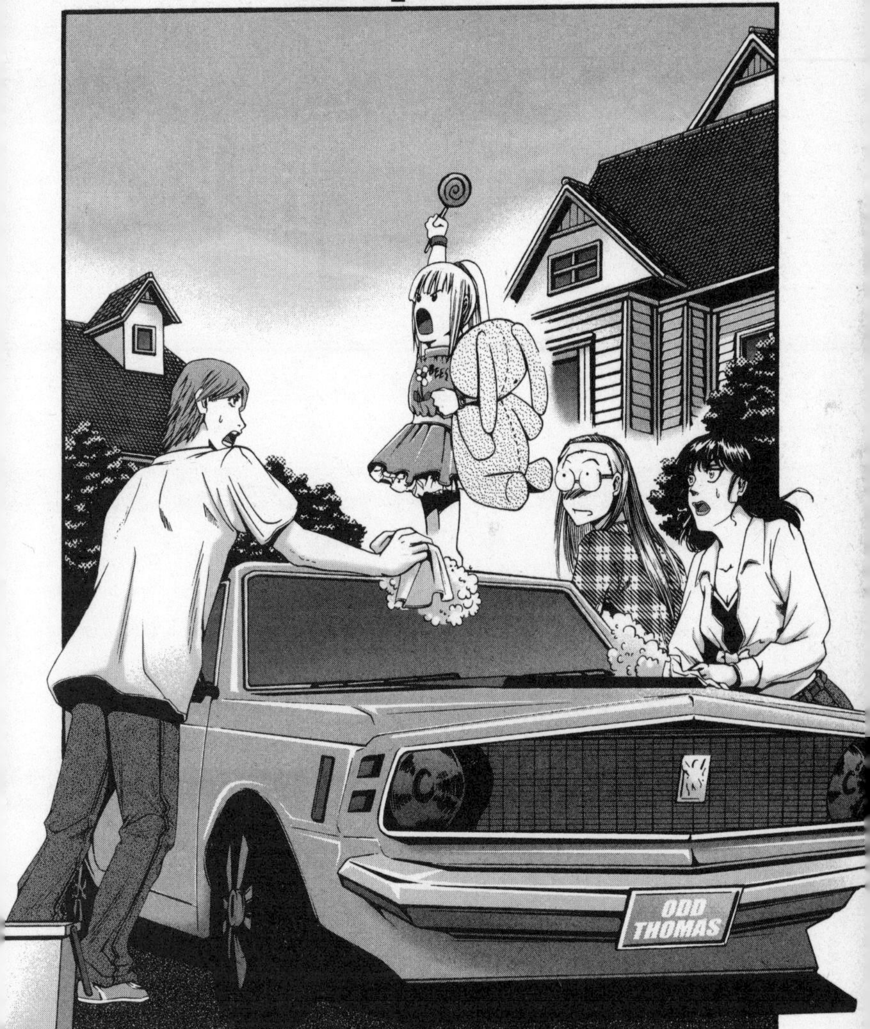

ODD
THOMAS

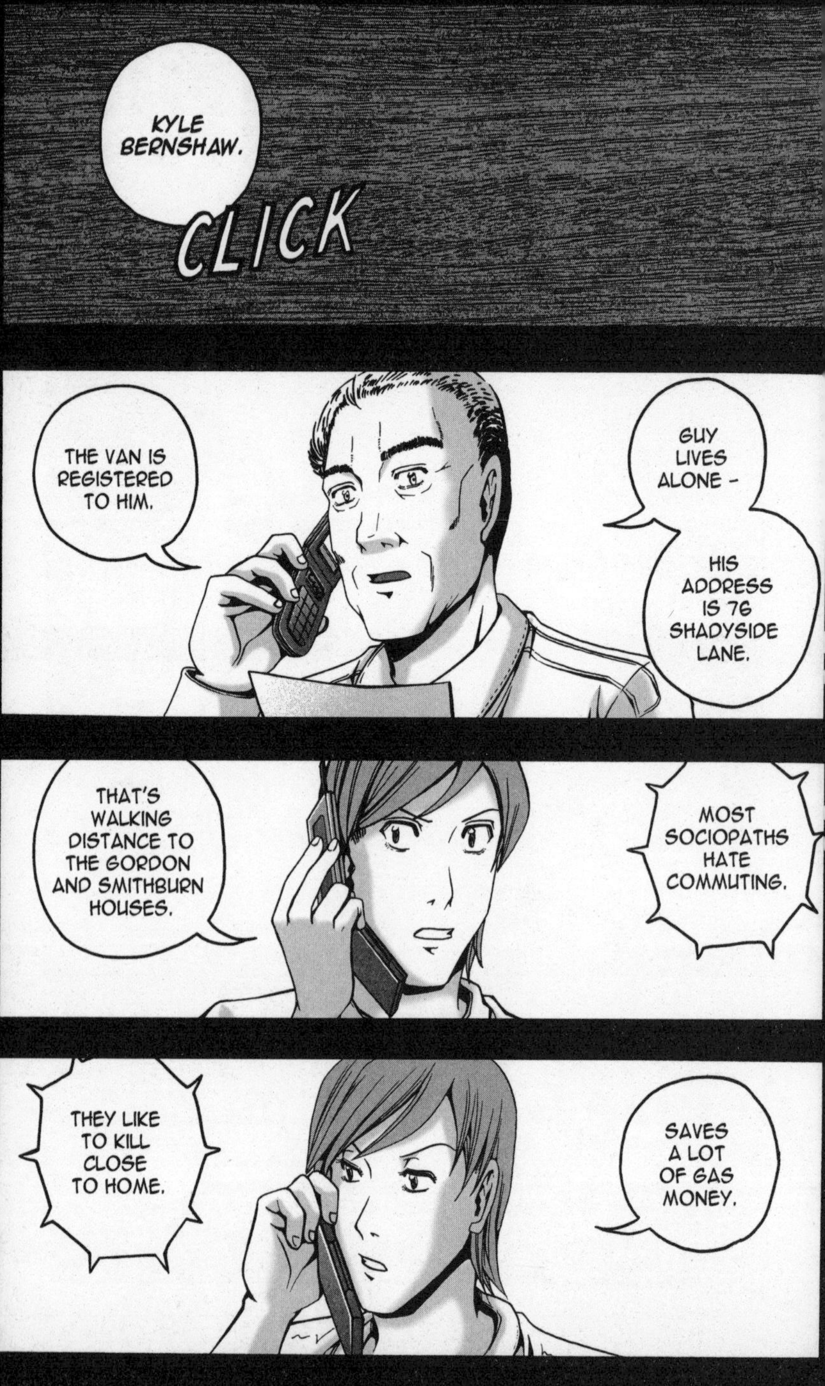
KYLE BERNSHAW.
CLICK
THE VAN IS REGISTERED TO HIM.
GUY LIVES ALONE -
HIS ADDRESS IS 76 SHADYSIDE LANE.
THAT'S WALKING DISTANCE TO THE GORDON AND SMITHBURN HOUSES.
MOST SOCIOPATHS HATE COMMUTING.
THEY LIKE TO KILL CLOSE TO HOME.
SAVES A LOT OF GAS MONEY.

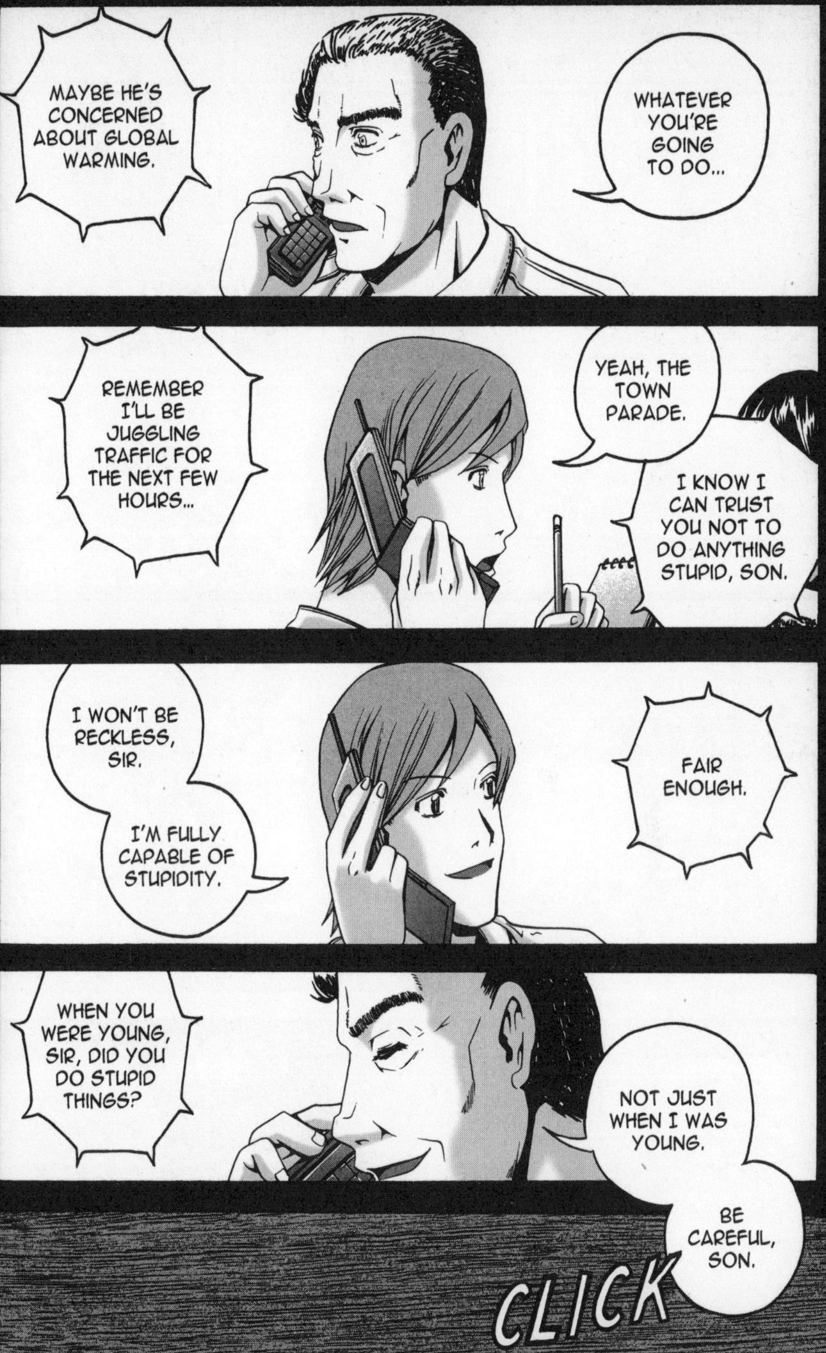
MAYBE HE'S CONCERNED ABOUT GLOBAL WARMING.
WHATEVER YOU'RE GOING TO DO...
REMEMBER I'LL BE JUGGLING TRAFFIC FOR THE NEXT FEW HOURS...
YEAH, THE TOWN PARADE.
I KNOW I CAN TRUST YOU NOT TO DO ANYTHING STUPID, SON.
I WON'T BE RECKLESS, SIR.
I'M FULLY CAPABLE OF STUPIDITY.
FAIR ENOUGH.
WHEN YOU WERE YOUNG, SIR, DID YOU DO STUPID THINGS?
NOT JUST WHEN I WAS YOUNG.
BE CAREFUL, SON.
CLICK

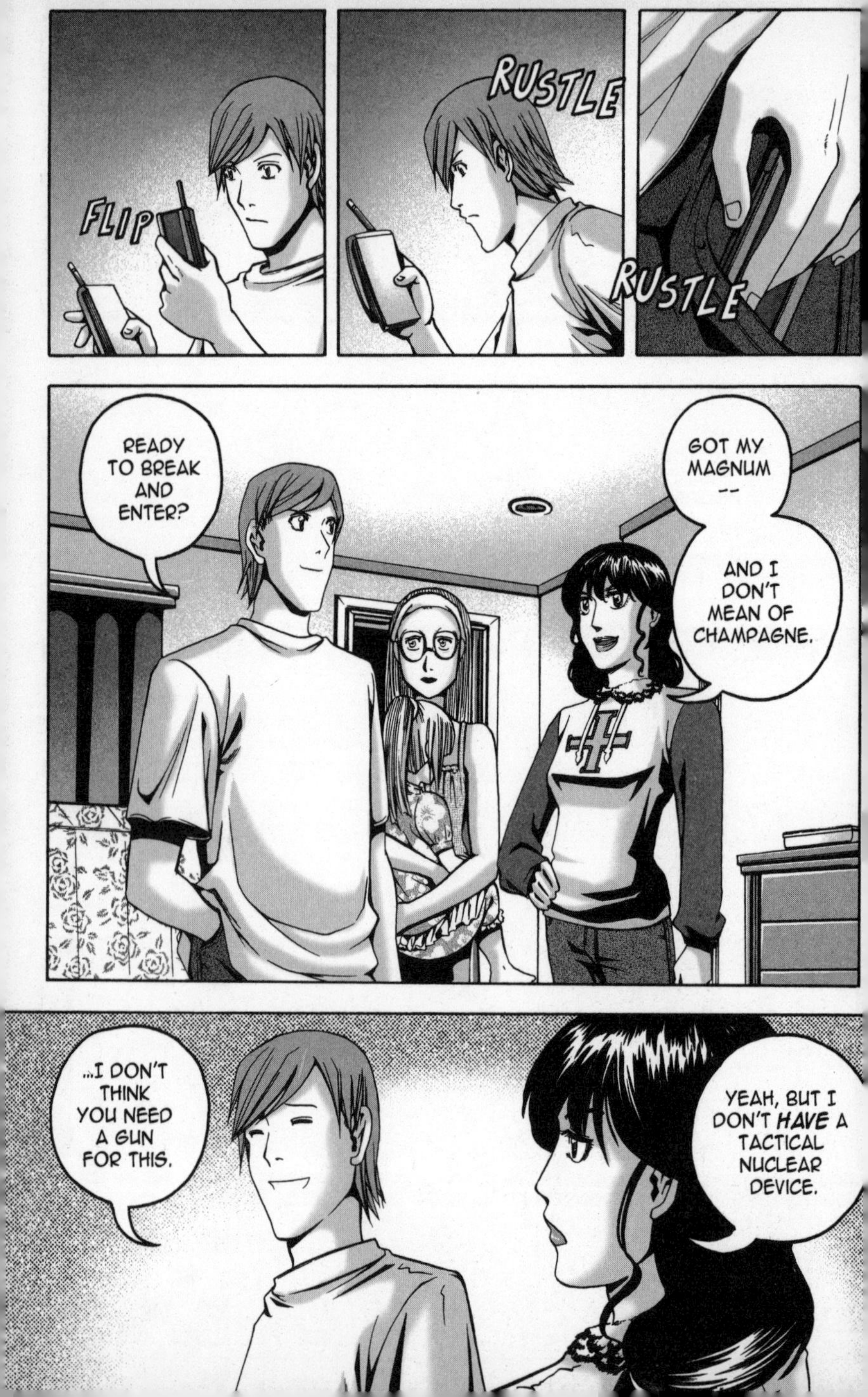
FLIP
RUSTLE
RUSTLE
READY TO BREAK AND ENTER?
GOT MY MAGNUM --
AND I DON'T MEAN OF CHAMPAGNE.
...I DON'T THINK YOU NEED A GUN FOR THIS.
YEAH, BUT I DON'T *HAVE* A TACTICAL NUCLEAR DEVICE.

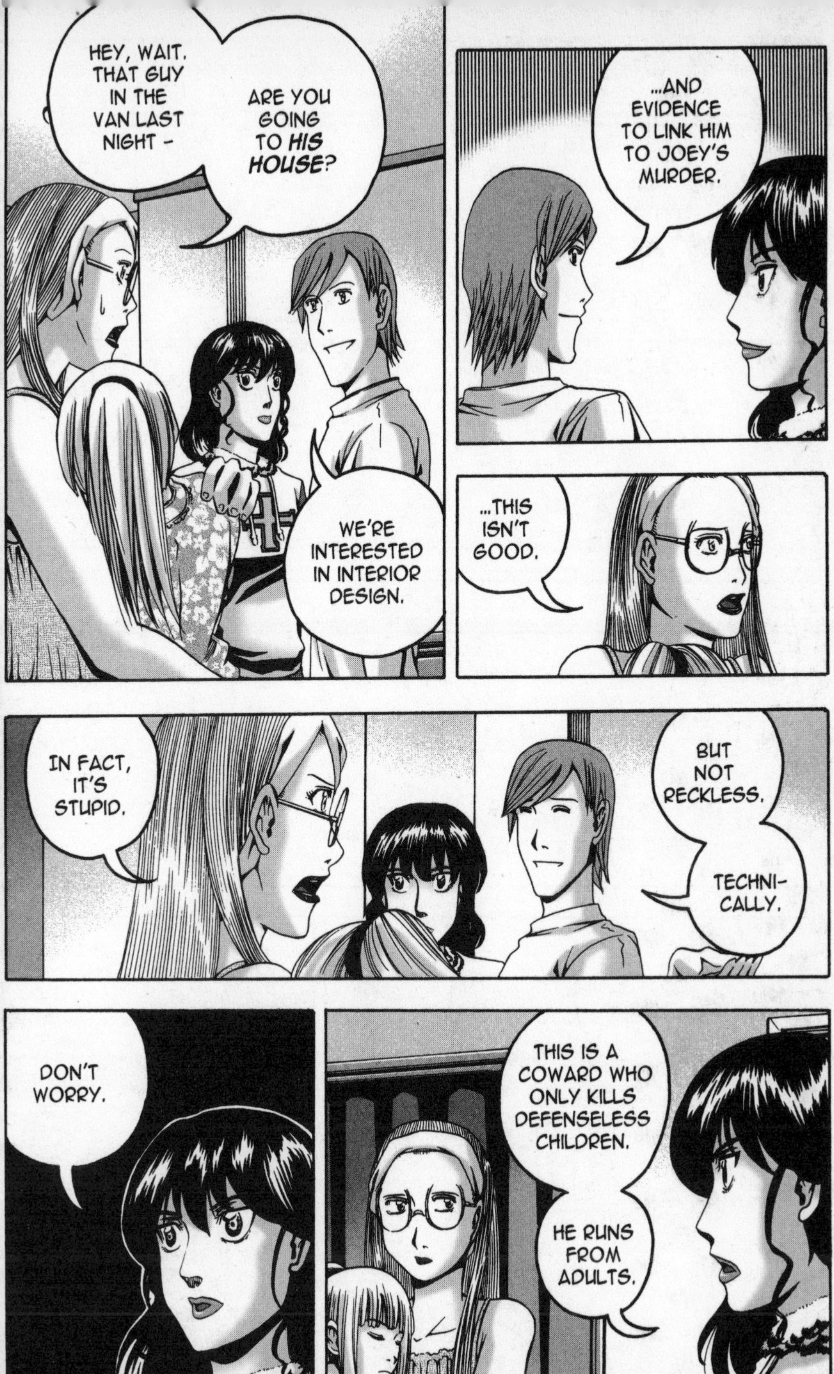
HEY, WAIT. THAT GUY IN THE VAN LAST NIGHT -
ARE YOU GOING TO *HIS HOUSE*?
WE'RE INTERESTED IN INTERIOR DESIGN.
...AND EVIDENCE TO LINK HIM TO JOEY'S MURDER.
...THIS ISN'T GOOD.
IN FACT, IT'S STUPID.
BUT NOT RECKLESS.
TECHNI-CALLY.
DON'T WORRY.
THIS IS A COWARD WHO ONLY KILLS DEFENSELESS CHILDREN.
HE RUNS FROM ADULTS.

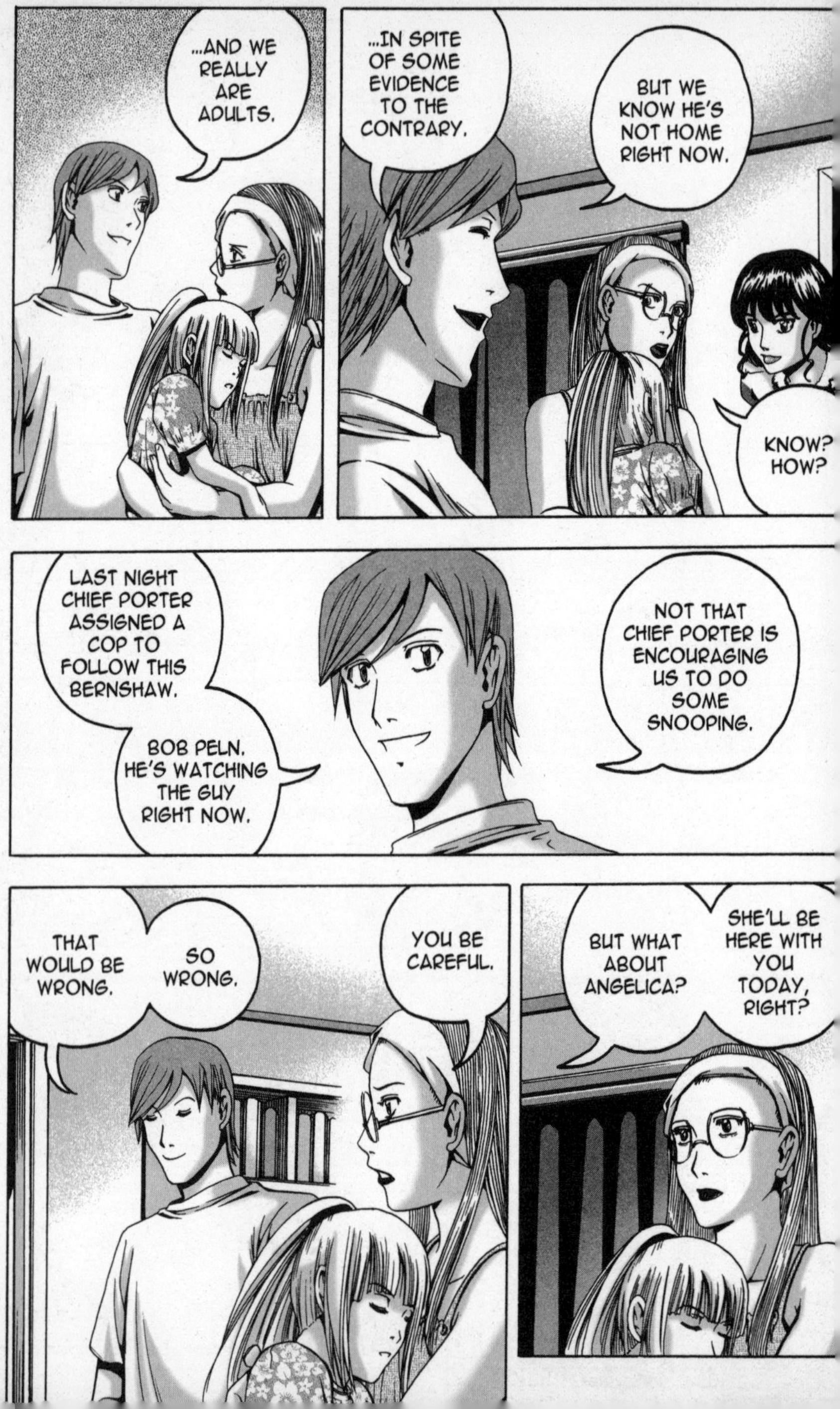
...AND WE REALLY ARE ADULTS.
...IN SPITE OF SOME EVIDENCE TO THE CONTRARY.
BUT WE KNOW HE'S NOT HOME RIGHT NOW.
KNOW? HOW?
LAST NIGHT CHIEF PORTER ASSIGNED A COP TO FOLLOW THIS BERNSHAW.
BOB PELN. HE'S WATCHING THE GUY RIGHT NOW.
NOT THAT CHIEF PORTER IS ENCOURAGING US TO DO SOME SNOOPING.
THAT WOULD BE WRONG.
SO WRONG.
YOU BE CAREFUL.
BUT WHAT ABOUT ANGELICA?
SHE'LL BE HERE WITH YOU TODAY, RIGHT?

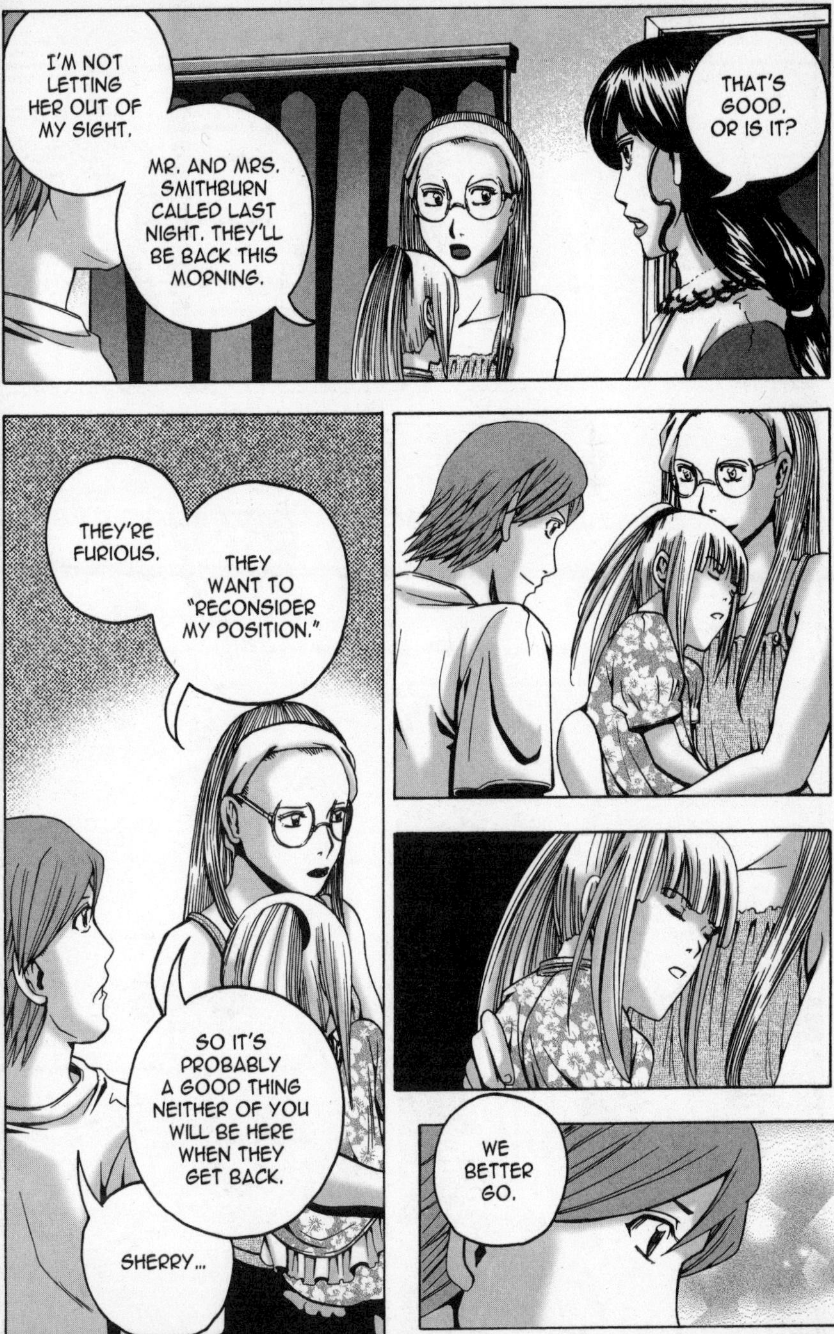
I'M NOT LETTING HER OUT OF MY SIGHT.
MR. AND MRS. SMITHBURN CALLED LAST NIGHT. THEY'LL BE BACK THIS MORNING.
THAT'S GOOD, OR IS IT?
THEY'RE FURIOUS.
THEY WANT TO "RECONSIDER MY POSITION."
SO IT'S PROBABLY A GOOD THING NEITHER OF YOU WILL BE HERE WHEN THEY GET BACK.
SHERRY...
WE BETTER GO.

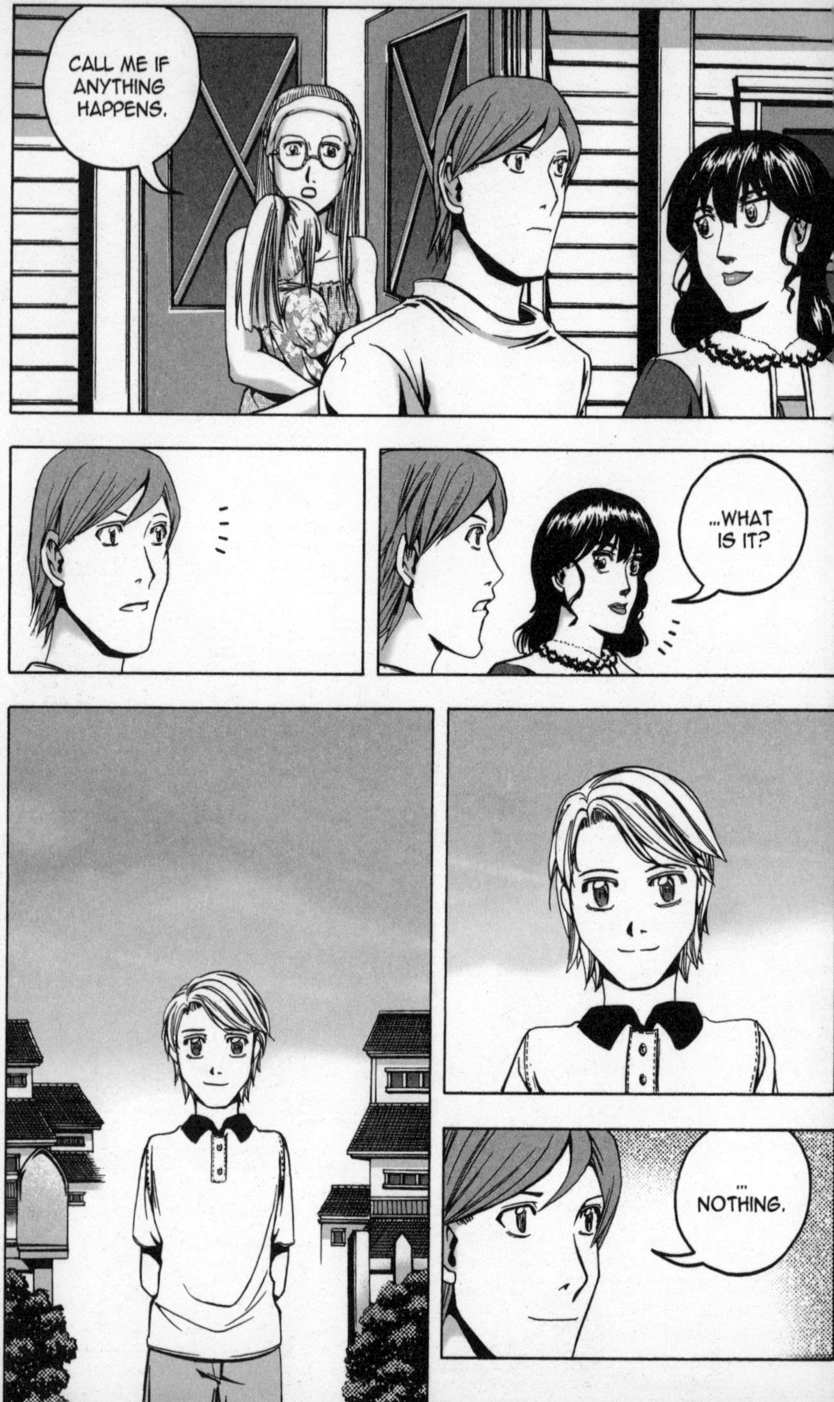
CALL ME IF ANYTHING HAPPENS.
...WHAT IS IT?
... NOTHING.

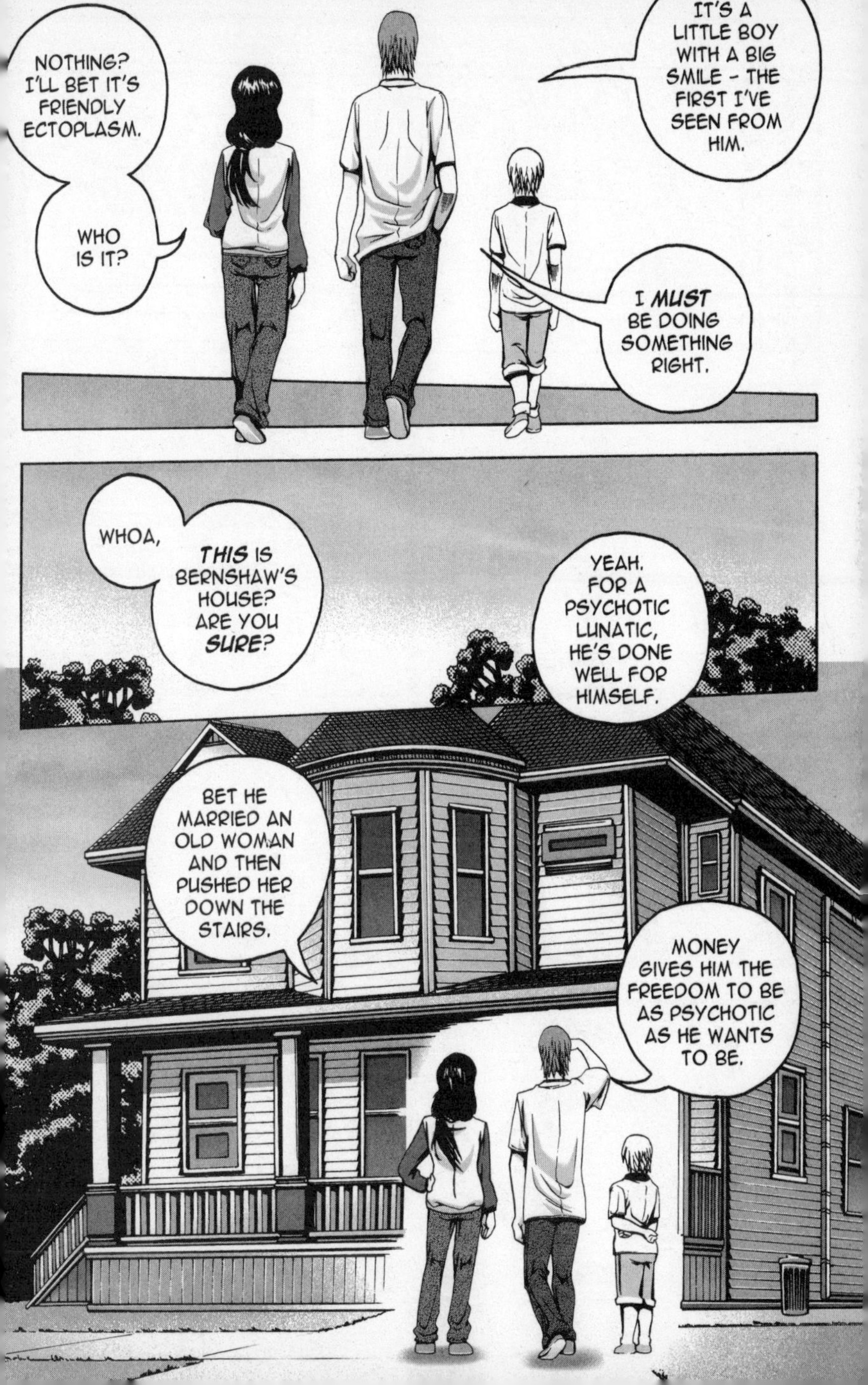
NOTHING? I'LL BET IT'S FRIENDLY ECTOPLASM.
WHO IS IT?
IT'S A LITTLE BOY WITH A BIG SMILE - THE FIRST I'VE SEEN FROM HIM.
I MUST BE DOING SOMETHING RIGHT.
WHOA,
THIS IS BERNSHAW'S HOUSE? ARE YOU SURE?
YEAH. FOR A PSYCHOTIC LUNATIC, HE'S DONE WELL FOR HIMSELF.
BET HE MARRIED AN OLD WOMAN AND THEN PUSHED HER DOWN THE STAIRS.
MONEY GIVES HIM THE FREEDOM TO BE AS PSYCHOTIC AS HE WANTS TO BE.

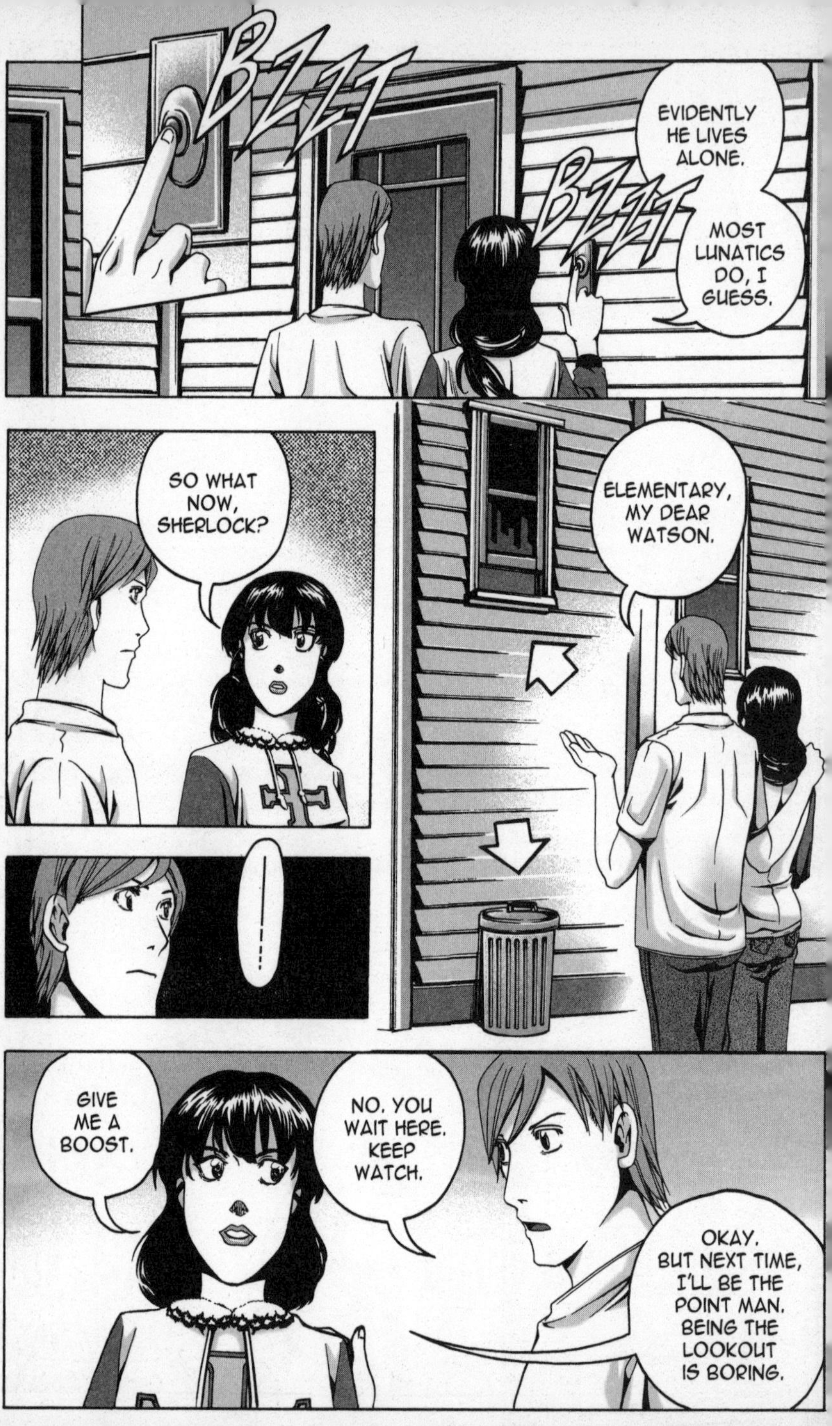
BZZT
BZZT
EVIDENTLY HE LIVES ALONE.
MOST LUNATICS DO, I GUESS.
SO WHAT NOW, SHERLOCK?
ELEMENTARY, MY DEAR WATSON.
!
GIVE ME A BOOST.
NO. YOU WAIT HERE. KEEP WATCH.
OKAY. BUT NEXT TIME, I'LL BE THE POINT MAN. BEING THE LOOKOUT IS BORING.

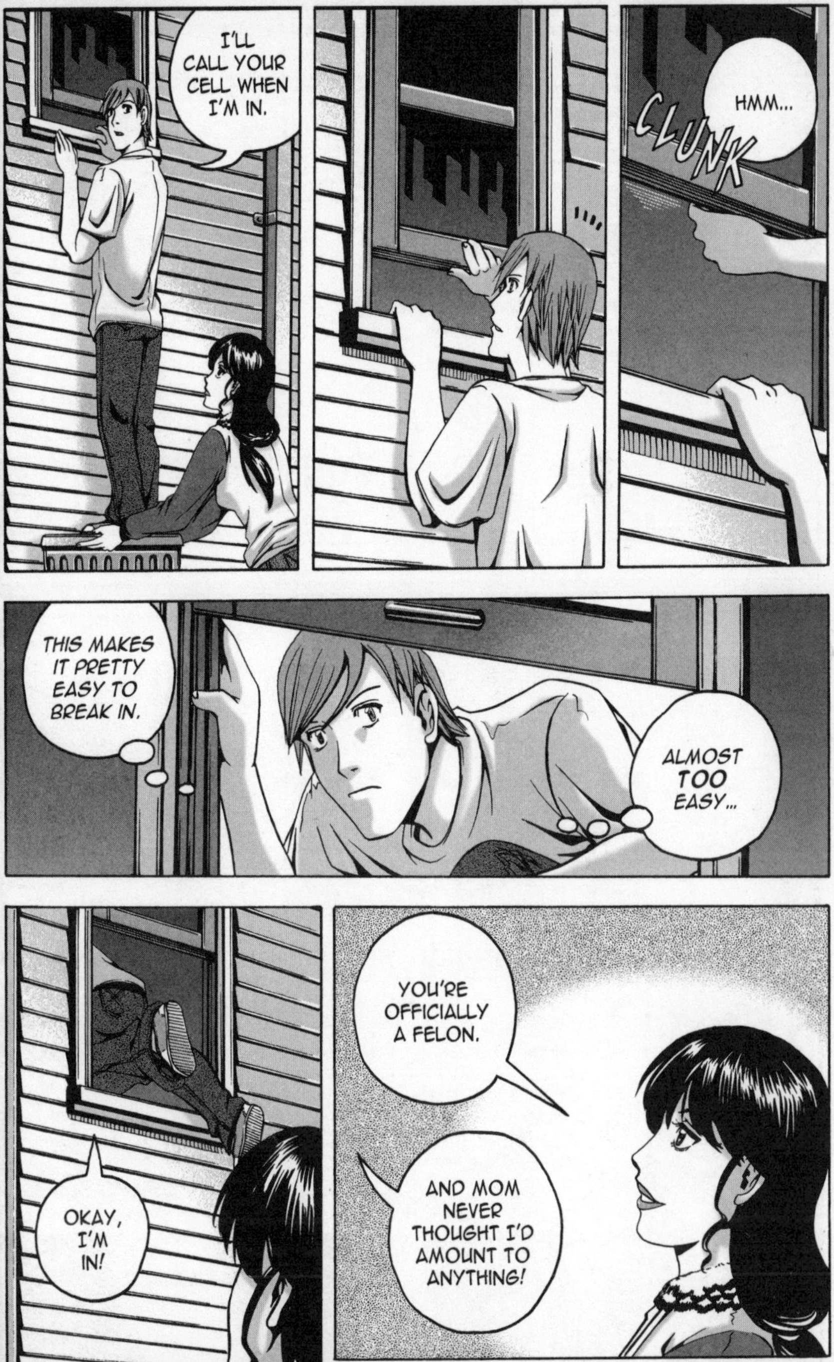
I'LL CALL YOUR CELL WHEN I'M IN.
...
CLUNK
HMM...
THIS MAKES IT PRETTY EASY TO BREAK IN.
ALMOST TOO EASY...
OKAY, I'M IN!
YOU'RE OFFICIALLY A FELON.
AND MOM NEVER THOUGHT I'D AMOUNT TO ANYTHING!

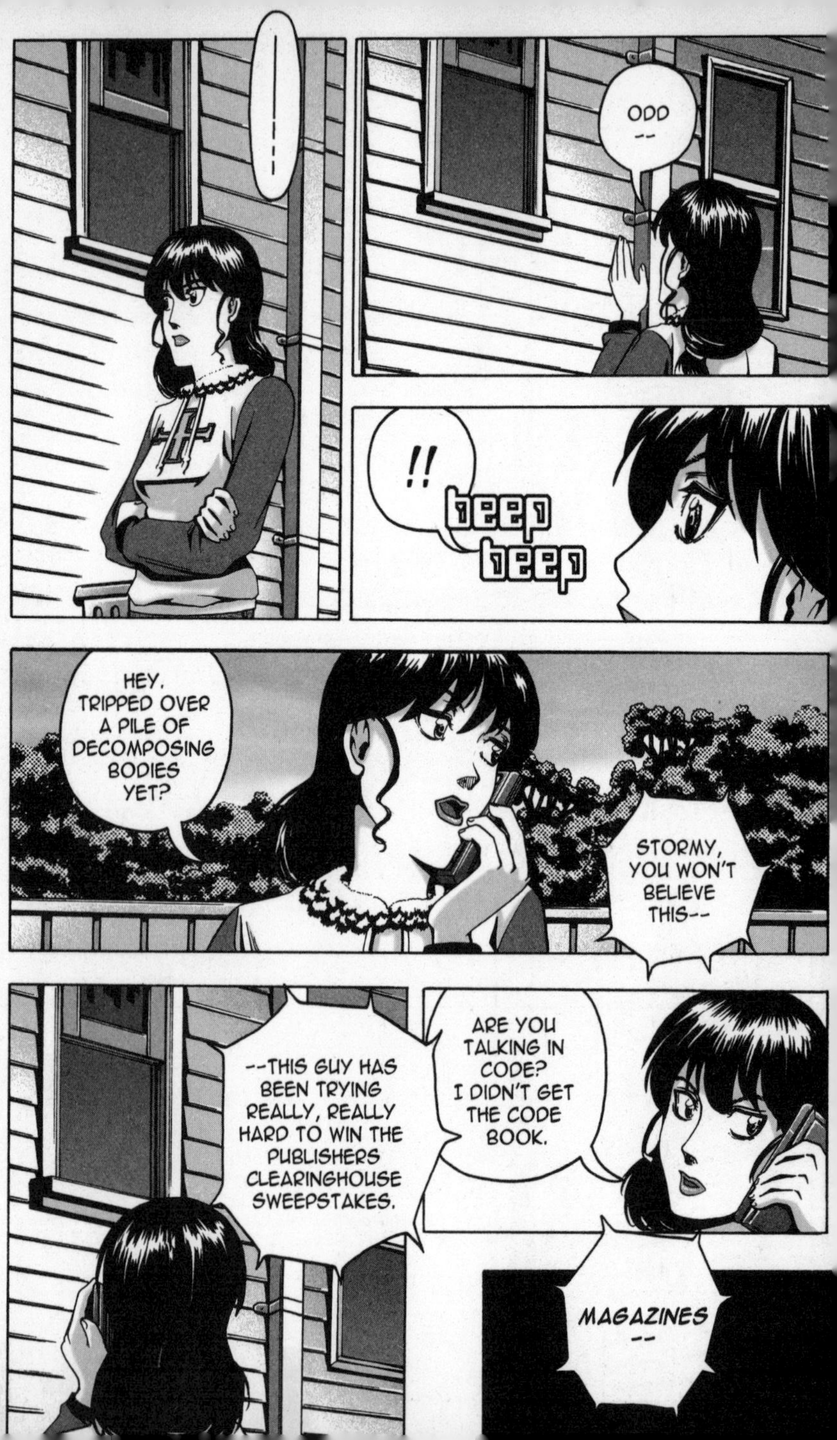
!
ODD --
!!
beep beep
HEY. TRIPPED OVER A PILE OF DECOMPOSING BODIES YET?
STORMY, YOU WON'T BELIEVE THIS--
--THIS GUY HAS BEEN TRYING REALLY, REALLY HARD TO WIN THE PUBLISHERS CLEARINGHOUSE SWEEPSTAKES.
ARE YOU TALKING IN CODE? I DIDN'T GET THE CODE BOOK.
MAGAZINES --

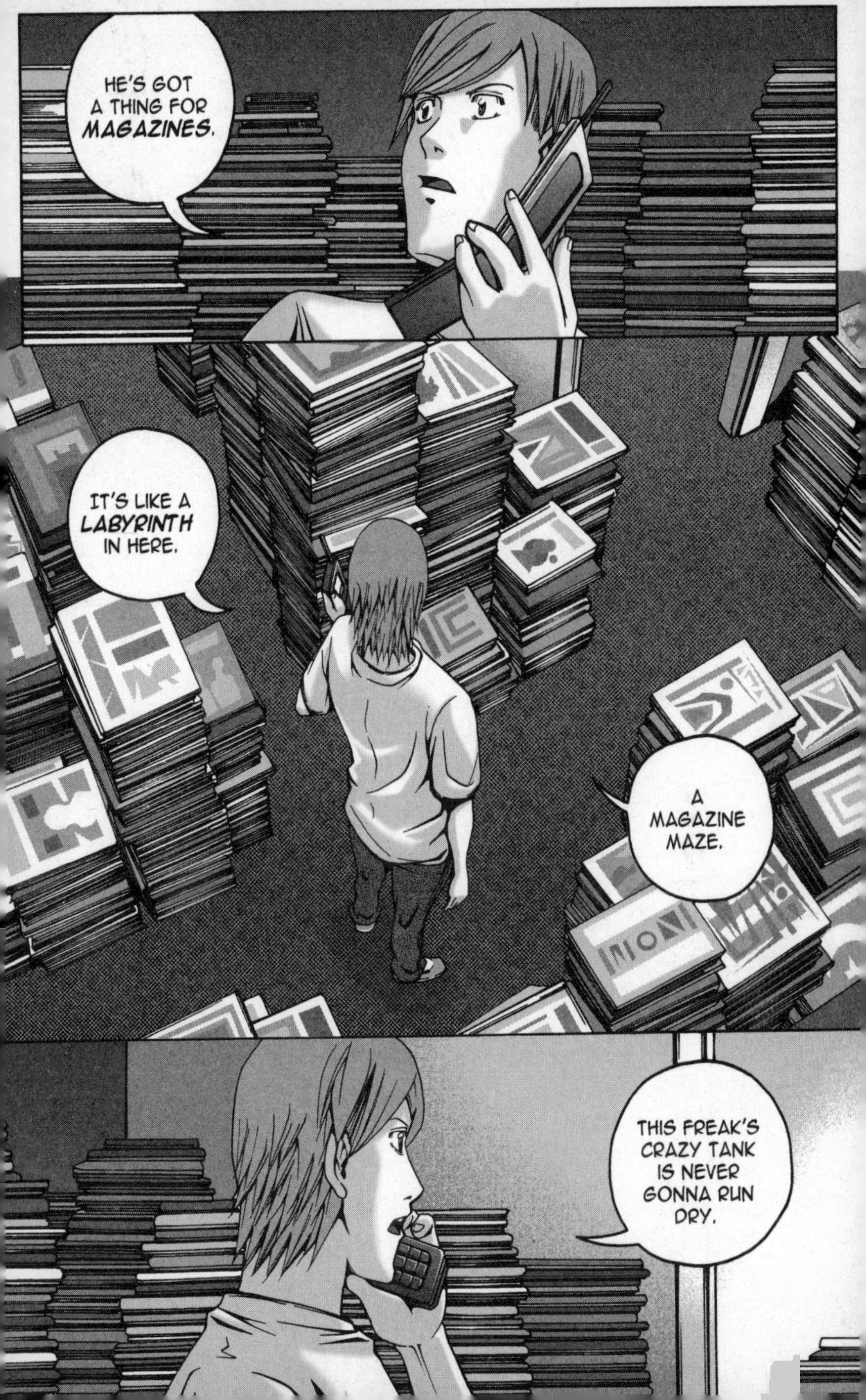
HE'S GOT A THING FOR MAGAZINES.
IT'S LIKE A LABYRINTH IN HERE.
A MAGAZINE MAZE.
THIS FREAK'S CRAZY TANK IS NEVER GONNA RUN DRY.

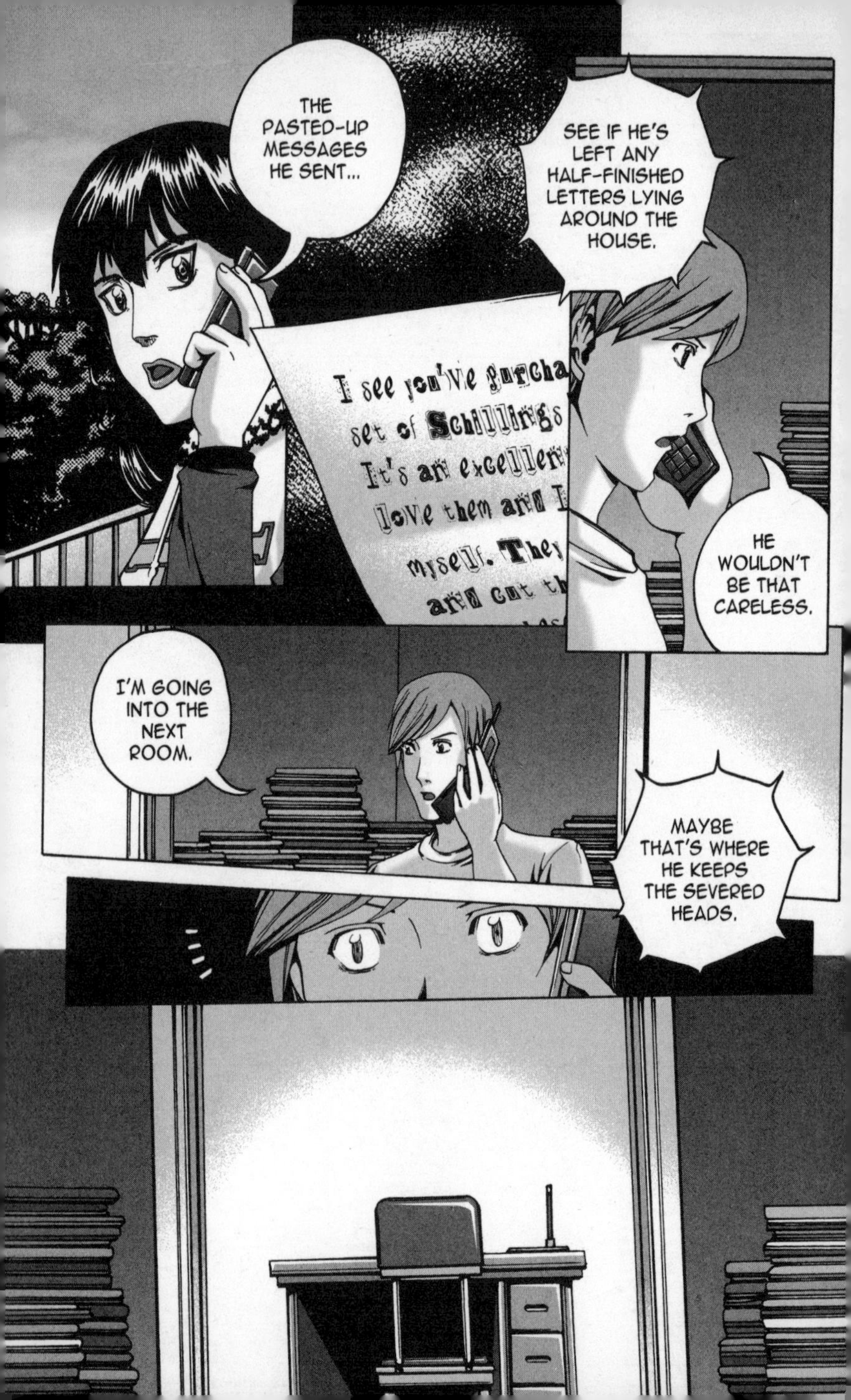
THE PASTED-UP MESSAGES HE SENT...
SEE IF HE'S LEFT ANY HALF-FINISHED LETTERS LYING AROUND THE HOUSE.
HE WOULDN'T BE THAT CARELESS.
I'M GOING INTO THE NEXT ROOM.
MAYBE THAT'S WHERE HE KEEPS THE SEVERED HEADS.

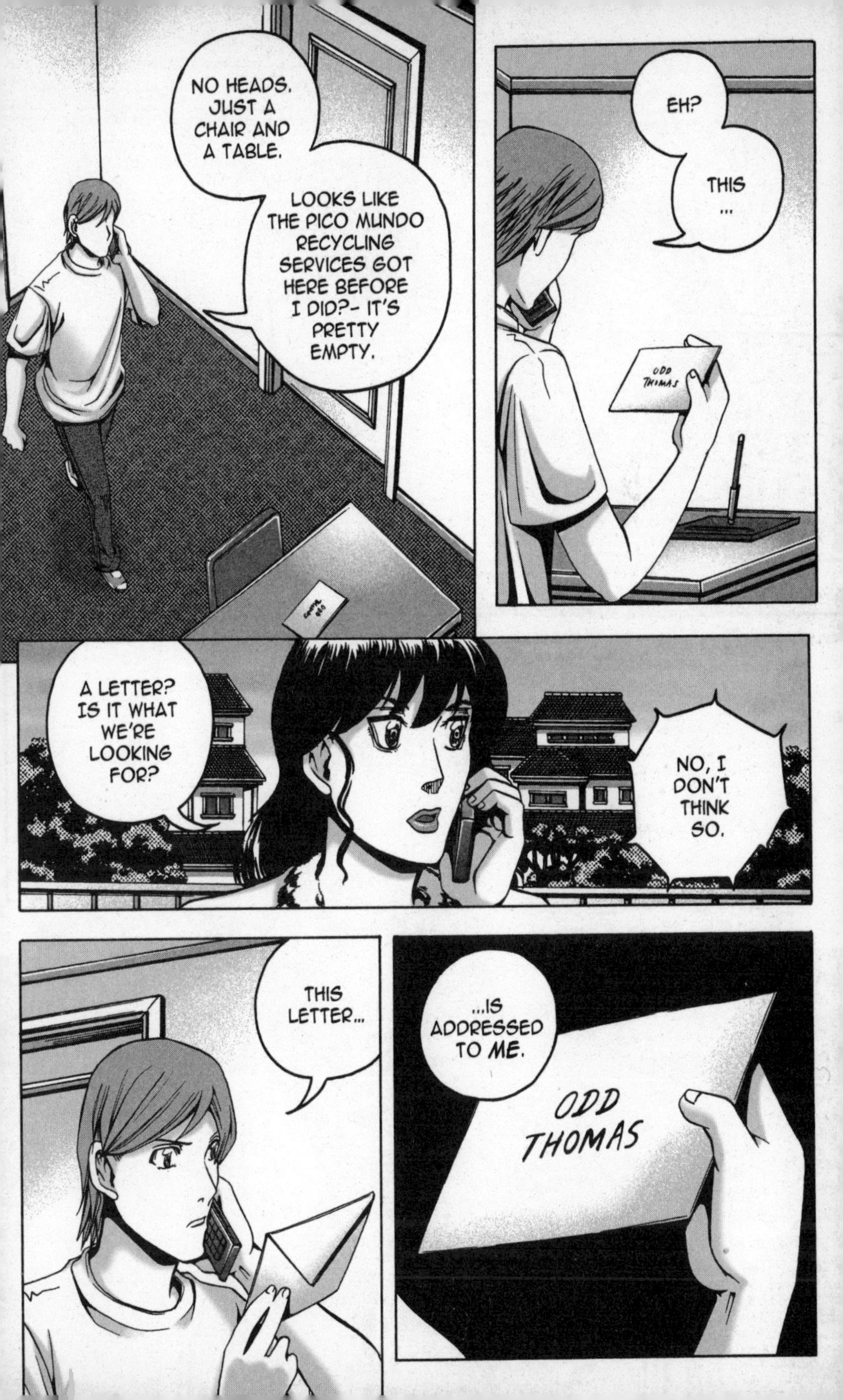
NO HEADS. JUST A CHAIR AND A TABLE.
LOOKS LIKE THE PICO MUNDO RECYCLING SERVICES GOT HERE BEFORE I DID?- IT'S PRETTY EMPTY.
EH?
THIS ...
ODD THOMAS
A LETTER? IS IT WHAT WE'RE LOOKING FOR?
NO, I DON'T THINK SO.
THIS LETTER...
...IS ADDRESSED TO ME.
ODD THOMAS

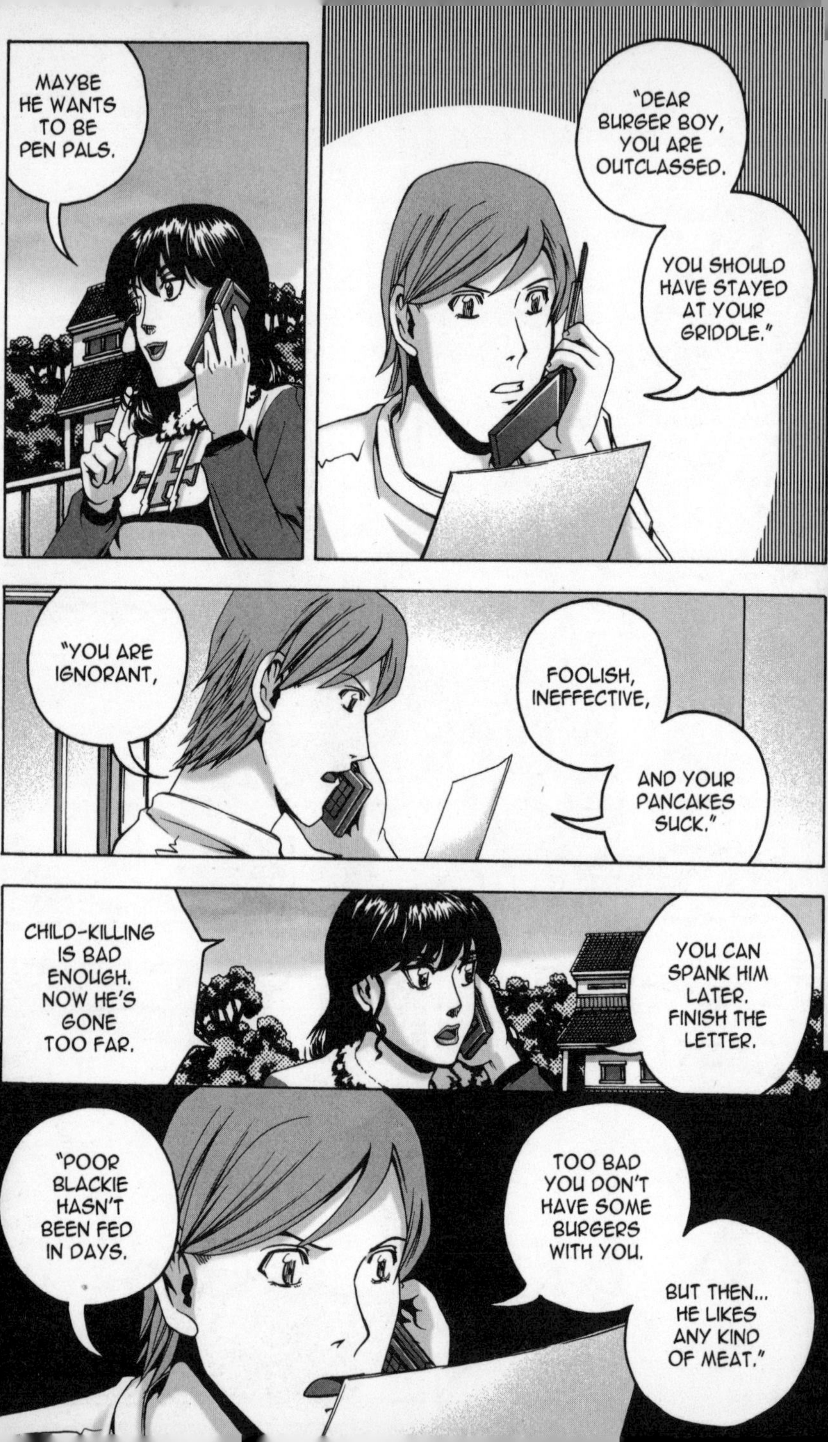
MAYBE HE WANTS TO BE PEN PALS.
"DEAR BURGER BOY, YOU ARE OUTCLASSED.
YOU SHOULD HAVE STAYED AT YOUR GRIDDLE."
"YOU ARE IGNORANT,
FOOLISH, INEFFECTIVE,
AND YOUR PANCAKES SUCK."
CHILD-KILLING IS BAD ENOUGH. NOW HE'S GONE TOO FAR.
YOU CAN SPANK HIM LATER. FINISH THE LETTER.
"POOR BLACKIE HASN'T BEEN FED IN DAYS.
TOO BAD YOU DON'T HAVE SOME BURGERS WITH YOU.
BUT THEN... HE LIKES ANY KIND OF MEAT."

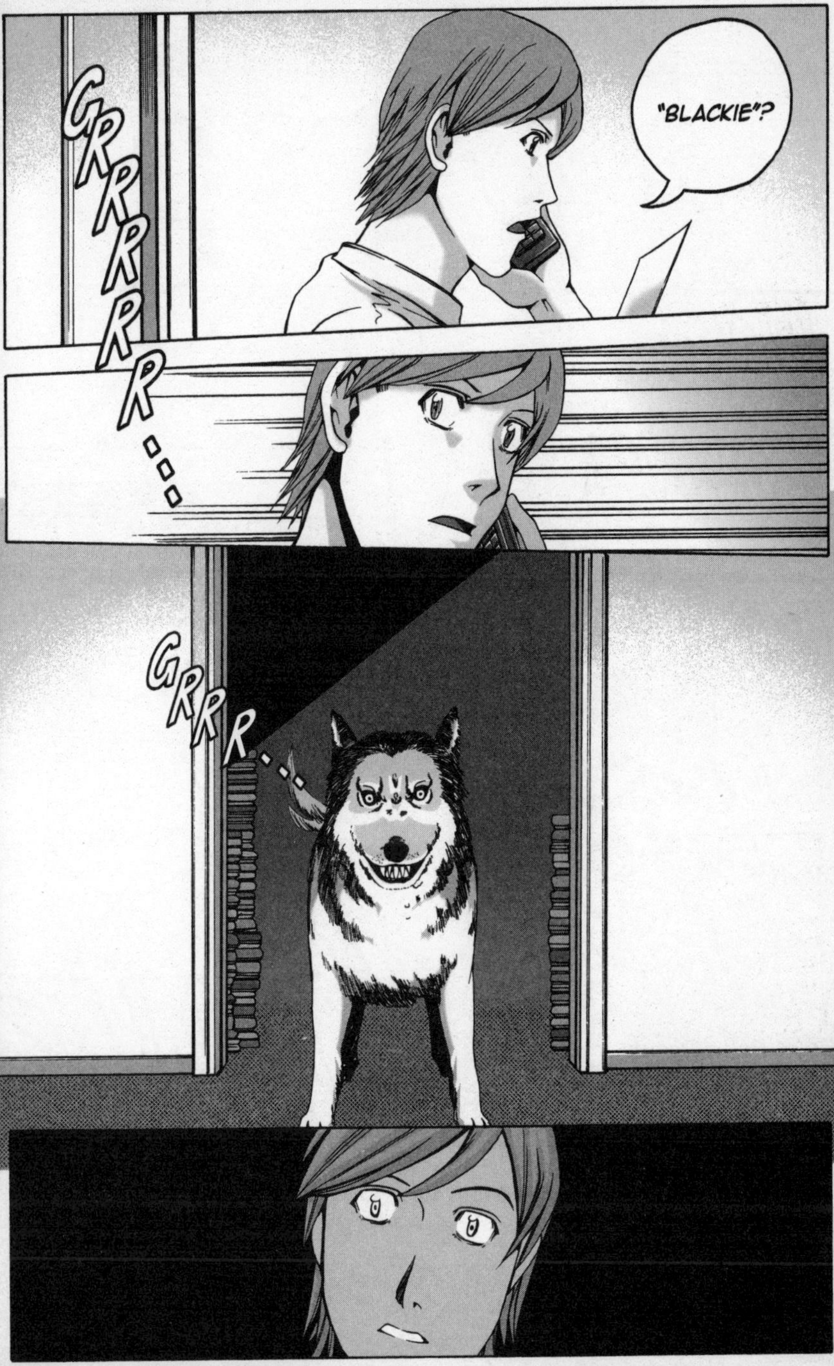
"BLACKIE"?
GRRRRRR...
GRRR...

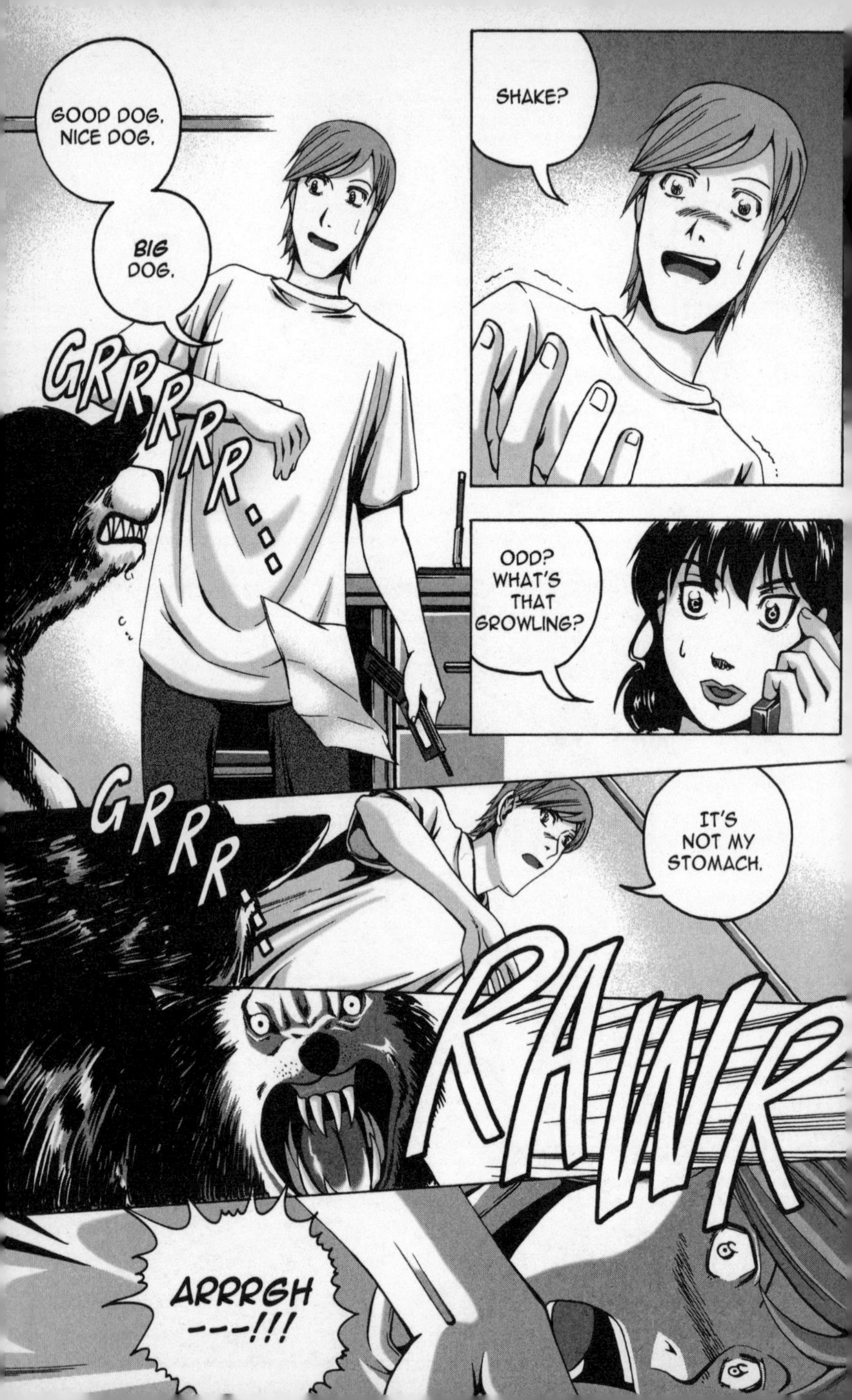
GOOD DOG. NICE DOG.
BIG DOG.
GRRRRR...
SHAKE?
ODD? WHAT'S THAT GROWLING?
GRRR...
IT'S NOT MY STOMACH.
RAWR
ARRRGH ---!!!

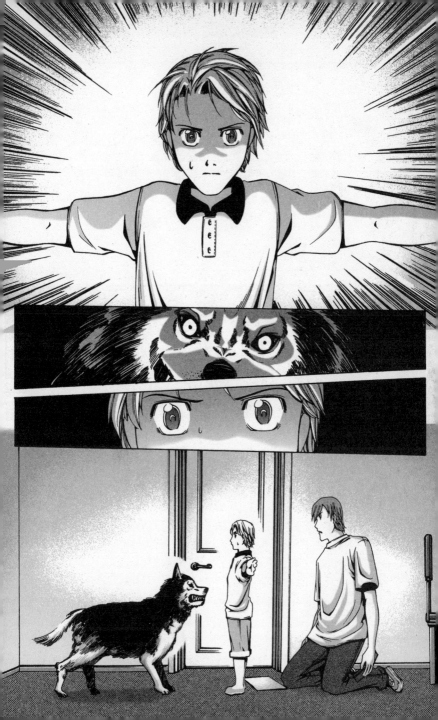

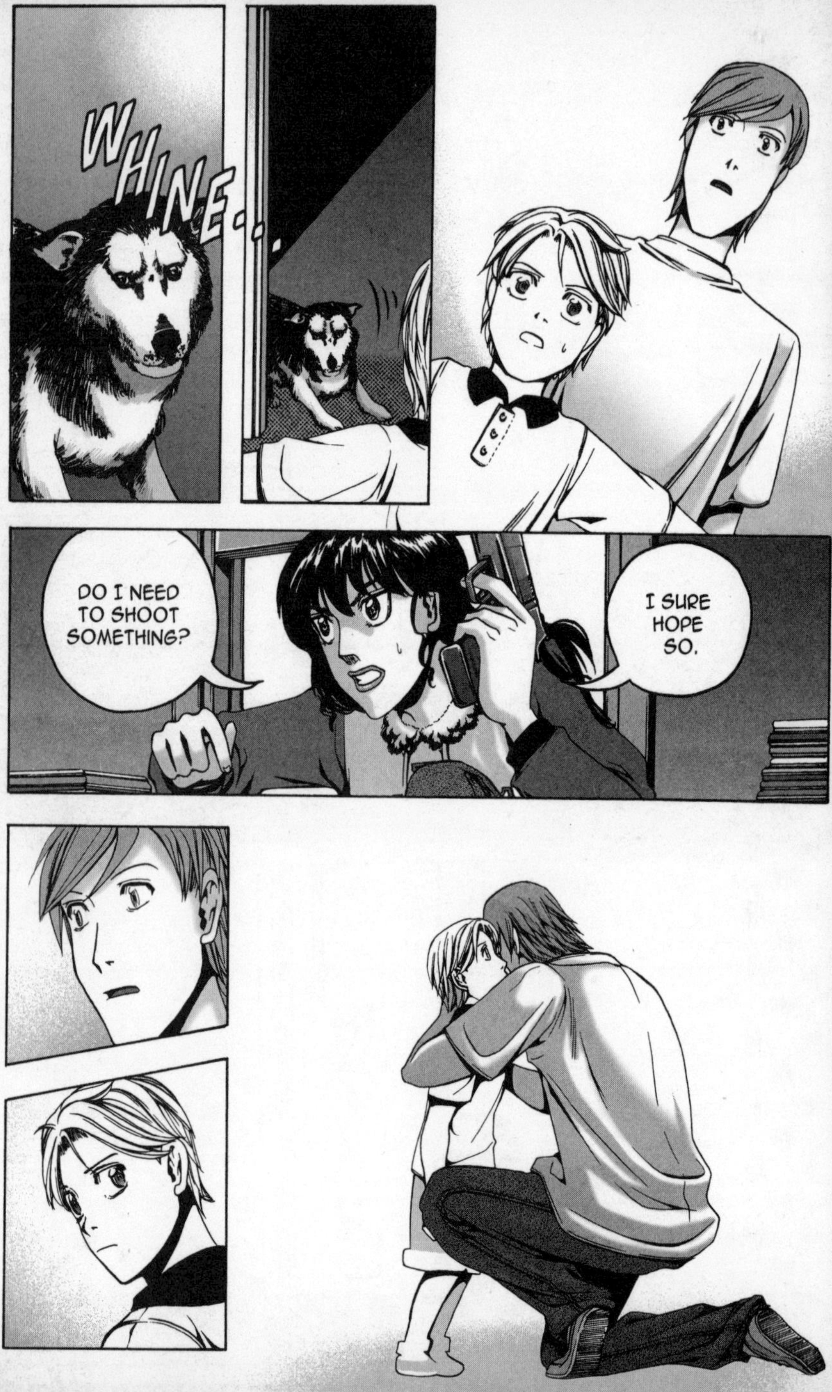
WHINE...
DO I NEED TO SHOOT SOMETHING?
I SURE HOPE SO.

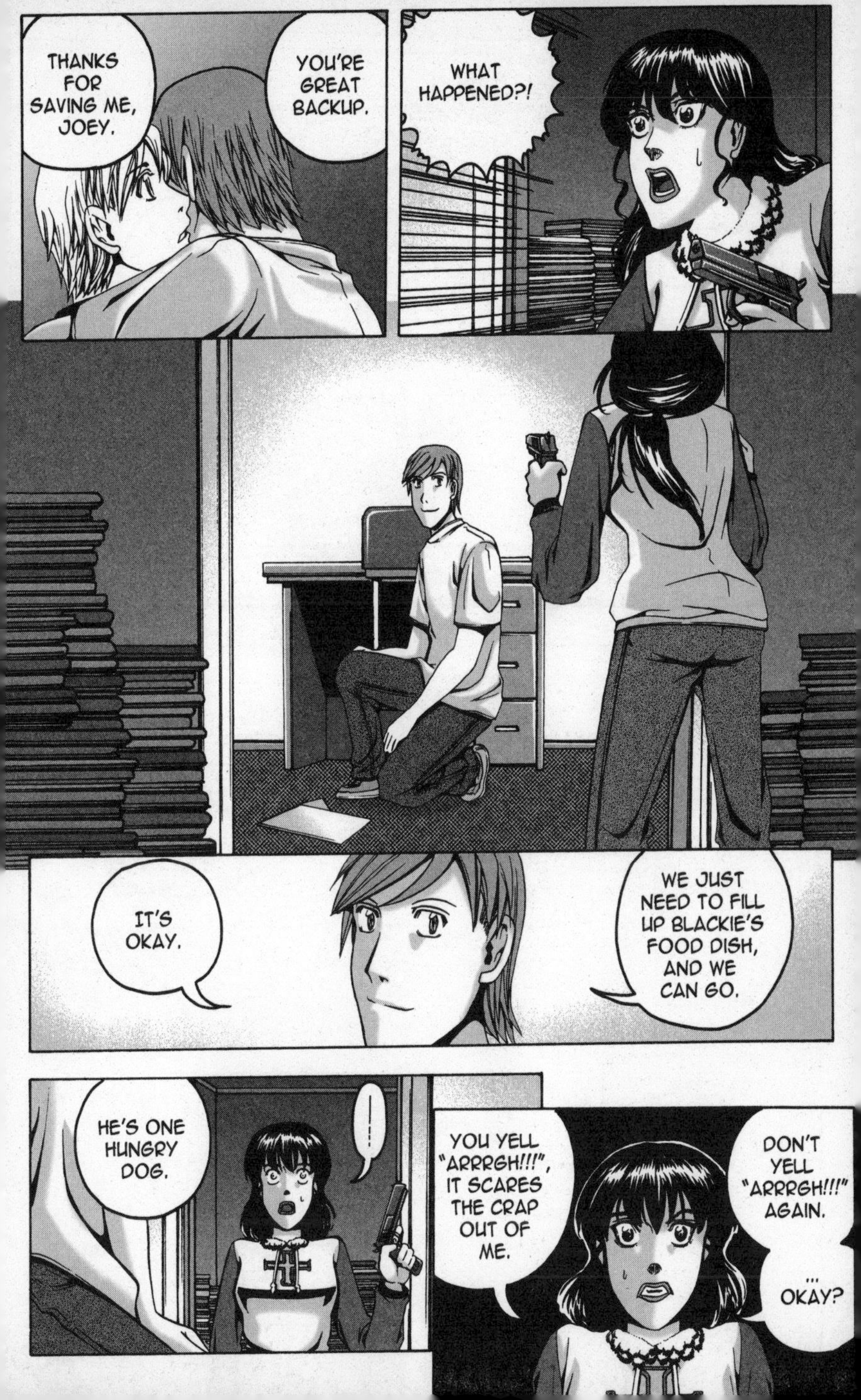
THANKS FOR SAVING ME, JOEY.
YOU'RE GREAT BACKUP.
WHAT HAPPENED?!
IT'S OKAY.
WE JUST NEED TO FILL UP BLACKIE'S FOOD DISH, AND WE CAN GO.
HE'S ONE HUNGRY DOG.
!
YOU YELL "ARRRGH!!!", IT SCARES THE CRAP OUT OF ME.
DON'T YELL "ARRRGH!!!" AGAIN.
... OKAY?

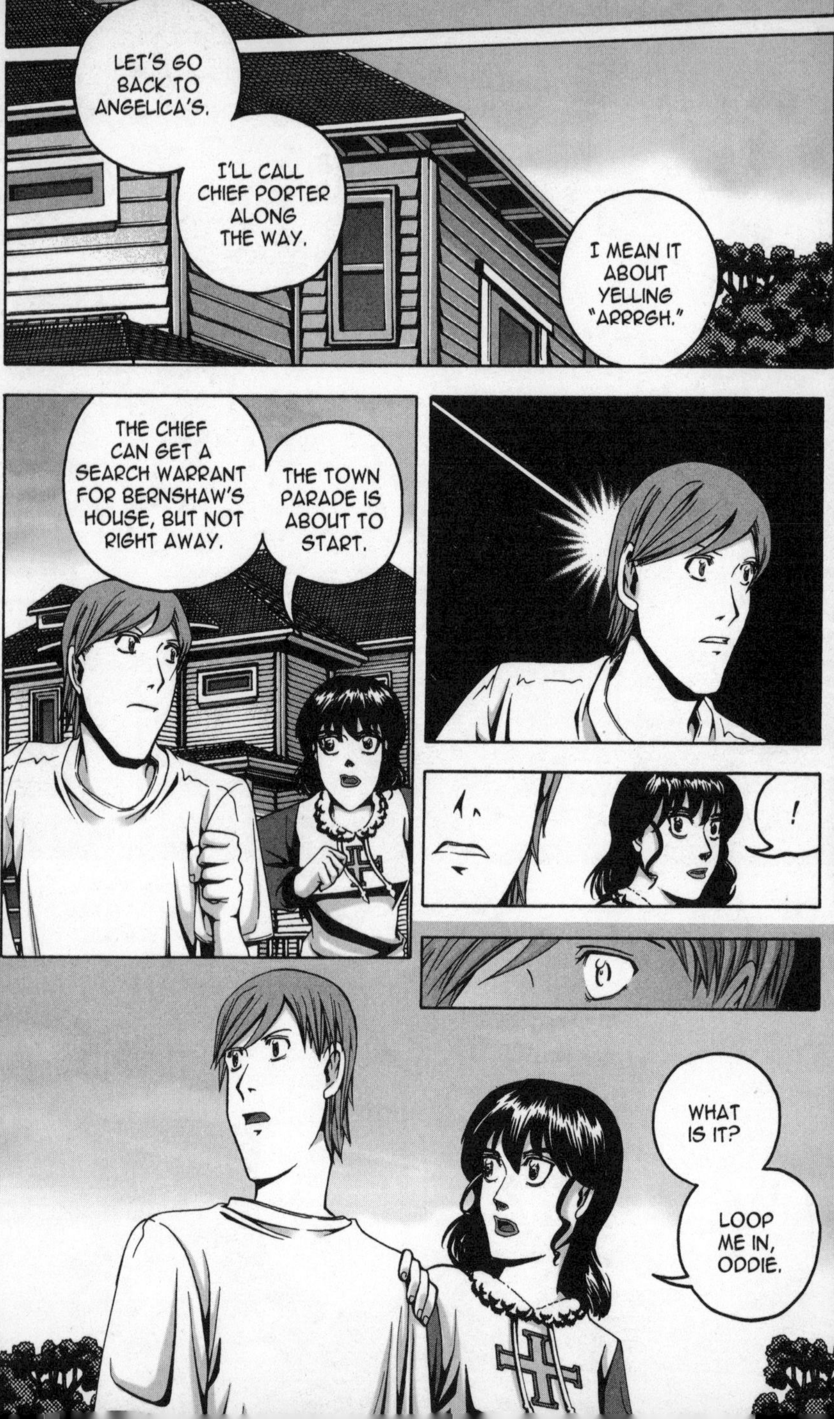
LET'S GO BACK TO ANGELICA'S.
I'LL CALL CHIEF PORTER ALONG THE WAY.
I MEAN IT ABOUT YELLING "ARRRGH."
THE CHIEF CAN GET A SEARCH WARRANT FOR BERNSHAW'S HOUSE, BUT NOT RIGHT AWAY.
THE TOWN PARADE IS ABOUT TO START.
!
WHAT IS IT?
LOOP ME IN, ODDIE.

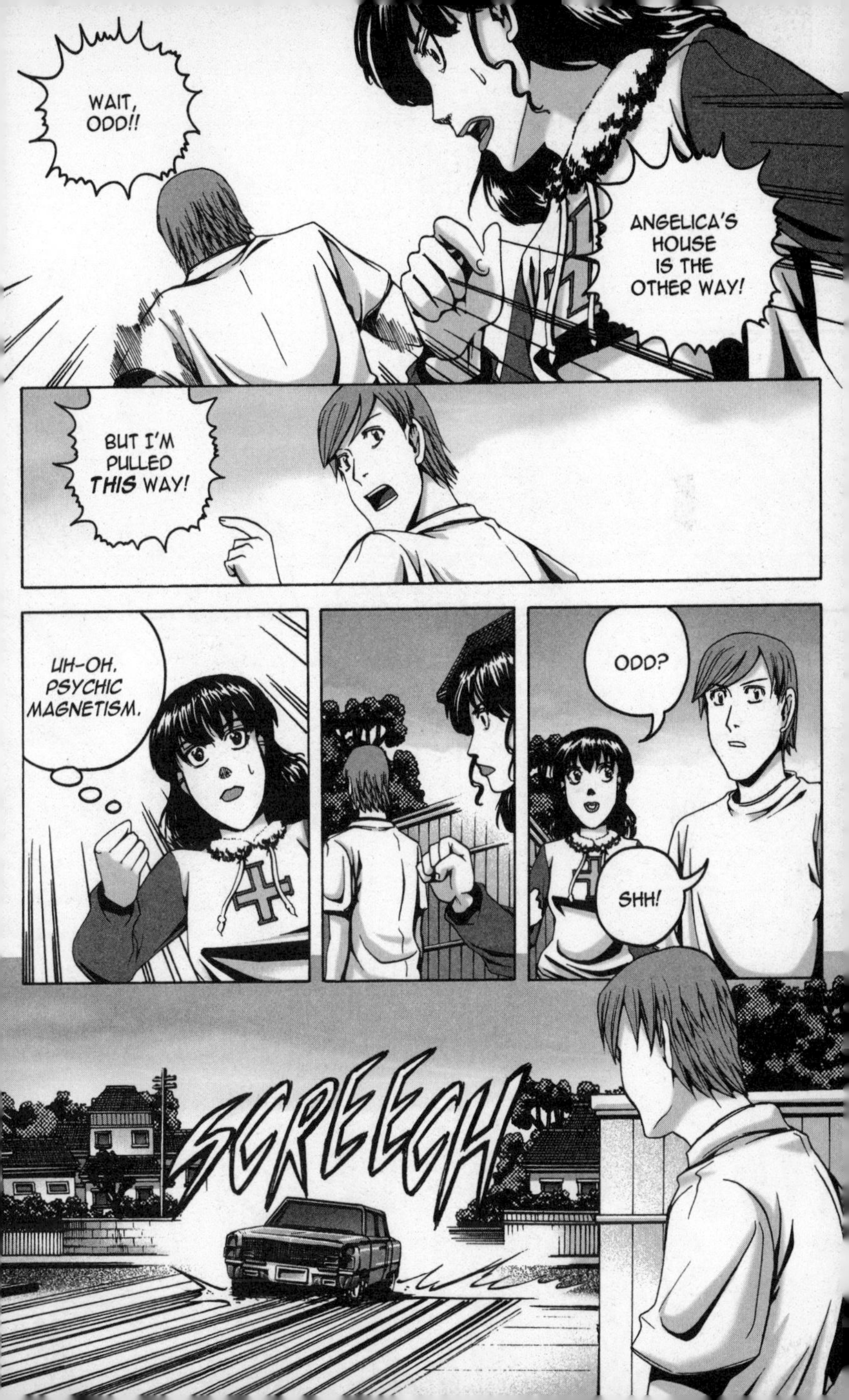
WAIT, ODD!!
ANGELICA'S HOUSE IS THE OTHER WAY!
BUT I'M PULLED THIS WAY!
UH-OH. PSYCHIC MAGNETISM.
ODD?
SHH!
SCREECH

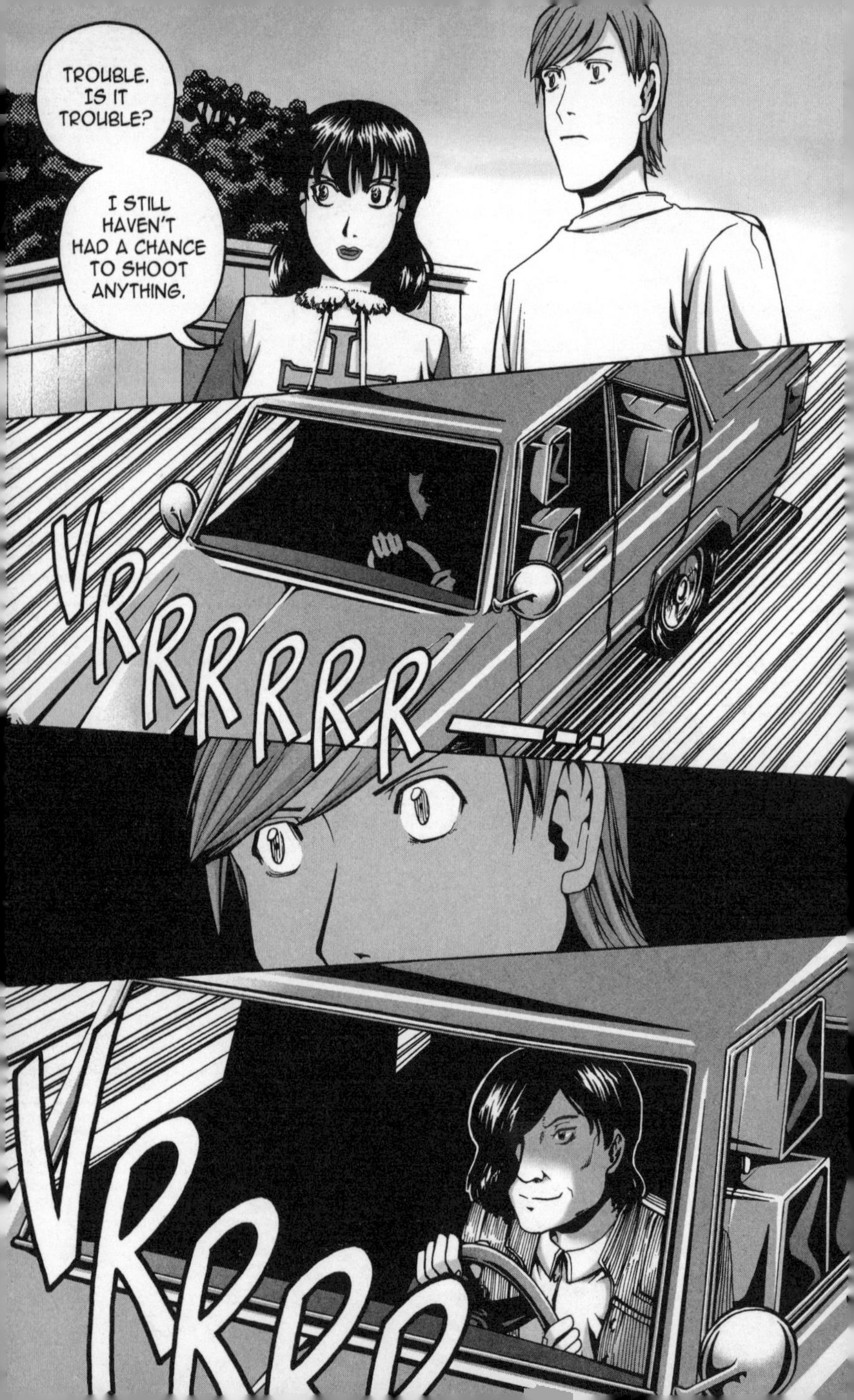
TROUBLE. IS IT TROUBLE?
I STILL HAVEN'T HAD A CHANCE TO SHOOT ANYTHING.
VRRRRRRR
VRRRR

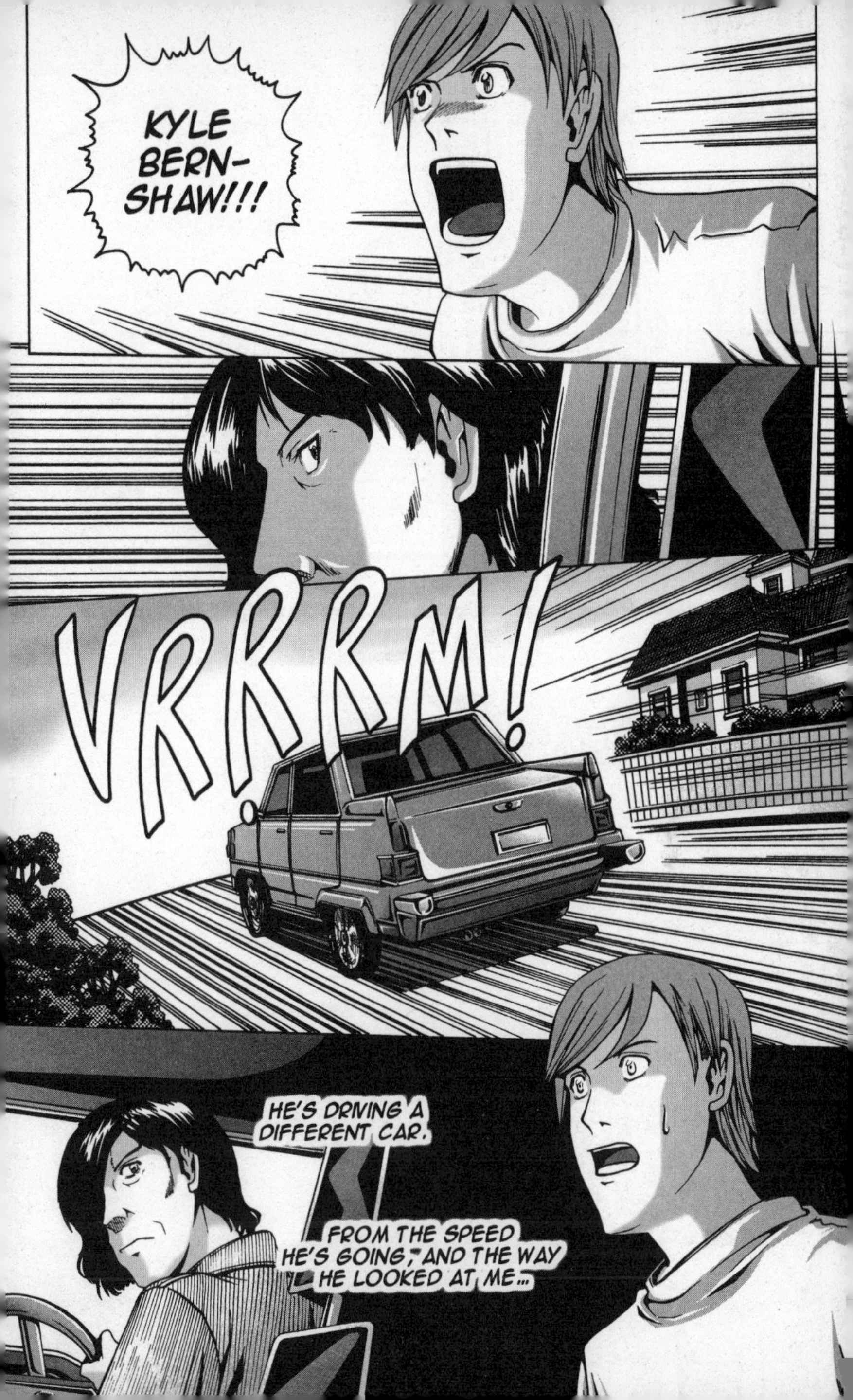
KYLE BERN-SHAW!!!
VRRRM!
HE'S DRIVING A DIFFERENT CAR.
FROM THE SPEED HE'S GOING, AND THE WAY HE LOOKED AT ME...

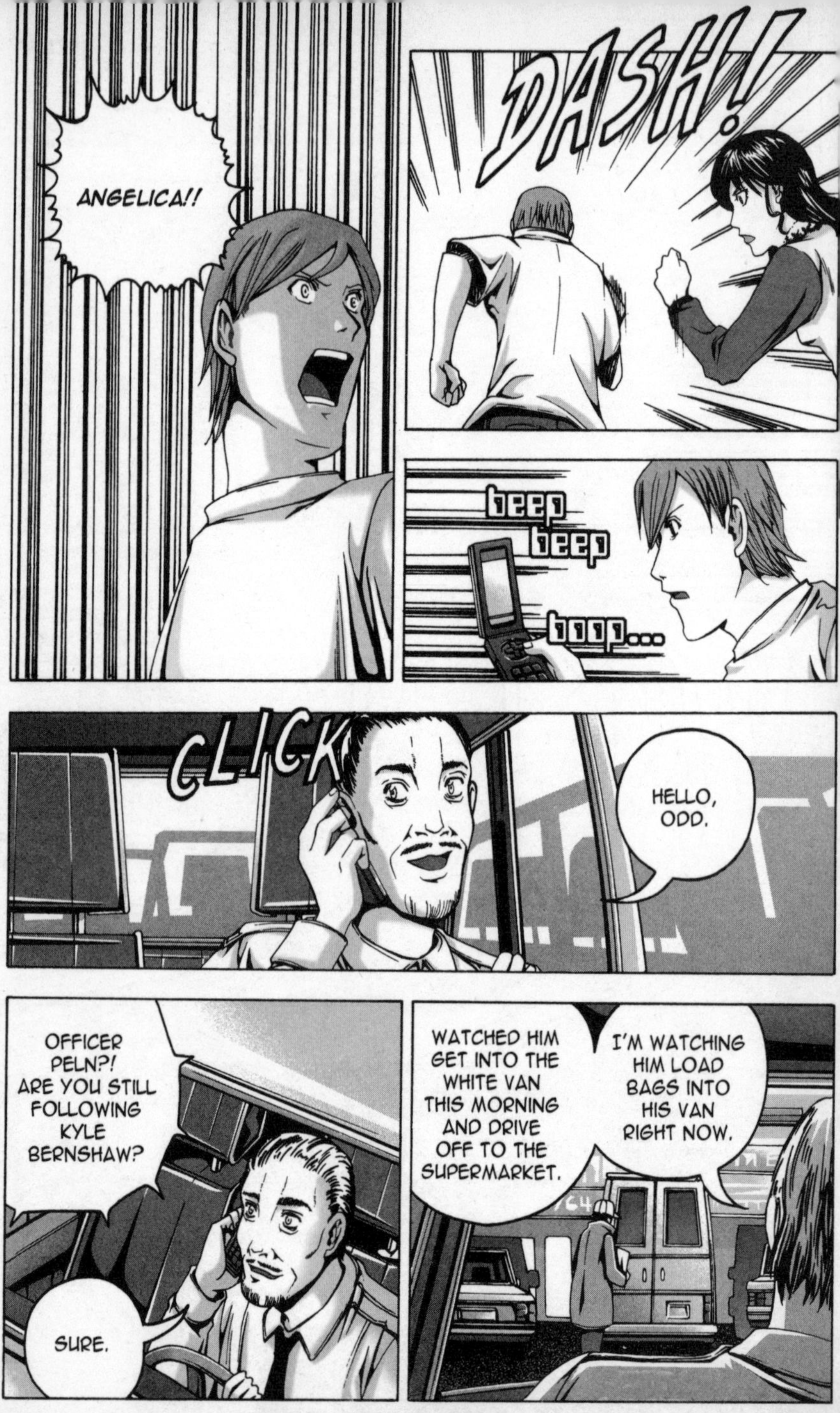
ANGELICA!!
DASH!
beep
beep
boop...
CLICK
HELLO, ODD.
OFFICER PELN?! ARE YOU STILL FOLLOWING KYLE BERNSHAW?
SURE.
WATCHED HIM GET INTO THE WHITE VAN THIS MORNING AND DRIVE OFF TO THE SUPERMARKET.
I'M WATCHING HIM LOAD BAGS INTO HIS VAN RIGHT NOW.

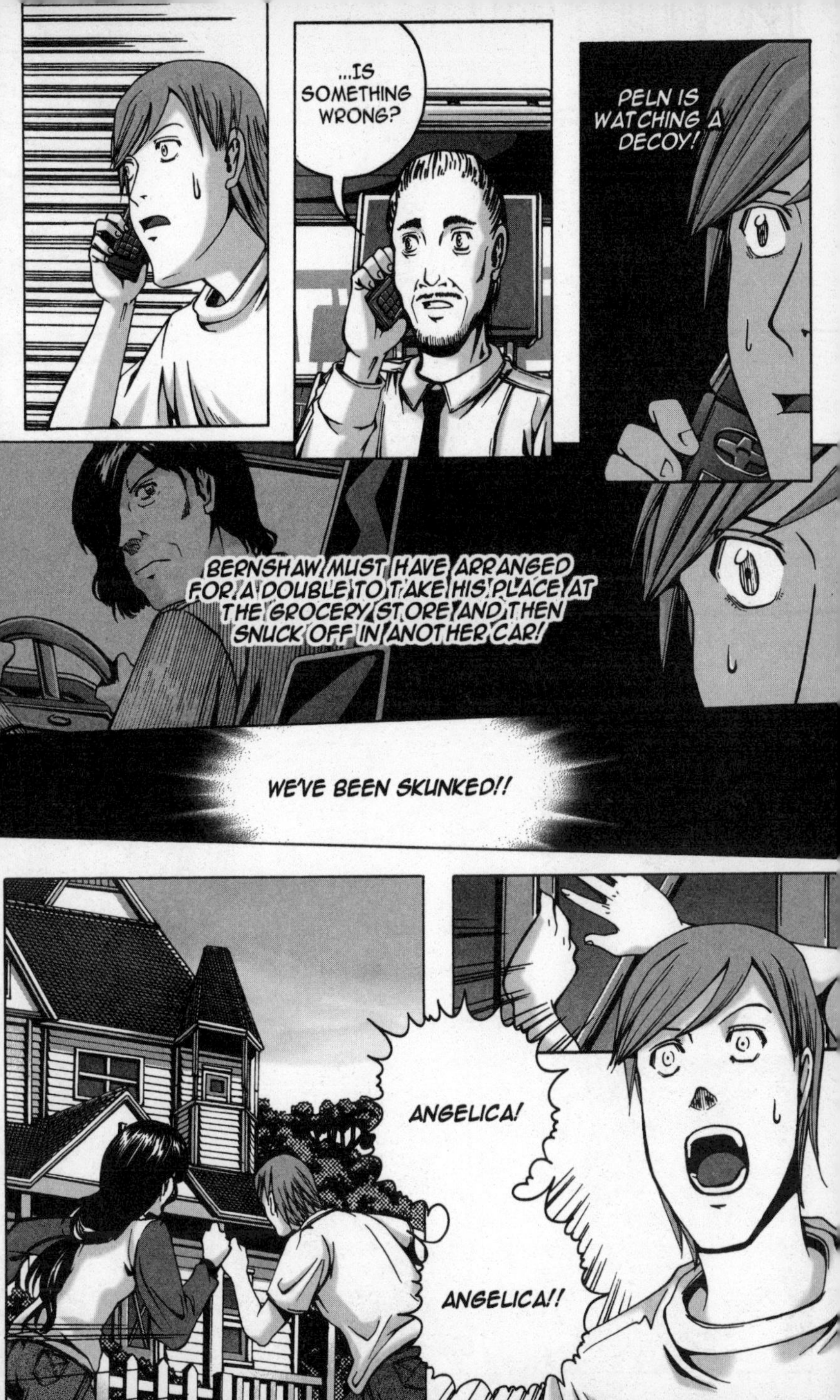
...IS SOMETHING WRONG?
PELN IS WATCHING A DECOY!
BERNSHAW MUST HAVE ARRANGED FOR A DOUBLE TO TAKE HIS PLACE AT THE GROCERY STORE AND THEN SNUCK OFF IN ANOTHER CAR!
WE'VE BEEN SKUNKED!!
ANGELICA!
ANGELICA!!

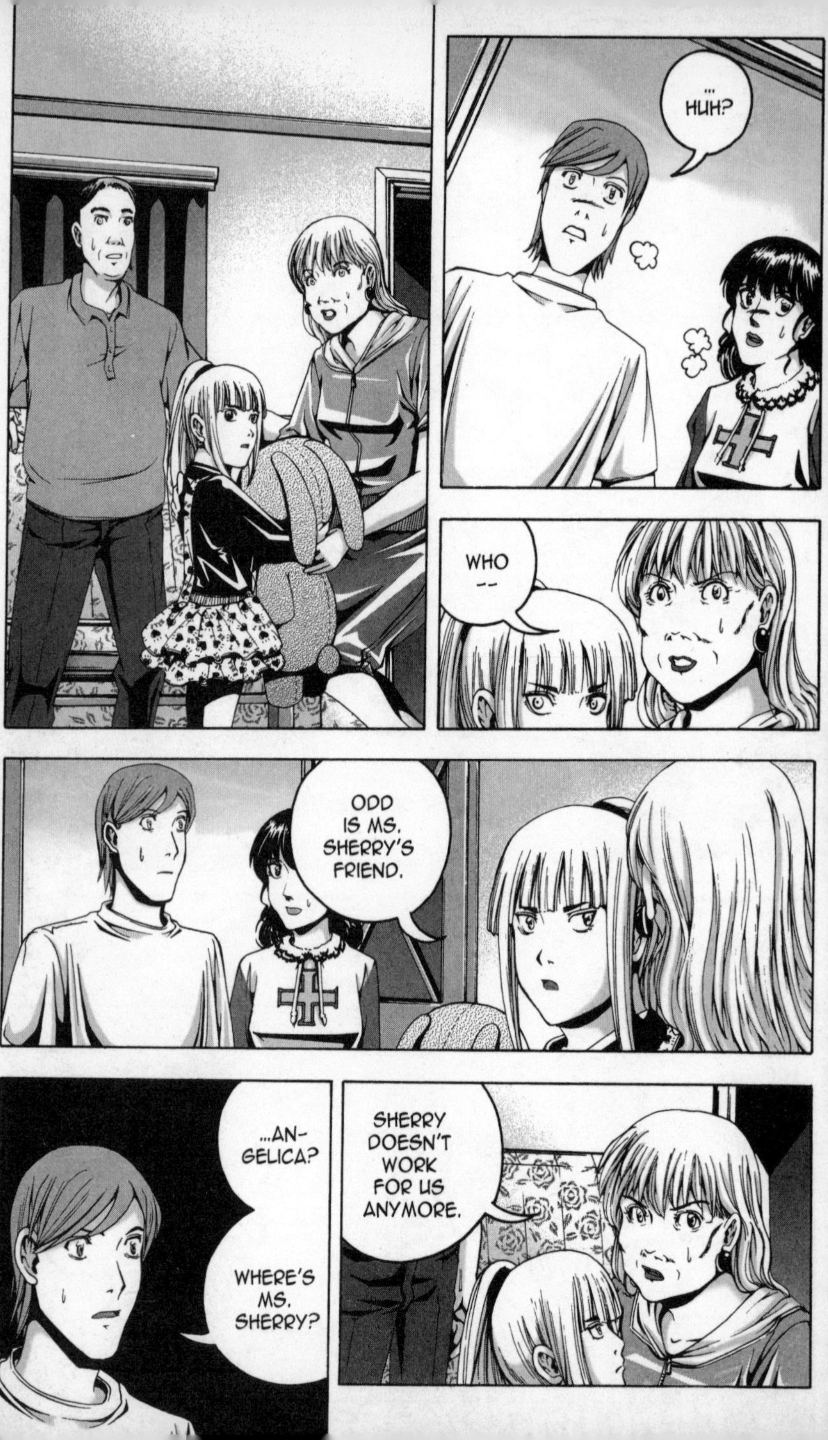

... HUH?
WHO --
ODD IS MS. SHERRY'S FRIEND.
...AN-GELICA?
WHERE'S MS. SHERRY?
SHERRY DOESN'T WORK FOR US ANYMORE.

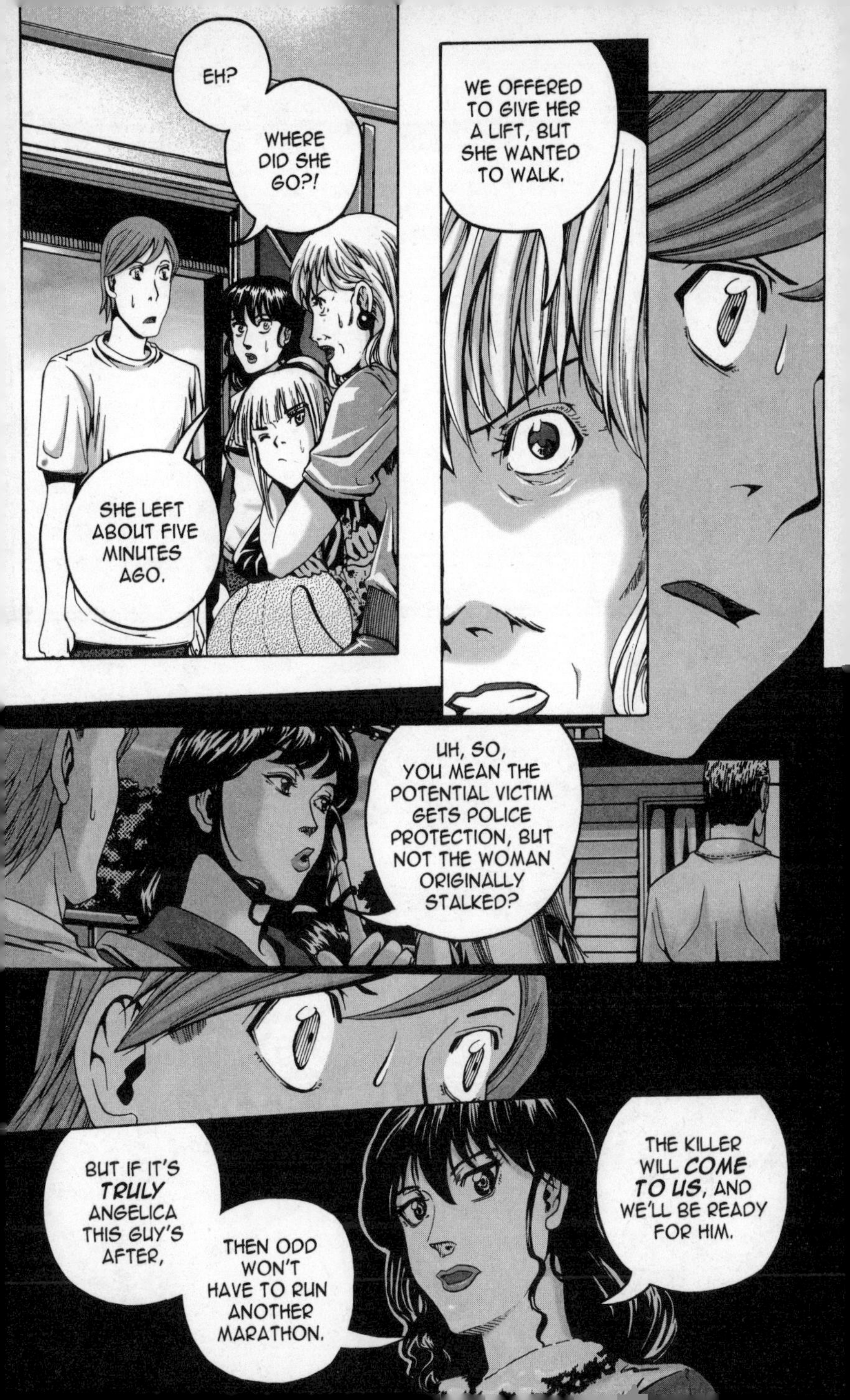
EH?
WHERE DID SHE GO?!
SHE LEFT ABOUT FIVE MINUTES AGO.
WE OFFERED TO GIVE HER A LIFT, BUT SHE WANTED TO WALK.
UH, SO, YOU MEAN THE POTENTIAL VICTIM GETS POLICE PROTECTION, BUT NOT THE WOMAN ORIGINALLY STALKED?
BUT IF IT'S TRULY ANGELICA THIS GUY'S AFTER,
THEN ODD WON'T HAVE TO RUN ANOTHER MARATHON.
THE KILLER WILL COME TO US, AND WE'LL BE READY FOR HIM.

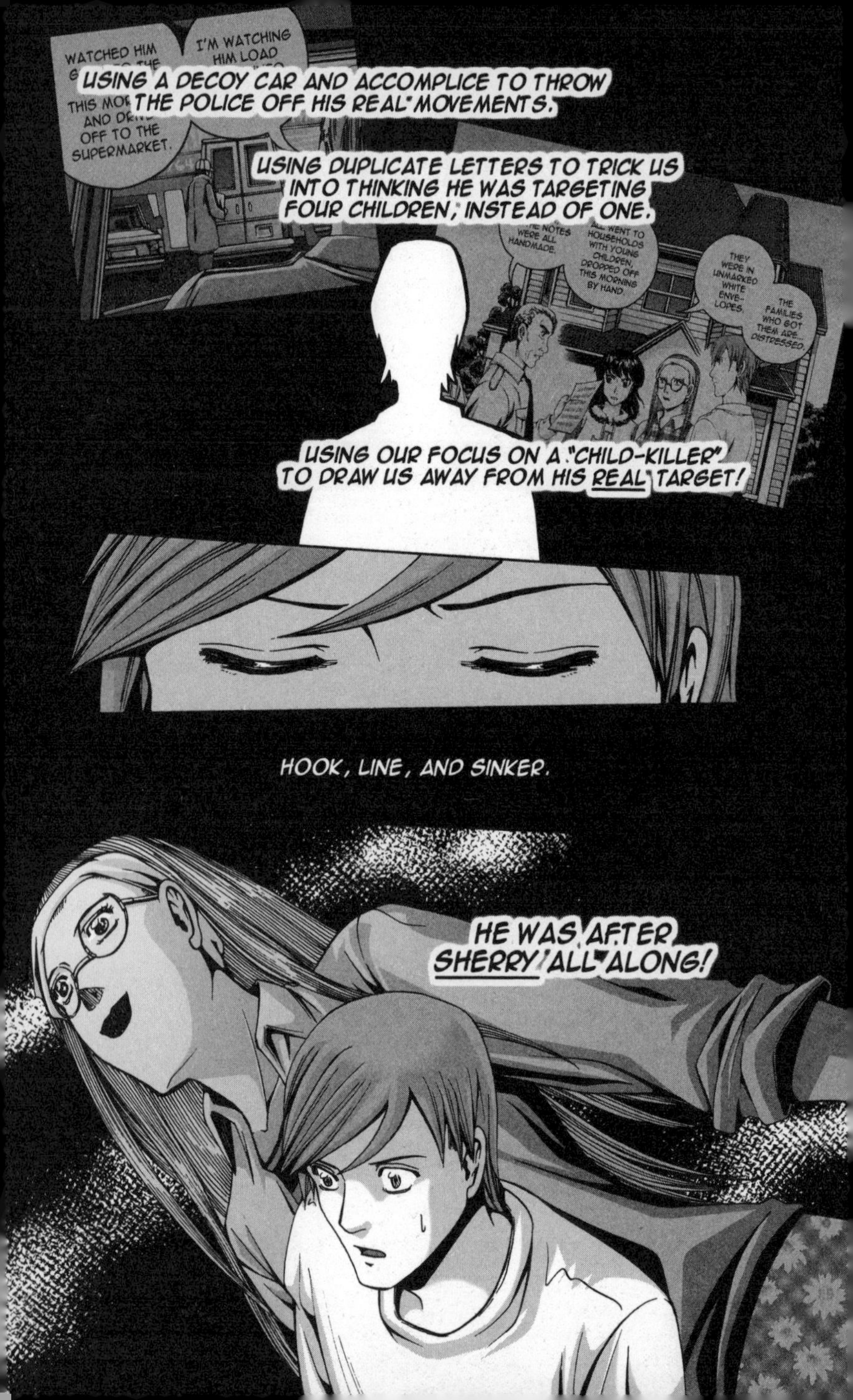
I'M WATCHING HIM LOAD
OFF TO THE SUPERMARKET.
USING A DECOY CAR AND ACCOMPLICE TO THROW THE POLICE OFF HIS REAL MOVEMENTS.
USING DUPLICATE LETTERS TO TRICK US INTO THINKING HE WAS TARGETING FOUR CHILDREN, INSTEAD OF ONE.
NOTES WERE ALL HANDMADE.
WENT TO HOUSEHOLDS WITH YOUNG CHILDREN, DROPPED OFF THIS MORNING BY HAND.
THEY WERE IN UNMARKED WHITE ENVE-LOPES.
THE FAMILIES WHO GOT THEM ARE... DISTRESSED.
USING OUR FOCUS ON A "CHILD-KILLER" TO DRAW US AWAY FROM HIS REAL TARGET!
HOOK, LINE, AND SINKER.
HE WAS AFTER SHERRY ALL ALONG!

In Odd We Trust
Chapter 6

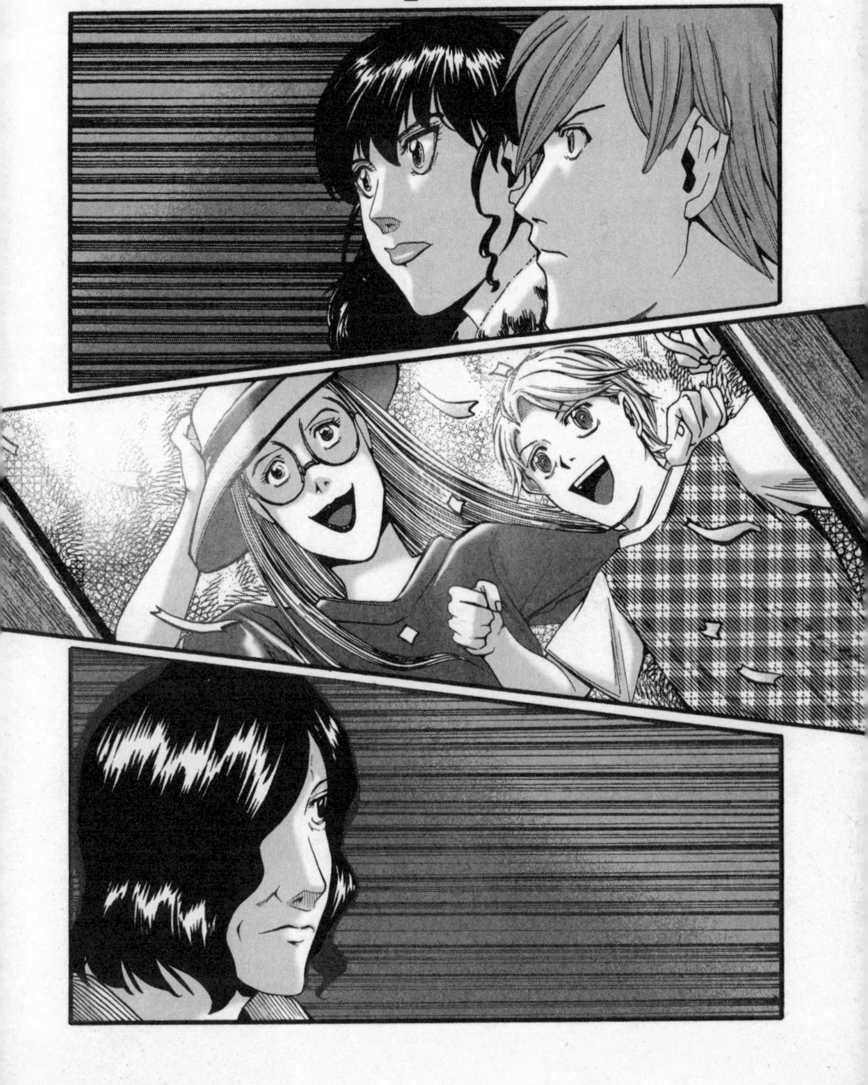

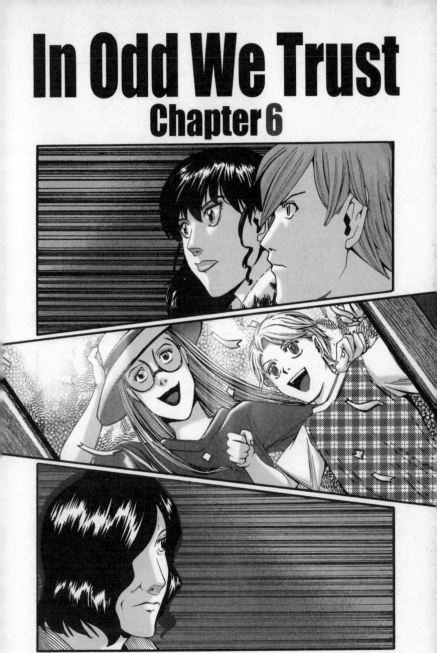

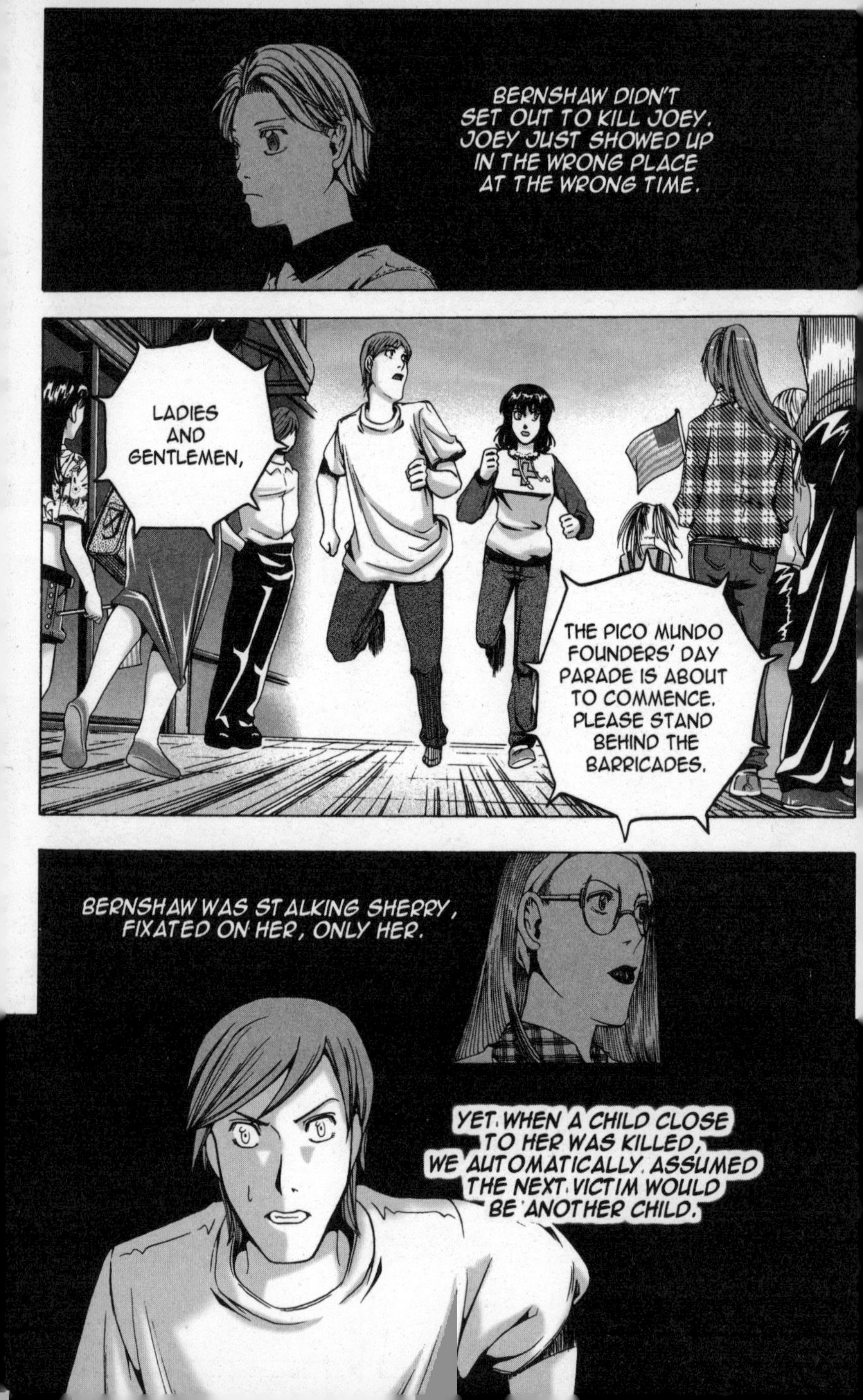
BERNSHAW DIDN'T SET OUT TO KILL JOEY. JOEY JUST SHOWED UP IN THE WRONG PLACE AT THE WRONG TIME.
LADIES AND GENTLEMEN,
THE PICO MUNDO FOUNDERS' DAY PARADE IS ABOUT TO COMMENCE. PLEASE STAND BEHIND THE BARRICADES.
BERNSHAW WAS STALKING SHERRY, FIXATED ON HER, ONLY HER.
YET WHEN A CHILD CLOSE TO HER WAS KILLED, WE AUTOMATICALLY ASSUMED THE NEXT VICTIM WOULD BE ANOTHER CHILD.

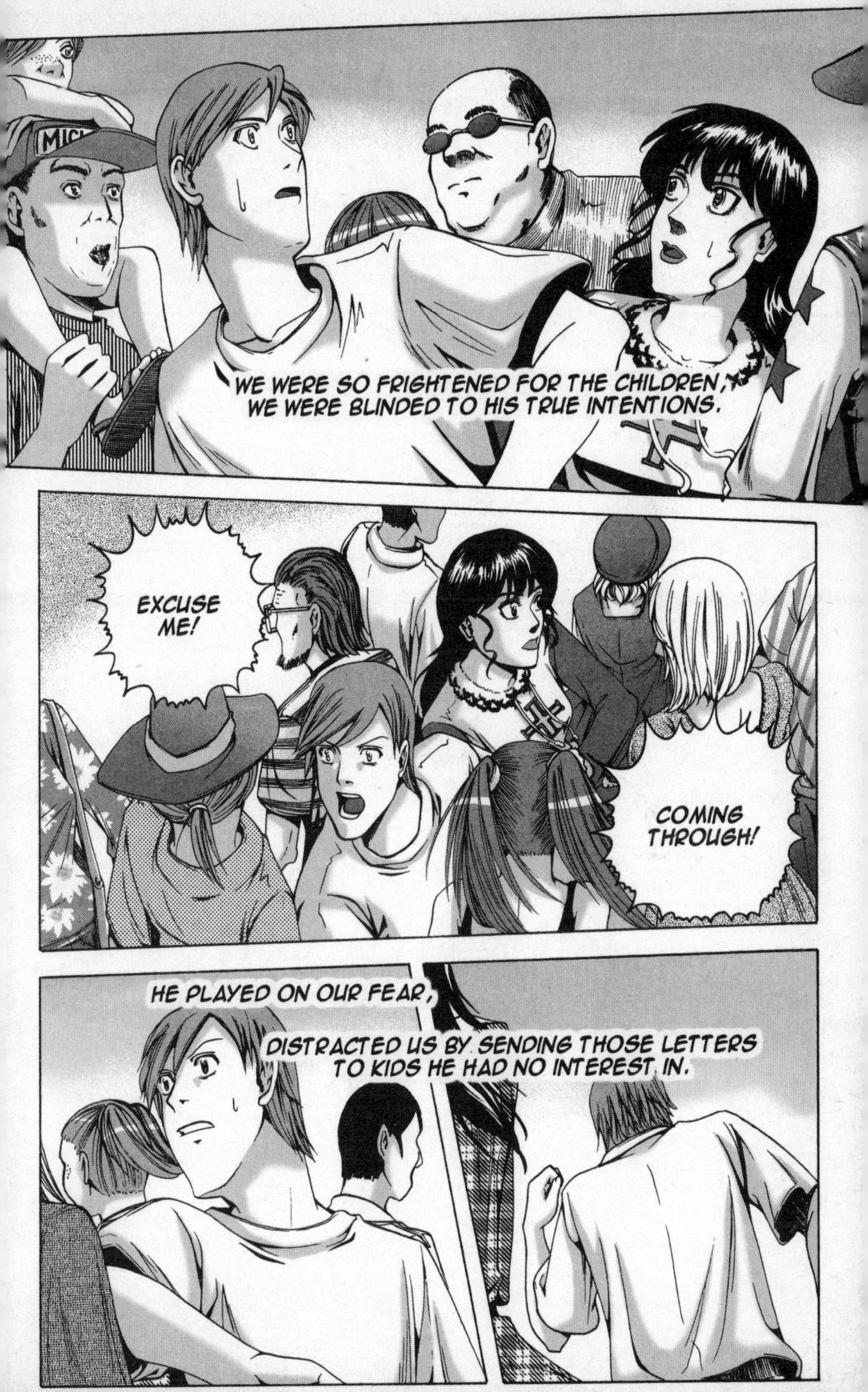
WE WERE SO FRIGHTENED FOR THE CHILDREN, WE WERE BLINDED TO HIS TRUE INTENTIONS.
EXCUSE ME!
COMING THROUGH!
HE PLAYED ON OUR FEAR,
DISTRACTED US BY SENDING THOSE LETTERS TO KIDS HE HAD NO INTEREST IN.

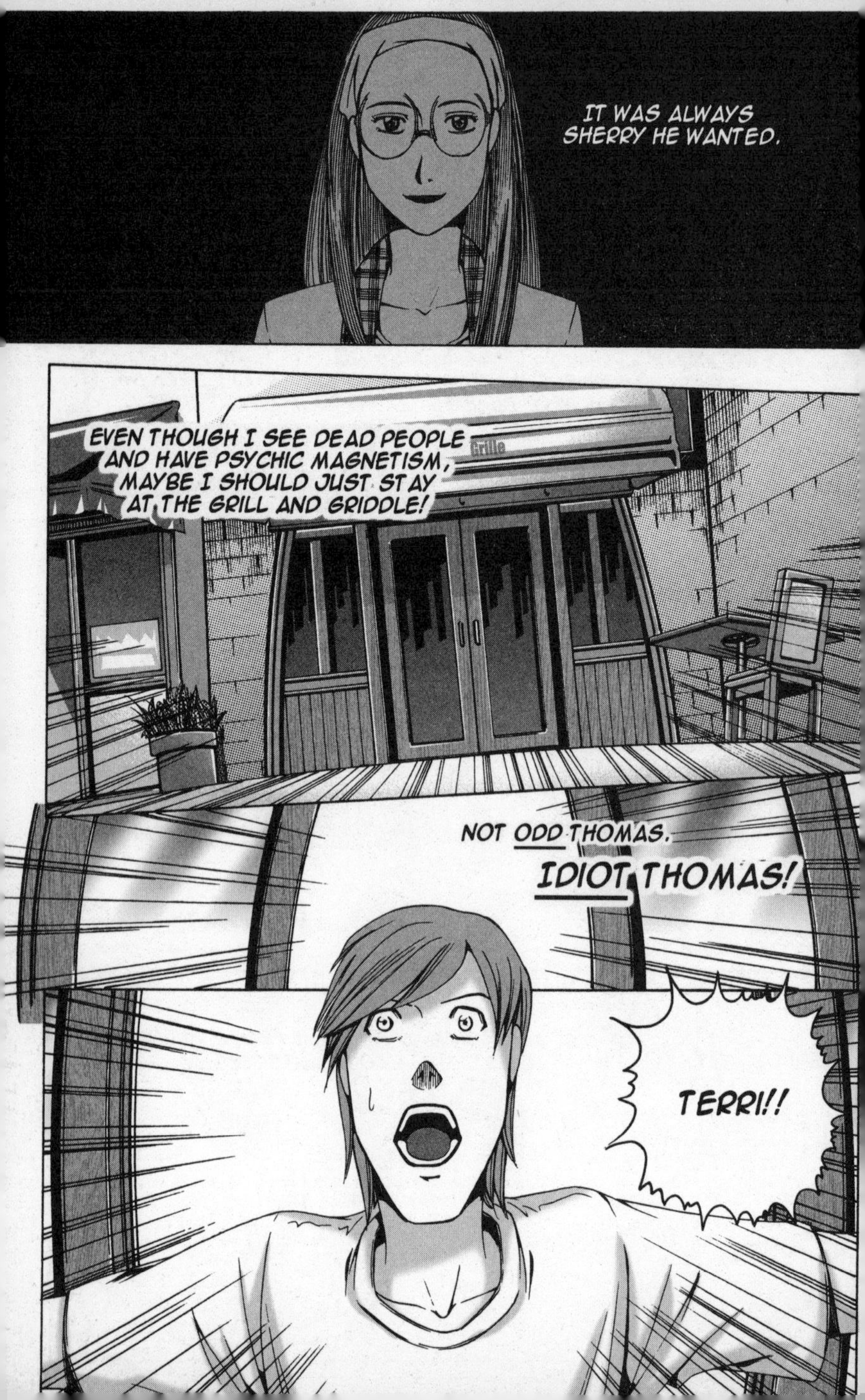
IT WAS ALWAYS SHERRY HE WANTED.
EVEN THOUGH I SEE DEAD PEOPLE AND HAVE PSYCHIC MAGNETISM, MAYBE I SHOULD JUST STAY AT THE GRILL AND GRIDDLE!
NOT ODD THOMAS.
IDIOT THOMAS!
TERRI!!

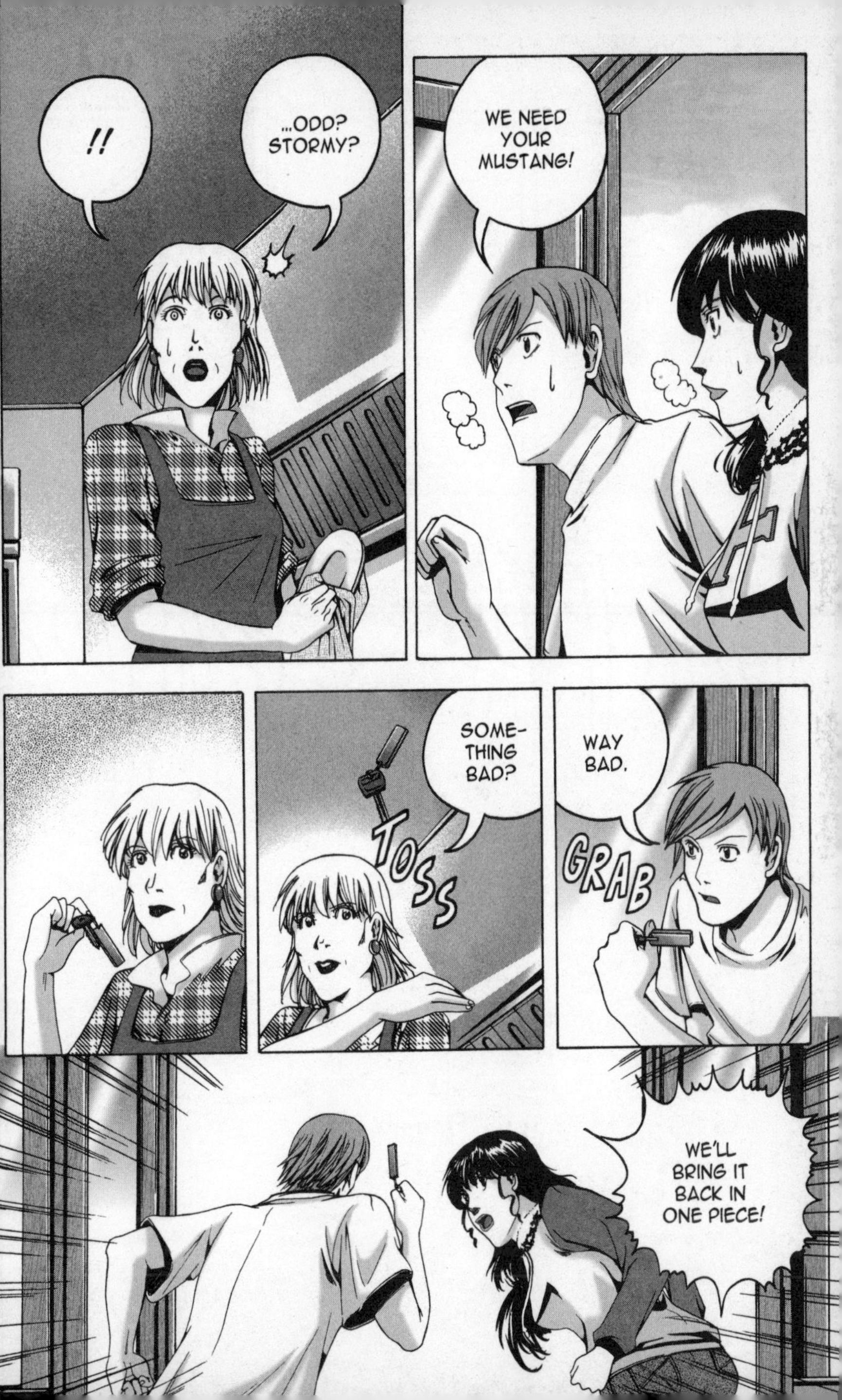
!!
...ODD? STORMY?
WE NEED YOUR MUSTANG!
SOME-THING BAD?
TOSS
WAY BAD.
GRAB
WE'LL BRING IT BACK IN ONE PIECE!

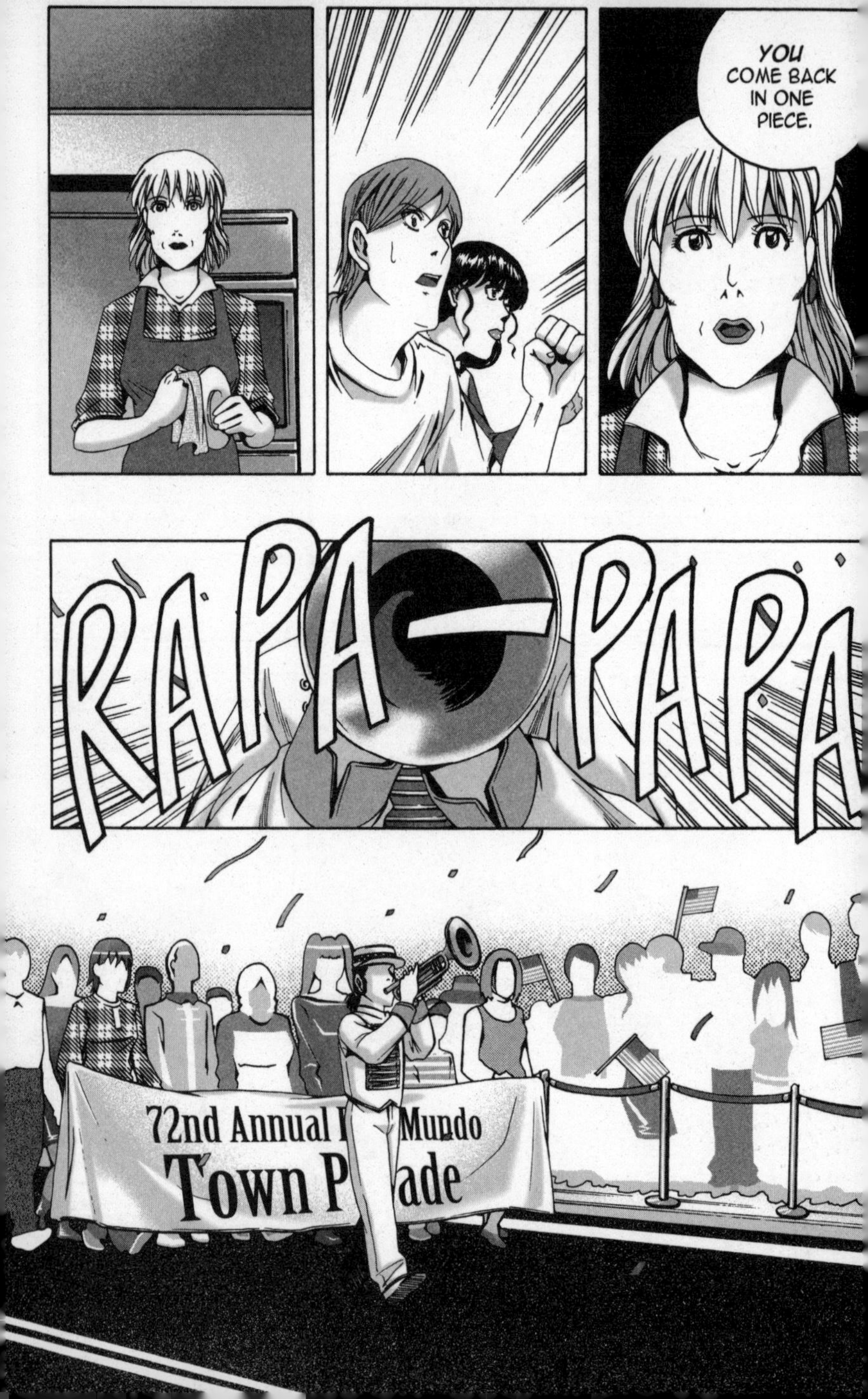
YOU COME BACK IN ONE PIECE.
RAPA-PAPA
72nd Annual
Mundo
Town P
ade

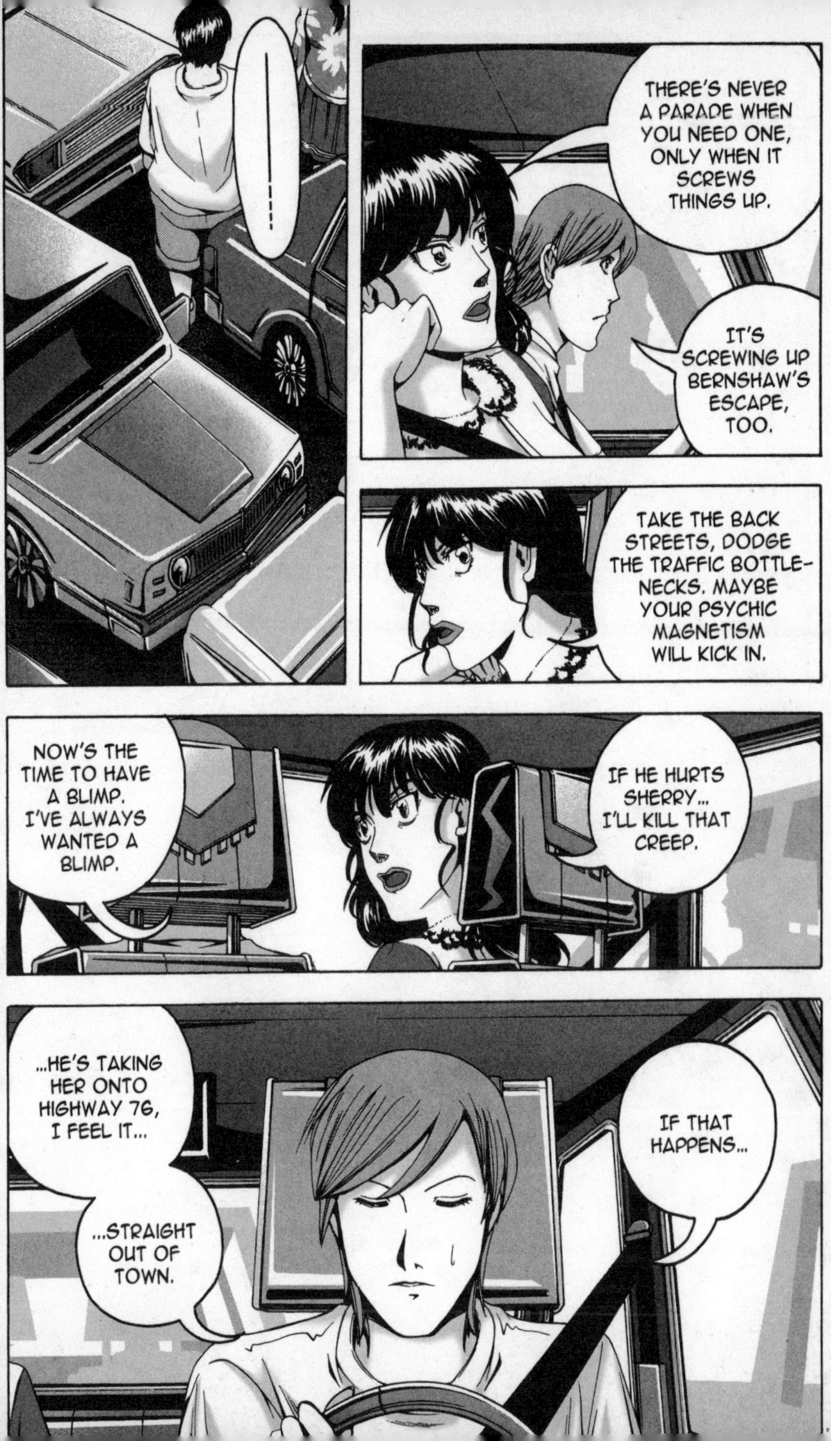
......
THERE'S NEVER A PARADE WHEN YOU NEED ONE, ONLY WHEN IT SCREWS THINGS UP.
IT'S SCREWING UP BERNSHAW'S ESCAPE, TOO.
TAKE THE BACK STREETS, DODGE THE TRAFFIC BOTTLE-NECKS. MAYBE YOUR PSYCHIC MAGNETISM WILL KICK IN.
IF HE HURTS SHERRY... I'LL KILL THAT CREEP.
NOW'S THE TIME TO HAVE A BLIMP. I'VE ALWAYS WANTED A BLIMP.
IF THAT HAPPENS...
...HE'S TAKING HER ONTO HIGHWAY 76, I FEEL IT...
...STRAIGHT OUT OF TOWN.

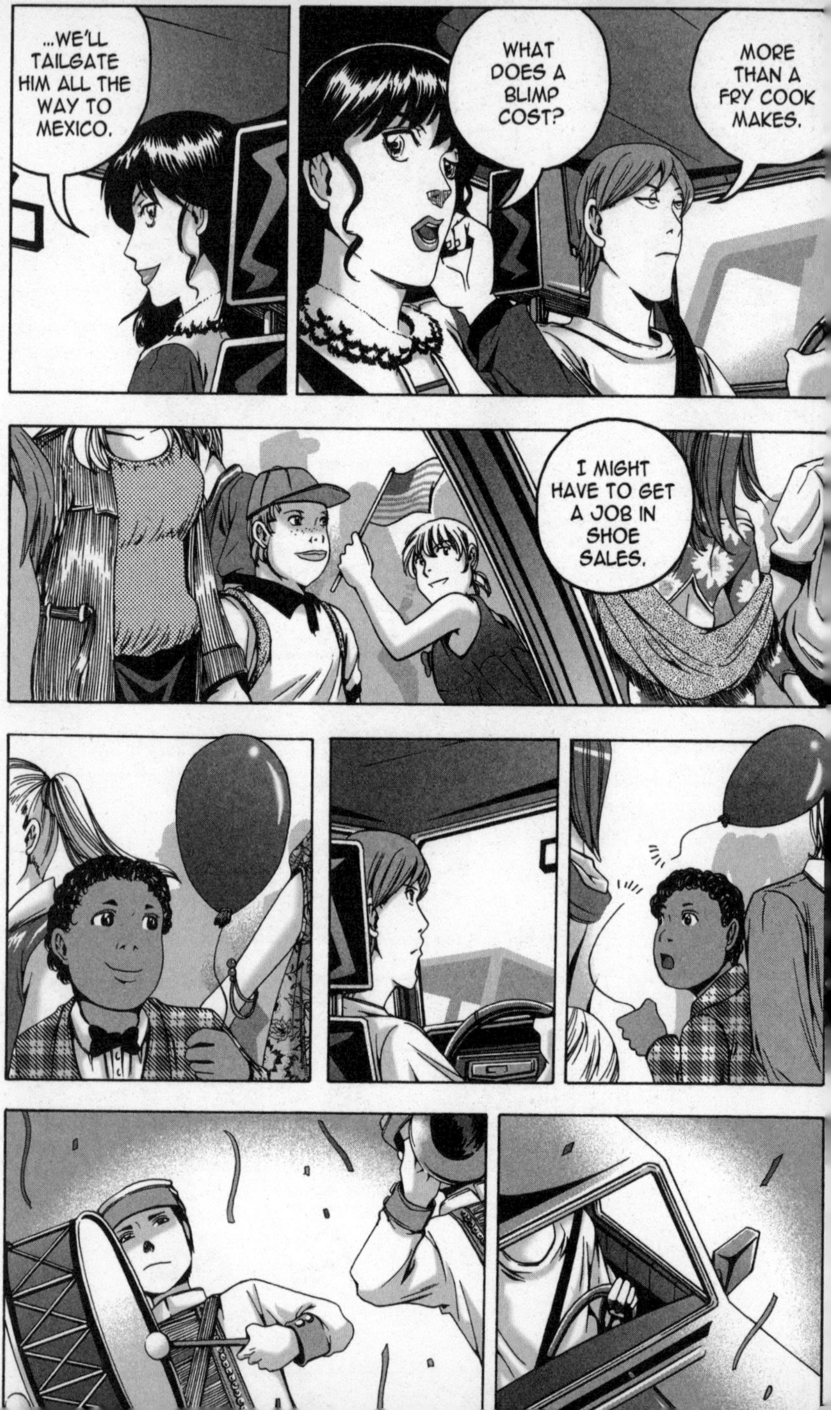
...WE'LL TAILGATE HIM ALL THE WAY TO MEXICO.
WHAT DOES A BLIMP COST?
MORE THAN A FRY COOK MAKES.
I MIGHT HAVE TO GET A JOB IN SHOE SALES.

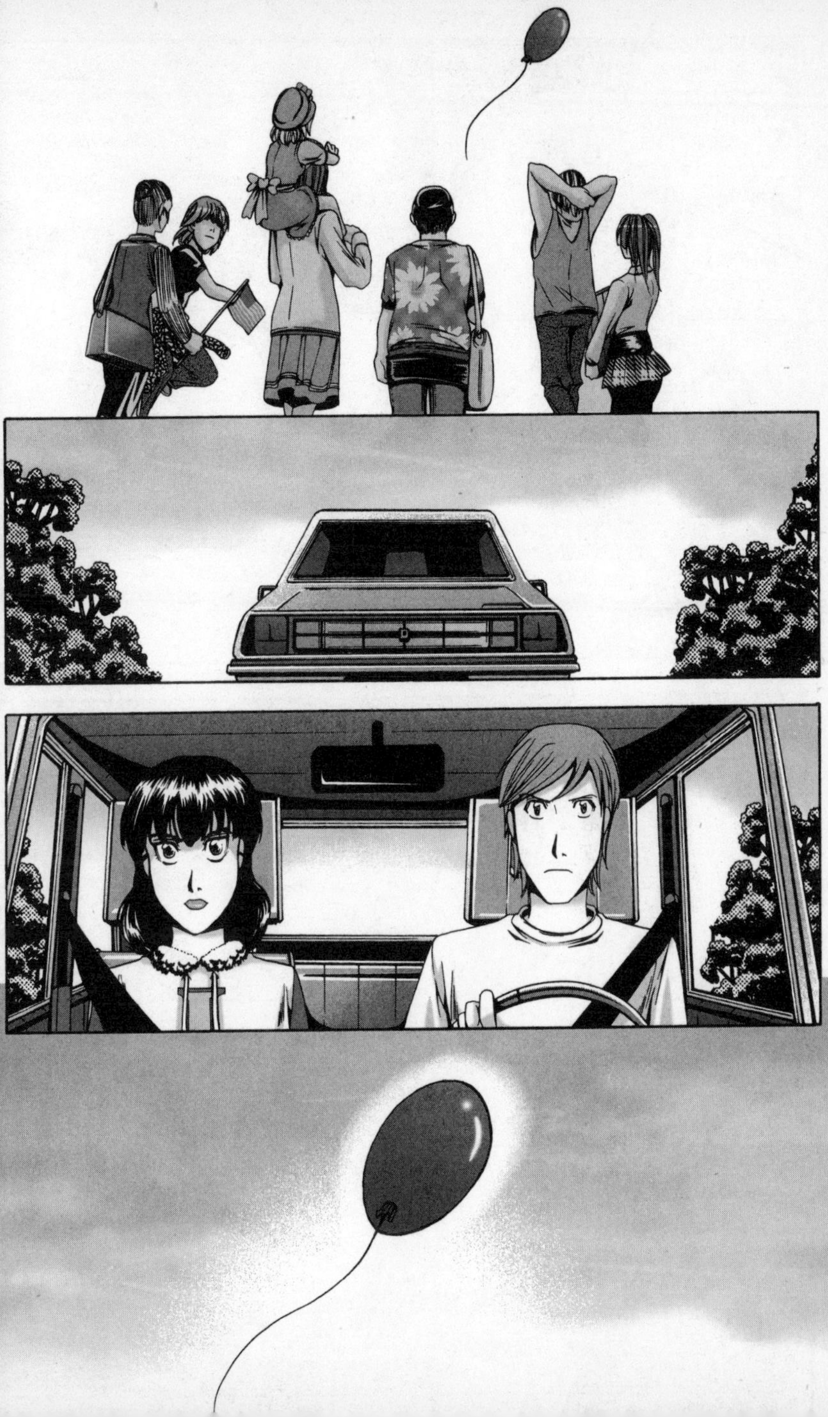

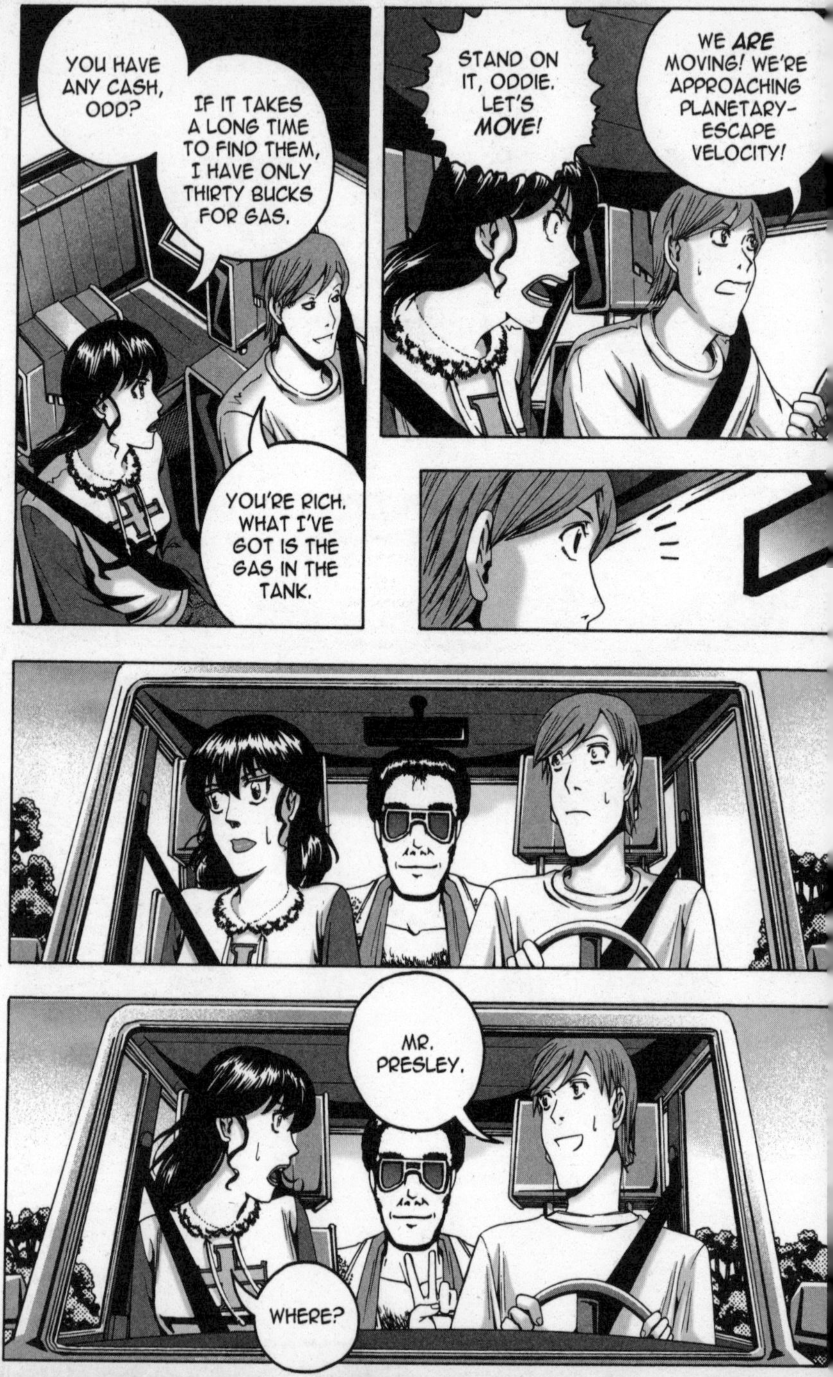
YOU HAVE ANY CASH, ODD?
IF IT TAKES A LONG TIME TO FIND THEM, I HAVE ONLY THIRTY BUCKS FOR GAS.
YOU'RE RICH. WHAT I'VE GOT IS THE GAS IN THE TANK.
STAND ON IT, ODDIE. LET'S MOVE!
WE ARE MOVING! WE'RE APPROACHING PLANETARY-ESCAPE VELOCITY!
MR. PRESLEY.
WHERE?

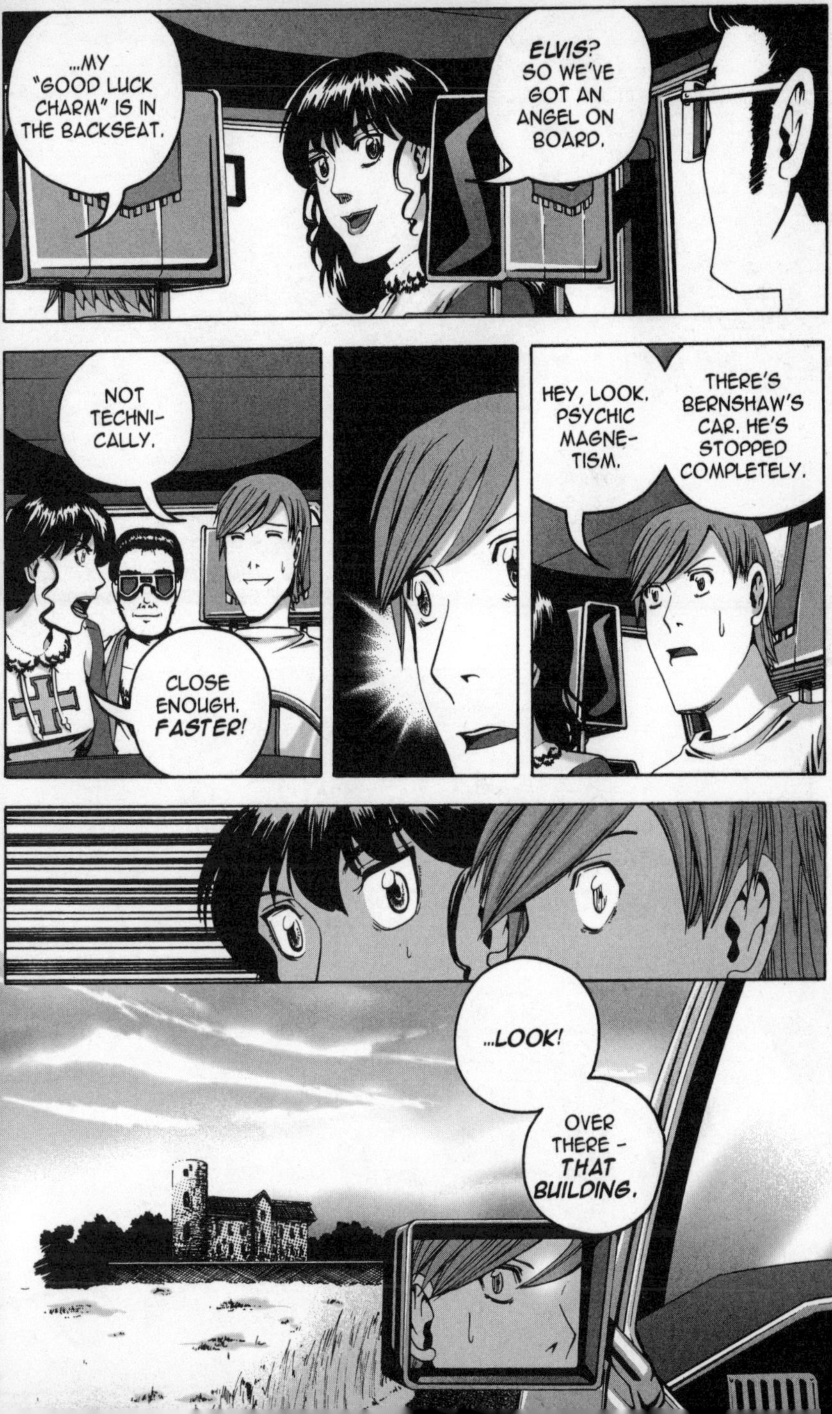

...MY "GOOD LUCK CHARM" IS IN THE BACKSEAT.
ELVIS? SO WE'VE GOT AN ANGEL ON BOARD.
NOT TECHNICALLY.
CLOSE ENOUGH. FASTER!
HEY, LOOK. PSYCHIC MAGNETISM.
THERE'S BERNSHAW'S CAR. HE'S STOPPED COMPLETELY.
...LOOK!
OVER THERE - THAT BUILDING.

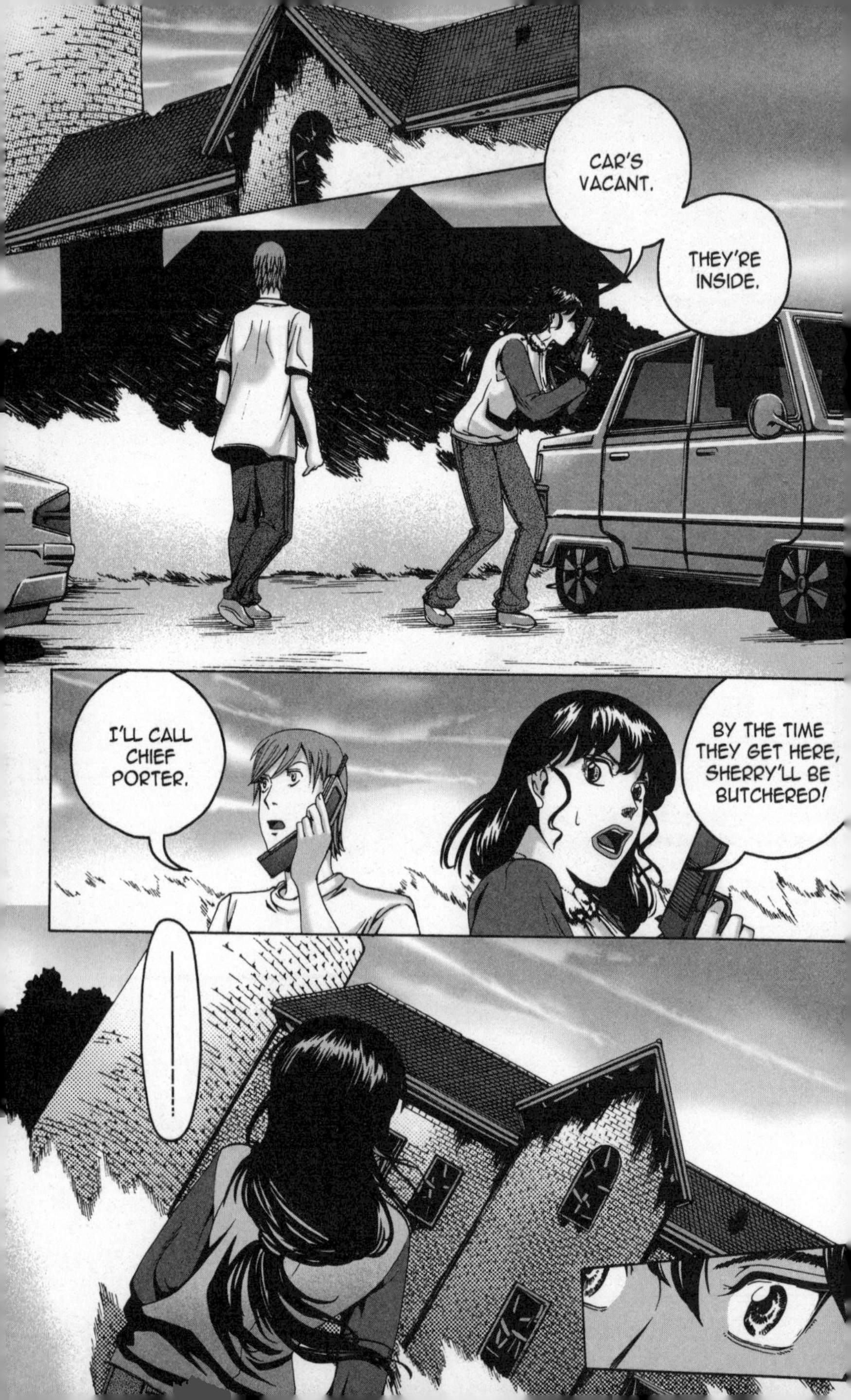
CAR'S VACANT.
THEY'RE INSIDE.
I'LL CALL CHIEF PORTER.
BY THE TIME THEY GET HERE, SHERRY'LL BE BUTCHERED!
......

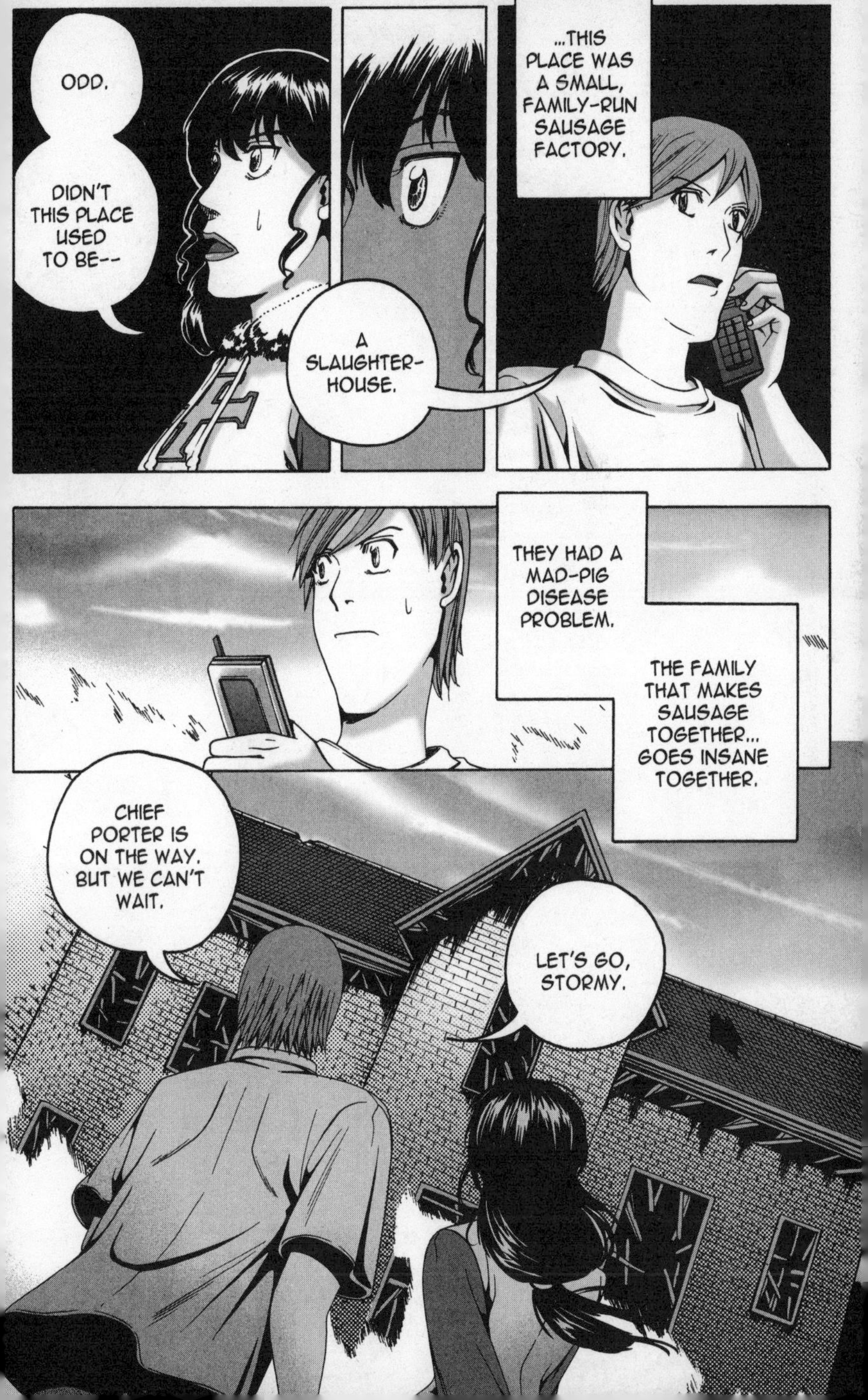
ODD.
DIDN'T THIS PLACE USED TO BE--
A SLAUGHTER-HOUSE.
...THIS PLACE WAS A SMALL, FAMILY-RUN SAUSAGE FACTORY.
THEY HAD A MAD-PIG DISEASE PROBLEM.
THE FAMILY THAT MAKES SAUSAGE TOGETHER... GOES INSANE TOGETHER.
CHIEF PORTER IS ON THE WAY. BUT WE CAN'T WAIT.
LET'S GO, STORMY.

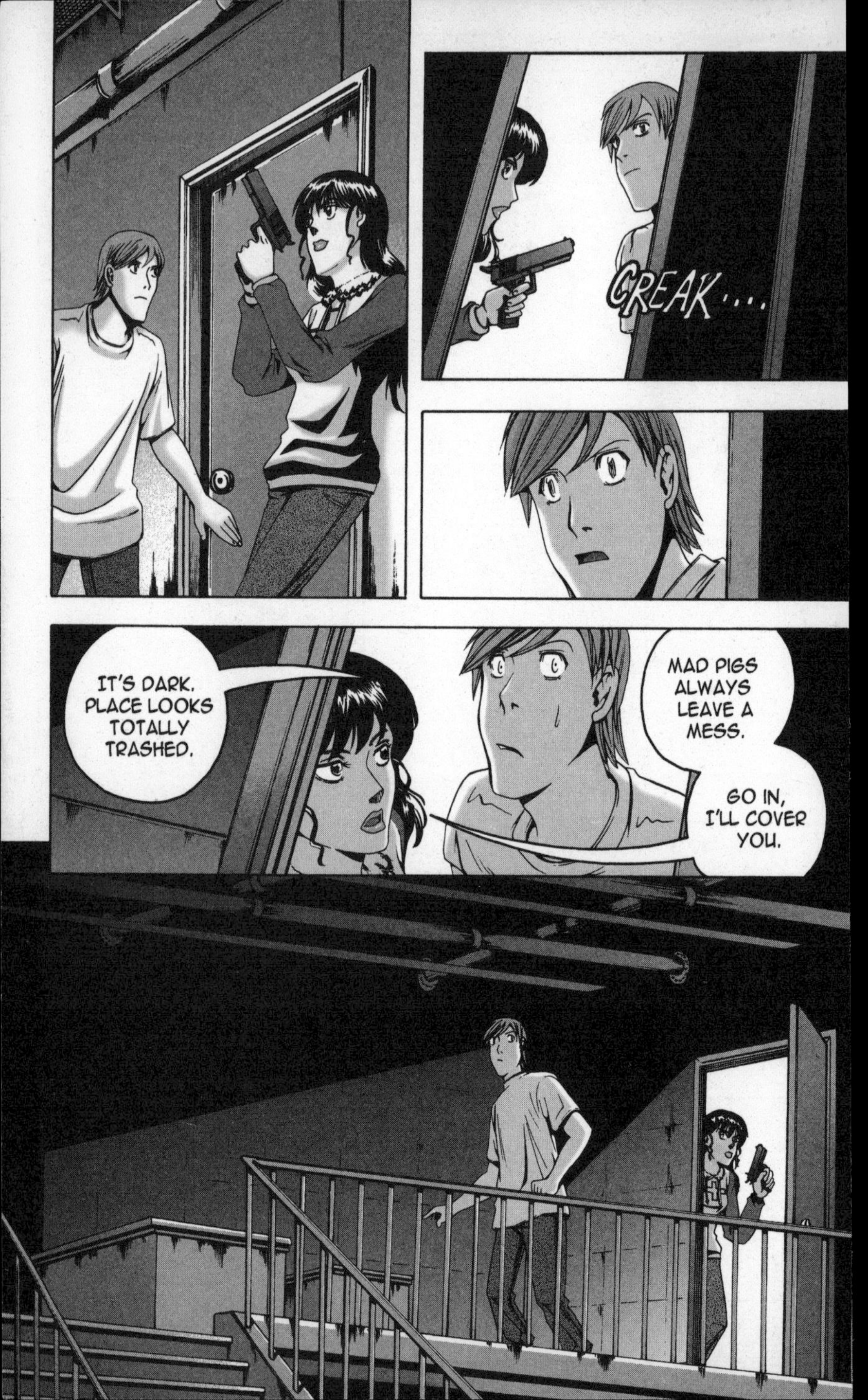
CREAK....
IT'S DARK. PLACE LOOKS TOTALLY TRASHED.
MAD PIGS ALWAYS LEAVE A MESS.
GO IN, I'LL COVER YOU.

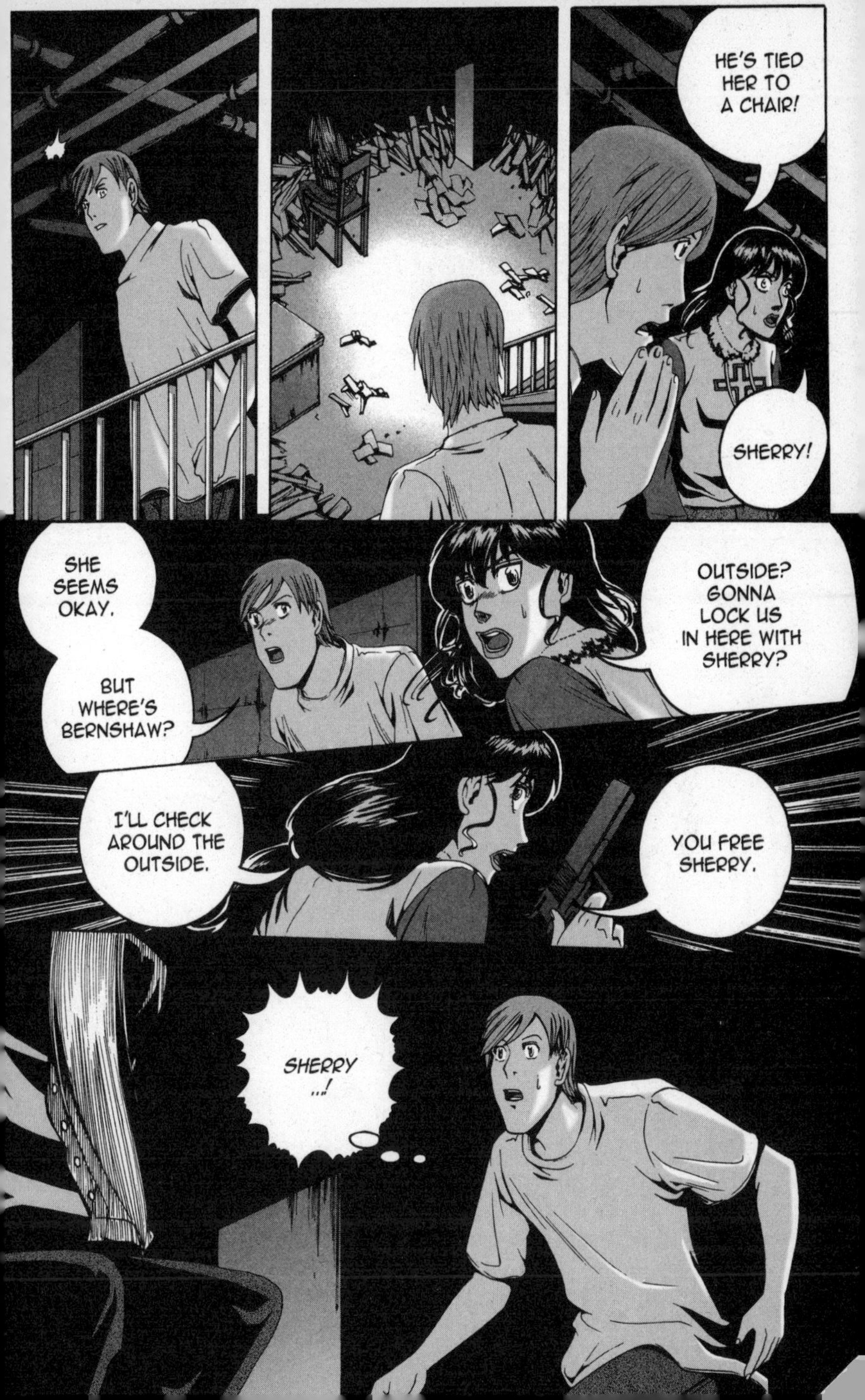
HE'S TIED HER TO A CHAIR!
SHERRY!
SHE SEEMS OKAY.
BUT WHERE'S BERNSHAW?
OUTSIDE? GONNA LOCK US IN HERE WITH SHERRY?
I'LL CHECK AROUND THE OUTSIDE.
YOU FREE SHERRY.
SHERRY ...!

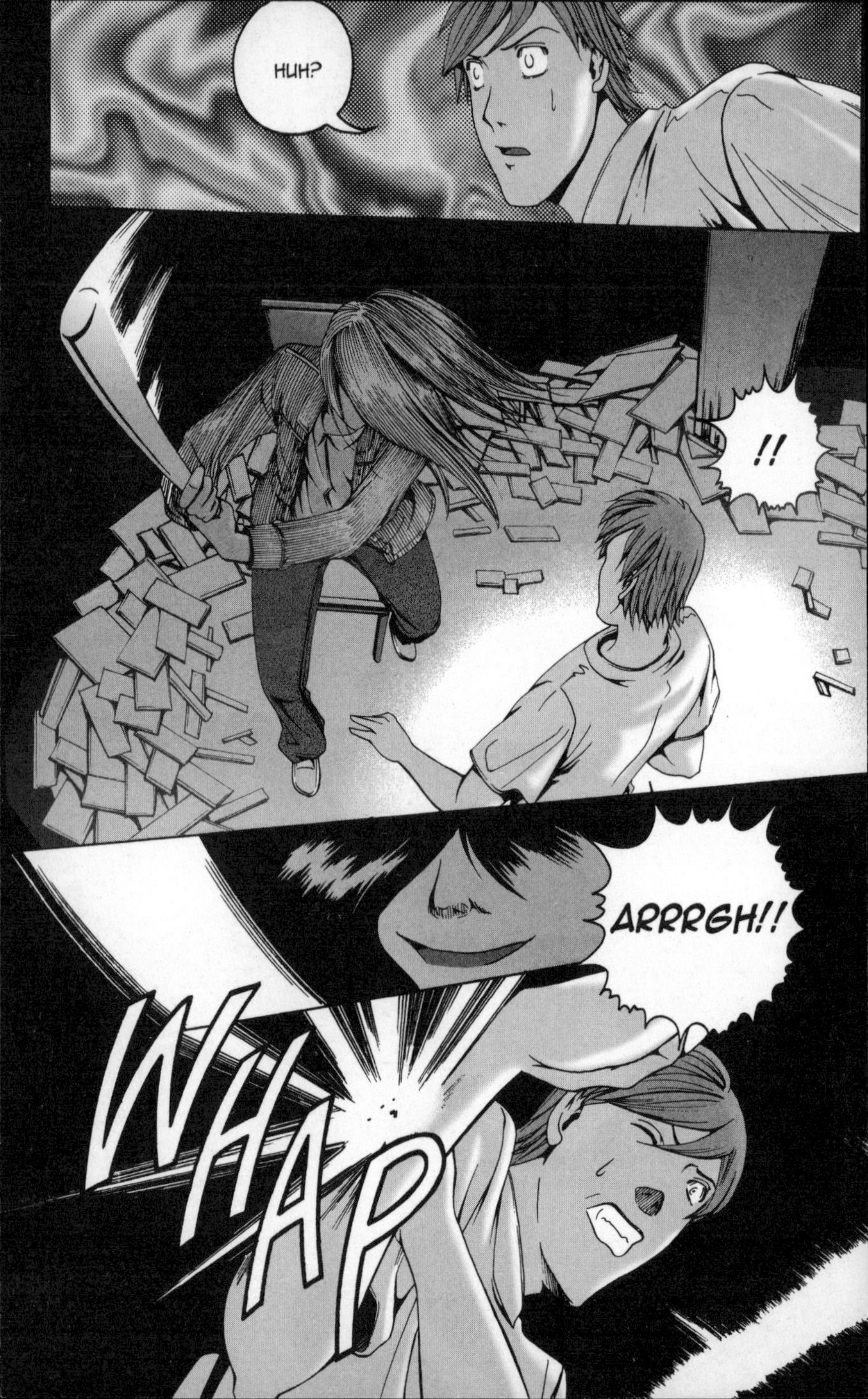
HUH?
!!
ARRRGH!!
WHAP

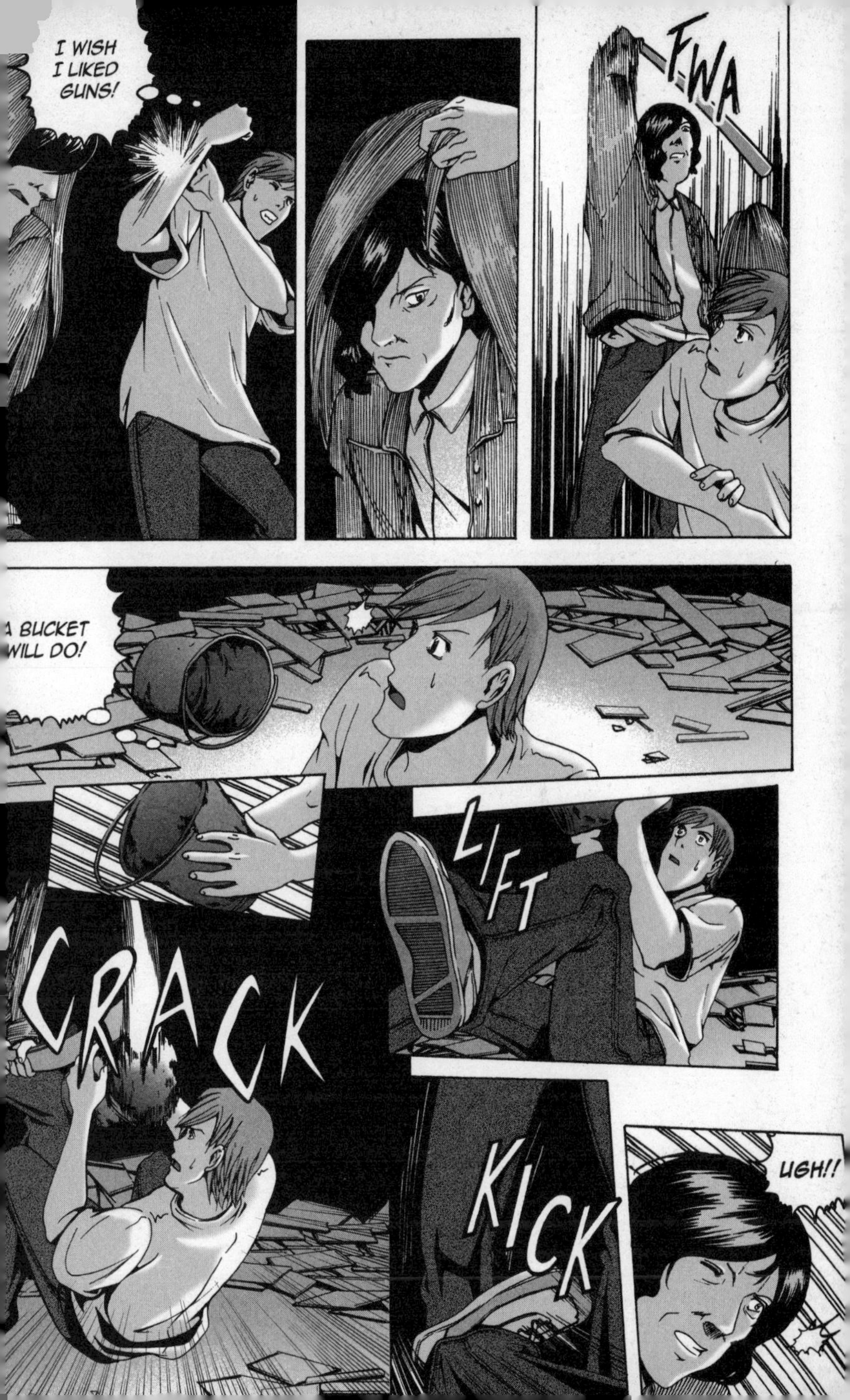
I WISH I LIKED GUNS!
FWA
A BUCKET WILL DO!
LIFT
CRACK
KICK
UGH!!

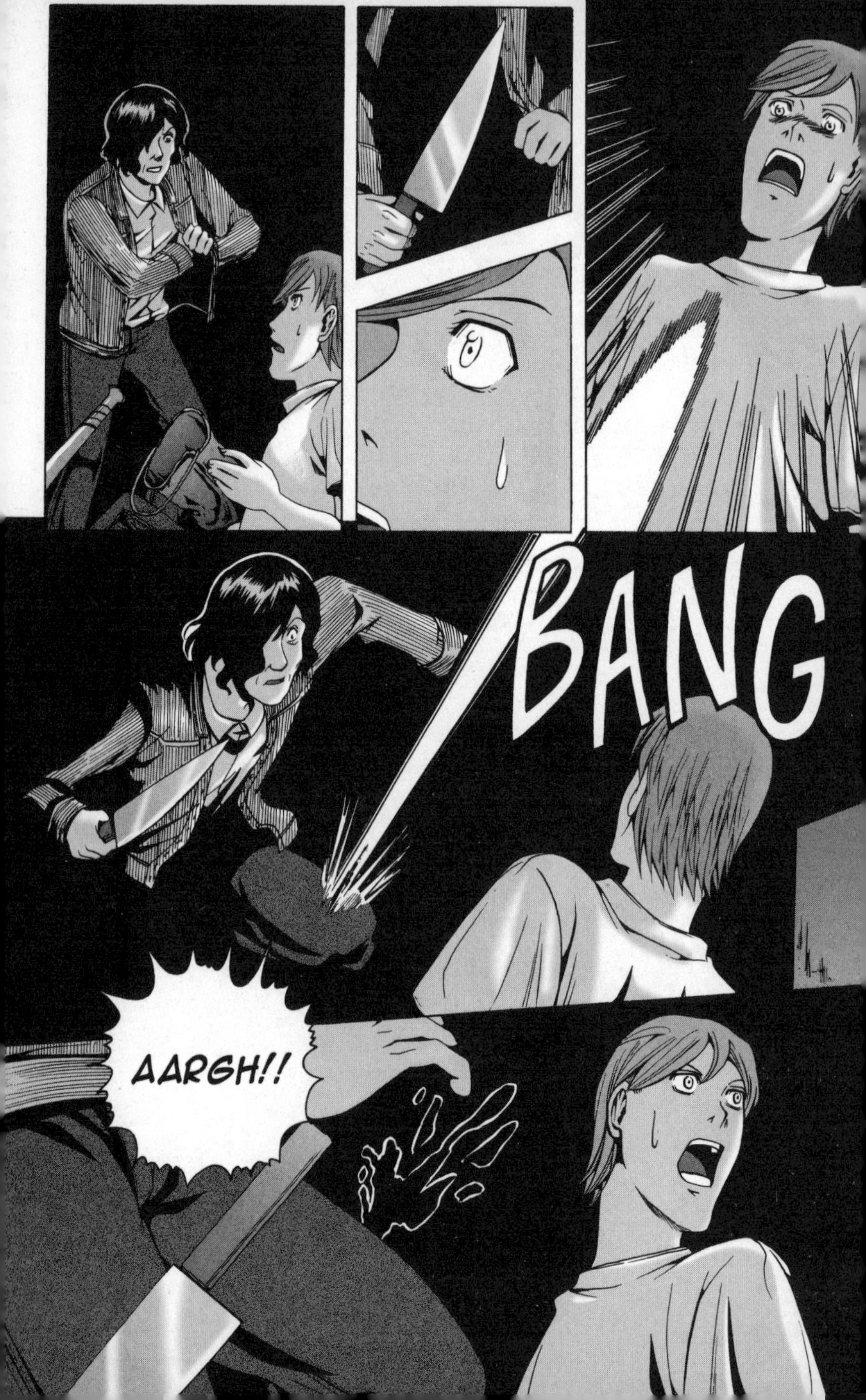
BANG
AARGH!!

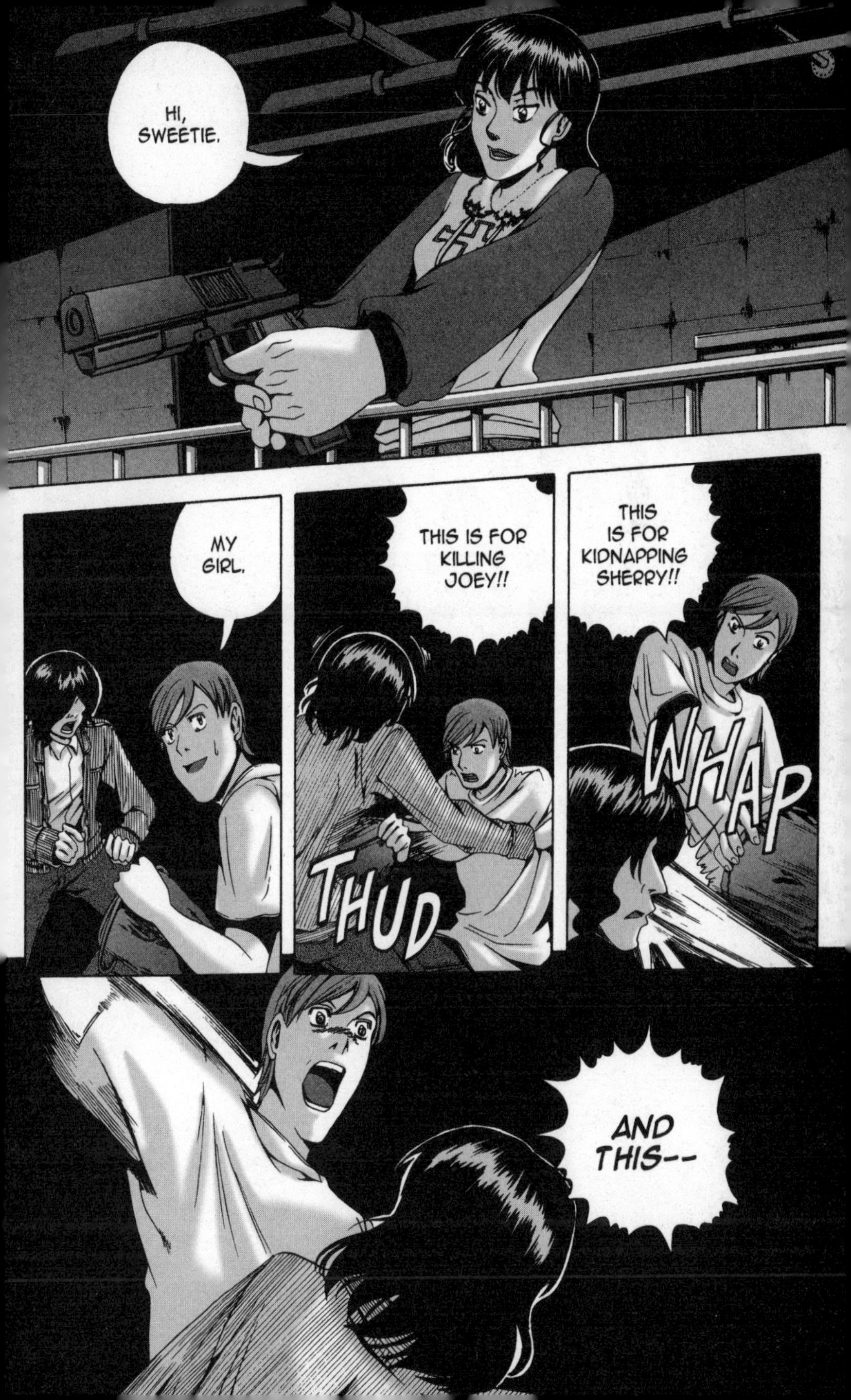
HI, SWEETIE.
MY GIRL.
THIS IS FOR KILLING JOEY!!
THUD
THIS IS FOR KIDNAPPING SHERRY!!
WHAP
AND THIS--

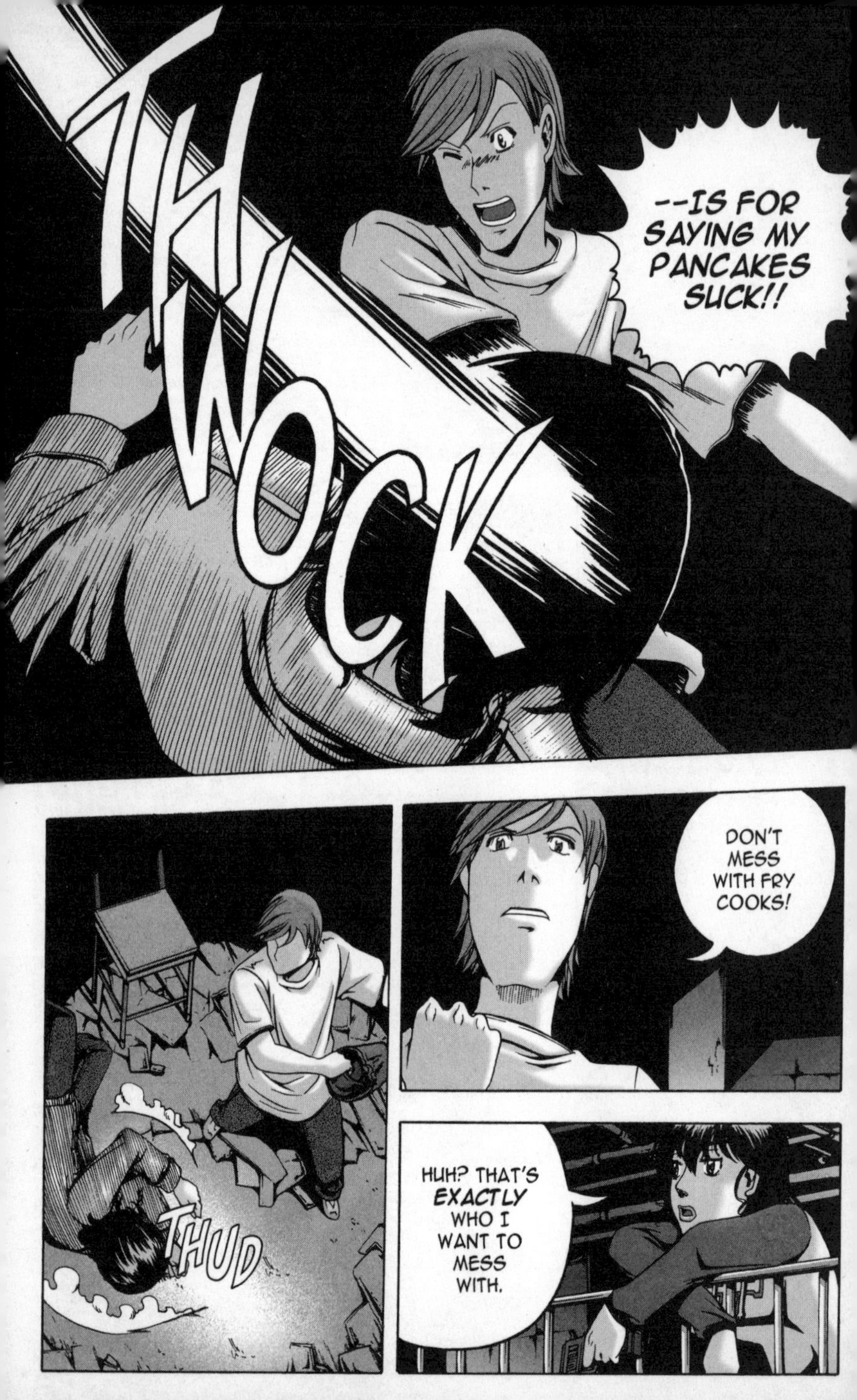
THWOCK
--IS FOR SAYING MY PANCAKES SUCK!!
THUD
DON'T MESS WITH FRY COOKS!
HUH? THAT'S ***EXACTLY*** WHO I WANT TO MESS WITH.

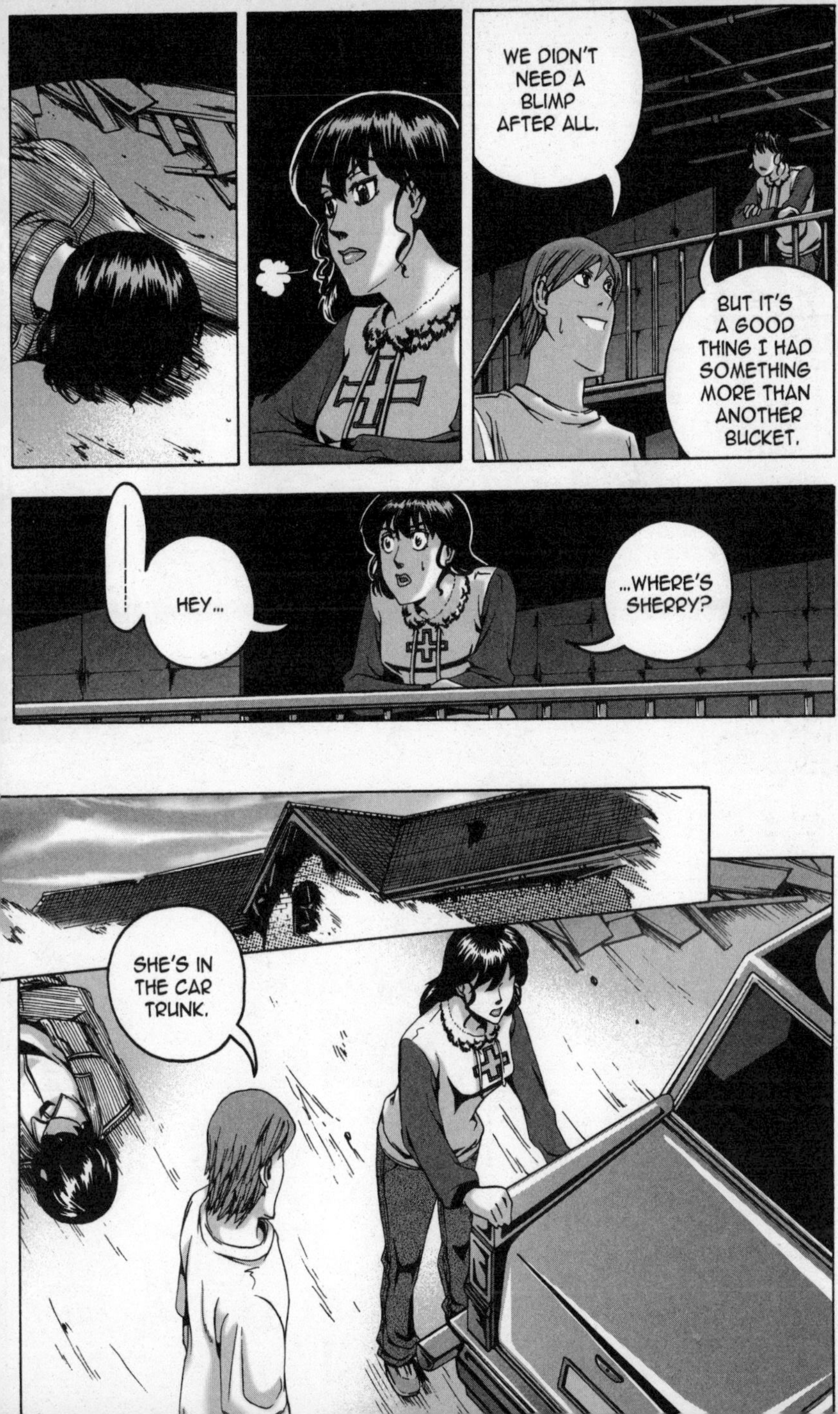

WE DIDN'T NEED A BLIMP AFTER ALL.
BUT IT'S A GOOD THING I HAD SOMETHING MORE THAN ANOTHER BUCKET.
HEY...
...WHERE'S SHERRY?
SHE'S IN THE CAR TRUNK.

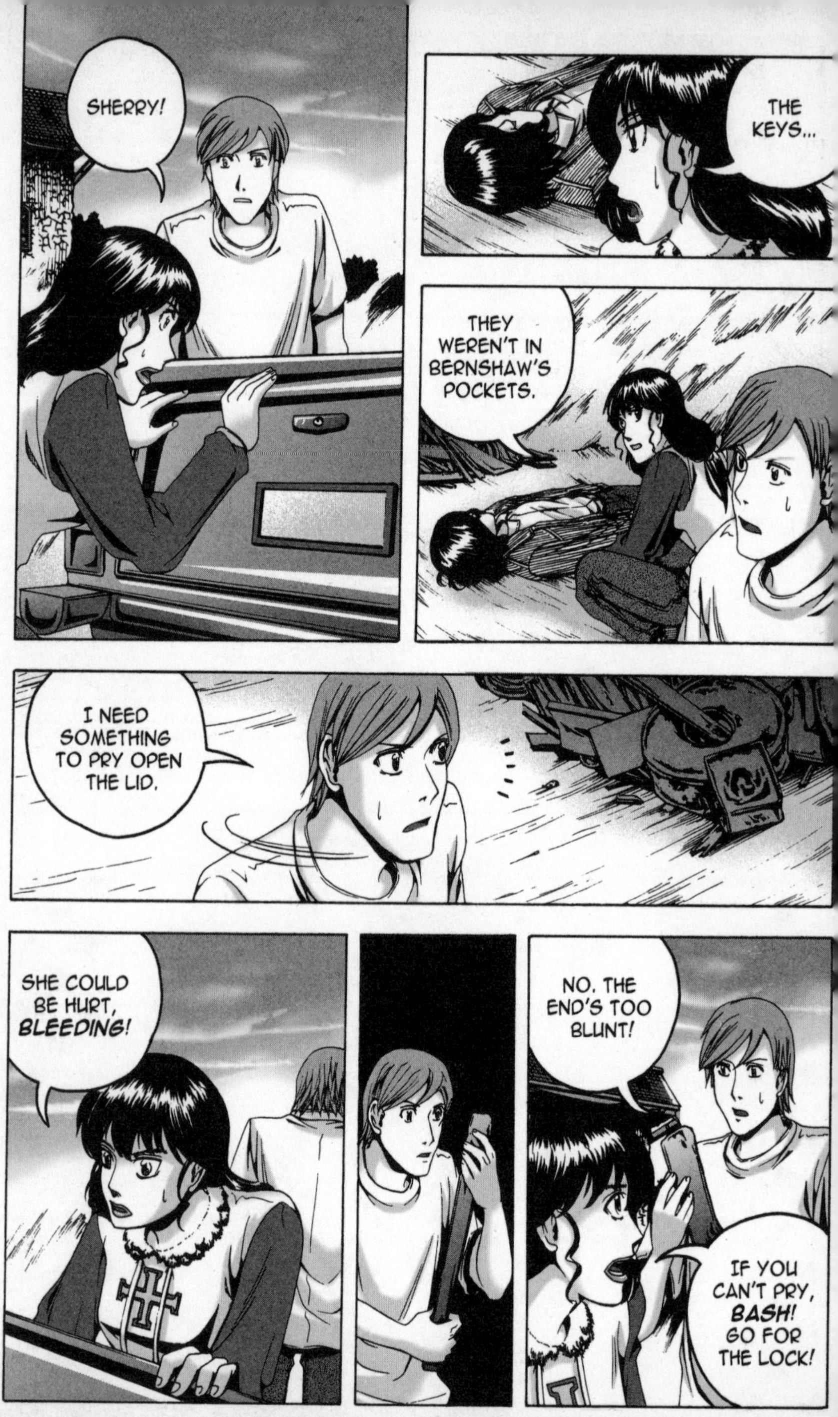
SHERRY!
THE KEYS...
THEY WEREN'T IN BERNSHAW'S POCKETS.
I NEED SOMETHING TO PRY OPEN THE LID.
SHE COULD BE HURT, **BLEEDING**!
NO. THE END'S TOO BLUNT!
IF YOU CAN'T PRY, **BASH**! GO FOR THE LOCK!

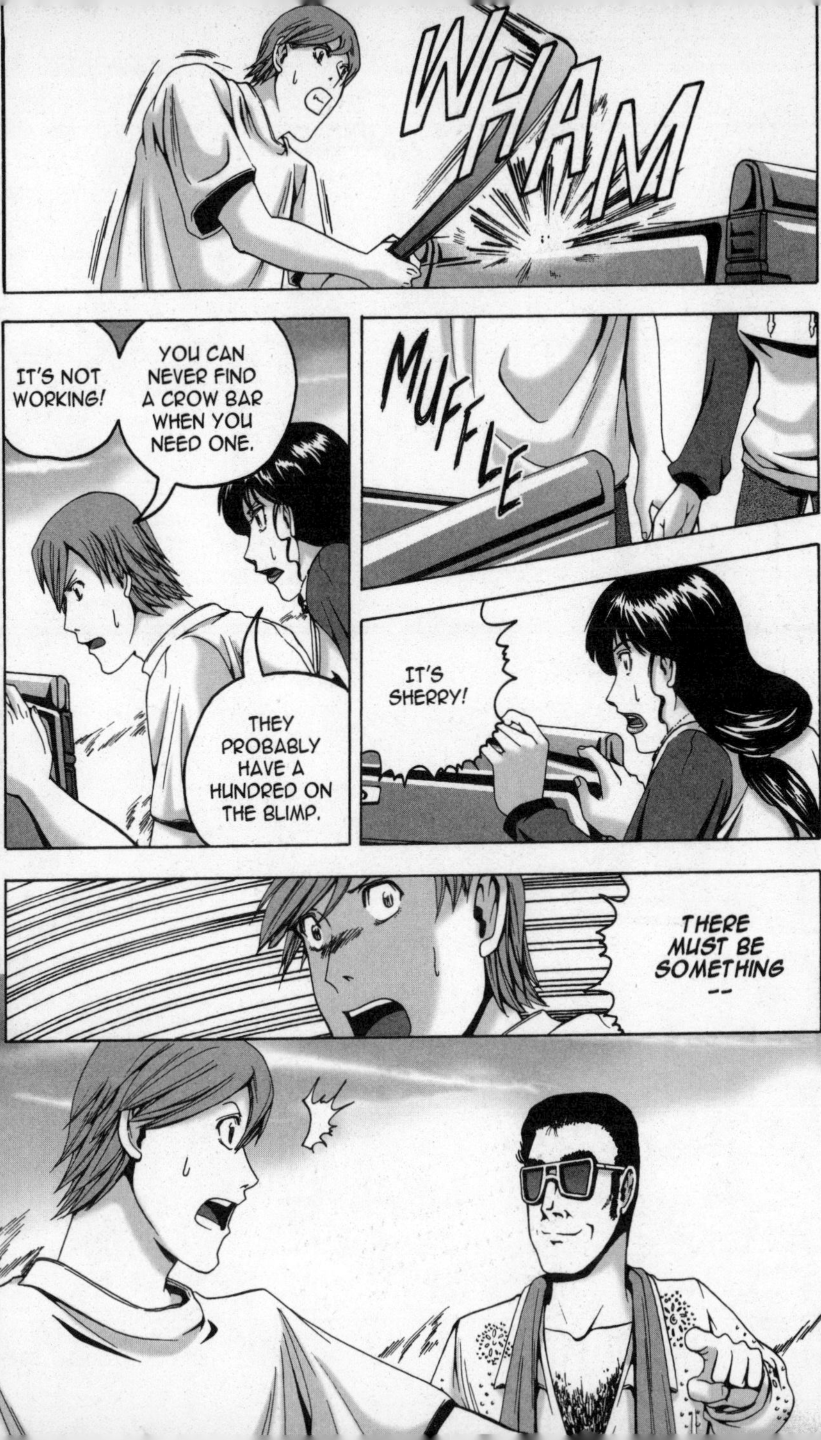
WHAM
IT'S NOT WORKING!
YOU CAN NEVER FIND A CROW BAR WHEN YOU NEED ONE.
THEY PROBABLY HAVE A HUNDRED ON THE BLIMP.
MUFFLE
IT'S SHERRY!
THERE MUST BE SOMETHING --

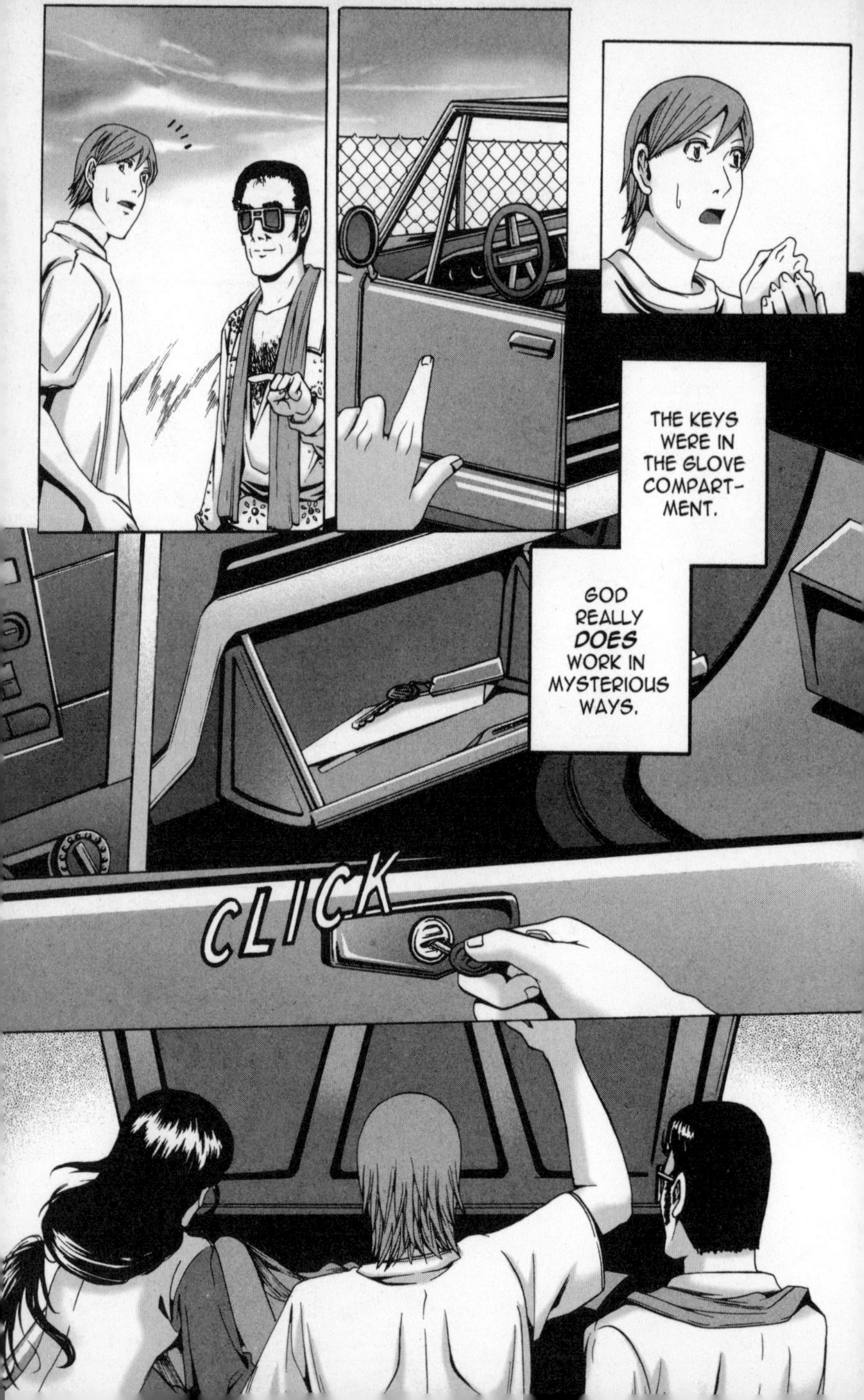
THE KEYS WERE IN THE GLOVE COMPART-MENT.
GOD REALLY **DOES** WORK IN MYSTERIOUS WAYS.
CLICK

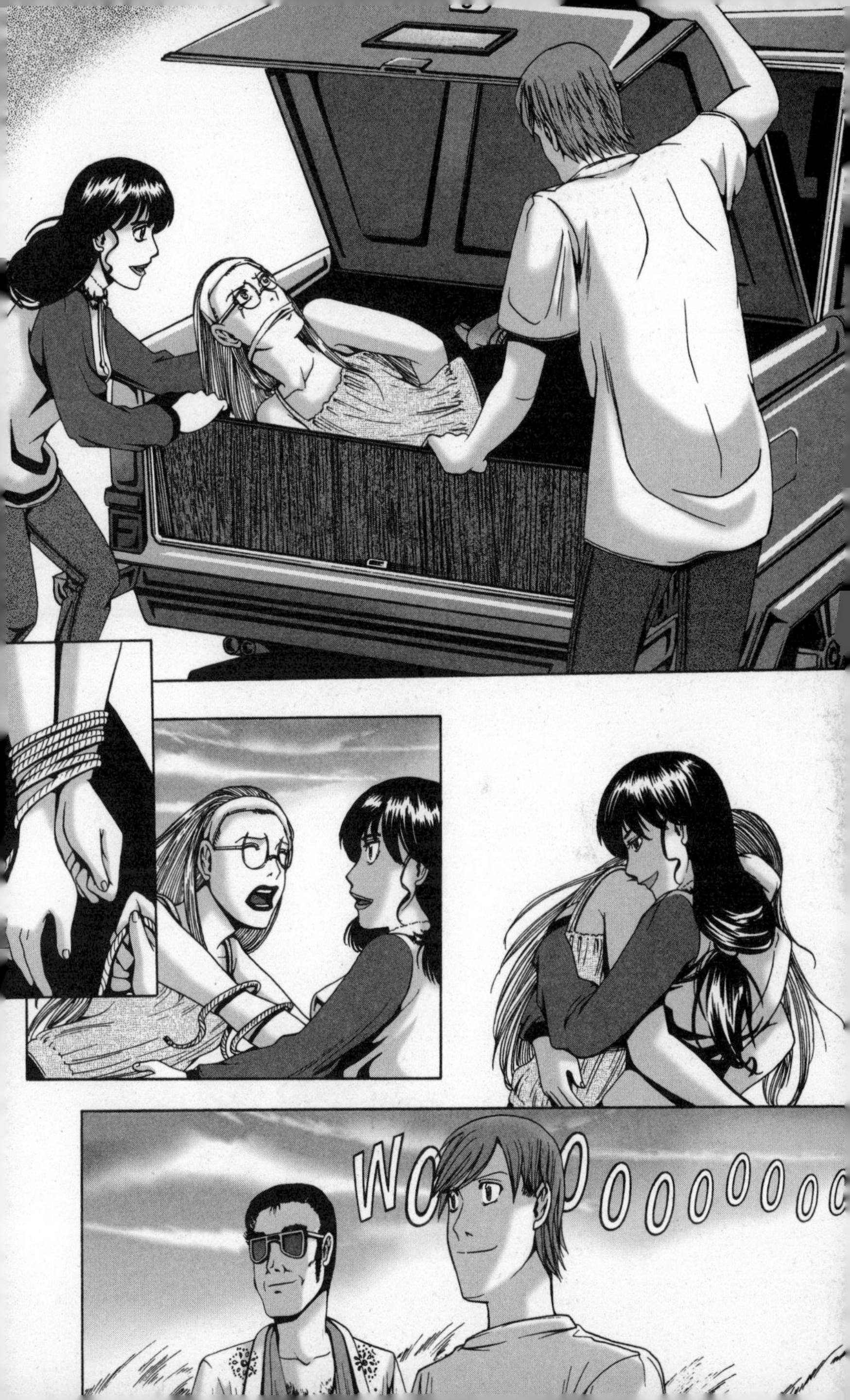
WOOOOOOOOO

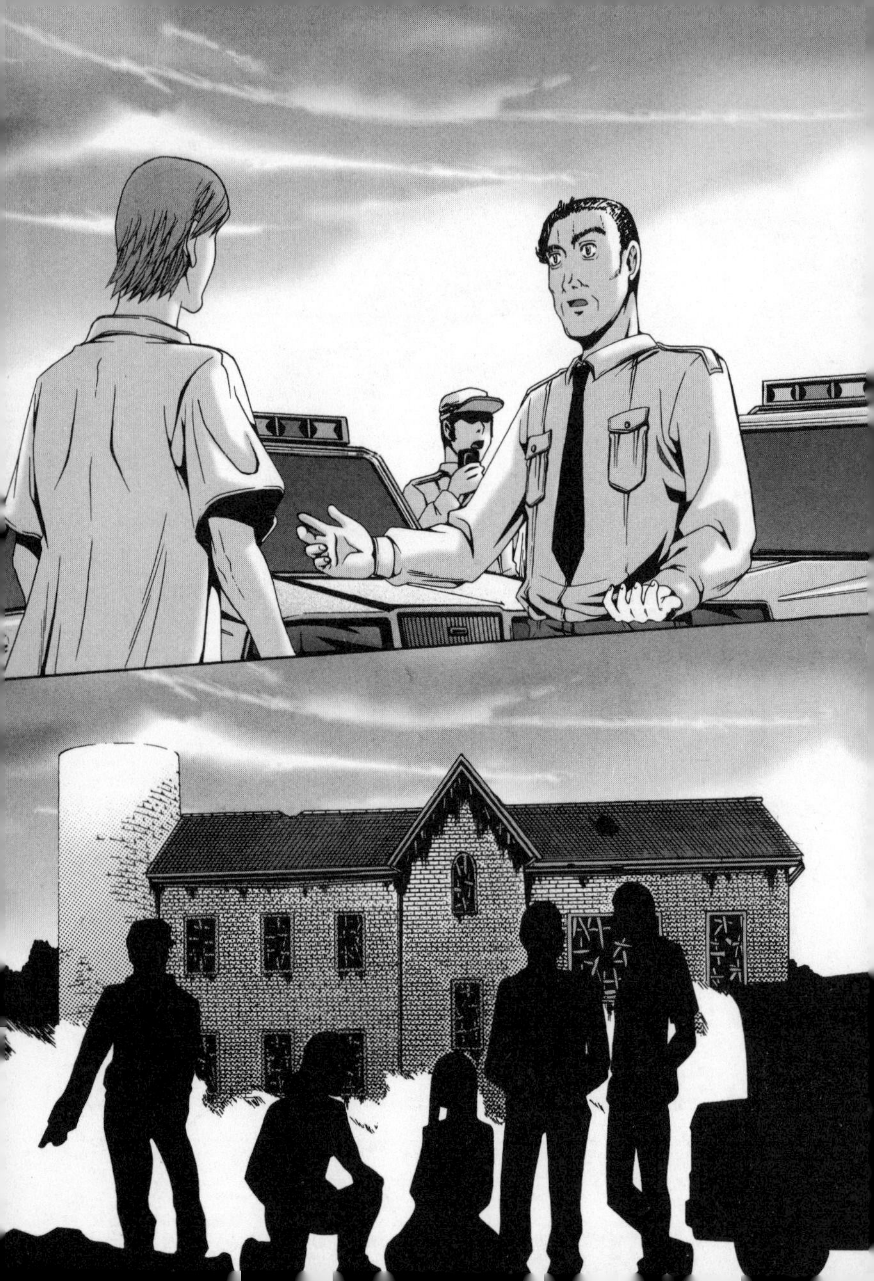

In Odd We Trust

Chapter 7

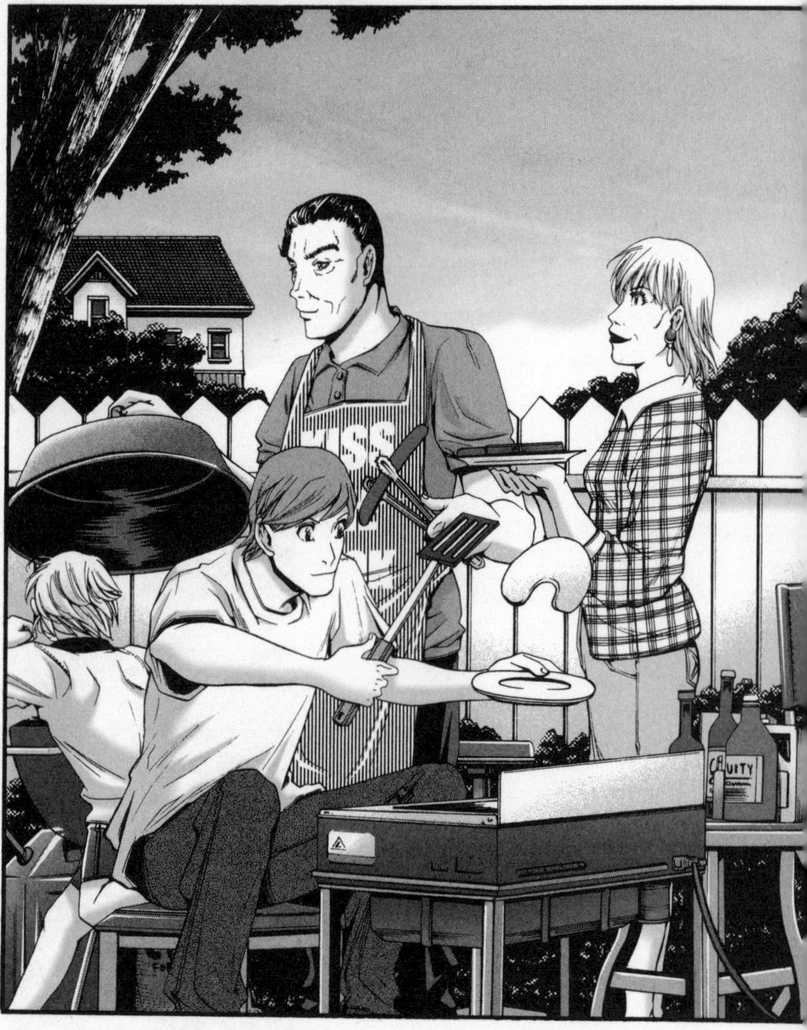

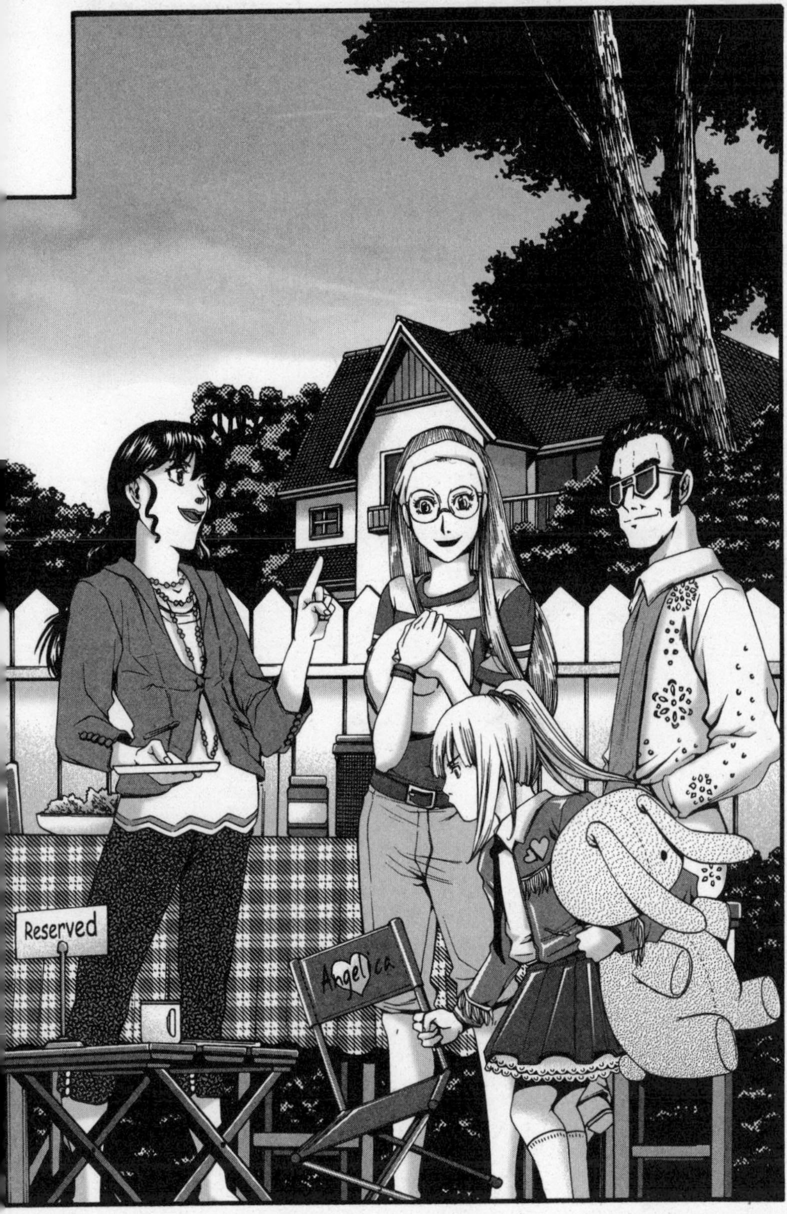
Reserved
Angelica

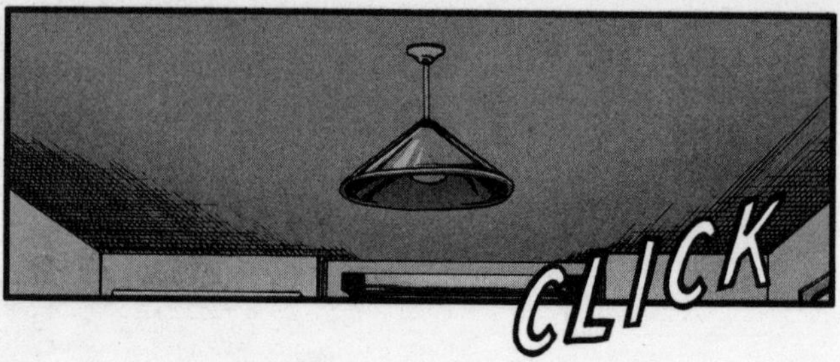
CLICK

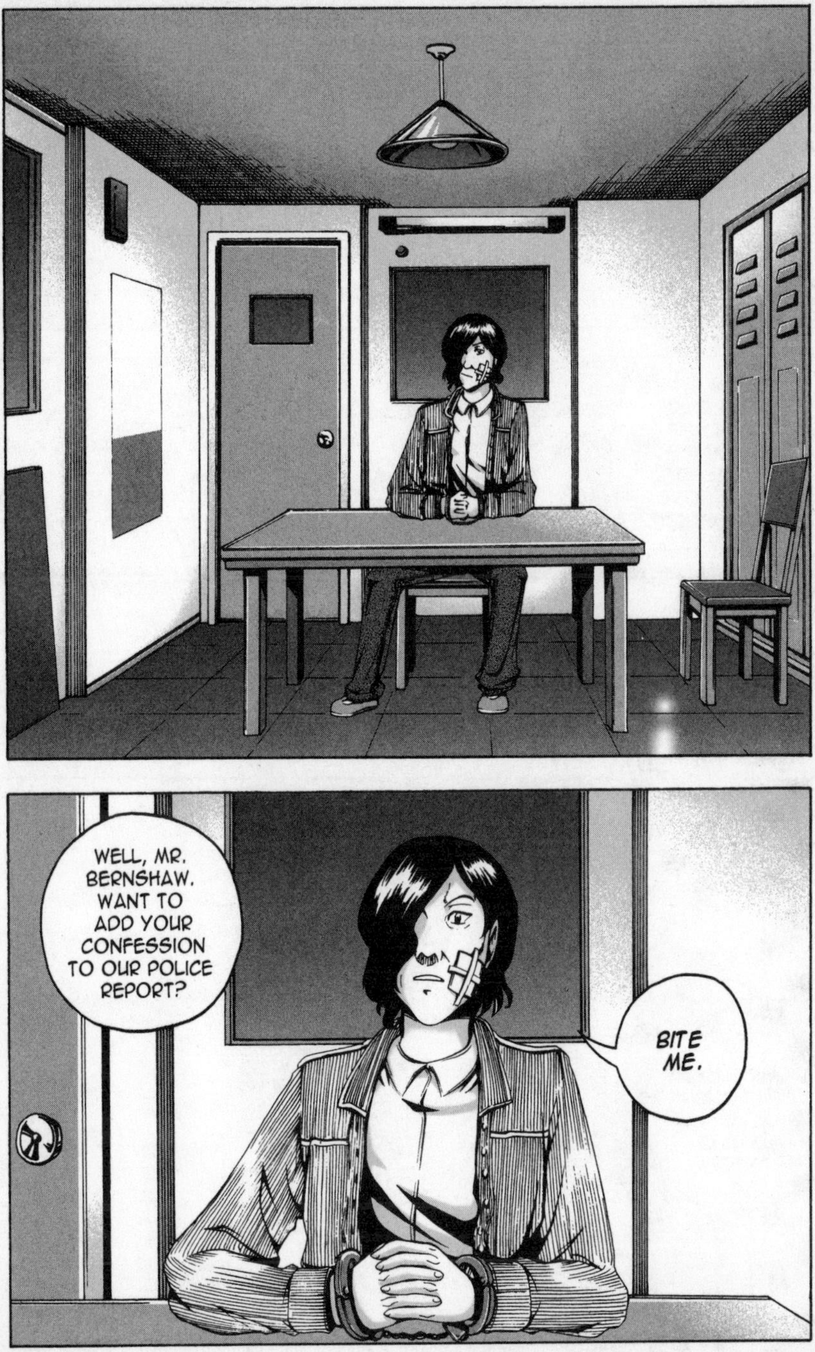
WELL, MR. BERNSHAW. WANT TO ADD YOUR CONFESSION TO OUR POLICE REPORT?
BITE ME.

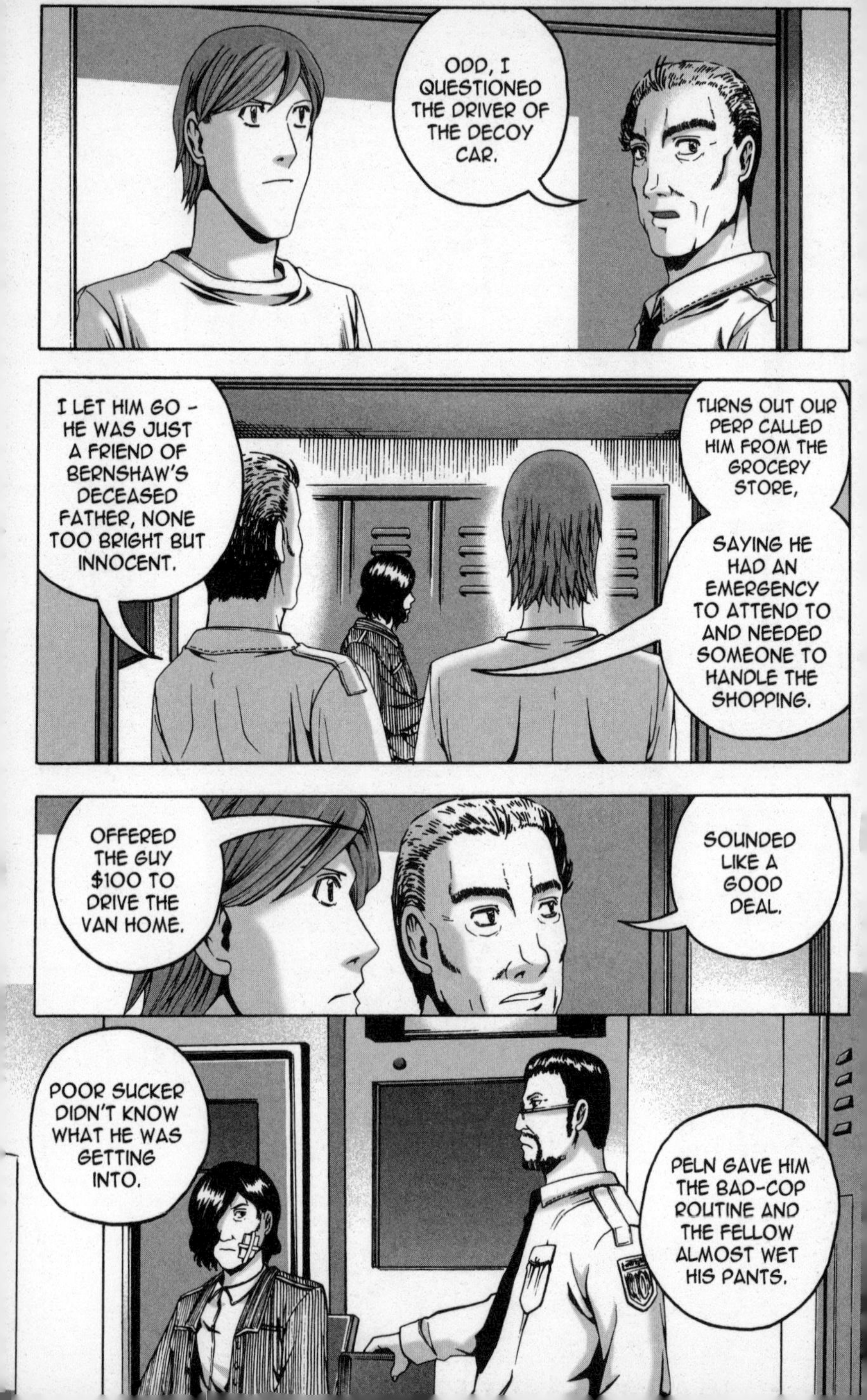
ODD, I QUESTIONED THE DRIVER OF THE DECOY CAR.
I LET HIM GO - HE WAS JUST A FRIEND OF BERNSHAW'S DECEASED FATHER, NONE TOO BRIGHT BUT INNOCENT.
TURNS OUT OUR PERP CALLED HIM FROM THE GROCERY STORE,
SAYING HE HAD AN EMERGENCY TO ATTEND TO AND NEEDED SOMEONE TO HANDLE THE SHOPPING.
OFFERED THE GUY $100 TO DRIVE THE VAN HOME.
SOUNDED LIKE A GOOD DEAL.
POOR SUCKER DIDN'T KNOW WHAT HE WAS GETTING INTO.
PELN GAVE HIM THE BAD-COP ROUTINE AND THE FELLOW ALMOST WET HIS PANTS.

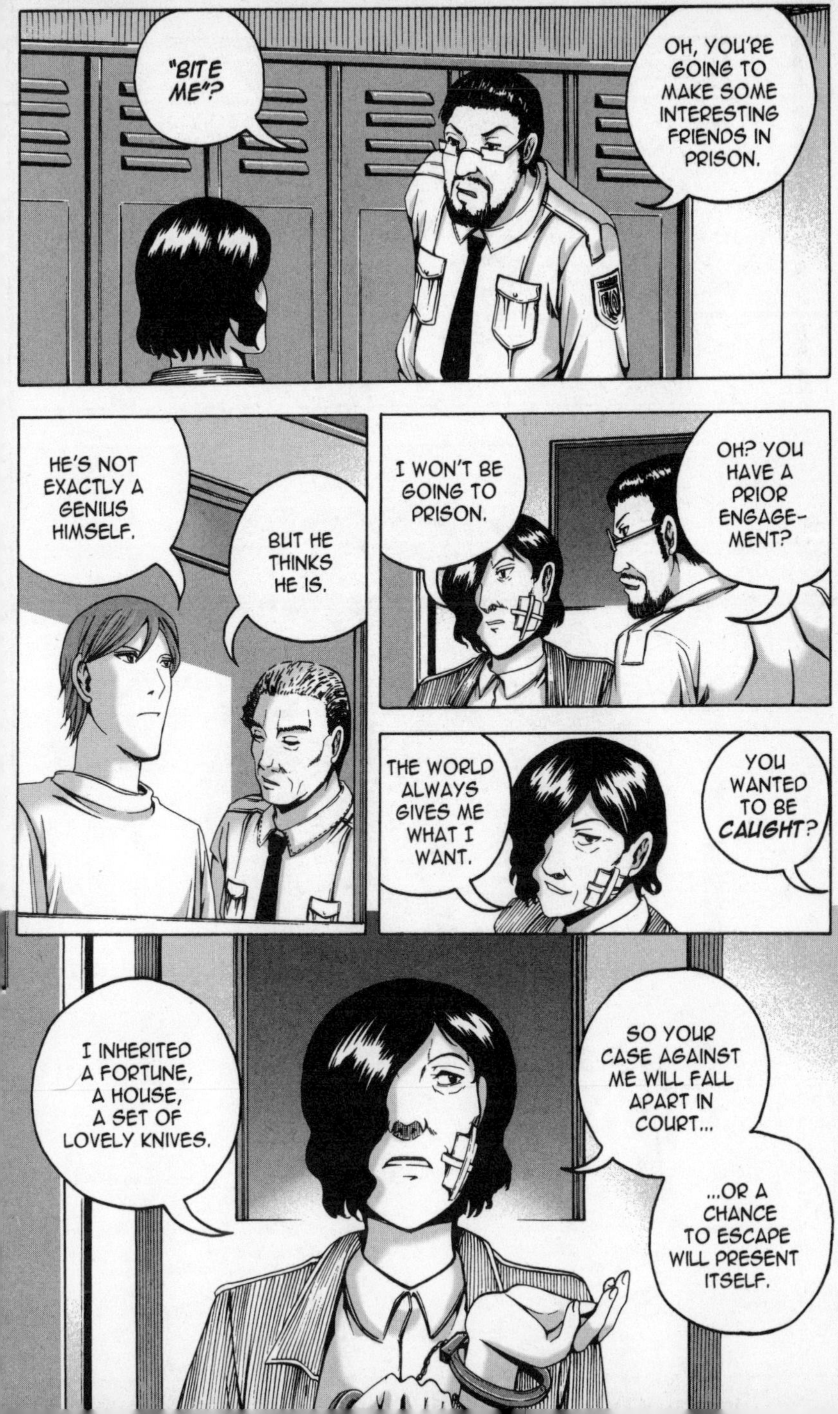
"BITE ME"?
OH, YOU'RE GOING TO MAKE SOME INTERESTING FRIENDS IN PRISON.
HE'S NOT EXACTLY A GENIUS HIMSELF.
BUT HE THINKS HE IS.
I WON'T BE GOING TO PRISON.
OH? YOU HAVE A PRIOR ENGAGE-MENT?
THE WORLD ALWAYS GIVES ME WHAT I WANT.
YOU WANTED TO BE *CAUGHT*?
I INHERITED A FORTUNE, A HOUSE, A SET OF LOVELY KNIVES.
SO YOUR CASE AGAINST ME WILL FALL APART IN COURT...
...OR A CHANCE TO ESCAPE WILL PRESENT ITSELF.

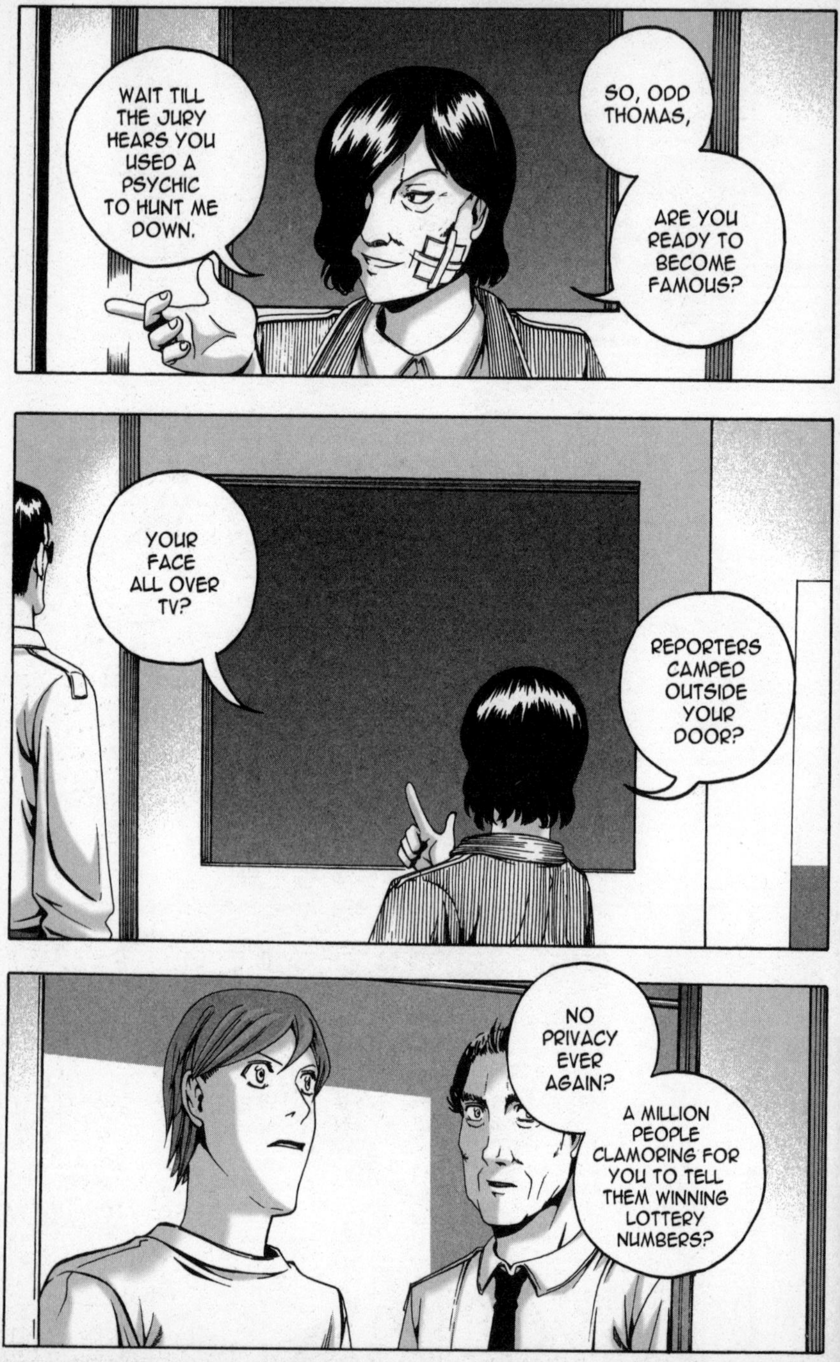
SO, ODD THOMAS,
ARE YOU READY TO BECOME FAMOUS?
WAIT TILL THE JURY HEARS YOU USED A PSYCHIC TO HUNT ME DOWN.
YOUR FACE ALL OVER TV?
REPORTERS CAMPED OUTSIDE YOUR DOOR?
NO PRIVACY EVER AGAIN?
A MILLION PEOPLE CLAMORING FOR YOU TO TELL THEM WINNING LOTTERY NUMBERS?

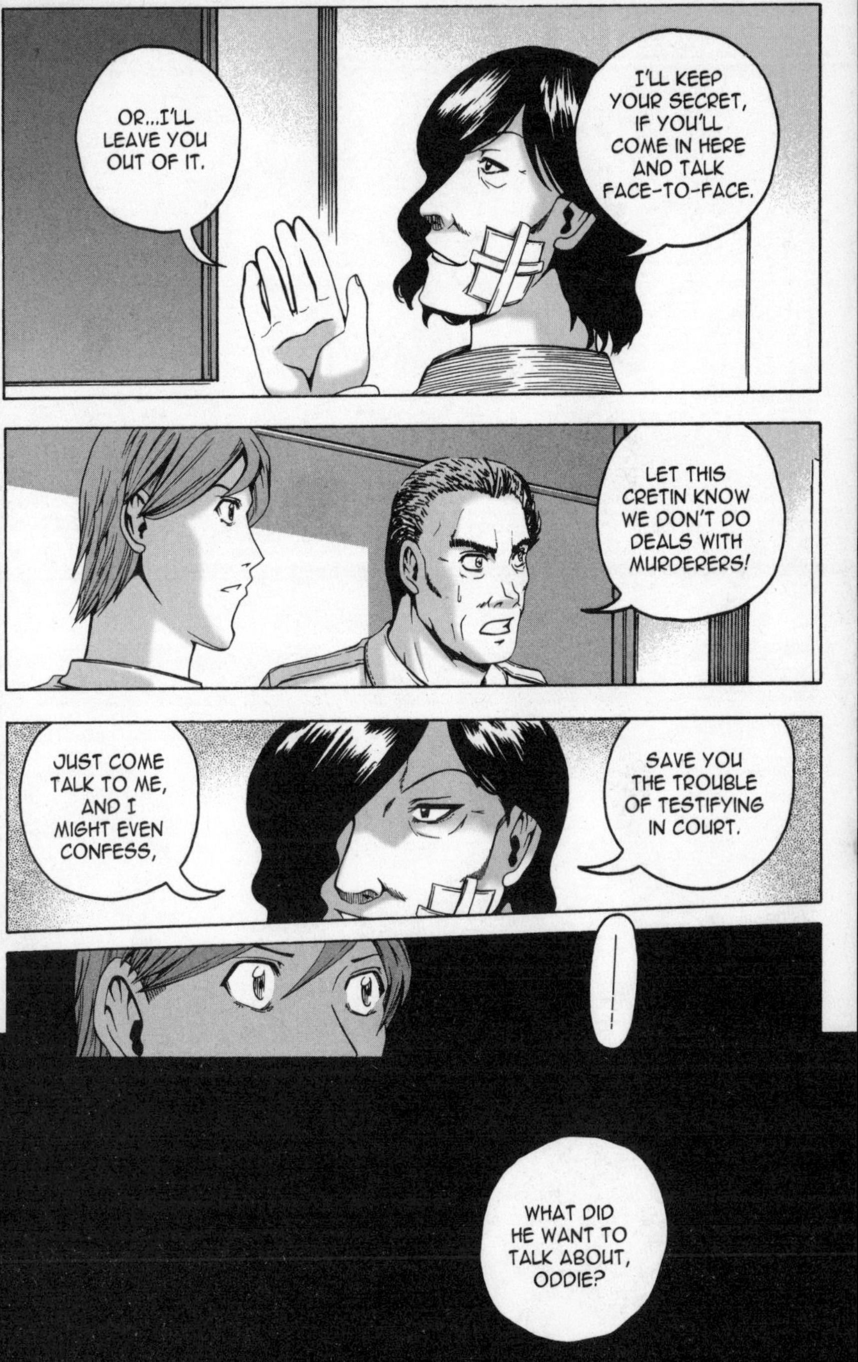
OR...I'LL LEAVE YOU OUT OF IT.
I'LL KEEP YOUR SECRET, IF YOU'LL COME IN HERE AND TALK FACE-TO-FACE.
LET THIS CRETIN KNOW WE DON'T DO DEALS WITH MURDERERS!
JUST COME TALK TO ME, AND I MIGHT EVEN CONFESS,
SAVE YOU THE TROUBLE OF TESTIFYING IN COURT.
WHAT DID HE WANT TO TALK ABOUT, ODDIE?

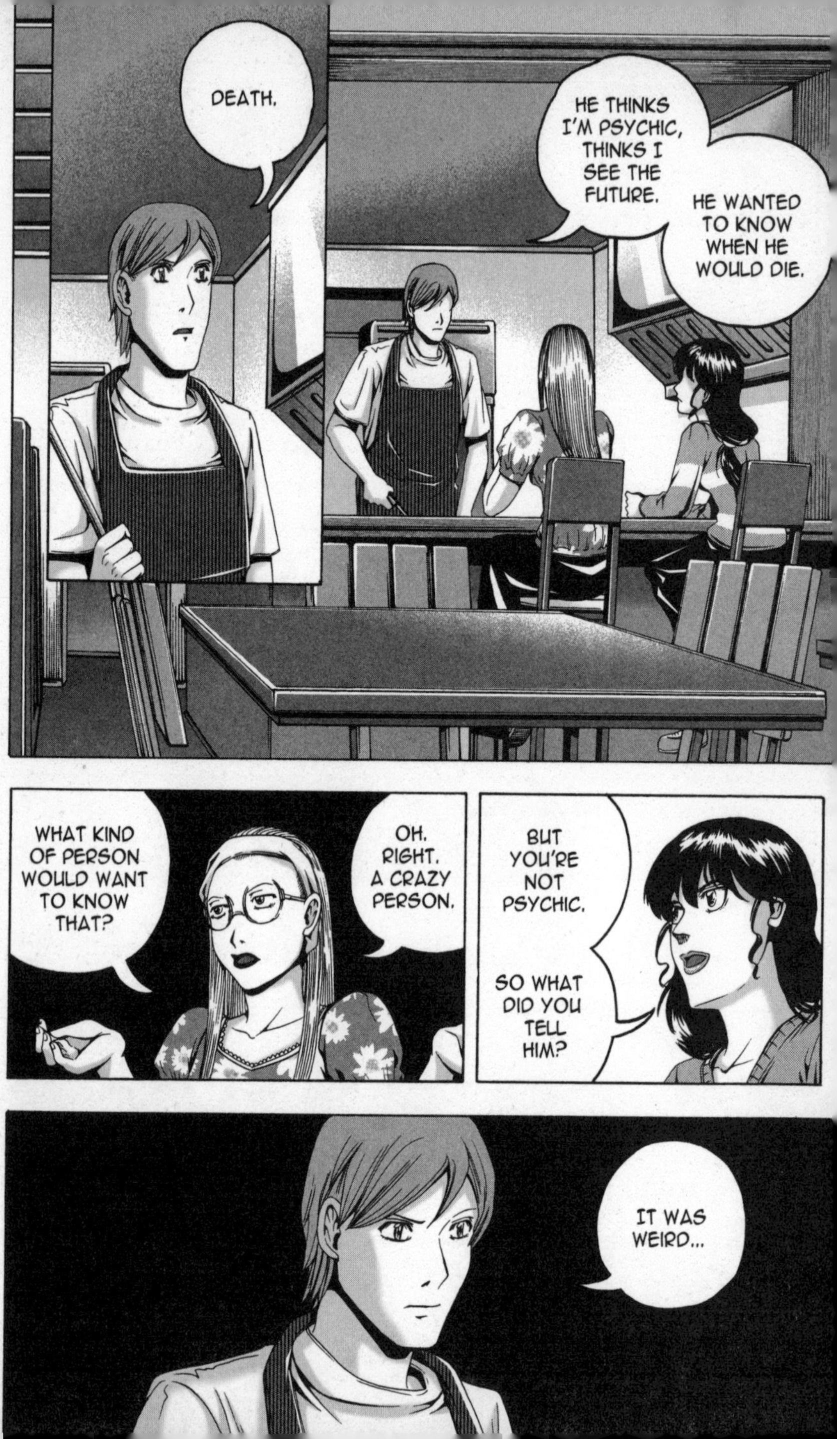
DEATH.
HE THINKS I'M PSYCHIC, THINKS I SEE THE FUTURE.
HE WANTED TO KNOW WHEN HE WOULD DIE.
WHAT KIND OF PERSON WOULD WANT TO KNOW THAT?
OH. RIGHT. A CRAZY PERSON.
BUT YOU'RE NOT PSYCHIC.
SO WHAT DID YOU TELL HIM?
IT WAS WEIRD...

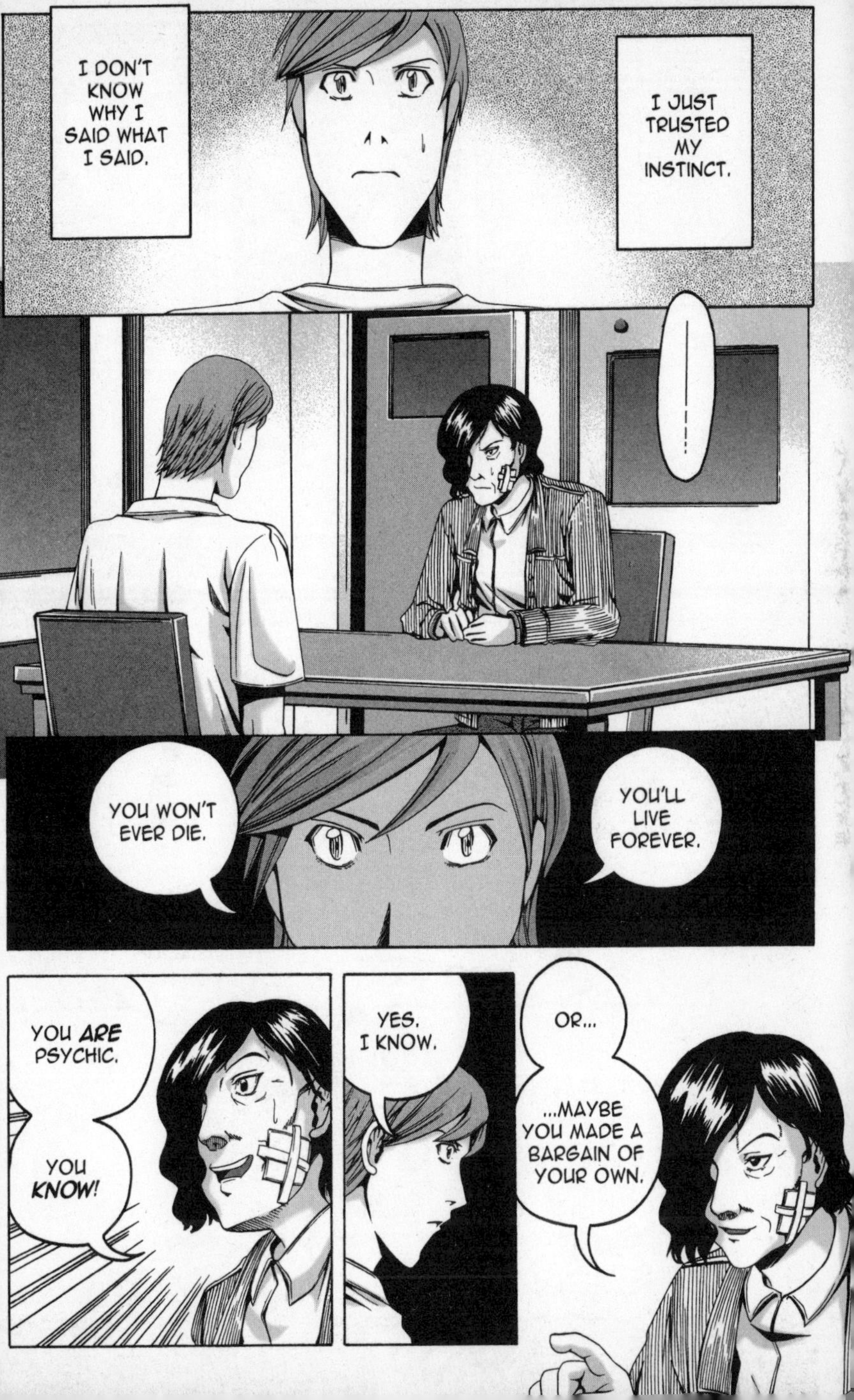
I DON'T KNOW WHY I SAID WHAT I SAID.
I JUST TRUSTED MY INSTINCT.
!
YOU WON'T EVER DIE.
YOU'LL LIVE FOREVER.
YOU ARE PSYCHIC.
YOU KNOW!
YES. I KNOW.
OR...
...MAYBE YOU MADE A BARGAIN OF YOUR OWN.

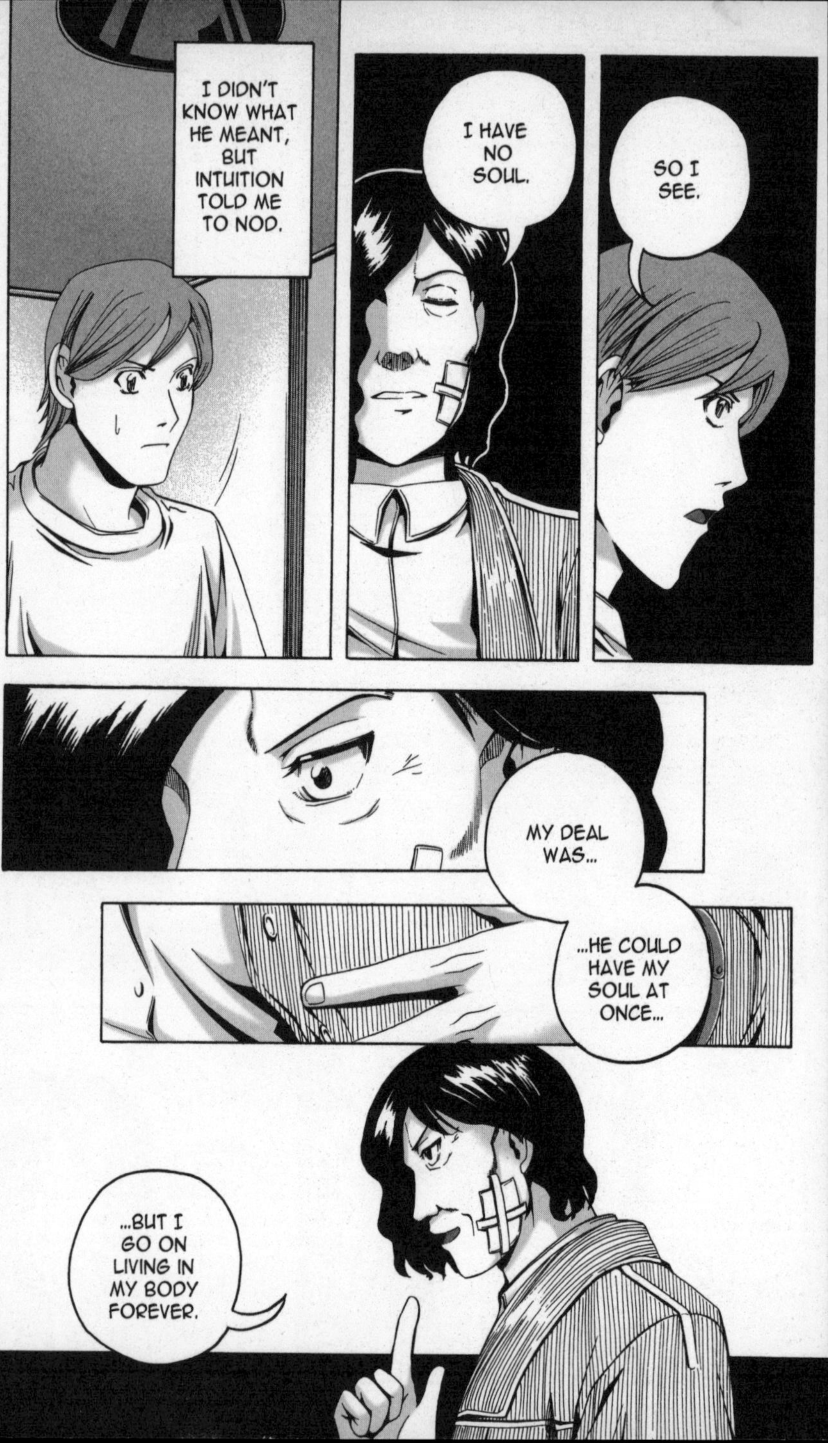
I DIDN'T KNOW WHAT HE MEANT, BUT INTUITION TOLD ME TO NOD.
I HAVE NO SOUL.
SO I SEE.
MY DEAL WAS...
...HE COULD HAVE MY SOUL AT ONCE...
...BUT I GO ON LIVING IN MY BODY FOREVER.

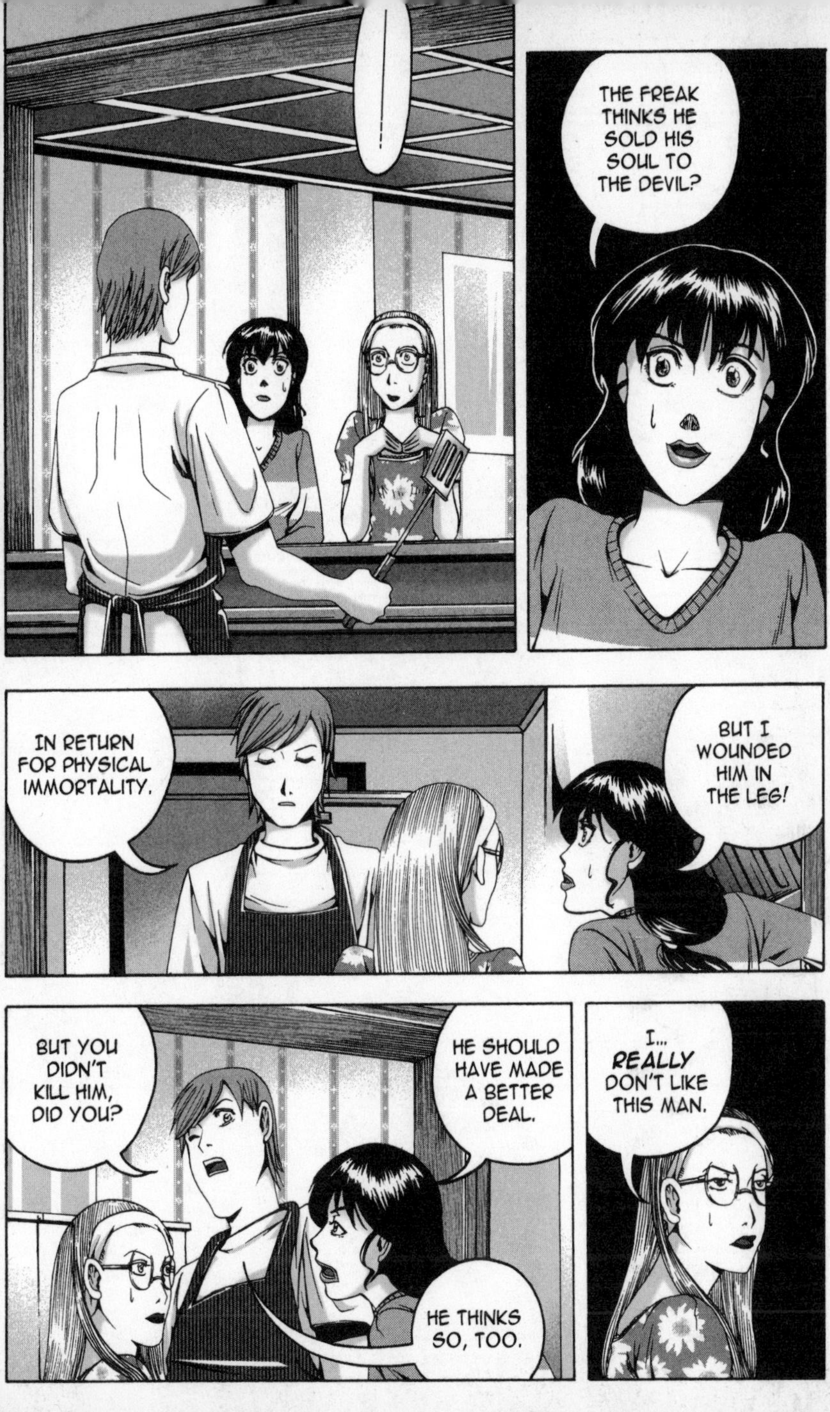
!
THE FREAK THINKS HE SOLD HIS SOUL TO THE DEVIL?
IN RETURN FOR PHYSICAL IMMORTALITY.
BUT I WOUNDED HIM IN THE LEG!
BUT YOU DIDN'T KILL HIM, DID YOU?
HE SHOULD HAVE MADE A BETTER DEAL.
HE THINKS SO, TOO.
I... REALLY DON'T LIKE THIS MAN.

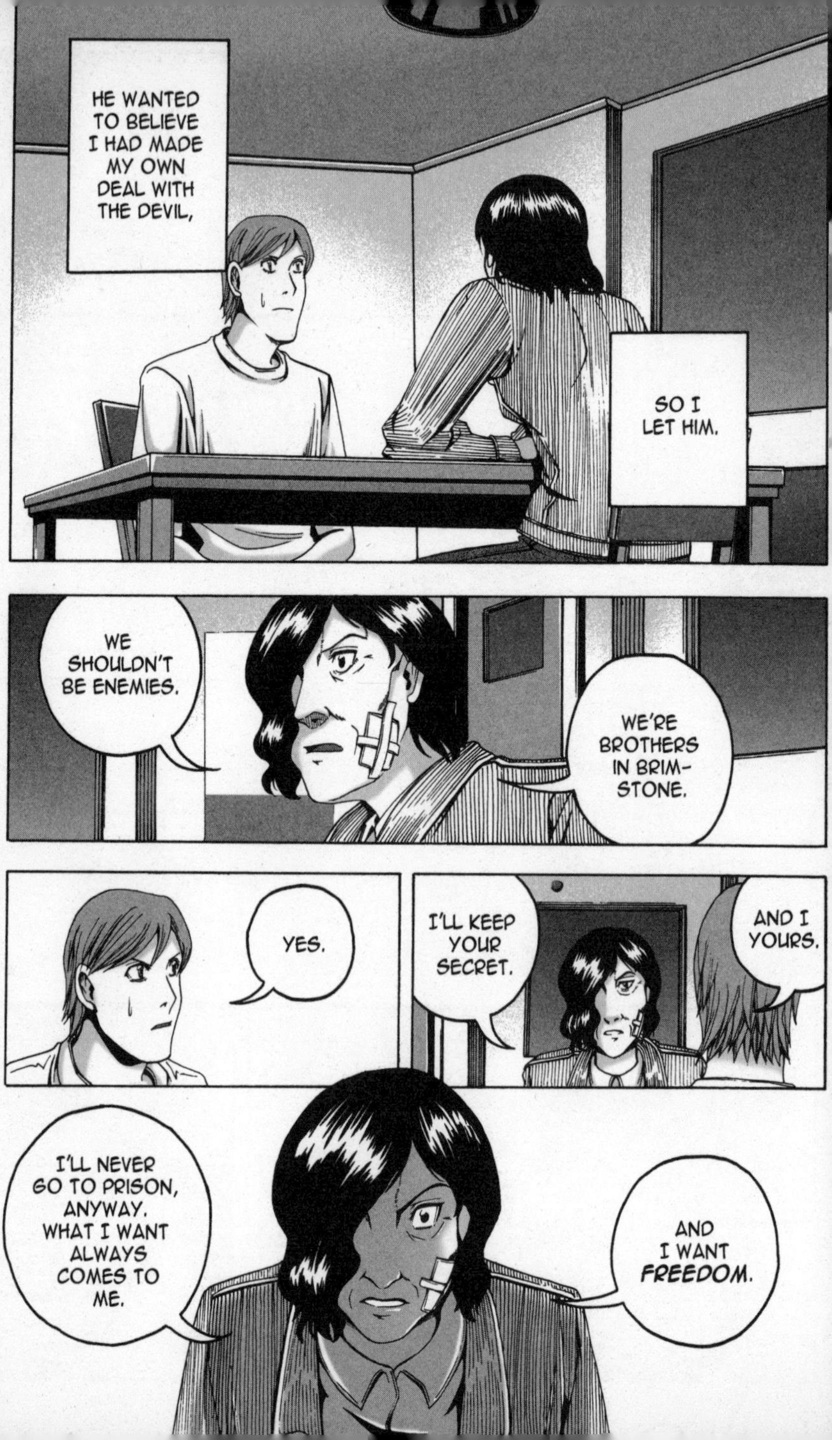
HE WANTED TO BELIEVE I HAD MADE MY OWN DEAL WITH THE DEVIL,
SO I LET HIM.
WE SHOULDN'T BE ENEMIES.
WE'RE BROTHERS IN BRIM-STONE.
YES.
I'LL KEEP YOUR SECRET.
AND I YOURS.
I'LL NEVER GO TO PRISON, ANYWAY. WHAT I WANT ALWAYS COMES TO ME.
AND I WANT *FREEDOM*.

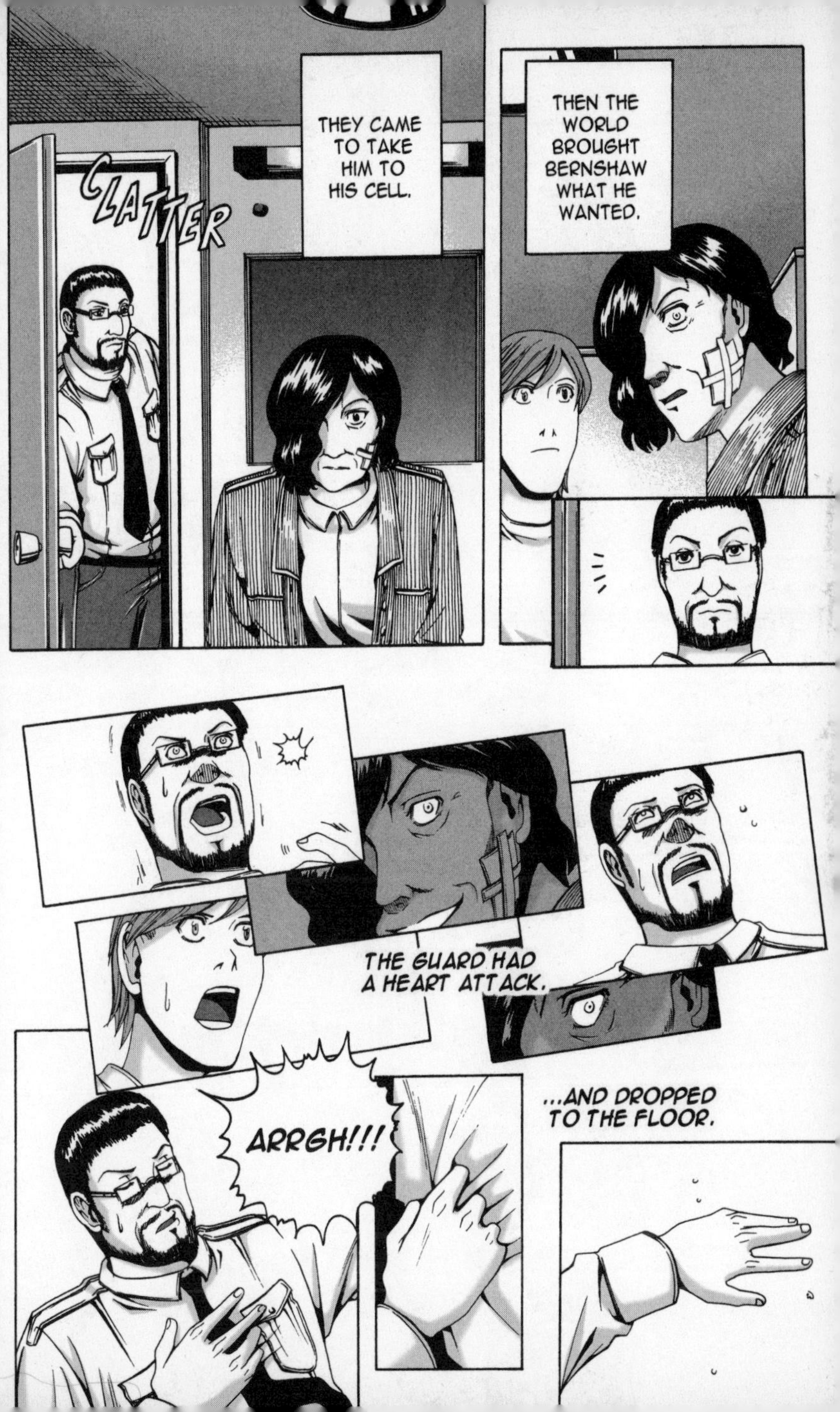
THEY CAME TO TAKE HIM TO HIS CELL.
CLATTER
THEN THE WORLD BROUGHT BERNSHAW WHAT HE WANTED.
THE GUARD HAD A HEART ATTACK.
ARRGH!!!
...AND DROPPED TO THE FLOOR.

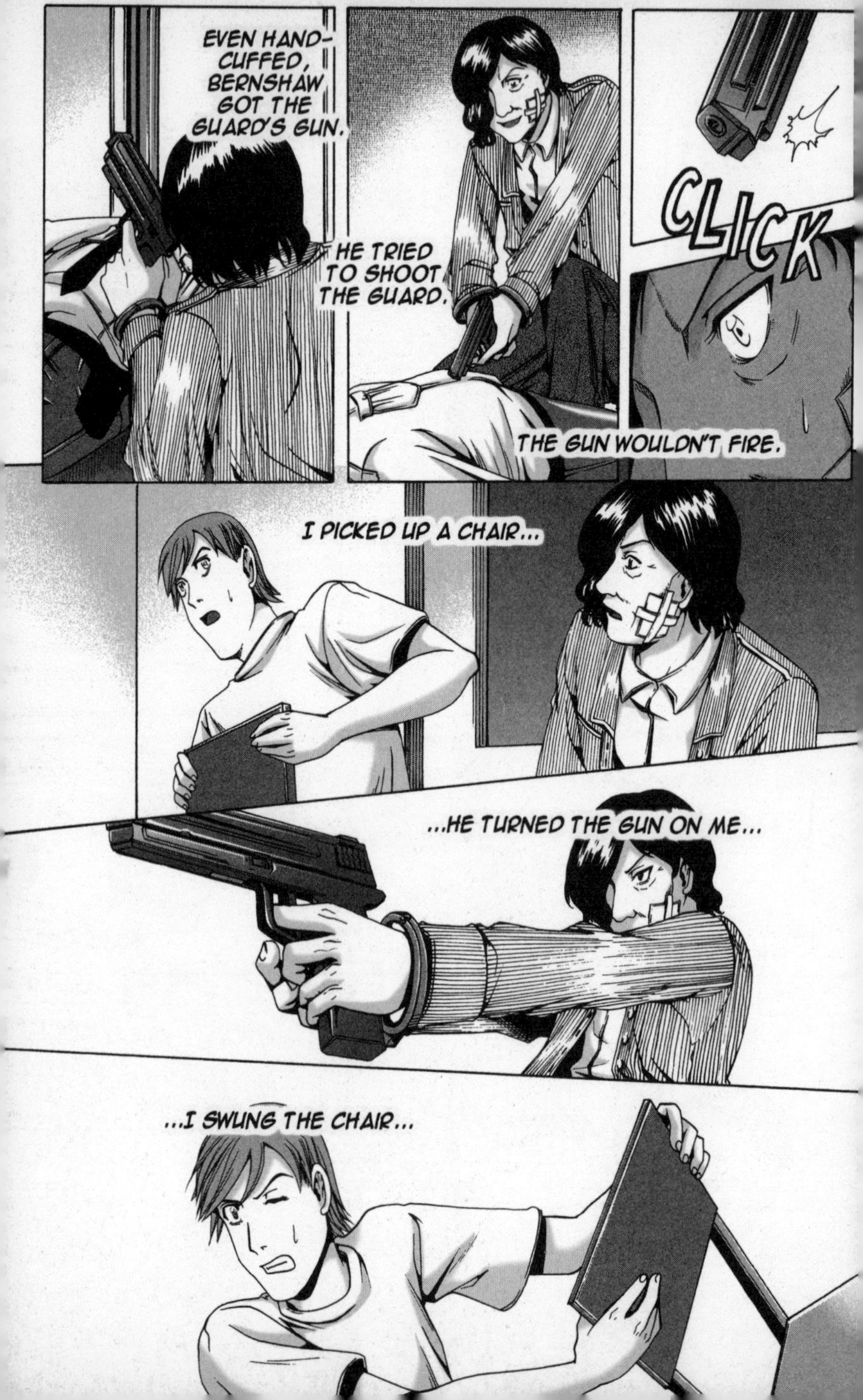
EVEN HAND-CUFFED, BERNSHAW GOT THE GUARD'S GUN.
HE TRIED TO SHOOT THE GUARD.
CLICK
THE GUN WOULDN'T FIRE.
I PICKED UP A CHAIR...
...HE TURNED THE GUN ON ME...
...I SWUNG THE CHAIR...

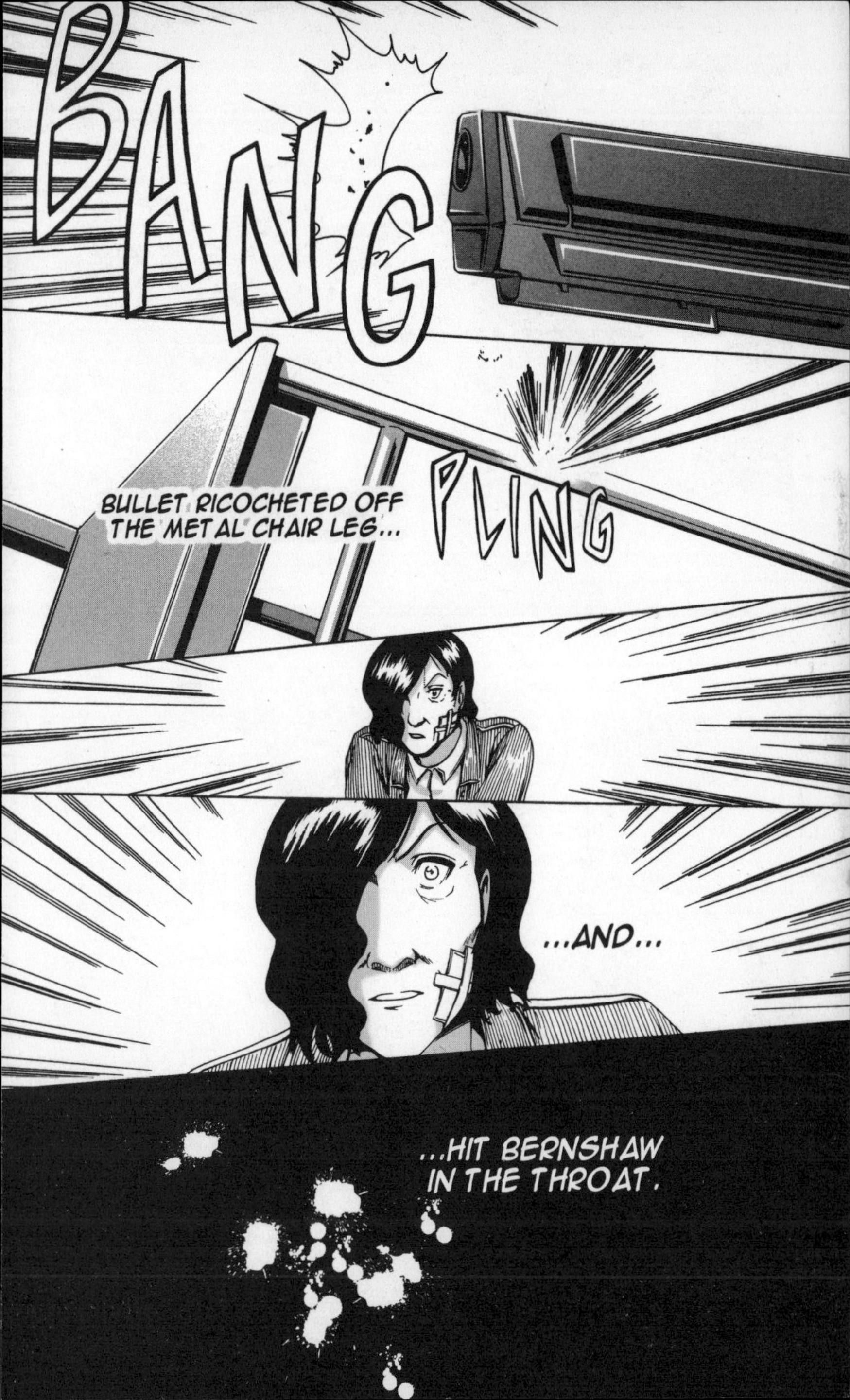
BANG
BULLET RICOCHETED OFF THE METAL CHAIR LEG...
PLING
...AND...
...HIT BERNSHAW IN THE THROAT.

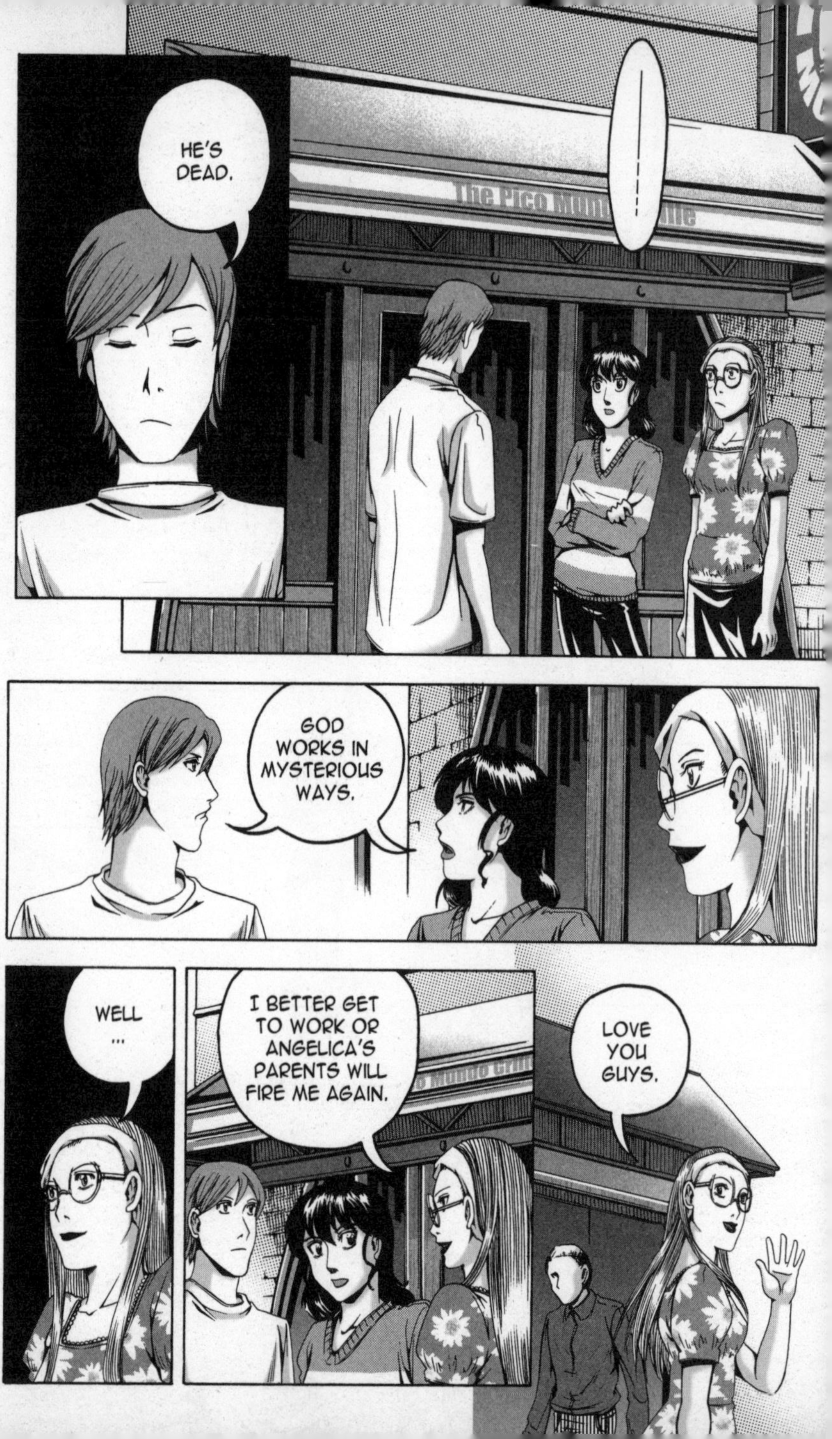
HE'S DEAD.
!
GOD WORKS IN MYSTERIOUS WAYS.
WELL ...
I BETTER GET TO WORK OR ANGELICA'S PARENTS WILL FIRE ME AGAIN.
LOVE YOU GUYS.

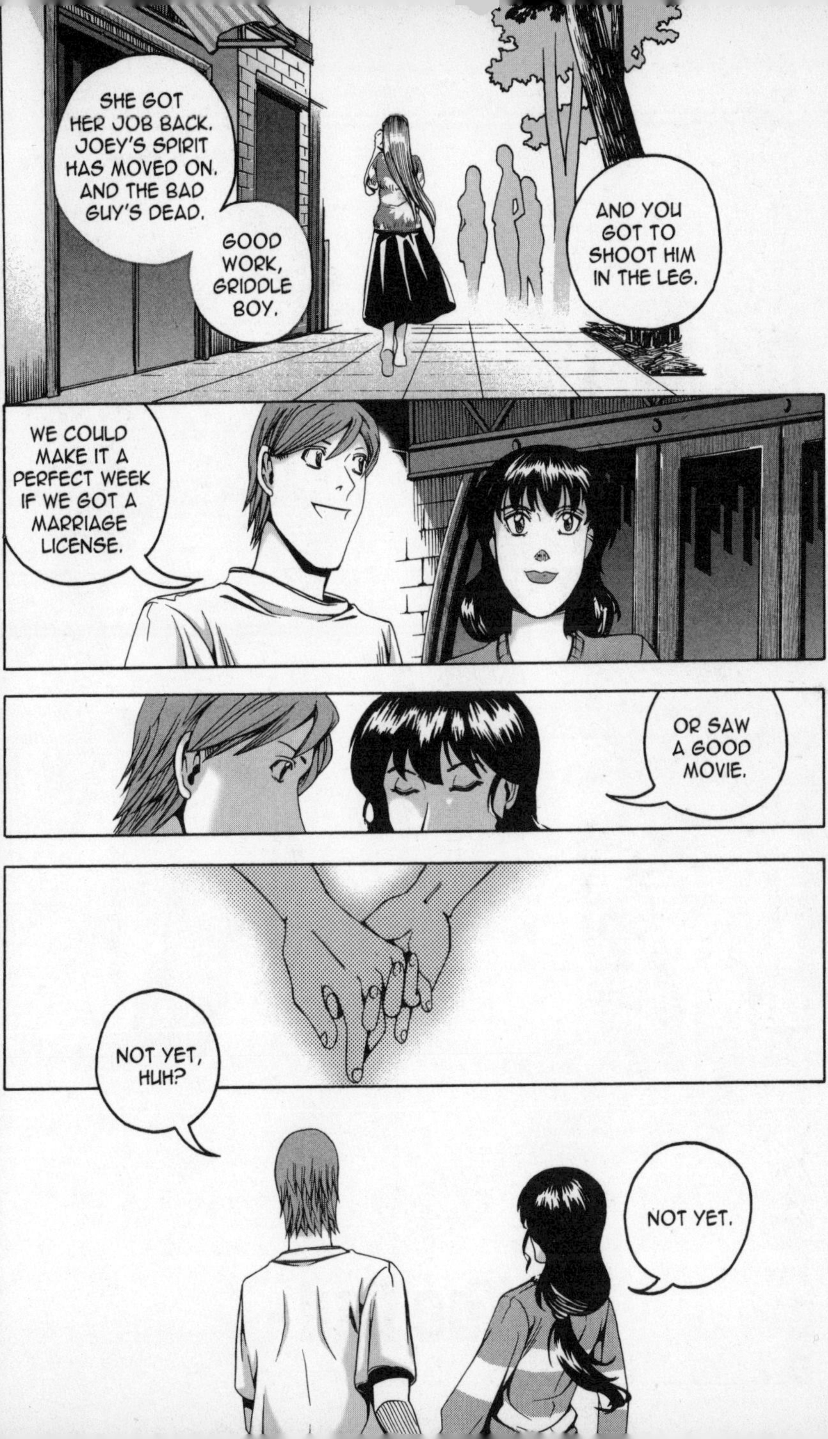
SHE GOT HER JOB BACK. JOEY'S SPIRIT HAS MOVED ON. AND THE BAD GUY'S DEAD.
GOOD WORK, GRIDDLE BOY.
AND YOU GOT TO SHOOT HIM IN THE LEG.
WE COULD MAKE IT A PERFECT WEEK IF WE GOT A MARRIAGE LICENSE.
OR SAW A GOOD MOVIE.
NOT YET, HUH?
NOT YET.

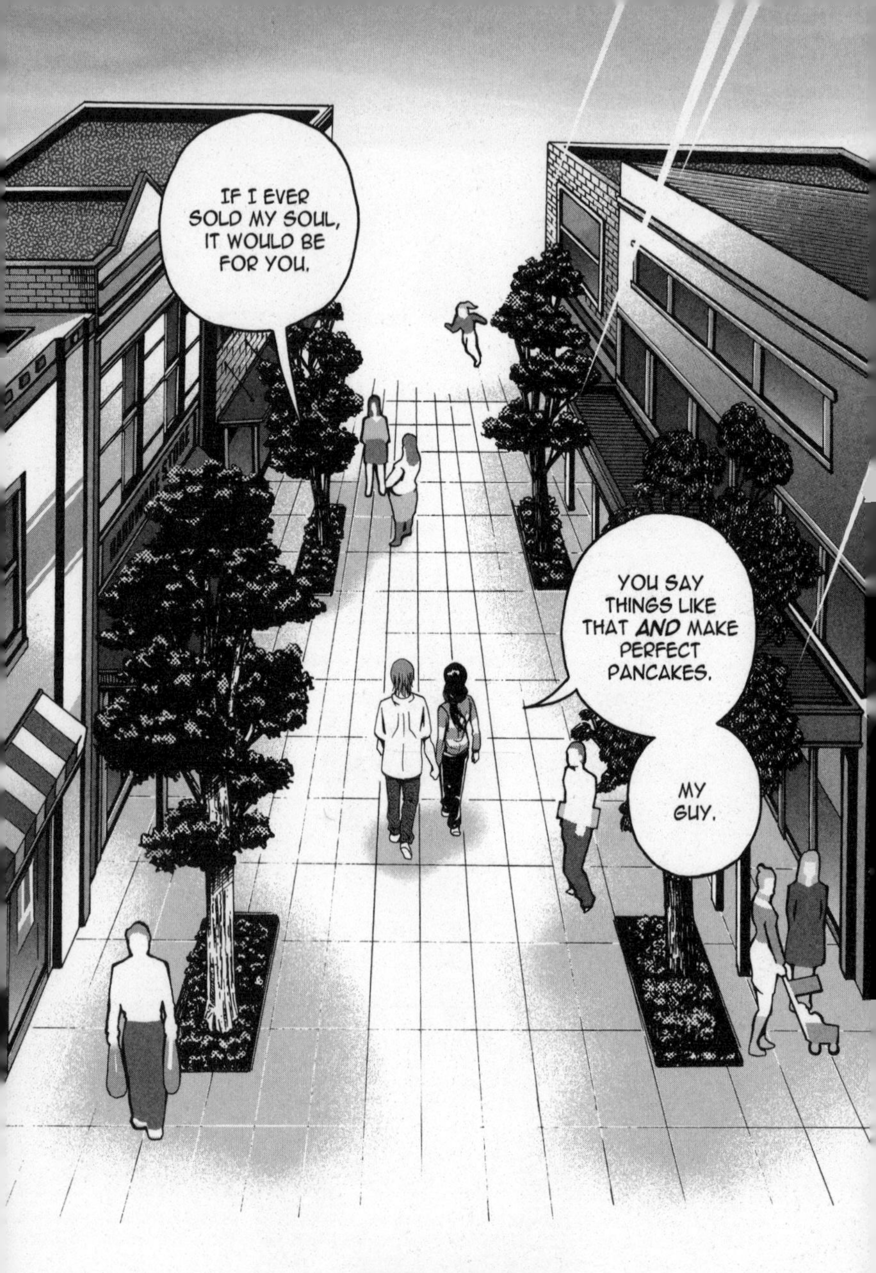
IF I EVER SOLD MY SOUL, IT WOULD BE FOR YOU.
YOU SAY THINGS LIKE THAT AND MAKE PERFECT PANCAKES.
MY GUY.

- The End -

ABOUT THE CREATORS

DEAN KOONTZ is the author of many #1 *New York Times* bestsellers. He lives with his wife, Gerda, in Southern California.

QUEENIE CHAN was born in 1980 in Hong Kong and emigrated to Australia when she was six years old. She began drawing at the age of 18 and graduated in 2002 with a degree in Information Systems. In 2004, she began drawing a mystery-horror series called *The Dreaming* for Los Angeles-based manga publisher Tokyopop, the three volumes of which are now available. It has been translated into four languages. Apart from her professional work, Queenie Chan also draws a number of online manga strips on her personal site:

http://www.queeniechan.com/

THE ODD FACE IN THE MIRROR

Dean Koontz

DURING MY CAREER, I HAVE WRITTEN A TOWNFUL OF CHARAC-
ters, maybe enough of them to populate Pico Mundo, California, in
which Odd Thomas lived his first twenty years. I have provided physical descriptions of those people, some in more detail than others. In
all but one case, during the writing of the books in which those people appeared, I had vivid images of their faces in my mind.

The exception was Odd Thomas. By page two, I *knew* Oddie more
intimately than I had ever known another character after writing so
few words about him. What I knew of Odd, however, was his heart,
every chamber of it, all its secrets, all the hopes and dreams that he
sheltered there, all his losses. I knew his goodness, his self-doubt, his
capacity for friendship and for love, his extraordinary humility. I did
not know what his face looked like.

Because the book employed a first-person point of view, I could
not describe him from the eyes of another character, and I did not
want to engage in any hokum like having him look in a mirror and describe himself. Rather than stop writing and brood about his face, I let
the narrative flow, certain that the details would accumulate until I
could see him clearly in my mind's eye.

By the time I finished *Odd Thomas*, the first novel in the series, I not only knew Odd's heart but also the singular workings of his mind, and not least of all the architecture of his soul. I knew him as well as—perhaps better than—I knew myself. I knew his body type. His physical qualities were clear: real strength without Schwarzeneggerian muscularity; masculinity without bravado; natural athleticism; the agility of a dancer; confidence in every pose and position, but never arrogance; self-effacement that expressed even in his physicality, so that he seemed unremarkable though he was in fact exceptional.

After three books—and a fourth in the works—I do not know his face. The actor to whom readers most often refer is Tobey Maguire, and I think Mr. Maguire—although soon too old for the part—would be terrific because he can project innocence without naiveté and can portray genuine goodness rather than the cloying kind. Yet Oddie's face is not Tobey Maguire's. It is nothing like the face of any actor anyone has named.

When we developed an avatar of Oddie for the website, we came up with one that I liked. But it's not his face. I thought at first that the limitations of avatar design would not allow us the detail necessary to capture the real Odd Thomas.

When the wonderful Queenie Chan presented her engaging sketches for the book you hold in your hands, I liked her Odd very much, and felt he worked perfectly for a manga. But this was not Odd's face any more than Tobey Maguire's face is Odd's.

As I write this, I am at work on *Odd Hours,* and I have begun to understand why Oddie's face will not materialize in my mind when I strive to envision it. The reason for this arises from Odd's destiny and from his fundamental nature, which have become apparent to me as I work on this book. Because he is an archetypal character in a way I did not fully understand until he revealed it to me during this fourth novel, no face is right for him; every face is his face, in one sense, and in another sense, he is not to be understood whatsoever by his appearance but only by what will prove to be his fundamental nature, which is why his face eludes me.

I now believe that, God willing, there will be six Odd Thomas novels. His end will prove to be there in his beginning, and his beginning in his end. When I get to the last page of the sixth book, I believe it will be apparent to me that everything in the series was to be foreseen in the first book, perhaps in the first chapter of the first book. And yet where I find this going is a great surprise to me and extremely exciting. Pulling off books five and six with the grace they require will be an epic challenge, and all I can do is follow my fry cook and hope that, when it's over, I will feel that the whole series was as much a gift to me as was the first book.

Odd's adventures continue in several full-length novels by Dean Koontz. Read on for a sample chapter from *Odd Thomas,* in which a stranger comes to Pico Mundo accompanied by a horde of hyena-like shades who herald an imminent catastrophe. Odd, Stormy, Chief Porter, and others must race against time to thwart the gathering evil. *Odd Thomas* is published by Bantam Books and © 2003 by Dean Koontz.

ONE

MY NAME IS ODD THOMAS, THOUGH IN THIS AGE WHEN FAME is the altar at which most people worship, I am not sure why you should care who I am or that I exist.

I am not a celebrity. I am not the child of a celebrity. I have never been married to, never been abused by, and never provided a kidney for transplantation into any celebrity. Furthermore, I have no desire to be a celebrity.

In fact I am such a nonentity by the standards of our culture that *People* magazine not only will never feature a piece about me but might also reject my attempts to subscribe to their publication on the grounds that the black-hole gravity of my noncelebrity is powerful enough to suck their entire enterprise into oblivion.

I am twenty years old. To a world-wise adult, I am little more than a child. To any child, however, I'm old enough to be distrusted, to be excluded forever from the magical community of the short and beardless.

Consequently, a demographics expert might conclude that my sole audience is other young men and women currently adrift between their twentieth and twenty-first birthdays.

In truth, I have nothing to say to that narrow audience. In my experience, I don't care about most of the things that other twenty-year-old Americans care about. Except survival, of course.

I lead an unusual life.

By this I do not mean that my life is better than yours. I'm sure that your life is filled with as much happiness, charm, wonder, and abiding fear as anyone could wish. Like me, you are human, after all, and we know what a joy and terror *that* is.

I mean only that my life is not typical. Peculiar things happen to me that don't happen to other people with regularity, if ever.

For example, I would never have written this memoir if I had not been commanded to do so by a four-hundred-pound man with six fingers on his left hand.

His name is P. Oswald Boone. Everyone calls him Little Ozzie because his father, Big Ozzie, is still alive.

Little Ozzie has a cat named Terrible Chester. He loves that cat. In fact, if Terrible Chester were to use up his ninth life under the wheels of a Peterbilt, I am afraid that Little Ozzie's big heart would not survive the loss.

Personally, I do not have great affection for Terrible Chester because, for one thing, he has on several occasions peed on my shoes.

His reason for doing so, as explained by Ozzie, seems credible, but I am not convinced of his truthfulness. I mean to say that I am suspicious of Terrible Chester's veracity, not Ozzie's.

Besides, I simply cannot fully trust a cat who claims to be fifty-eight years old. Although photographic evidence exists to support this claim, I persist in believing that it's bogus.

For reasons that will become obvious, this manuscript cannot be published during my lifetime, and my effort will not be repaid with royalties while I'm alive. Little Ozzie suggests that I should leave my literary estate to the loving maintenance of Terrible Chester, who, according to him, will outlive all of us.

I will choose another charity. One that has not peed on me.

Anyway, I'm not writing this for money. I am writing it to save my sanity and to discover if I can convince myself that my life has purpose and meaning enough to justify continued existence.

Don't worry: These ramblings will not be insufferably gloomy. P. Oswald Boone has sternly instructed me to keep the tone light.

"If you don't keep it light," Ozzie said, "I'll sit my four-hundred-pound ass on you, and that's *not* the way you want to die."

Ozzie is bragging. His ass, while grand enough, probably weighs no more than a hundred and fifty pounds. The other two hundred fifty are distributed across the rest of his suffering skeleton.

When at first I proved unable to keep the tone light, Ozzie suggested that I be an unreliable narrator. "It worked for Agatha Christie in *The Murder of Roger Ackroyd*," he said.

In that first-person mystery novel, the nice-guy narrator turns out to be the murderer of Roger Ackroyd, a fact he conceals from the reader until the end.

Understand, I am not a murderer. I have done nothing evil that I am concealing from you. My unreliability as a narrator has to do largely with the tense of certain verbs.

Don't worry about it. You'll know the truth soon enough.

Anyway, I'm getting ahead of my story. Little Ozzie and Terrible Chester do not enter the picture until after the cow explodes.

This story began on a Tuesday.

For you, that is the day after Monday. For me, it is a day that, like the other six, brims with the potential for mystery, adventure, and terror.

You should not take this to mean that my life is romantic and magical. Too much mystery is merely an annoyance. Too much adventure is exhausting. And a little terror goes a long way.

Without the help of an alarm clock, I woke that Tuesday morning at five, from a dream about dead bowling-alley employees.

I never set the alarm because my internal clock is so reliable. If I wish to wake promptly at five, then before going to bed I tell myself three times that I must be awake sharply at 4:45.

While reliable, my internal alarm clock for some reason runs fifteen minutes slow. I learned this years ago and have adjusted to the problem.

The dream about the dead bowling-alley employees has troubled my sleep once or twice a month for three years. The details are not yet specific enough to act upon. I will have to wait and hope that clarification doesn't come to me too late.

So I woke at five, sat up in bed, and said, "Spare me that I may serve," which is the morning prayer that my Granny Sugars taught me to say when I was little.

Pearl Sugars was my mother's mother. If she had been my father's mother, my name would be Odd Sugars, further complicating my life.

Granny Sugars believed in bargaining with God. She called Him "that old rug merchant."

Before every poker game, she promised God to spread His holy word or to share her good fortune with orphans in return for a few unbeatable hands. Throughout her life, winnings from card games remained a significant source of income.

Being a hard-drinking woman with numerous interests in addition to poker, Granny Sugars didn't always spend as much time spreading God's word as she promised Him that she would. She believed that God expected to be conned more often than not and that He would be a good sport about it.

You can con God and get away with it, Granny said, if you do so with charm and wit. If you live your life with imagination and verve, God will play along just to see what outrageously entertaining thing you'll do next.

He'll also cut you some slack if you're astonishingly stupid in an amusing fashion. Granny claimed that this explains why uncountable millions of breathtakingly stupid people get along just fine in life.

Of course, in the process, you must never do harm to others in any serious way, or you'll cease to amuse Him. Then payment comes due for the promises you didn't keep.

In spite of drinking lumberjacks under the table, regularly winning at poker with stone-hearted psychopaths who didn't like to lose, driving fast cars with utter contempt for the laws of physics (but never while intoxicated), and eating a diet rich in pork fat, Granny Sugars died peacefully in her sleep at the age of seventy-two. They found her with a nearly empty snifter of brandy on the nightstand, a book by her favorite novelist turned to the last page, and a smile on her face.

Judging by all available evidence, Granny and God understood each other pretty well.

Pleased to be alive that Tuesday morning, on the dark side of the dawn, I switched on my nightstand lamp and surveyed the chamber that served as my bedroom, living room, kitchen, and dining room. I never get out of bed until I know who, if anyone, is waiting for me.

If visitors either benign or malevolent had spent part of the night watching me sleep, they had not lingered for a breakfast chat. Sometimes simply getting from bed to bathroom can take the charm out of a new day.

Only Elvis was there, wearing the lei of orchids, smiling, and pointing one finger at me as if it were a cocked gun.

Although I enjoy living above this particular two-car garage, and though I find my quarters cozy, *Architectural Digest* will not be seeking an exclusive photo layout. If one of their glamour scouts saw my place, he'd probably note, with disdain, that the second word in the magazine's name is not, after all, *Indigestion.*

The life-size cardboard figure of Elvis, part of a theater-lobby display promoting *Blue Hawaii,* was where I'd left it. Occasionally, it moves—or is moved—during the night.

I showered with peach-scented soap and peach shampoo, which were given to me by Stormy Llewellyn. Her real first name is Bronwen, but she thinks that makes her sound like an elf.

My real name actually is Odd.

According to my mother, this is an uncorrected birth-certificate error. Sometimes she says they intended to name me Todd. Other times she says it was Dobb, after a Czechoslovakian uncle.

My father insists that they always intended to name me Odd, although he won't tell me why. He notes that I don't have a Czechoslovakian uncle.

My mother vigorously asserts the existence of the uncle, though she refuses to explain why I've never met either him or her sister, Cymry, to whom he is supposedly married.

Although my father acknowledges the existence of Cymry, he is adamant that she has never married. He says that she is a freak, but what he means by this I don't know, for he will say no more.

My mother becomes infuriated at the suggestion that her sister is any kind of freak. She calls Cymry a gift from God but otherwise remains uncommunicative on the subject.

I find it easier to live with the name Odd than to contest it. By the time I was old enough to realize that it was an unusual name, I had grown comfortable with it.

Stormy Llewellyn and I are more than friends. We believe that we are soul mates.

For one thing, we have a card from a carnival fortune-telling machine that says we're destined to be together forever.

We also have matching birthmarks.

Cards and birthmarks aside, I love her intensely. I would throw myself off a high cliff for her if she asked me to jump. I would, of course, need to understand the reasoning behind her request.

Fortunately for me, Stormy is not the kind of person to ask such a thing lightly. She expects nothing of others that she herself would not do. In treacherous currents, she is kept steady by a moral anchor the size of a ship.

She once brooded for an entire day about whether to keep fifty cents that she found in the change-return slot of a pay phone. At last she mailed it to the telephone company.

Returning to the cliff for a moment, I don't mean to imply that I'm afraid of Death. I'm just not ready to go out on a date with him.

Smelling like a peach, as Stormy likes me, not afraid of Death, having eaten a blueberry muffin, saying good-bye to Elvis with the words "Taking care of business" in a lousy imitation of his voice, I set off for work at the Pico Mundo Grille.

Although the dawn had just broken, it had already flash-fried into a hard yellow yolk on the eastern horizon.

The town of Pico Mundo is in that part of southern California where you can never forget that in spite of all the water imported by the state aqueduct system, the true condition of the territory is desert. In March we bake. In August, which this was, we broil.

The ocean lay so far to the west that it was no more real to us than the Sea of Tranquility, that vast dark plain on the face of the moon.

Occasionally, when excavating for a new subdivision of tract homes on the outskirts of town, developers had struck rich veins of seashells in their deeper diggings. Once upon an ancient age, waves lapped these shores.

If you put one of those shells to your ear, you will not hear the surf breaking but only a dry mournful wind, as if the shell has forgotten its origins.

At the foot of the exterior steps that led down from my small apartment, in the early sun, Penny Kallisto waited like a shell on a shore. She wore red sneakers, white shorts, and a sleeveless white blouse.

Ordinarily, Penny had none of that preadolescent despair to which some kids prove so susceptible these days. She was an ebullient twelve-year-old, outgoing and quick to laugh.

This morning, however, she looked solemn. Her blue eyes darkened as does the sea under the passage of a cloud.

I glanced toward the house, fifty feet away, where my landlady, Rosalia Sanchez, would be expecting me at any minute to confirm that she had not disappeared during the night. The sight of herself in a mirror was never sufficient to put her fear to rest.

Without a word, Penny turned away from the stairs. She walked toward the front of the property.

Like a pair of looms, using sunshine and their own silhouettes, two enormous California live oaks wove veils of gold and purple, which they flung across the driveway.

Penny appeared to shimmer and to darkle as she passed through this intricate lace of light and shade. A black mantilla of shadow dimmed the luster of her blond hair, its elaborate pattern changing as she moved.

Afraid of losing her, I hurried down the last of the steps and followed the girl. Mrs. Sanchez would have to wait, and worry.

Penny led me past the house, off the driveway, to a birdbath on the front lawn. Around the base of the pedestal that supported the basin, Rosalia Sanchez had arranged a collection of dozens of the seashells, all shapes and sizes, that had been scooped from the hills of Pico Mundo.

Penny stooped, selected a specimen about the size of an orange, stood once more, and held it out to me.

The architecture resembled that of a conch. The rough exterior was brown and white, the polished interior shone pearly pink.

Cupping her right hand as though she still held the shell, Penny brought it to her ear. She cocked her head to listen, thus indicating what she wanted me to do.

When I put the shell to my ear, I did not hear the sea. Neither did I hear the melancholy desert wind that I mentioned previously.

Instead, from the shell came the rough breathing of a beast. The urgent rhythm of a cruel need, the grunt of mad desire.

Here in the summer desert, winter found my blood.

When she saw from my expression that I had heard what she wished me to hear, Penny crossed the lawn to the public sidewalk. She stood at the curb, gazing toward the west end of Marigold Lane.

I dropped the shell, went to her side, and waited with her.

Evil was coming. I wondered whose face it would be wearing.

Old Indian laurels line this street. Their great gnarled surface roots have in places cracked and buckled the concrete walkway.

Not a whisper of air moved through the trees. The morning lay as uncannily still as dawn on Judgment Day one breath before the sky would crack open.

Like Mrs. Sanchez's place, most houses in this neighborhood are Victorian in style, with varying degrees of gingerbread. When Pico Mundo was founded, in 1900, many residents were immigrants from the East Coast, and they preferred architectures better suited to that distant colder, damper shore.

Perhaps they thought they could bring to this valley only those things they loved, leaving behind all ugliness.

We are not, however, a species that can choose the baggage with which it must travel. In spite of our best intentions, we always find that we have brought along a suitcase or two of darkness, and misery.

For half a minute, the only movement was that of a hawk gliding high above, glimpsed between laurel branches.

The hawk and I were hunters this morning.

Penny Kallisto must have sensed my fear. She took my right hand in her left.

I was grateful for this kindness. Her grip proved firm, and her hand did not feel cold. I drew courage from her strong spirit.

Because the car was idling in gear, rolling at just a few miles per hour, I didn't hear anything until it turned the corner. When I recognized the vehicle, I knew a sadness equal to my fear.

This 1968 Pontiac Firebird 400 had been restored with loving care. The two-door, midnight-blue convertible appeared to glide toward us with all tires a fraction of an inch off the pavement, shimmering like a mirage in the morning heat.

Harlo Landerson and I had been in the same high-school class. During his junior and senior years, Harlo rebuilt this car from the axles up, until it looked as cherry as it had in the autumn of '67, when it had first stood on a showroom floor.

Self-effacing, somewhat shy, Harlo had not labored on the car with the hope either that it would be a babe magnet or that those who had thought of him as tepid would suddenly think he was cool enough to freeze the mercury in a thermometer. He'd had no social ambitions. He had suffered no illusions about his chances of ever rising above the lower ranks of the high-school caste system.

With a 335-horsepower V-8 engine, the Firebird could sprint from zero to sixty miles per hour in under eight seconds. Yet Harlo wasn't a street racer; he took no special pride in having wheels of fury.

He devoted much time, labor, and money to the Firebird because the beauty of its design and function enchanted him. This was a labor of the heart, a passion almost spiritual in its purity and intensity.

I sometimes thought the Pontiac figured so large in Harlo's life because he had no one to whom he could give the love that he lavished on the car. His mom died when he was six. His dad was a mean drunk.

A car can't return the love you give it. But if you're lonely enough, maybe the sparkle of the chrome, the luster of the paint, and the purr of the engine can be mistaken for affection.

Harlo and I hadn't been buddies, just friendly. I liked the guy. He was quiet, but quiet was better than the boast and bluster with which many kids jockeyed for social position in high school.

With Penny Kallisto still at my side, I raised my left hand and waved at Harlo.

Since high school, he'd worked hard. Nine to five, he unloaded trucks at Super Food and moved stock from storeroom to shelves.

Before that, beginning at 4:00 AM, he dropped hundreds of newspapers at homes on the east side of Pico Mundo. Once each week, he also delivered to *every* house a plastic bag full of advertising flyers and discount-coupon books.

This morning, he distributed only newspapers, tossing them with a snap of the wrist, as though they were boomerangs. Each folded and bagged copy of the Tuesday edition of the *Maravilla County Times* spun through the air and landed with a soft *thwop* on a driveway or a front walk, precisely where the subscriber preferred to have it.

Harlo was working the far side of the street. When he reached the house opposite me, he braked the coasting Pontiac to a stop.

Penny and I crossed to the car, and Harlo said, "Good mornin', Odd. How're you this fine day?"

"Bleak," I replied. "Sad. Confused."

He frowned with concern. "What's wrong? Anything I can do?"

"Something you've already done," I said.

Letting go of Penny's hand, I leaned into the Firebird from the passenger's side, switched off the engine, and plucked the key from the ignition.

Startled, Harlo grabbed for the keys but missed. "Hey, Odd, no foolin' around, okay? I have a tight schedule."

I never heard Penny's voice, but in the rich yet silent language of the soul, she must have spoken to me.

What I said to Harlo Landerson was the essence of what the girl revealed: "You have her blood in your pocket."

An innocent man would have been baffled by my statement. Harlo stared at me, his eyes suddenly owlish not with wisdom but with fear.

"On that night," I said, "you took with you three small squares of white felt."

One hand still on the wheel, Harlo looked away from me, through the windshield, as if willing the Pontiac to move.

"After using the girl, you collected some of her virgin blood with the squares of felt."

Harlo shivered. His face flushed red, perhaps with shame.

Anguish thickened my voice. "They dried stiff and dark, brittle like crackers."

His shivers swelled into violent tremors.

"You carry one of them with you at all times." My voice shook with emotion. "You like to smell it. Oh, God, Harlo. Sometimes you put it between your teeth. And bite on it."

He threw open the driver's door and fled.

I'm not the law. I'm not vigilante justice. I'm not vengeance personified. I don't really know what I am, or why.

In moments like these, however, I can't restrain myself from action. A kind of madness comes over me, and I can no more turn away from what must be done than I can wish this fallen world back into a state of grace.

As Harlo burst from the Pontiac, I looked down at Penny Kallisto and saw the ligature marks on her throat, which had not been visible when she had first appeared to me. The depth to which the garroting cloth had scored her flesh revealed the singular fury with which he had strangled her to death.

Pity tore at me, and I went after Harlo Landerson, for whom I had no pity whatsoever.

ARTIST'S SKETCHBOOK

Queenie Chan worked closely with Dean Koontz to arrive at the visual representation of each character. Some of her preliminary sketches appear on the pages that follow, along with her comments on the creation process.

Odd Thomas

ODD, AS THE EPONYMOUS CHARACTE
WAS THE MOST IMPORTANT AND
THE MOST DIFFICULT DESIGN I HAD
TO DO.

ODD IS MEANT TO BE AN
EVERYMAN, AN AVERAGE-LOOKING
GUY WHO IS QUIET AND GENTLE,
YET CAPABLE OF GREAT STRENGTH
(BOTH INNER AND OUTER) WHEN
REQUIRED.

THIS MEANS HIS DESIGN CAN'T
BE OUTLANDISH, BUT STILL HAS
TO BE UNIQUE AND EASILY
RECOGNIZABLE. HE ALSO HAS TO
BE ATTRACTIVE-LOOKING FOR THE
BENEFIT OF THE READERS, BUT NOT
TOO GOOD-LOOKING, SINCE HE'S
NOT MEANT TO BE HANDSOME.

IN THE END, I'M VERY HAPPY WITH
THIS DESIGN OF ODD, WHICH HAS A
HAIRSTYLE MORE SUITED TO DEAN'S
VISION OF THIS CHARACTER. HE HAS
AN EXPRESSIVE FACE IN THIS DESIGN,
BOTH OPEN AND HONEST, AS WELL
AS AN EASYGOING AND HUMBLE
APPEARANCE.

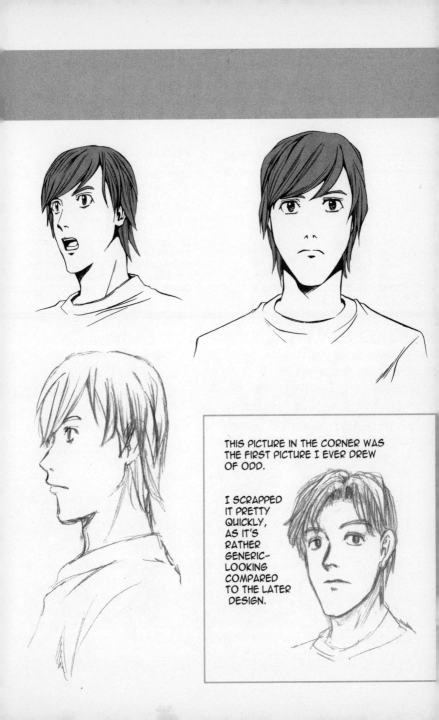

THIS PICTURE IN THE CORNER WAS THE FIRST PICTURE I EVER DREW OF ODD.

I SCRAPPED IT PRETTY QUICKLY, AS IT'S RATHER GENERIC-LOOKING COMPARED TO THE LATER DESIGN.

Stormy Llewellyn

I HAD AN IMAGE OF WHAT STORMY LOOKED LIKE FROM THE VERY BEGINNING – A DARK, MYSTERIOUS, ASS-KICKING BABE OF MEDITERRANEAN DESCENT. SHE HAS STRIKING EYES AND A CALM, KNOWING GAZE.

BECAUSE HER NICKNAME IS "STORMY," I WANTED TO GIVE HER WISPY HAIR, MUCH LIKE ANGRY STORM CLOUDS. IT'S ONLY FITTING THAT SHE HAS BLACK HAIR.

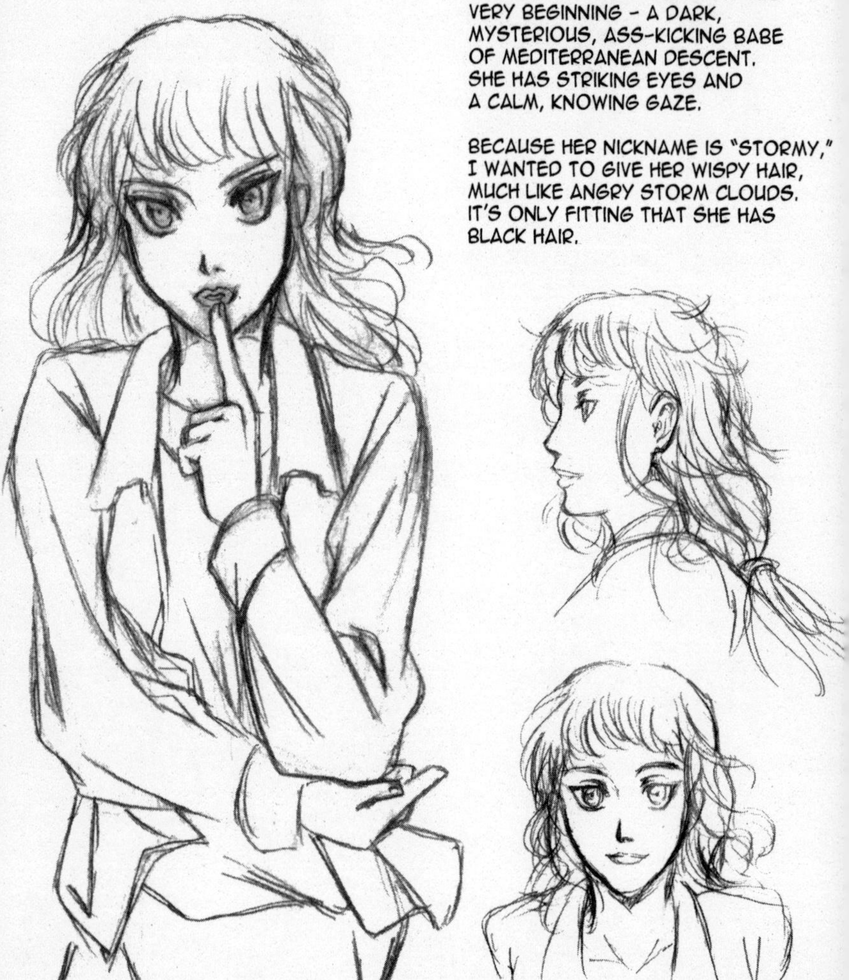

Police Chief Wyatt Porter

CHIEF PORTER'S INITIAL DESIGN WAS WILDLY OFF THE MARK – HE WAS THE ONLY CHARACTER WHO REQUIRED MAJOR DESIGN REVISIONS. HE WENT THROUGH 1.5 RE-DESIGNS BEFORE I SLIMMED HIM DOWN TO THE PRESENT VERSION.

THE NOVELS DESCRIBED CHIEF PORTER AS HAVING "DROOPY FACIAL MUSCLES," BUT HE'S REALLY MEANT TO BEAR A STRONG RESEMBLANCE TO ACTOR KURT RUSSELL (SO IT'S MEANT TO BE FLESHY MIDDLE-AGED HANDSOMENESS).

IRONICALLY, THE PICTURE OF KURT RUSSELL I USED AS REFERENCE WAS FROM THE QUENTIN TARANTINO MOVIE "DEATH PROOF," WHERE HE PLAYED A SERIAL KILLER.

REJECTED

AMENDED

Sherry Sheldon

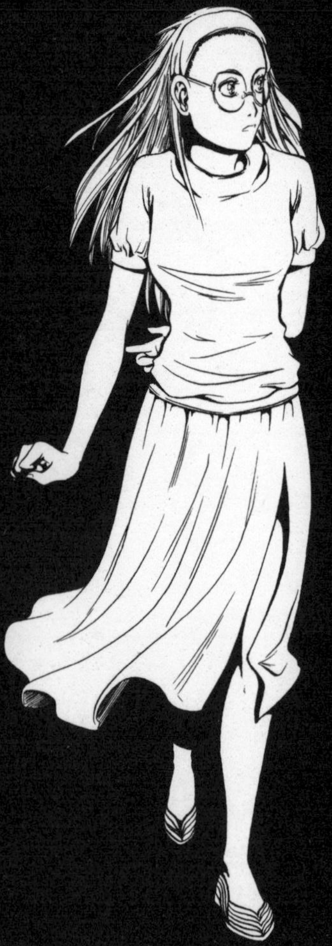

SHERRY'S DESIGN IS A COUNTERPOINT TO STORMY'S - SHE AND STORMY ARE MEANT TO LOOK LIKE POLAR OPPOSITES.

SHERRY IS AN ATTRACTIVE GIRL, BUT SHE COULD EASILY MAKE HERSELF MORE ATTRACTIVE BY DOING SOMETHING ABOUT HER HAIR AND HER GLASSES.

HER LOOKS ARE APPROPRIATE FOR HER PROFESSION, THOUGH - A NANNY SHOULDN'T BE ***TOO*** ATTRACTIVE.

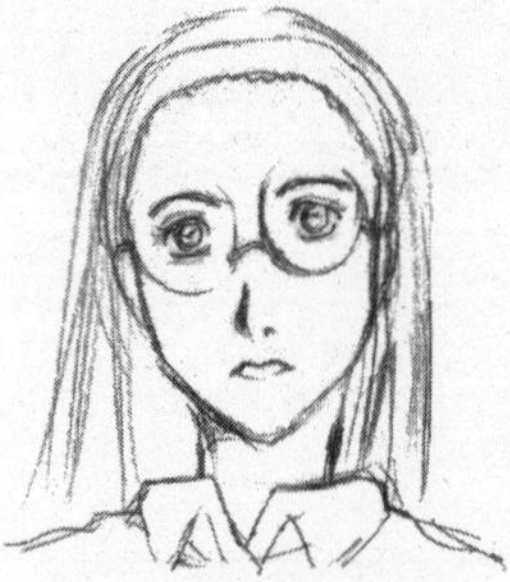

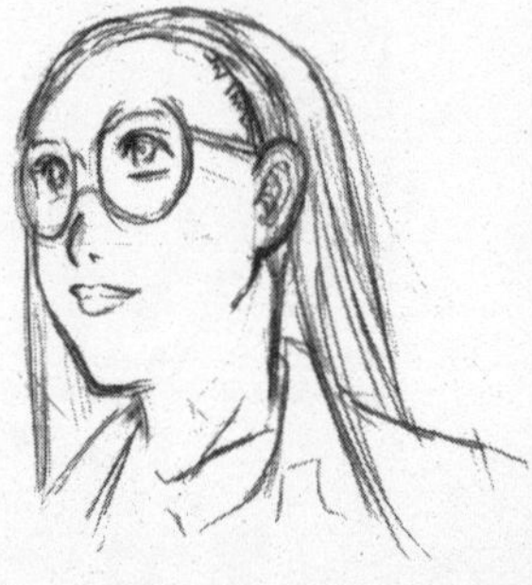

Terri Stambaugh

TERRI'S DESIGN WAS PRETTY
STRAIGHTFORWARD - SHE'S A NICE
MIDDLE-AGED LADY AND SHE LOOKS
THE PART. I GAVE HER BRIGHT,
GENTLE EYES TO EXEMPLIFY THAT.

SINCE HER MOST IMPORTANT ROLE
IS AS ODD'S SURROGATE MOTHER,
I TRIED TO GIVE HER A "MOTHERLY" FEEL,
COMPLETE WITH JEANS AND AN APRON
AROUND HER WAIST.

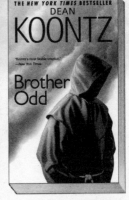

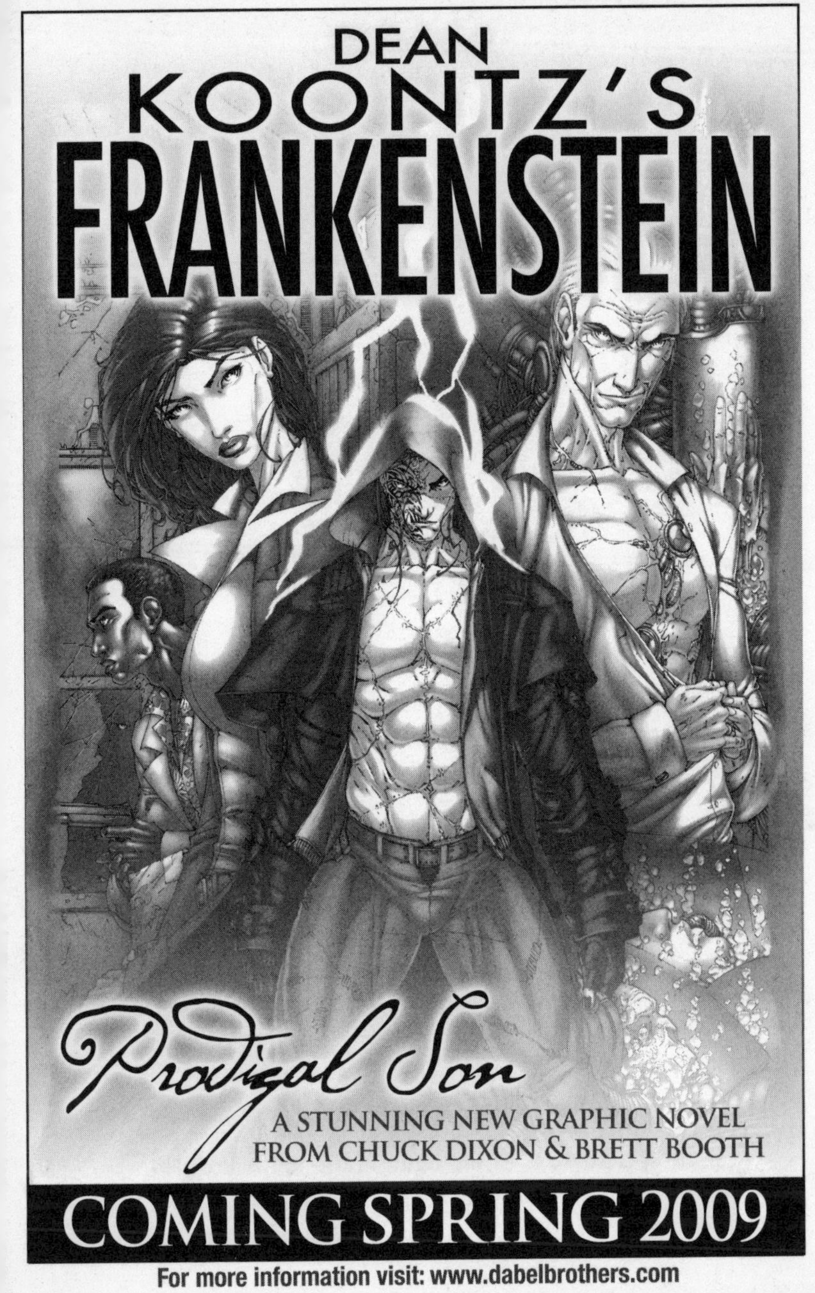
DEAN
KOONTZ'S
FRANKENSTEIN
Prodigal Son
A STUNNING NEW GRAPHIC NOVEL
FROM CHUCK DIXON & BRETT BOOTH
COMING SPRING 2009